ATLAS
OF WESTWARD
EXPANSION

ATLAS OF WESTWARD EXPANSION

Alan Wexler

MAPS AND PEN-AND-INK DRAWINGS BY
Molly Braun

Carl Waldman
EDITORIAL CONSULTANT

Facts On File®

AN INFOBASE HOLDINGS COMPANY

To Nathan and Minnie Wexler

Atlas of Westward Expansion
Text copyright © 1995 by Alan Wexler
Original maps and pen-and-ink drawings copyright © 1995 by Molly Braun
All rights reserved. No part of this book may be reproduced or utilized in
any form or by any means, electronic or mechanical, including photocopying,
recording, or by any information storage or retrieval systems, without
permission in writing from the publisher. For information contact:

Facts On File, Inc.
460 Park Avenue South
New York NY 10016

Library of Congress Cataloging–in–Publication Data

Wexler, Alan.
    The atlas of westward expansion / Alan Wexler ; maps and pen and
ink drawings, Molly Braun ; Carl Waldman, editorial consultant.
        p.   cm.
    Mainly covers the period 1754–1917.
    Includes bibliographical references and index.
    HC ISBN 0-8160-2660-2
    PB ISBN 0-8160-3206-8
    1. United States—Historical geography—Maps.   2. United States—
Territorial expansion—Maps.   3. United States—Territorial
expansion—Chronology.   I. Braun, Molly.   II. Waldman, Carl.
III. Title.   IV. Title: Westward expansion.
G1201.S1W44   1995 ⟨G&M⟩
911'.73—dc20   94-756

Facts On File books are available at special discounts when purchased in
bulk quantities for businesses, associations, institutions or sales
promotions. Please call our Special Sales Department in New York at
212/683-2244 or 800/322-8755.

Text design by Ellen Levine
Printed in the United States of America

QB VC 10 9 8 7 6 5 4 3 2 1

This book is printed on acid-free paper

"Go West, young man,
and grow up with the country."
　　　　　—Horace Greeley (1857)

"Whoever controls the past
controls the future.
Whoever controls the present
controls the past."
　　　　　—George Orwell (1949)

Contents

List of Maps

A TRANSCONTINENTAL REPUBLIC (1846–1853)

WEALTH OF THE WEST (1854–1860)

RESHAPING THE WEST (1861–1867)

FRONTIER'S END (1868–1900s)

THE REAL SIGNIFICANCE OF THE FRONTIER

Introduction

Walk into any city or small town's hall of records and you'll find maps and data revealing who owns what land, who owned it before, how much it was sold for, who holds judgments and liens against property and what disputes there may have been over easements and boundaries.

But that is only half the story. The official record does not tell of the tawdry affair between a homeowner and his neighbor, and the ensuing messy divorce that ultimately led to the sale of his house. Nor do these mute "libers" speak of how a landowner was able to enlarge his holdings by acquiring the adjoining property through subterfuge and deceit.

A county's official maps do not relate how a property got to be shaped a particular way. They do not depict the human events that caused a huge estate of several thousand acres to be reduced over the years, through misfortunes and bad marriages, to a small plot containing little more than an old house with a front lawn and a tiny backyard.

In much the same way, the map of a nation is a historical "footprint" that outlines the end result of that nation's fortunes over the course of its existence. It is the aim of a historical atlas to shed light on the story behind the map. The shape of the earth's land masses has changed very little in the last five or six thousand years. Yet the boundaries of empires and nations have fluctuated with every social and political upheaval of recorded human history. In our own time, the map of the world has changed so rapidly that contemporary atlases are soon out of date. But a historical atlas has the advantage of history's 20/20 hindsight to ensure its accuracy. It can show things as they were, and relate how they came to change.

Territorial growth was a central factor in the history of the United States during the first seventy-five years of its existence. The territorial changes that occurred between 1776 and 1850 not only transformed the nation on the map, but also had a tremendous impact on nearly every facet of the nation's political and social life. Over the next 50 years, after it had grown to encompass the land "from sea to shining sea," much of the nation's energy was directed at the settlement and organization of its vast new domain. To tell the story of how the nation came to occupy its present boundaries is to show how seemingly diverse events, both at home and abroad, coalesced to shape the nation's geographic history.

The United States began as a string of loosely allied British colonies along the Atlantic seaboard of North America. Those colonies had been established as political and social outposts of European society. In a sense, they were 18th-century Europe's "suburbs," a long commute from the mother country, but nonetheless existing primarily for the sake of the mother country.

Other European nations had colonies in North America as well. France and Spain controlled the bulk of the continent at one time or another. Yet it was only the British colonists who valued the land as a resource. For the French, "New France" was essentially a huge game preserve valued mainly as an abundant source of furs. For the Spanish, "New Spain" held the promise of an "El Dorado" of mineral wealth. There was also a strong evangelical motive for the Spanish: The American Indians were a fertile source of new souls to be won for Christ.

U.S. territorial expansion has its roots in the conflict between the British and the French over which nation was to dominate the continent. The new American nation inherited the desire for territorial growth, which it fulfilled through a series of diplomatic and military adventures. Through wars and real estate deals, through Indian treaties and campaigns of conquest, the nation acquired more and more land. Meanwhile, Spain lost its empire, its economy undone by the influx of too much American gold and silver. The animals that the French had depended on for furs were eventually hunted to near-extinction, while the demand for fur in Europe dropped dramatically due to changes in fashion.

Yet the American demand for new lands to settle was

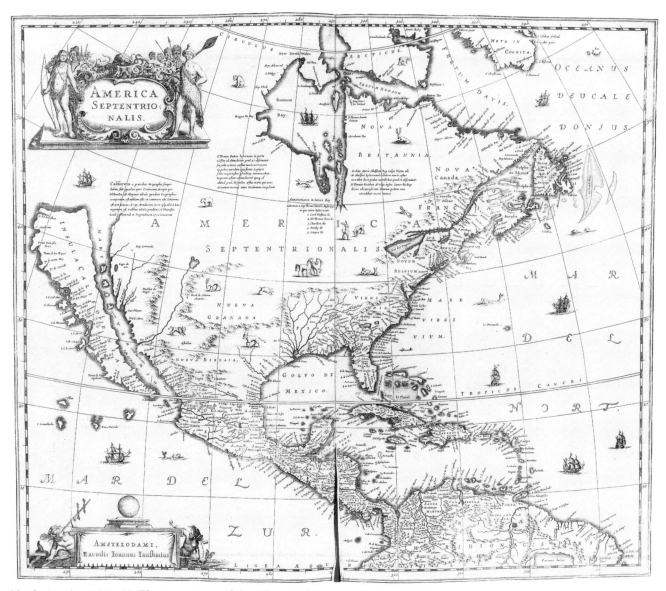

North America, 1646–49 (Photo courtesy of the Library of Congress)

insatiable. For more than a century after 1776, the United States was mainly an agricultural nation. Most of its people were employed as farmers, and to them land was an even more valuable resource than gold or furs. Unsettled wilderness, once settled, became real estate. Wealth could be created from virtually nothing, and would continue to be created until every acre of available land was accounted for. Unlike gold or furs, settled land increased in value and created more wealth.

America's westward expansion continued until the early years of the 20th century when the last western territories were organized into states. Not coincidentally, the nation's territorial growth and development climaxed at about the same time that industry replaced agriculture as the focus of the country's economic life.

America's westward expansion is a multi-faceted story intertwined with the major issues of the nation's history. At its inception, the United States was created as a na-

tion in which "all men are created equal." Yet through most of the first 100 years of its existence, many of its inhabitants were held as slaves in the Southern States. And, in the case of American westward expansion, the American Indians were virtually wiped out by European arrival and conquest. When Christopher Columbus first landed on an obscure island in the Bahamas in 1492, the North American continent was home to over 1,000,000 Native Americans (some scholars estimate as many as 10 million). By 1820, their numbers had dwindled to scarcely 200,000. First decimated by alien diseases borne by European visitors, they later suffered additional destruction wrought by the relentless encroachment on their hunting grounds by white settlers.

In his novel *Ulysses*, Irish author James Joyce has his young hero, Stephen Daedelus, remark to a bigoted university professor that "History is a nightmare from which I have been trying to awaken for twenty years."

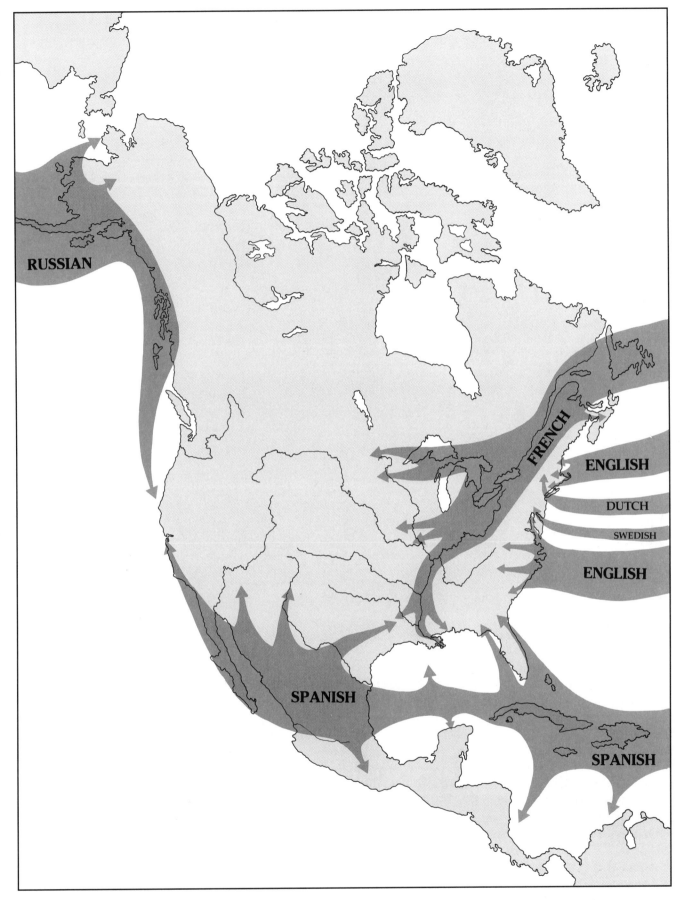

I.1 EUROPEAN INCURSIONS ONTO INDIAN LANDS

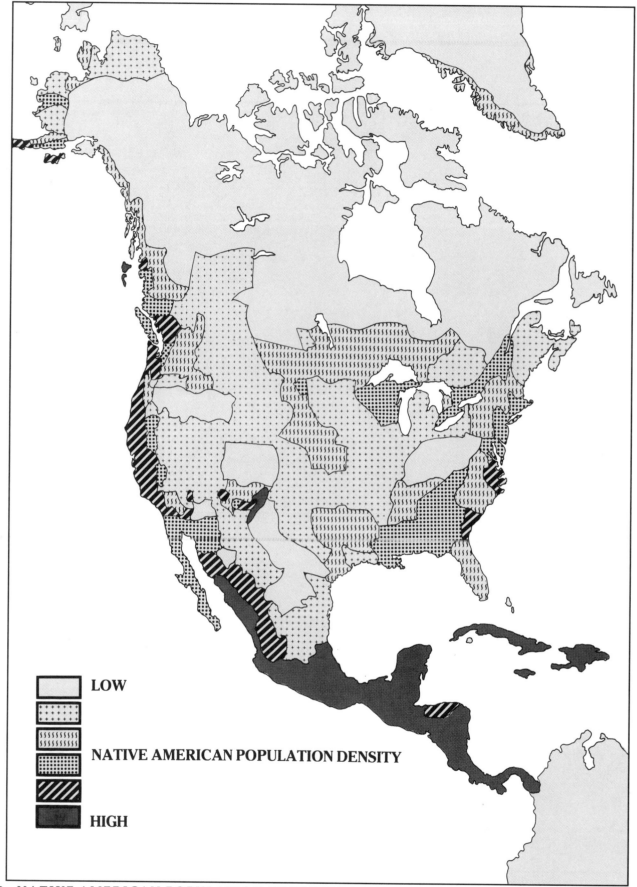

LOW

NATIVE AMERICAN POPULATION DENSITY

HIGH

I.2 NATIVE AMERICAN POPULATION DENSITY IN 1500

Acoma Pueblo, Continually Inhabited Long before the Arrival of Europeans in North America (Photo courtesy of the National Archives)

The American Indians' experience of U.S. westward expansion was similarly nightmarish; it was an ordeal that did not end until most of their ancestral domains had been absorbed and their way of life nearly erased from the face of the earth.

By the time Americans began to settle the continent beyond the Appalachians, Indians had already adopted many modern innovations from their contacts with Europeans. Their skills as hunters had been augmented by the introduction of firearms. Fur trading had opened up new avenues of commerce that greatly expanded their formerly subsistence economic life. By the early 1700s, in the Trans-Mississippi West, horses and guns introduced by Europeans had already transformed the life of the Plains Indians to make them a formidable presence on the frontier.

Yet Native Americans did not adopt the European idea of the nation-state. Although armed with rifles, and equipped with iron and steel implements obtained in trade with whites, the Indians remained loosely orga-nized, their leaders commanding scattered bands. They failed to view themselves as a political entity, and this left them extremely vulnerable to the piecemeal dismemberment of their homelands.

Despite its inequities and horror, its trials and conflicts, the westward expansion of the United States inevitably came about. The process of expansion was generated by a chain of events that began long before the first European set foot in the New World. Originally, America was made in the image of Europe, but over the years that image underwent a series of metamorphoses; many additional cultures also came to this country and became part of the unique national entity that is the United States of America.

In 1732, Anglo-Irish philosopher and churchman George Berkeley, who lived in the American colonies from 1728 to 1731, made an accurate prophesy when he wrote:

Westward the course of empire takes its way . . .

Chapter 1

COLONIAL AMERICA LOOKS WEST (1754–1795)

THE FRENCH AND INDIAN WAR

IN THE LATE 1740s, IN both England and her North American colonies, land development schemes had begun to hatch, the most notable of which was initiated by the Ohio Company. Chartered in 1747 by a group of land speculators in London and Virginia, the Ohio Company planned to subdivide and sell a half-million acres of land in the upper Ohio River region acquired in a grant from King George II of England. Among the principal stockholders were members of Virginia's prominent Lee and Fairfax families, George Washington's family (and later Washington himself) as well as Governor Robert Dinwiddie.

Christopher Gist, a frontiersman and guide from North Carolina's Yadkin Valley, knowledgeable about the Native Americans of the region, was soon hired by the Ohio Company to explore the company's lands along the upper Ohio River. In 1750–51, his travels took him southward to the Falls of the Ohio, now the site of Louisville, Kentucky, and as far westward as the Kanawha River in western Ohio.

The next year, Gist established a small plantation for the Ohio Company on the Younghiogheny River, south of the Forks of the Ohio, the point where the Allegheny and Monongahela join to form the Ohio River. William Trent, another professional pioneer employed by the Ohio Company, set up a storehouse at the confluence of the Monongahela and Redstone Creek, while company agent John Frazier opened a blacksmith shop within five miles of the Forks of the Ohio.

Gist was by no means the first non-Indian to penetrate the Appalachian Plateau on behalf of the Virginia colony. Starting in the early 1670s, 60 years after the founding of the Jamestown settlement, explorations across the southern Appalachians had been undertaken by John Lederer, followed by Abraham Woods, Thomas Batts, Robert Fallam and Gabriel Arthur. In addition, English fur traders had long been active in the Ohio Valley, and by the late 1740s had established commercial relations with Delaware, Miami and Shawnee bands, centered around Pickawillany, a Miami village on the Miami River.

Nonetheless, until the mid-1700s, European penetration into the Ohio country had been mainly the work of fur traders from French Canada. Europeans relied on the natural highway of the Ohio River and its tributaries to ship furs and trade goods throughout Quebec, the eastern Great Lakes, the Illinois country, and, by way of the Mississippi River to New Orleans, their main southern shipping center on the Gulf of Mexico.

French claims on the Ohio country stemmed from the explorations of Samuel de Champlain, Jacques Marquette and Louis Joliet, among others. French traders and explorers continued to probe southward from the Great Lakes, culminating in Robert Cavelier de La Salle's 1682 voyage down the Mississippi River to the Gulf of Mexico. At that time, La Salle named the region Louisiana, in honor of French monarch Louis XIV.

UNEXPLORED

Hudson Bay

BRITISH

Quebec

Montreal
Sault Ste. Marie
St. Lawrence R.

LOUISIANA

SPANISH

Missouri R.

Boston

NEW FRANCE

St. Louis

New York
Philadelphia

ENGLISH COLONIES

PACIFIC OCEAN

Colorado R.

Santa Fe

Arkansas R.

Red R.

Mississippi R.

Williamsburg

Charleston
Savannah

ATLANTIC OCEAN

Rio Grande

Natchez
Fort Biloxi
New Orleans

St. Augustine

Gulf of Mexico

CUBA

HISPANIOLA

Mexico City

BRITISH

JAMAICA

1.1 EUROPEAN CLAIMS TO NORTH AMERICA IN 1754

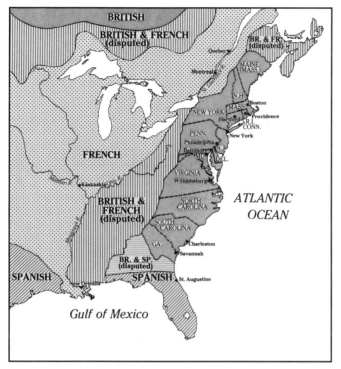

1.2 THE ORIGINAL THIRTEEN COLONIES

The underlying motive of French colonization in North America was to support and expand the fur trade. As a consequence, the French limited immigration and settlement to trading forts along the river system so that Native Americans could continue to harvest pelts and sell them to traders.

The pattern was different among the English colonies along the mid-Atlantic coast and southward. These colonies were maintained as overseas agricultural enterprises, dedicated to the production of cash crops—especially tobacco—grown on large-scale plantations for export to England. Unlike the fur-trading monopolies developed over vast, unknown ranges of wilderness, as in the cases of French Canada and Louisiana, the English colonies were organized around the private ownership of lands and the production of agricultural wealth.

Although they carried on some fur trading with the Indians, the English colonists generally viewed the tribes on the Virginia frontier—such as the bands in the Powhatan Confederacy—as a hindrance to further expansion of the plantation economy.

As for the Native American viewpoint, the Indians of the Ohio and Mississippi valleys for the most part maintained good relations with the French, regarding them as trading partners. By contrast, they tended to view the westward movement of settlers from the English colonies as an invasion, threatening to upset the natural equilibrium of their lives.

The geographical barriers of the Blue Ridge Mountains and the Appalachians, together with the threat of Indian resistance, limited the growth of the Virginia colony to the region between the Atlantic coastal plain and the upland Piedmont region. Yet despite Indian efforts to repel the movement of English settlers westward, the accelerated demand for new agricultural lands in the English colonies increased the potential value of the Appalachian Plateau, providing additional commercial incentives for the English.

In July of 1748, at Logstown, an Indian village near the Forks of the Ohio, a conference took place between leaders of the Ohio tribes and English colonial officials. By that time, some of the Ohio tribes had grown dissatisfied with the quality of French trade goods, and resented the restrictions the French had placed on their trade with the English, who offered better goods at a more generous rate of exchange. As a result, leaders of the Delaware, Shawnee, Iroquois and Wyandot (Huron), meeting with colonial Indian agents George Groghan and Conrad Weiser, entered into the Treaty of Logstown proclaiming their allegiance to the English.

The treaty allowed the Virginia colony to assert its claims to the region south of the Ohio River, the prelude to Colonial America's first territorial expansion west of the Appalachians. Virginia immediately transferred a large piece of this territory to the Ohio Company. In re-

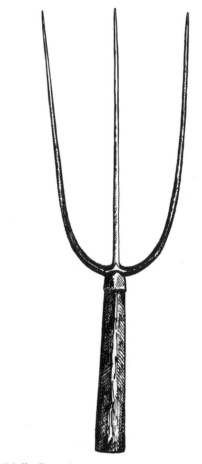

Hayfork (Molly Braun)

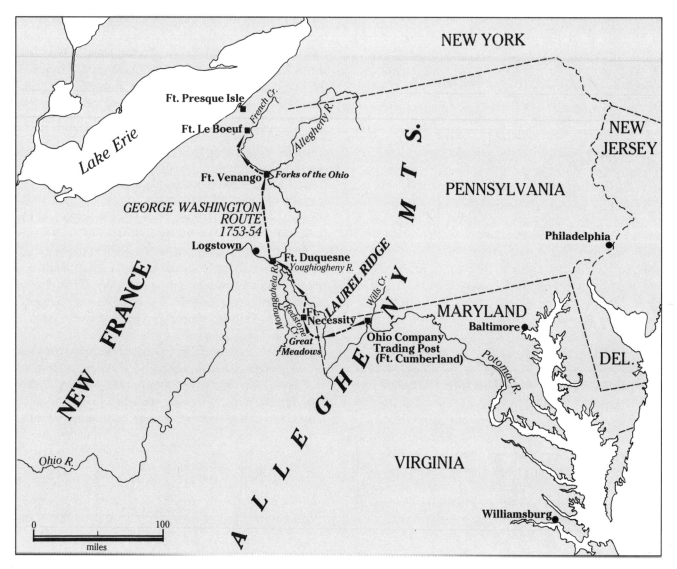

1.3 GEORGE WASHINGTON'S ROUTE IN 1753–54

turn, the Ohio Company, in accordance with its charter, agreed to provide for the defense of its proposed Ohio Valley settlements, opening the way for an acceleration of English trade and settlement from the Atlantic colonies into the Ohio Valley.

The treaty prompted French action. Response was sporadic at first, with French-led Indian raids on outlying English settlements in the Ohio country; it began in July of 1752 with an attack on the English trading post at Pickawillany on the Miami River. French fur trader Charles Langlade led a party of Chippewas (Ojibways) and Ottawas from northern Lake Michigan and captured the settlement after killing a white trader and 15 native inhabitants.

The French were especially concerned that the strategic Forks of the Ohio would fall under British control, cutting off France's eastern access to the Ohio–Mississippi river system so vital to the fur trade of the Louisiana country and French Canada. In April of 1753, the

Marquis Duquesne, governor of French Canada, dispatched a military expedition southward from Niagara that established a chain of forts between Lake Erie and the Forks of the Ohio, hoping to safeguard French interests in the Ohio Valley and drive out the British. Among these were Fort Presque Isle near the southeastern corner of Lake Erie, Fort Le Boeuf on French Creek and Fort Venango near the junction of the Allegheny River and French Creek.

In the autumn of 1753, a 21-year-old Virginia militia officer, Major George Washington, was sent on a diplomatic mission by Virginia's governor, Robert Dinwiddie, to investigate reports of an increased French military presence in the territory south of Lake Erie. Washington left the colonial capital at Williamsburg on October 31, 1753. He followed the Potomac upstream, traveling northwestward into the eastern slopes of the Appalachian Mountains. He carried Dinwiddie's letter to the region's French military commander reminding the French that the Ohio country had long been claimed by the colony of Virginia, and demanding the immediate removal of their forces.

At Wills Creek, the head of navigation on the Potomac, the young major was joined by five frontiersman, including Christopher Gist, who served as his guide and interpreter. Traveling on horseback, Washington and his party made their way northwestward into the Appalachian Plateau by way of Laurel Ridge, arriving at a large clearing known as Great Meadows. From there, they followed the Younghiogheny and Monongahela rivers to the upper Ohio, where they stopped at the Indian settlement at Logstown. Washington learned from the Mingo (Seneca) chief Half King (Tanacharison), an ally of the British, that the French had constructed forts between Lake Erie and the Forks of the Ohio. With his own concerns over the French military build-up in his domain, Half King and a small escort of warriors agreed to accompany the Virginia delegation to meet with the French at Fort Venango.

The French officer in charge at Fort Venango advised Washington that he had no authority to accept Dinwiddie's warning letter. Instead, he sent him to speak with the region's chief French military commander, Captain Legardeur de Saint-Pierre, at Fort Le Boeuf near the head of French Creek to the north, the command center for French forces in the Ohio country. There Washington soon met with Saint-Pierre, who refused to comply with Dinwiddie's demand for withdrawal of French forces. He recognized neither British nor Virginia sovereignty over the region, announcing that he was in the Ohio country on orders of the governor-general of New France.

In January of 1754, Washington was back at Williamsburg, Virginia, where he informed Governor Dinwiddie that the French had decided to defy his demand to withdraw. Dinwiddie immediately began raising support for a military response to the French invasion of the Ohio Valley. A force of several hundred colonials was organized, spurred on by the promise of generous land grants in return for their services. Command of the expedition went to Colonel Joshua Fry of the Virginia Militia, with George Washington—now a lieutenant-colonel—as his second-in-command.

In May of 1754, Washington, leading an advance force of about 300 colonists and Indian allies, engaged the French near Fort Duquesne, their newly established stronghold at the Forks of the Ohio. Realizing that a much larger French force was on its way down the Allegheny, Washington withdrew to Great Meadows, where he set up a defensive outpost with improvised materials, which he dubbed "Fort Necessity." Soon besieged by the French and hopelessly outnumbered, Washington agreed to surrender in return for a promise that he and his men would be permitted to return to Virginia.

News of these events brought a strong response from British officials, who resolved to meet the French threat in the Ohio Valley head on. A counteroffensive was launched, with 1,000 regular army troops under the leadership of General Edward Braddock deployed to Virginia. In the spring of 1755, Braddock's forces, supported by George Washington—who was in command of 500 Virginia Militia volunteers and 50 Indian scouts—set out from Baltimore for Fort Cumberland, the British outpost at Wills Creek. Braddock ordered the construction of a wagon road along the route to haul supplies for his intended assault on Fort Duquesne.

In early July of 1755, British forces were ambushed by the French and their Indian allies just eight miles from Fort Duquesne, in what came to be known as the Battle of the Wilderness or "Braddock's Defeat." After Braddock himself was mortally wounded, and with nearly two-thirds of the 1,500-man army lost, Washington managed to lead the survivors of the battle back to eastern Virginia.

The next year, 1756, the war erupted into a worldwide conflict, played out in Europe and India in addition to North America. The struggle was later known as the Seven Years' War.

In 1758, the British tried to regain the Ohio country with another campaign against Fort Duquesne. Again Washington took part, this time under the command of General John Forbes. Forbes and his troops made their way westward along a more northern route than that taken by Braddock. He ordered a wagon road cut from Philadelphia across Pennsylvania into the Appalachians. With an overwhelming force of 7,000 troops, the British moved on Fort Duquesne in November of 1758. The French withdrew without an engagement; as Forbes' column approached, they blew up Fort Duquesne to keep it from falling to the British. Now in control of the vital Forks of the Ohio, the British constructed Fort Pitt on the former site of Fort Duquesne, around which developed what is now Pittsburgh, Pennsylvania.

George Washington Raising the British Flag at Fort Duquesne in 1758 (Photo courtesy of the New York Public Library)

Lake Huron

NEW FRANCE

Lake Ontario

■ Ft. Oswego

■ Ft. Niagara

NEW YORK

MAINE (MASS.)

N.H.

MASS.

CONN.

R.I.

Lake Erie

■ Ft. Presque Isle

■ Ft. Le Boeuf

Ft. Venango ■

PENNSYLVANIA

NEW

Logstown

Ft. Duquesne

Forbes Road

Philadelphia

N.J.

ATLANTIC OCEAN

Ft. Necessity ■ *Braddock's Road*

BRADDOCK'S DEFEAT 1755

Ft. Cumberland

Baltimore

MD.

DEL

Miami R.

Ohio R.

VIRGINIA

Kanawha R.

Williamsburg

0   200

miles

1.4   THE FRENCH AND INDIAN WAR OF 1754–63 ON THE WESTERN FRONTIER

Although the French and Indian War continued to rage along a front ranging from Nova Scotia to the Great Lakes, Forbes' victory at Fort Duquesne marked the end of France's hold on the Ohio Valley. Settlers from Pennsylvania and Virginia, encouraged by the British victory, resumed their westward movement along the Ohio River, with Forbes Road and Braddock's Road developing into major routes of migration into the Appalachian Plateau.

Meanwhile, the main thrust of British strategy in the Seven Years' War in North America turned to the St. Lawrence River region and the Great Lakes. Louisburg, Nova Scotia had fallen to the British in July of 1758, fol-

lowed by Fort Frontenac on Lake Ontario one month later.

In September of 1759, the British sealed their victory over the French in North America with General James Wolfe's triumph over the French commander Louis Montcalm at Quebec, a battle in which both the French and British generals lost their lives. The following year, Montreal was taken, and the British took possession of all of French Canada. Soon afterward, the French were defeated at Detroit.

In November of 1762, the French, hoping to retain some control over their remaining lands in North America, entered into a secret treaty with their allies, the

DISPUTED
&
UNEXPLORED

Hudson Bay

BRITISH

THIRTEEN COLONIES

ATLANTIC OCEAN

PACIFIC OCEAN

SPANISH

Mississippi R.

Gulf Of Mexico

CUBA (Sp.)

FR.

BRITISH

1.5 NON-INDIAN NORTH AMERICA IN 1763

Spanish, in which they agreed to cede to them all of he Louisiana country west of the Mississippi, as well as the port of New Orleans.

The Seven Years' War and the French and Indian War in North America officially came to a close with the Treaty of Paris in 1763. Under its terms, France yielded its claim to the Ohio Valley and French Canada, virtually all of its North American empire. Spain, which had allied itself with France during the war, lost Florida to Great Britain. The end of nine years of frontier warfare in the Ohio Valley and along the Appalachian frontier soon inspired a renewed interest in westward migration.

Although they had won a final victory over the French, the British still faced the problem of keeping the peace with the Indian tribes of the Ohio frontier, most of them formerly allied with the French. As early as 1758, colonial authorities in Pennsylvania, seeking to allay Delaware and Iroquois fears of English encroachment from the east, had entered into a treaty with tribal leaders at Easton. Under the terms of the Treaty of Easton, the colonial government agreed to limit further white incursion onto Indian lands in western Pennsylvania.

This treaty and other prohibitions against westward settlement were ignored by many colonists seeking affordable new lands on which to settle, and, by May of 1763, less than six months after the Treaty of Paris, Indian resistance to English settlement in the West erupted in a well-organized Indian rebellion.

United under Ottawa chief Pontiac, the Ohio Valley tribes launched attacks against British forts and settlements from Lake Michigan and Detroit to Oswego in western New York. But in August of 1763, at the Battle of Bushy Run near Fort Pitt, Pontiac's forces suffered a major defeat, and, the next year, his rebellion ended with a decisive victory by British and colonial forces on the Muskingum River in Ohio.

Meanwhile, English westward expansion beyond the Appalachians continued on an even grander scale. In September of 1763, the Mississippi Company, headed by George Washington, was granted 2.5 million acres between the Ohio and Wisconsin rivers to distribute to Virginia colonists who had fought in the French and Indian War.

Hoping to avert further costly warfare with the Indians of the Ohio Valley and the Trans-Appalachian region to the south, King George III issued a proclamation on October 7, 1763 forbidding English settlement west of the Appalachians. The Proclamation Line of 1763, running along the crest of the Appalachians from New York through southern Georgia, marked the official limit beyond which further settlement was prohibited. This move contradicted the claims of colonial land speculators, who had ignored Indian ancestral land use and had already acquired lands west of the Alleghenies. It also nullified the claims of Virginia, Massachusetts, the Carolinas and Georgia, maintaining that this area belonged to them by virtue of the terms of their original colonial charters, some of which had granted them rights to western territory extending as far as the "Western Ocean."

Colonial opposition to these restrictions soon led to a relaxation of British policy, so that by 1766, colonists who had settled west of the Proclamation Line prior to 1763 were permitted to remain on their lands. In August of 1768, in the Treaty of Hard Labor, the Cherokees were coerced into allowing South Carolina colonists to extend settlement into their lands along the southern Appalachian frontier. Less than three months later in New York's Mohawk Valley, the Iroquois entered into the Treaty of Fort Stanwix, under which they sold their lands in southwestern New York, western Pennsylvania, and portions of present-day West Virginia, Kentucky and Tennessee.

More land speculation syndicates were organized, including the Indiana Company, which purchased 2 million acres southeast of the Ohio River from the Iroquois. On the southern frontier, the Creeks agreed to allow settlement into their lands as far westward as the Ogeechee River, extending the western limits of South Carolina and Georgia. The Virginia frontier was extended farther westward in 1770, when the Cherokees agreed to the Treaty of Lochabar.

The cycle of warfare, treaties and land cessions would continue in the 18th century. More and more Indian families would be displaced and their cultures dispossessed.

DANIEL BOONE AND THE SETTLEMENT OF KENTUCKY

With the expulsion of the French, and the Indians pacified for a time, the way was now open for British settlement of the Trans-Appalachian West. The decade preceding the American Revolution saw the first great migration of settlers across the Appalachians and Alleghenies into the Ohio Valley and the Illinois country.

The Proclamation of 1763 proved to be largely unenforceable. Land speculators, ignoring the prohibitions against settlement beyond the Proclamation Line, continued to purchase lands from the Indians or squat on them without the approval of the English crown or any of the colonial governments. Pioneers from Virginia and Pennsylvania streamed across the northern Alleghenies into the Ohio Valley. The military trails cut by Braddock and Forbes became major avenues of migration into the interior. Fort Pitt, where the roads led, soon grew from a military outpost to become the first permanent English

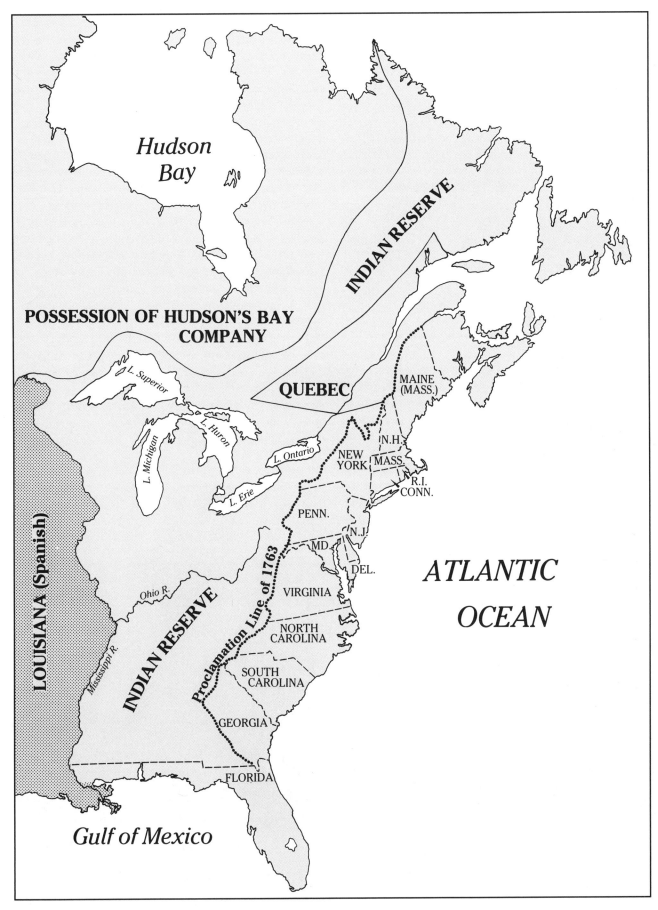

Hudson
Bay

POSSESSION OF HUDSON'S BAY
COMPANY

INDIAN RESERVE

L. Superior

QUEBEC

MAINE
(MASS.)

N.H.

L. Huron

L. Michigan

L. Ontario

NEW
YORK

MASS.

R.I.
CONN.

L. Erie

PENN.

N.J.

MD.

DEL.

LOUISIANA (Spanish)

Ohio R.

INDIAN RESERVE

Proclamation Line of 1763

VIRGINIA

ATLANTIC

OCEAN

NORTH
CAROLINA

Mississippi R.

SOUTH
CAROLINA

GEORGIA

FLORIDA

Gulf of Mexico

1.6   EUROPEAN CLAIMS TO NORTH AMERICA IN 1763

Log Cabin in the Late 18th Century (Photo courtesy of the New York Public Library)

settlement west of the Alleghenies in what is now the United States.

The lands south of the Ohio River, however, were much less accessible to the colonial pioneers. The powerful Iroquois Confederacy still held control over the frontier separating this segment of the Appalachian Plateau from the established English colonies to the east. Moreover, mountain passes, rivers and trails leading across the mountains into the interior were few. For this reason, in the years immediately following the end of the French and Indian War, only a small number of white traders and hunters ventured into the country west of the Cumberland Mountains, now the state of Kentucky.

Kentucky or *Ken Tapke,* Iroquoian for "splendid fields"—had long been a favorite hunting ground for the Indians, attracting the Cherokees, Chickasaws and Yuchis from the south and the Iroquois and Shawnees from the north, among others, but none of these groups regularly inhabited the region or claimed it as part of their tribal territory. The minimal Indian resistance consequently made Kentucky attractive to colonial land speculators and pioneers. With conflicting claims over the region held by Virginia and the Carolinas, it was not clear which would prevail. The confusion made it easy for land speculators to circumvent colonial authorities and deal directly with the Indians for acquisition of lands in this region.

One of the leading figures in the white exploration and settlement of Kentucky was Daniel Boone. Originally from Reading, Pennsylvania, Boone's family had settled in the Yadkin Valley in western North Carolina. Raised on the frontier, he grew to be a seasoned woodsman and hunter. In 1755, Boone had been a 21-year-old volunteer with British and colonial forces in the first assault on Fort Duquesne, narrowly surviving the ensuing rout of General Edward Braddock's forces.

After 1763, Boone went on long hunting trips into the wilderness, exploring the southern Appalachians from present-day eastern Tennessee to northwestern Florida. In 1769–71, Boone, his brother Squire and a small party of "long-hunters" probed what is now eastern Kentucky. They crossed the Alleghenies by way of the Cumberland Gap, a natural passage through the mountains near the point where present-day Tennessee, Kentucky and Virginia meet.

Boone and his companions were not the first non-Indians to use this pass to cross the mountains. The Cumberland Gap had been first reported in 1750 by Dr. Thomas Walker who came upon it while surveying for the Loyal Land Company. But Boone was the first to realize the Cumberland Gap's great potential as a conduit for settlement across the Alleghenies into eastern Kentucky's Bluegrass Country and territory to the West.

In 1773, Boone made his first attempt to bring settlers through the mountains and into eastern Kentucky, guiding a small group of pioneer families, including his own, into the Alleghenies. Near the Cumberland Gap, they

Daniel Boone (Photo courtesy of the New York State Library)

The Wilderness Road, 1774 (Photo courtesy of the National Archives)

were forced to turn back after Cherokees attacked the group, killing several of them, including Boone's own son.

In 1774, Indian resistance to Virginia's expansion into the Ohio Valley once again erupted into warfare. Virginia colonial governor Lord Dunmore had antagonized the Shawnees and Delawares by establishing a fort in lands reserved for them. The Indians were decisively defeated in October of 1774 at the Battle of Point Pleasant on the Kanawha River in southern Ohio. That same month, in the Treaty of Camp Charlotte that ended Lord Dunmore's War, Shawnee leaders agreed to allow settlement south of the Ohio. Immediately, land speculators resumed their activities, acquiring huge tracts of lands beyond the Alleghenies.

Richard Henderson, a North Carolina lawyer and judge, and a friend of Daniel Boone, saw the opening of Kentucky as an opportunity to create a proprietary colony of his own beyond the mountains. In August of 1774, he had organized the Transylvania Company, and in March of 1775, in the Treaty of Sycamore Shoals, he purchased from the Cherokees the territory between the Kentucky and Cumberland rivers, a region comprising most of what eventually became the state of Kentucky.

Henderson then commissioned Daniel Boone to blaze a trail through the Cumberland Gap as far as the Kentucky River as a first step in bringing settlers into the region. By April of 1775, Boonesborough, the Transylvania Company's first settlement, had been established on the Kentucky River. Boone's trail through the Cumberland Gap, later known as the Wilderness Road, soon brought thousands of more settlers into Kentucky, heading for Boonesborough as well as for settlements at Boiling Spring, St. Asaph's and Harrodsburg.

With the rapid growth of these Kentucky settlements came the need for local governments. Deeds and wills had to be recorded, marriage licenses issued and local regulations created for the welfare of the community. Since the colonial governments in North Carolina and Virginia were too far away to handle these affairs, the settlers decided to undertake local governing themselves. Led by Judge Henderson, a group petitioned the Continental Congress in Philadelphia for recognition of Kentucky as the 14th colony. Virginia, which still claimed Kentucky and did not recognize Henderson's title to the region, voiced strong opposition to this plan. The Continental Congress, not wanting to alienate any of the colonies now loosely allied against Great Britain, voted to reject the proposal.

By the summer of 1776, the authority of the Transylvania Company and other proprietary companies came to be questioned by the inhabitants of the Kentucky settlements. Land prices had begun to increase, with the better tracts available only to company stockholders. The outbreak of the American Revolution the previous year further weakened the hold of the land companies. The Shawnees and other tribes of the southern Ohio Valley, supported by the British, used that conflict as an opportunity to drive white settlers from lands the crown had reserved for them.

In need of protection from the Indians, the settlers of Harrodsburg and Boiling Spring initiated a movement for annexation to Virginia. A delegation headed by a leading Kentucky settler, George Rogers Clark, traveled to Williamsburg to ask the Virginia government to take a direct role. Before the close of 1776, the Virginia legislature voted to officially annex Kentucky as a county. Although the Transylvania Company's holdings were now legally invalid, Judge Henderson was nevertheless compensated for his contribution to westward settlement with a 200,000 acre land grant in Kentucky's Cumberland Valley.

Daniel Boone went on to play a major role in the defense of the Kentucky settlements during the American Revolution. In 1777, he was captured by the Shawnees and brought to Chillicothe, their stronghold in southern Ohio. He managed to win the confidence of the Shawnee leader Black Fish, who adopted him as his son and took him into the tribe under the name Big Turtle. Later, the Indians took him to Detroit, where he met with British lieutenant governor Henry Hamilton and pretended to pledge his loyalty to the British. On his return to Chillicothe, he managed to escape from the Shawnees, who had come to trust him, then make his way back to Boonesborough, where he led in the defense of the settlement against the British-backed Indians.

After the American Revolution, Boone lost his lands in Kentucky and western Virginia when his claims were declared invalid, having been improperly surveyed and recorded. He remained in Kentucky until 1799, then moved westward into Spanish Louisiana, settling in the lower Missouri River Valley just west of St. Louis.

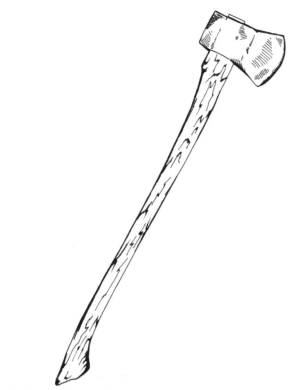

Felling Ax (Molly Braun)

Even in his advanced years, Daniel Boone continued to probe westward on hunting trips. In 1814, at the age of 80, he traveled into the Rocky Mountains to the banks of the Yellowstone River. His death in 1820 marked the end of a life-long career on the frontier in which he had been a major participant in the early expansion of the United States, and an eyewitness to the new nation's territorial push westward in the first decades of the 19th century.

The annexation of Kentucky by Virginia at the outset of the American Revolution was the first territorial western acquisition of the United States. In 1792, Kentucky was admitted to the Union, the first state to be carved out of the Trans-Appalachian West.

THE FRONTIER IN THE AMERICAN REVOLUTION

As the first great pioneer migration began to stream over the Appalachians from western Pennsylvania into Kentucky and Tennessee, relations between the English colonies and the mother country had begun to unravel. In April of 1775, fighting had broken out in Massachusetts between British forces and colonial militia, marking the start of the American Revolution.

Underlying the colonists' dissatisfaction with British rule—along with unfair taxation and other abuses of their "rights as Englishmen"—was the British govern-ment's prohibition against western settlement. Settlers on the Appalachian frontier had become disgruntled by the British government's reluctance to provide protection against the Indians. Opposition to British frontier policy, before expressed in a flagrant disregard of the Proclamation Line of 1763, now galvanized the Trans-Appalachian population behind the movement for independence. On July 4, 1776, the colonies proclaimed their separation from Great Britain in the Declaration of Independence.

The Revolutionary War in the West may well have seemed to the frontier population more like the "British and Indian War." Just as the French had won the allegiance of the native tribes in their struggle against the British in North America 20 years before (in the French and Indian War), so now did the British win Indian support against the colonists.

In the early years of the war, Cherokees launched attacks on the North Carolina–Tennessee frontier. In 1778, the Iroquois, led by the Mohawk leader Thayendanegea (also known as Joseph Brant) along with a Tory forces under John Butler and his son Walter, attacked settlements along New York's Mohawk Valley and Pennsylvania's Wyoming Valley. On July 3, 1778, John Butler and a force of Tory Rangers and allied Iroquois captured and burned a post known as Forty Fort in Pennsylvania. On November 11, Joseph Brant and his warriors, along with Tories under Walter Butler, attacked the small frontier

Thayendanegea (Joseph Brant) (Photo courtesy of the New York State Library)

North America, 1778 (Photo courtesy of the Library of Congress)

settlement of Cherry Valley, New York, about 50 miles west of Albany.

To counter the Tory and Iroquois threat, in the summer of 1779 George Washington, now a general and commander of the Continental Army, dispatched an expeditionary force into Iroquois country. General John Sullivan commanded a column out of Easton, Pennsylvania, and up the Susquehanna Valley into New York. General James Clinton led a column out of Albany to a staging point on the Mohawk River, then southward to Otsego Lake and the northern end of the Susquehanna. Colonel Daniel Brodhead led a third column from Ft. Pitt (Pittsburgh) in western Pennsylvania along the Allegheny. The more than 4,000-troop army marched across Iroquoia, burning entire villages and crops. The only battle of any size occurred at Newtown on August 29, 1779,

near the present-day New York–Pennsylvania border. The Indians lost 22 warriors; the rest retreated into the wilderness. But as a result of the destructive campaign, British-backed Indian and Tory activity on that segment of the northwestern frontier was effectively halted for the rest of the war.

Meanwhile, the settlements in Kentucky found themselves under perpetual siege. The Shawnees and Delawares, supported and supplied by the British in the Illinois country, forced most of the Kentucky pioneers to flee eastward across the mountains to Virginia or seek refuge at Boonesborough, St. Asaph's and Harrodsburg.

In late 1776, while in Williamsburg petitioning for Kentucky's annexation by Virginia, George Rogers Clark managed to secure military aid for the beleaguered Kentucky settlements. With the help of Virginia governor

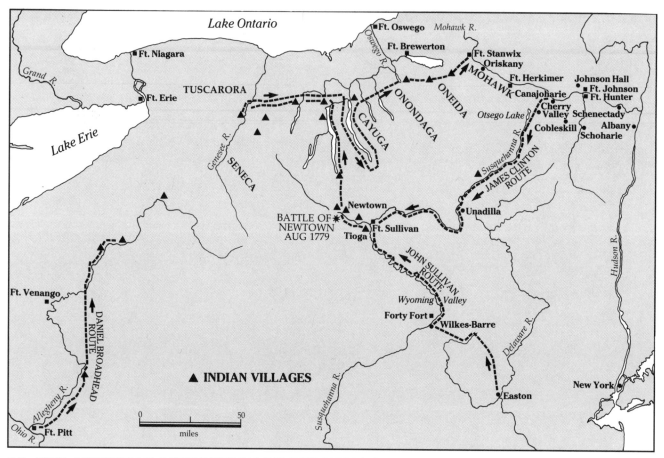

1.7 THE AMERICAN REVOLUTION ON THE NEW YORK FRONTIER: 1779

Patrick Henry, he brought a vital shipment of gunpowder down the Ohio River from Pittsburgh and overland to Boonesborough and Harrodsburg, enabling the Kentucky frontier militia to mount a successful stand against the Delawares and Shawnees.

A year later, Clark was back in the Virginia capital where he won Governor Henry's support for a counteroffensive against Kaskaskia and Vincennes in the Old Northwest—the region bounded by the Appalachians, the Great Lakes, the Ohio River and the Mississippi River. These British strongholds in the Illinois country served as bases for the British-allied Indians in their raids against Kentucky and the Ohio Valley. Clark reasoned that the only effective way to defend the Kentucky frontier was with a long-distance strike against these settlements, and ultimately with the capture of the main British frontier garrison at Detroit.

Clark mustered a force of 175 Kentucky riflemen, largely equipped at his own expense, and set out by boat down the Ohio from Fort Pitt. Some of his contingent, who had brought their families along, intended to use Clark's campaign in the West to carve out new homes and farms. Clark established Fort Massac, which was located below the Falls of the Ohio. Some of his soldier-settlers and their families remained there, and founded the new settlement of Louisville, named in honor of America's new ally, French monarch Louis XVI.

In late June of 1778, Clark and his command left Fort Massac, traveling down the Ohio as far as its junction with the Tennessee River, in what is now southeastern Illinois. From there, he set out overland for Kaskaskia on the Mississippi River, a former French settlement now held by the British. On July 4, 1778, Kaskaskia fell to Clark and his patriot forces with little resistance, the British garrison there having been removed the previous year. He soon won the allegiance of the settlement's French inhabitants, and at the nearby Indian village of Cahokia, succeeded in gaining the support of some leaders among the Chippewa, Fox, Illinois, Kickapoo, Miami, Ottawa, Potawatomi, Seneca, Shawnee and Wyandot bands.

Soon afterward, Clark and his forces took Vincennes on the Wabash River to the east. Later that year, the region was officially incorporated into the United States as a county of Virginia.

Meanwhile, a large British and Indian force commanded by British lieutenant governor Henry Hamilton marched southward from Detroit and recaptured Vincennes. In response, Clark left from Kaskaskia and undertook an overland counter-assault against the Brit-

1.8   THE AMERICAN REVOLUTION ON THE WESTERN FRONTIER: 1778

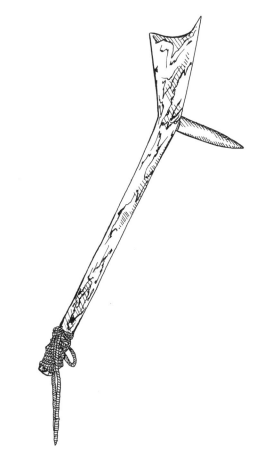

Chippewa Warclub (Molly Braun)

son's proposal; 20 years later, however, Clark's younger brother William would take part in the first official U.S. exploration into the Trans-Mississippi West as co-leader of the Lewis and Clark Expedition.

While General George Washington's victory at Yorktown effectively ended the Revolutionary War on the East Coast, the conflict with the Indians still raged on the frontier, especially in the Ohio country. In 1782, a force of Kentucky riflemen suffered a defeat in the Battle of Blue Licks. Later that year, Clark again mounted a military response with a victory against the Indians and their British allies at Chillicothe.

In the years after the Revolution, George Rogers Clark fell on hard times, impoverished after the Virginia legislature failed to reimburse him for the costs he had incurred in his campaign in the Illinois country. He became involved with the Spanish government in Louisiana and later settled in what is now Indiana, where he died in 1818.

The Revolutionary War officially ended with the Treaty of Paris in 1783. Although the Americans had triumphed in the region that would become known as the Old Northwest, the British still maintained a strong military presence at Detroit and other Great Lakes posts.

ish advance position at Vincennes, 180 miles to the east. In February of 1779, he led his men across what is now southern Illinois toward the Wabash, trudging through country at times flooded to shoulder level.

After three weeks, Clark and his Kentuckians reached Vincennes and launched a surprise attack against Hamilton's British and Indian forces. Clark persuaded the Indian allies of the British to desert, and Hamilton, deceived into thinking he was outnumbered by the patriot forces, surrendered Vincennes.

Clark had planned a major new offensive against Detroit, hoping to remove the British-backed Indian threat on the frontier and seize control of the region for the Americans. Yet support for Clark's plan was not forthcoming from the Continental Congress. Moreover, Clark's men had enlisted only for the assault on the Illinois settlements; many of them began returning to their homes in Kentucky.

Before the end of 1779, Clark himself withdrew eastward to the Falls of the Ohio where he directed defensive operations against the Indians. At the conclusion of hostilities in 1783, Thomas Jefferson, Clark's influential neighbor from his native Virginia, proposed to Congress that the hero of the campaign on the western frontier be commissioned to lead an exploring expedition into the Far West. The government declined to follow up Jeffer-

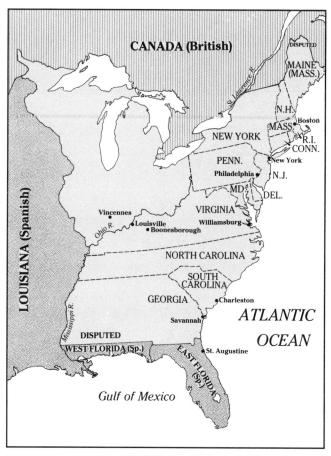

1.9 THE UNITED STATES AFTER THE TREATY OF 1783

SIBERIA
(Russian)

GREENLAND

ALASKA
(Russian)

UNCHARTED

Hudson
Bay

BRITISH

St. Lawrence R.

CLAIMED
BY
RUSSIA,
SPAIN,
&
GREAT
BRITAIN

UNITED
STATES

SPANISH

Mississippi R.

PACIFIC
OCEAN

ATLANTIC
OCEAN

Gulf of Mexico

BAHAMA ISLANDS (Br.)

CUBA (Sp.)

SANTO DOMINGO
(Sp.)

JAMAICA (Br.)

HAITI (Fr.)

BRITISH

Caribbean Sea

1.10   NORTH AMERICA IN 1783 (NON-INDIAN CLAIMS)

1.11 WESTERN LAND CLAIMS AFTER 1781

In negotiating the Treaty of Paris, the American representatives found themselves at odds with their ally, France, now itself allied with Spain. The Spanish, wishing to restrict the new American nation's expansion westward, devised a plan with France whereby the territory between the Appalachians and the Mississippi was to be reserved for the Indians. Such a move contradicted not only American territorial claims on the Old Northwest, but also threatened to bring the American territory in Tennessee, Kentucky and western Georgia under Spanish sovereignty.

The American diplomats in Paris, including Benjamin Franklin and John Jay, responded by disregarding the interests of France and Spain and instead dealt directly with the British. In the East, the border with Canada was established much as it exists today. (The Webster-Ashburton Treaty of 1842 would resolve the border dispute between Maine and New Brunswick and border disputes in the Great Lakes region.) The United States also received the lands of the Old Northwest as far as the Mississippi. The new nation's northwestern boundary was defined as running from Lake Superior to the Lake of the Woods, with the Mississippi River designating its western boundary. Southward, its territory ran as far as the 31st Parallel, along what is now Florida's northern

limit, eastward to the Atlantic coast. Ironically, Florida, which had remained loyal to Great Britain throughout the Revolution, was ceded to Spain.

THE OLD NORTHWEST

The Treaty of Paris, ratified by the Continental Congress in January of 1784, confirmed the status of the United States as a sovereign nation. Nonetheless, while Spain, France and Great Britain now recognized the new nation's territorial boundaries, how the United States was to assert and maintain its authority over its dominion in the Trans-Appalachian West was an issue still not resolved.

Even before hostilities with Great Britain had officially ended, the question of claims on western land held by some states had posed an obstacle to unifying the new nation. Maryland's delegation to the Continental Congress, leading the opposition of those states with no such claims, argued that it was unfair to expect all the states to take part in liberating the western region from British control if only some of the states were to benefit. Furthermore, it was feared that after independence was finally won, if these states were to retain their hold on the West, they would grow to dominate the smaller Atlantic states without western lands.

Only after New York, Connecticut, Massachusetts, North Carolina and Georgia had consented to cede to the Congress their claims to territory between the Appalachians and the Mississippi did Maryland agree to the Articles of Confederation—the final state to do so.

Starting in 1781, land cessions by the individual states brought the vast Trans-Appalachian West under the control of the central government. The Continental Congress then began to develop a plan for the development and administration of the region north of the Ohio River between the Appalachians and the Mississippi, which came to be known as the Northwest Territory.

In May of 1785, Congress enacted what became known as the Land Ordinance of 1785. This was the first

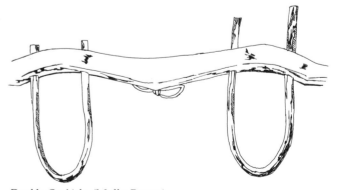

Double Ox Yoke (Molly Braun)

step in organizing the Northwest Territory. The pattern of prior settlement in the region had been haphazard, with land companies claiming title to huge tracts of largely unsurveyed Indian territory, often on lands already settled by squatters, giving rise to numerous disputes over which party actually had title to the land.

Under the Ordinance of 1785, the central government authorized the division of the Old Northwest into individual townships of 36 square miles each. Each township was then subdivided into 36 individual square mile sections (640 acres) and sold to the public. In each township, revenues derived from the sale of one square mile were reserved for the establishment of a public school, while four other square mile sections were set aside for use by the U.S. government.

The plan, however, did not make the lands of the Northwest Territory readily available to individual settlers. The minimum size of lots sold was 640 acres—one square mile—with a minimum selling price of one dollar an acre, plus survey costs. A square mile lot was far greater than most individual farmers could possibly need or manage. In addition, pioneer land seekers rarely had enough cash to buy even one section, and consequently much of the Northwest Territory was promptly bought up by land speculators and resold to settlers for a tremendous profit.

One such group was the Ohio Company of Associates, headed by Massachusetts governor Rufus Putnam, a former high-ranking Revolutionary War officer, along with the Reverend Manasseh Cutler, Benjamin Tupper and Samuel Parsons. The Ohio Company acquired 6.5 million acres of land in the Ohio country after Putnam and his associates took advantage of the depreciation of Continental currency. Their actual purchase price amounted to less than 10 cents an acre, far below the one dollar an acre asking price intended by the central government. In 1788, the Ohio Company of Associates established its first settlement in the Northwest Territory at the confluence of the Muskingum and Ohio rivers. Named Marietta, in honor of the French queen Marie Antoinette, it was the first planned permanent settlement in the Northwest Territory, and that year it became the region's first territorial capital. The first governor of the Northwest Territory was Arthur St. Clair, a Revolutionary War officer and former president of the Continental Congress.

Although the initial land offerings in the Northwest Territory mainly benefited land speculators, it was through the secondary sales of the lands to settlers that the region came to be surveyed and developed with a minimum of conflict over valid land titles. The subsequent Land Act of 1800 provided for the government's sale of smaller-sized lots with credit terms available, making the lands of the region more accessible to individual settlers.

The Continental Congress wanted to avoid maintaining the western region as a colonial empire, subject to the direct rule of the central government in the East. They feared this would eventually lead to resentment and revolt among the inhabitants, leading to a break with the United States in much the same way the United States had separated itself from England 10 years before.

In an effort to create a local government for the Northwest Territory, Congress enacted the Northwest Ordinance of 1787. Under this plan, the region's first governor was appointed by Congress, along with three judges. The ordinance further provided that the Northwest Territory was to be divided into three to five territories. When any of these territories attained a population of 5,000 free, white males, it could elect a territorial legislature empowered to enact local laws. Eventually, when the population of any of these territories reached 60,000 free inhabitants, a constitution could be drafted, and if approved by the U.S. Congress, that territory would be admitted into the Union as a state, with the same rights as any of the original 13 states.

The Northwest Ordinance of 1787 openly banned the extension of slavery into any of the new territories, except for those slaves already in the territory. This marked one of the earliest attempts by the central government to deal with the issue of slavery, setting a precedent that was to have a far-reaching impact on future developments in westward expansion.

In 1803, Ohio became the first state carved from the Northwest Territory to be admitted to the Union, followed by Indiana in 1816, Illinois in 1818, Michigan in 1837 and Wisconsin in 1848. From the Northwest Ordinance of 1787 evolved the system of organizing newly acquired lands first into territories, then incorporating them into the Union as states—a policy that would be generally followed throughout the 19th century and into the 20th, until the admission of Hawaii in 1959.

While the issues involving the administration of the Northwest Territory had now been resolved, there still remained the problem of asserting U.S. sovereignty over the region's indigenous population.

A series of meetings with tribal leaders began in October of 1784, under which the Indians ceded their territories to the United States. Representatives of the Iroquois, Wyandots, Delawares, Chippewas, Miamis, Ottawas and other tribes of the region recognized the sovereignty of the United States and gave up territorial claims in return for payments from the central government.

These treaties established the precedent that the United States government had the authority to purchase Indian lands. Soon afterward, a number of these land cessions were refuted by some tribal leaders, such as the Miami chief Little Turtle, who claimed they had not understood that they were actually giving up the right to co-inhabit their traditional homelands. These misunder-

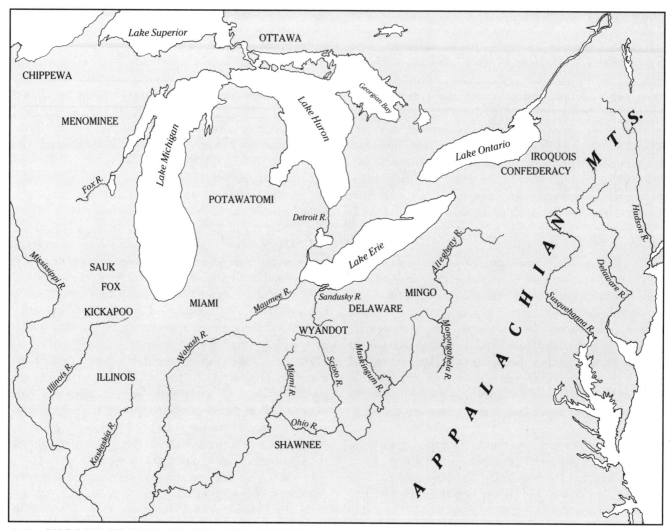

1.12 INDIAN TRIBES OF THE OLD NORTHWEST

standings fueled hostilities and soon led to a major armed conflict between the United States and the Indians of the Northwest Territory.

Initially, the central government attempted, under the Articles of Confederation, to prevent whites from encroaching upon the lands that, under the provisions of the treaties, had been reserved for the Indians. In 1785, it sent Colonel Josiah Harmar and a small military force into the Ohio country where Harmar established Fort Harmar at the confluence of the Muskingum and Ohio rivers, a strategic point on the usual river route taken by prospective white settlers on their way into the lands north of the Ohio. Harmar's efforts to turn back newly arrived pioneers and remove those that had already illegally encroached upon Indian lands proved to be less than effective. Squatters persisted in streaming into the protected area, many of them Revolutionary War veterans eager to stake claims to lands promised to them as a reward for their military service.

Moreover, some Indian bands themselves ignored the restrictions the treaties had placed upon them. Raids on authorized white settlements north of the Ohio continued, prompting a strong military response from the government. With the ratification of the U.S. Constitution in 1789, Indian resistance in the Northwest Territories became the concern of the newly empowered federal government. The following year, President George Washington ordered an armed force of federal troops and Kentucky, Pennsylvania and Virginia militia to undertake a punitive expedition against the region's tribes.

In September of 1790, Harmar, now a brigadier general, led a combined force of about 2,000 men from Fort Washington, the site of present-day Cincinnati, up the Little Miami River northward along what is now the Ohio–Indiana state line. At an Indian village near what is now Fort Wayne, Indiana, Harmar's men routed the inhabitants, destroying homes and crops. Within days, however, Indians of allied bands under Little Turtle

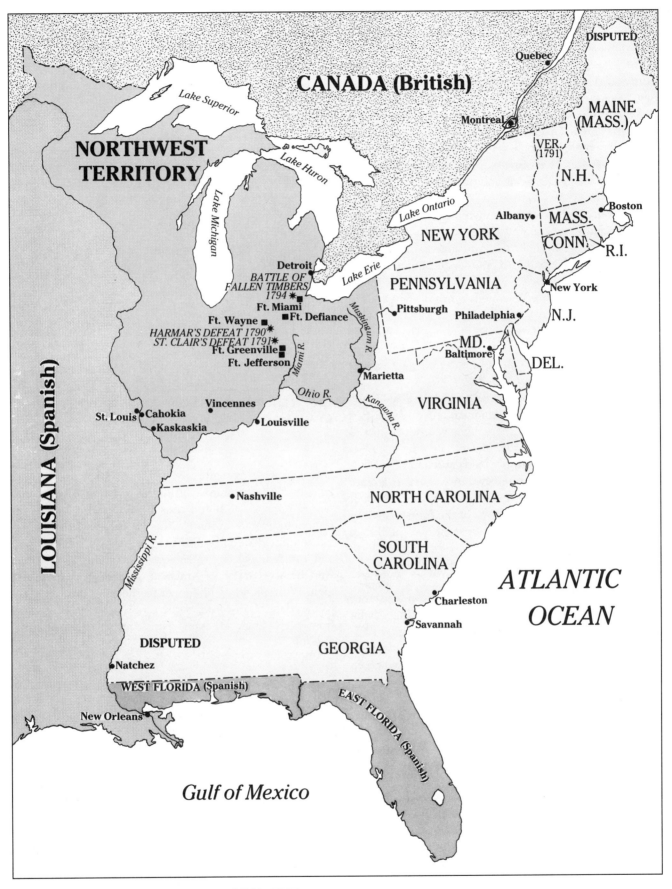

1.13   THE NORTHWEST TERRITORY: 1787

counterattacked with devastating results. With more than 200 of his men killed and many wounded, Harmar was compelled to withdraw southward to Fort Washington.

Encouraged by this victory, the Indians stepped up their raids on the Ohio frontier. In addition, the British, who still occupied garrisons at Detroit, Michilimackinac and other Great Lakes sites, also sought to discourage American settlement in the region, viewing it as a threat to the fur trade. They gave support to the Indians by providing trade goods, arms and protection in their frontier forts.

In response to the setback suffered by Harmar's expedition, Washington ordered the governor of the Northwest Territory, Arthur St. Clair, to take command of a new and larger campaign to counter the Indian threat. St. Clair first established Fort Hamilton and Fort Jefferson as fortified advanced positions north of the Ohio. In November of 1791, his forces made their way northward toward present-day Greenville, Ohio. The Indians launched a surprise attack. In the battle near the Wabash River, St. Clair lost fully half his entire force, with about 600 men killed and 300 wounded.

The next year, Revolutionary War hero General "Mad" Anthony Wayne was given command. He established Fort Greenville, and from there advanced northward to the site of St. Clair's earlier defeat. By July of 1794, Wayne had established supply roads and additional outposts to support a major offensive. In August, at a place known as Fallen Timbers, he won a decisive victory over the Indians who fled to the safety of the British garrison at Fort Miami. When it became apparent that the British would not lend their support this time, many of the Indians gave up the struggle and retreated back into the wilderness.

Wayne went on to destroy Native American resistance in what is now northeastern Indiana, eradicating Miami villages in the surrounding area. By the spring of 1795, the Indians were ready to negotiate a peace settlement. At the ensuing Treaty of Greenville, the Indians agreed to give up their claims to most of what is now southeastern Ohio and southeastern Indiana.

The Treaty of Greenville marked the first time the U.S. government had won concessions from the Indians as a result of a military victory. As a result, much of the Northwest Territory was open to extensive white settlement.

The British meanwhile still held forts in the region, maintained in flagrant violation of the Treaty of Paris of 1783. In November of 1794, a few months after Wayne's victory at Fallen Timbers, American diplomat John Jay was in London where he finalized a treaty with British officials that provided for the surrender of all British garrisons in the Trans-Appalachian West. In return, the

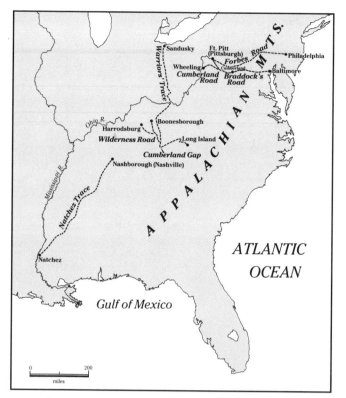

1.14 ROADS IN COLONIAL AND POST-REVOLUTIONARY TIMES

U.S. agreed to recognize as valid all debts and claims held by British commercial interests dating back to the period prior to 1783, and consented to allow British fur traders to operate in the Northwest Territory.

The immediate impact of the victory over the Indians, and the removal of British forts under the Jay Treaty, was the acceleration of American settlement into the region. With migration no longer restricted to the southern Cumberland Gap route, settlers now poured westward from New England, New York and the mid-Atlantic region.

THE OLD SOUTHWEST

West of the southern Appalachian frontier, the United States had to win a similar struggle to assert its sovereignty in the region known as the Old Southwest. Again, the nation's westward movement faced opposition from a European power—in this case Spain, which then held the Louisiana country. In Georgia, the Carolinas and Kentucky, the southeastern Indian nations—the Choctaw, Cherokee, Chickasaw and Creek—with the encouragement of the Spanish, continued to resist westward settlement. This situation was further complicated in 1786, when Spain closed the lower Mississippi and the

Georgia, 1797 (Photo courtesy of Library of Congress)

port of New Orleans to American ships, cutting off the main outlet for agricultural products from Kentucky and Tennessee.

Although this step soon prompted a movement among Tennessee and Kentucky settlers to join with Spain in order to regain use of the vital trade route, Spain reversed its position three years later, opening New Orleans to American traders. In 1795, in the Treaty of San Lorenzo, negotiated by U.S. diplomat Thomas Pinckney, Spain settled its disputes with the United States over the western boundaries of Georgia and assured American rights to navigation on the Mississippi. In addition, Spain agreed to curb the Indian attacks on the southern frontier and recognized U.S. claims over the region now comprising Mississippi and Alabama.

SOVEREIGNTY BY FORCE

At the conclusion of the American Revolution in 1783, the United States found itself only nominally in control of the Trans-Appalachian West. Only through a series of diplomatic struggles and military triumphs did the new nation actually achieve sovereignty over the territory stretching westward to the Mississippi.

The Mississippi River (Photo courtesy of the National Archives of Canada)

FRANKLIN: THE STATE
THAT NEVER WAS

South of the Ohio River, in what was then the Old Southwest, the first attempt was made to create a new state west of the Appalachians. In 1780, after he had lost title to his lands in the Kentucky country, Richard Henderson, together with frontiersman James Robertson, established the settlement of Nashborough (present-day Nashville) in what was then North Carolina's western territory. Attracted by cheap lands in the surrounding region, speculators bought up huge tracts and sold them to frontier settlers who soon flocked into the area.

In 1784, after North Carolina had ceded the Tennessee country to the central government, a move-

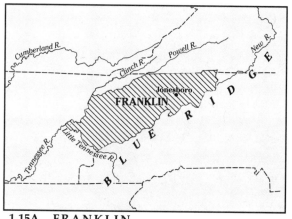

1.15A FRANKLIN

ment for statehood got under way, led by land speculator John Sevier. Many of Tennessee's inhabitants, although glad to be independent of North Carolina, did not look forward to administration by Congress and the new central government. Wishing to avoid an interim period as a territory, a convention of representatives of the frontier communities was held at Jonesboro. They voted to organize the Tennessee country as a new state and apply to Congress for admission to the Union. The proposed state was named "Franklin," in honor of Benjamin Franklin, in an effort to win the support of that influential Pennsylvania statesman.

Congress was slow to act, and North Carolina decided to reclaim the Tennessee country. In 1788, a brief revolt broke out between supporters of Franklin statehood and those wanting to rejoin with North Carolina, with the North Carolina faction ultimately winning out. Sevier went on to serve in the North Carolina legislature until 1790, when North Carolina again ceded Tennessee to the central government. Six years later, the territory of Tennessee was admitted to the Union, with Sevier as its first governor.

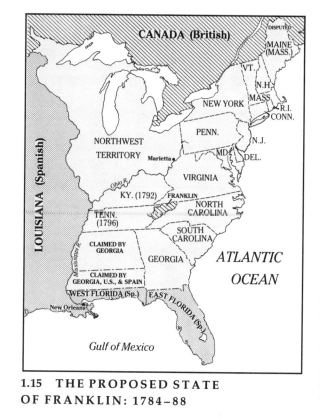

**1.15 THE PROPOSED STATE
OF FRANKLIN: 1784–88**

Chapter 2

THE UNITED STATES EXTENDS ITS EMPIRE (1796–1811)

IN THE 1790s, THE United States emerged as a sovereign nation under its newly formulated Constitution and federal government. The era also saw a new eruption of conflicts among the European powers, ushered in by the French Revolution and the rise of Napoleon. These events in Europe contributed to U.S. territorial expansion.

At the close of the French and Indian War in 1763, France ceded its central North American domain to Spain to keep it out of the hands of Great Britain. Known as Louisiana, it enveloped a vast expanse of territory to the west of the Mississippi River, stretching westward to the Rocky Mountains and northward to British Canada.

With U.S. independence from Great Britain in 1783, the nation's western territorial boundary was designated as the Mississippi River, with Spanish Louisiana bordering its western frontier. Spanish control of the lower Mississippi, and especially of New Orleans, became a problem for western settlers when the Spanish would often close that port to American shipping. There were then few roads connecting the Trans-Appalachian West with the East. Consequently, the southern Ohio Valley regions of Kentucky and western Tennessee, and the American settlements of the lower Mississippi Valley relied on the Mississippi River and the port of New Orleans as a trade route to markets in the eastern United States, the West Indies and Europe.

In 1795, the Treaty of San Lorenzo temporarily resolved this issue. Within five years, however, French designs on Louisiana posed an even greater threat, not only to America's vital access to New Orleans, but to the security of the nation's entire western region.

On October 1, 1800, France and Spain entered into the Treaty of San Ildefonso in which Spain agreed to cede Louisiana to France. In return, France promised to secure a kingdom in northern Italy for the Spanish king's son-in-law. Although an attempt was made to keep the terms of the San Ildefonso treaty secret, a report in a Paris newspaper soon brought these developments to the attention of American diplomats in Spain and France, who relayed the news to President Thomas Jefferson.

The United States could cope with a relatively weak foreign power like Spain on its western border. Yet the prospect of France—then one of the strongest military powers in the world—taking its place was a cause of great concern. Further fueling the impending crisis, on October 18, 1802 Spanish authorities, still nominally in control at New Orleans, once again closed that port to American trade.

For President Jefferson, the news that New Orleans had been closed to American trade signaled an even greater threat from abroad, and compelled him to take action, either diplomatic or military.

2.1   THE UNITED STATES IN 1800

THE LOUISIANA PURCHASE

Aware of Napoleon's plan to regain Louisiana and reestablish a French overseas empire in North America, Jefferson faced a three-fold challenge. First, he had to calm agitation among Congressional representatives of the western regions whose response to the latest closure of New Orleans was a cry for war with Spain, France or both countries. Secondly, he had to regain the right of American traders to deposit and trans-ship goods from New Orleans. Finally, to avoid the same conditions in the future, he needed to achieve U.S. possession of New Orleans and possibly the Spanish territory of East and West Florida. This last measure would assure that access to the Gulf Coast, essential to the economic well-being of America's western states and territories, would no longer be subject to the course of events in Europe.

Earlier in 1802, Jefferson had instructed Robert R. Livingston, his minister to France, to offer to buy New Orleans from the French, and possibly some adjoining territory in West Florida. Concerned over the implications of the impending cession of New Orleans and Louisiana to France, Jefferson stressed the urgency of the situation to Livingston.

Meanwhile, Napoleon was engaged in a campaign to retake Haiti following a successful slave insurrection led by Toussaint L'Ouverture. The restoration of French control in Haiti was crucial to Napoleon's vision of a renewed French empire in North America. He planned to use Louisiana as a source of food supplies and other necessities to support Haiti's lucrative sugar and coffee plantations. The French First Consul at that time declined any American overtures to buy New Orleans or any portion of Louisiana.

Within a few months, however, events in Haiti and in Europe led Napoleon to change his mind. Rather than the swift re-conquest that had been envisioned, French forces commanded by Napoleon's brother-in-law, Charles V.E. Leclerc, had been decimated. Although the Haitian insurrectionists had inflicted a fair share of the casualties, it was the ravages of yellow fever that caused the most French losses. By November of 1802, even Leclerc himself had succumbed to the disease. Moreover, by that time the tenuous peace with England and her allies was about to come apart, and it became apparent that France would soon be embroiled in a resumption of hostilities on the European continent, ruling out the continuing colonial venture in the Western Hemisphere.

In April of 1803, James Monroe, Jefferson's special envoy, joined Livingston in Paris. Monroe had been instructed to offer France as much as $10 million for the purchase of New Orleans and the Floridas. If that did not come about, he had been directed to visit London in order to form an alliance with Great Britain.

Without French control of Haiti, the Louisiana country and New Orleans were a useless drain on France's resources. Selling the territory to the United States would bring much needed cash into the French national coffers for the upcoming war with England. Monroe also knew that Louisiana would be difficult to defend against a British offensive from Canada.

Shortly before Monroe's arrival in Paris, Napoleon's foreign minister, Talleyrand, had approached Livingston with an offer to sell not only New Orleans but all of Louisiana. Immediately, Livingston and Monroe began negotiations over the price with French treasury minister François Barbé-Marbois. After a few weeks of bargaining, it was finally agreed that the U.S. would purchase Louisiana and the port of New Orleans for $15 million, an amount which also covered the assumption of American claims against France stemming from the undeclared naval war of 1797–98.

Both Livingston and Monroe believed they had probably overstepped their authority in having purchased half a continent rather than merely a city. The actual extent of the new territory was more than 800,000 square miles, making the purchase price about three cents an acre.

The prompt transfer of Louisiana came about in two stages. On November 30, 1803, Spain formally ceded Louisiana to France. On December 20, France officially turned the territory over to the United States in a ceremony in New Orleans.

Jefferson had his doubts over whether the federal government had the authority to purchase foreign territory, a move not in keeping with his own strict constructionist interpretation of the U.S. Constitution. Despite criticism from his political adversaries, the president succeeded in winning Congressional ratification of the purchase by an overwhelming vote in October of 1803.

Most Americans—especially the inhabitants of the West—were exuberant about the acquisition of territory, which virtually doubled the size of the nation overnight. Many hailed it as "America's Extension of Empire."

Nonetheless, some members of Congress, especially those representing the Northern states, as well as a number of important government officials, expressed

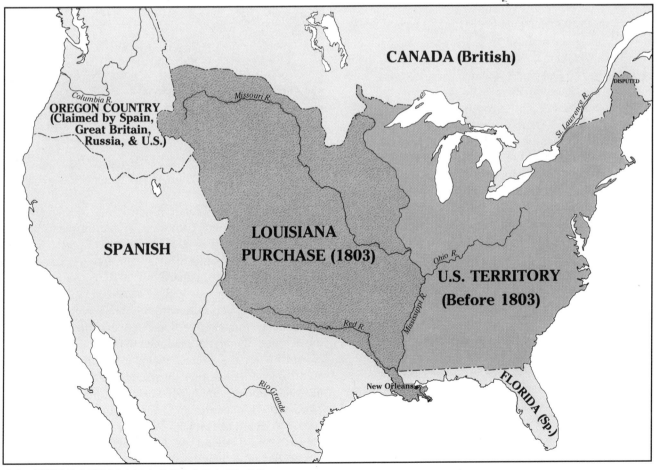

2.2 THE LOUISIANA PURCHASE OF 1803

their doubts over the legality underlying the transaction. Did the French actually have the right to sell Louisiana? In return for Louisiana, Napoleon had originally promised King Charles IV of Spain that he would secure the throne of the Kingdom of Tuscany for his son-in-law, a promise he failed to keep. Moreover, Napoleon had accepted Louisiana from Spain on the condition that he would never transfer it to a third nation, a pledge he promptly broke by selling it the United States.

In 1828, the legitimacy of the Louisiana Purchase was upheld indirectly by Chief Justice John Marshall of the Supreme Court. Ruling in *American Insurance Company v. Cantner*, Marshall implied that the Louisiana Purchase was consistent with the president's authority to make treaties with the consent of Congress, as expressed in the U.S. Constitution.

Dividing the newly acquired domain into U.S. territories began immediately. On March 26, 1804, Congress designated the region south of the 33rd parallel and west of the Mississippi as the Territory of Orleans. North of that boundary, the area was proclaimed as the District of Louisiana. Although initially placed under the jurisdiction of Indiana Territory, it was reorganized as the Territory of Louisiana in 1805.

In 1812, the Territory of Orleans was admitted to the Union as the state of Louisiana, and what had been the Louisiana Territory was renamed the Territory of Missouri. Other states that eventually formed from the lands of the Louisiana Purchase were the states of Arkansas, Missouri, Oklahoma, Kansas, Nebraska, Iowa, South Dakota, North Dakota, Montana, part of Minnesota, northeastern Colorado and most of Wyoming.

The Louisiana Purchase proved to be a great political triumph for both Jefferson and the newly created federal government. The entire Mississippi Valley was now under the sovereignty of the United States. With their access to the vital Mississippi River trade route and the port of New Orleans assured, western settlers set aside the sectional differences that had once fueled separatist sentiments in the southern Trans-Appalachian West.

THE LEWIS AND CLARK EXPEDITION

As early as 20 years before the Louisiana Purchase, Thomas Jefferson had been an enthusiastic proponent of American exploration of the Trans-Mississippi West. Prompted by his interest in the region's natural history, and concerned over British designs on the West, he had contacted Revolutionary War hero George Rogers Clark in 1783, with a suggestion that he lead an exploring expedition into the country between the Mississippi River and California.

Meriwether Lewis (Photo courtesy of Library of Congress)

Although Congressional funding was not forthcoming, Jefferson's interest for such a venture persisted. In Paris, while serving as U.S. minister to France in 1786, he had met the Connecticut adventurer John Ledyard. Eight years earlier, Ledyard had visited the northwest coast of North America with British naval explorer Captain James Cook, and knew first-hand of potential profits to be made from the fur trade between that region and the Orient. Ledyard planned to explore the Pacific Northwest for the United States, intending to reach the area by first traveling eastward across Siberia, crossing to Alaska and continuing his eastward march across the North American continent to the Atlantic coast. Jefferson helped Ledyard obtain travel documents for the journey. Nevertheless, Ledyard had only reached as far as central Siberia before he was stopped by suspicious Russian authorities, who deported him back to Western Europe.

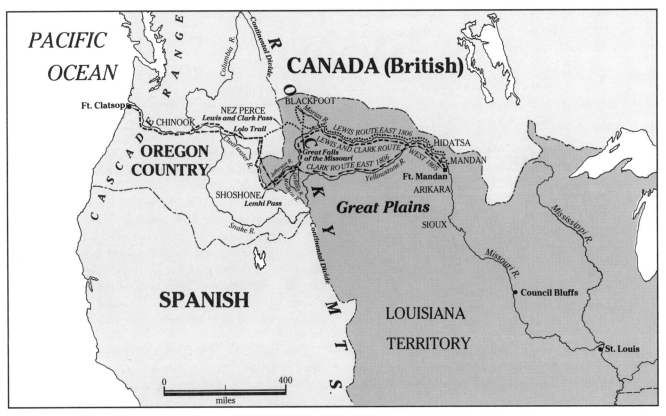

2.3 THE LEWIS AND CLARK EXPEDITION: 1804–06

In 1792, as vice president of the American Philosophical Society, Jefferson supported French naturalist Andre Michaux in his plan to explore Spanish Louisiana. This project was abandoned two years later, however, when it became apparent that Michaux was actually a secret agent for the French Revolutionary government and was in league with citizen Edmond Genet's schemes to seize the Louisiana country from Spain.

With his election as the third U.S. president in 1800, Jefferson was in a better position to promote a federally funded expedition into the vast region lying between the Mississippi and the Cascade Range. In January of 1803, he succeeded in gaining a secret appropriation from Congress to finance a probe into the West "for the purpose of extending the external commerce of the United States."

On the surface, the proposed expedition was to be scientific in scope, with the aim of collecting information on the region's animal and plant life. Yet Jefferson had underlying political and economic motives as well. He knew of the exploits of British explorer-fur trader Alexander Mackenzie, who had trekked across western Canada's Continental Divide to reach the Pacific coast of present-day British Columbia in 1793. Jefferson was also acquainted with Mackenzie's published account of the voyage in which he recommended that the British seize control of the mouth of the Columbia and monopolize the fur trade.

U.S. claims on the Pacific Northwest were based on the explorations of American sea captain Robert Gray, who had reached the mouth of the Columbia River in 1792. Jefferson hoped that an overland expedition to the Pacific Northwest would counter any British designs and reaffirm U.S. territorial claims over the Pacific Northwest.

Jefferson also speculated that as a result of American exploration in the Trans-Mississippi West, the Canadian-dominated fur trade of the Saskatchewan River region might be diverted southward via the Missouri River into the United States, adding to the growth of commerce in the American West.

To lead the expedition, Jefferson chose his 28-year-old private secretary, Captain Meriwether Lewis, a veteran of General "Mad" Anthony Wayne's campaign against the Indians of the Old Northwest. Lewis was given the responsibility of recruiting the other members of the exploring team himself, a group that eventually numbered nearly 50 men. As co-leader, he chose William Clark, younger brother of George Rogers Clark, an army officer who, like Lewis, had also seen frontier service in the Old Northwest. Technically, Captain Lewis outranked Clark, who held a commission as an artillery lieutenant; so that both men could lead exploring parties when the need arose, they were deemed to have equal standing as captains. Nonetheless, in order that both men could lead independent exploring parties when the need arose,

SACAJAWEA

Painting of Sacajawea Leading the Lewis and Clark Expedition (Photo courtesy of the National Archives)

The success of the Lewis and Clark Expedition may have hinged on the assistance provided by its only female member—the Shoshone Indian woman Saca-jawea. Sacajawea, or "Birdwoman," provided the important services of guide and interpreter to the Lewis and Clark Expedition, making her one of the earliest women to play a significant role in the history of America's territorial expansion into the Trans-Mississippi West.

Sacajawea was born in the tribe's homelands in what is now western Montana and central Idaho. When she was about 16, she was captured by a Hi-datsa raiding party and taken eastward to their vil-lages on the Missouri River in present-day North Dakota. Soon afterward, she became the wife of a French-Canadian trader named Toussaint Charbon-neau, who had won her as a prize in a gambling game.

Over the winter of 1804–05, Charbonneau and Sa-cajawea lived at the Mandan villages near present-day Bismarck, North Dakota. Also encamped in win-

Lewis agreed that both he and Clark would have equal standing as captains.

Lewis set out from Pittsburgh in mid-summer of 1803, floating down the Ohio River on a 55-foot long keelboat. With the U.S. acquisition of the Louisiana country a few months earlier, the character and purpose of the expedi-tion had dramatically altered. No longer merely a scien-tific probe into the wilds of a foreign land, it was now undertaken as an exploration into territory newly incor-porated into the United States. It also had a diplomatic purpose. Lewis and Clark were to inform the region's Indian tribes that they were now under U.S. sovereignty and assert U.S. authority over any British traders still op-erating in the region.

Lewis joined up with Clark near Louisville, and to-gether they continued down the Ohio to the Mississippi. After wintering on the east bank of the Mississippi River opposite St. Louis, Lewis and Clark and their Corps of Discovery (as the expedition came to be known) set out on their historic journey on May 14, 1804. The initial phase of the voyage up the Missouri took them through territory already known to French and British traders and trappers. Along the way, they stopped to hold a ma-jor conference with Native American leaders of the cen-tral Missouri, announcing that the United States was now in control of trade in the region; the site of that meeting became known as Council Bluffs.

At the end of October of 1804, Lewis and Clark arrived at the villages of the Mandan Indians, near the site of present-day Bismarck, North Dakota. They established winter quarters there at Fort Mandan, and spent the en-suing months preparing for the rest of the journey.

Natural history samples were sent downstream with some of the men in April of 1805, while Lewis and Clark and the rest of the expedition resumed the westward journey up the Missouri. Joining them was an Indian woman named Sacajawea, a Shoshone from the eastern Rockies who had been captured by the Hidatsas some years before, and married to a somewhat disreputable French trader named Toussaint Charbonneau. She had been recruited because of her knowledge of the territory along the upper Missouri. Her French husband was also engaged as the expedition's interpreter to the region's tribes.

Mandan Earthlodge (Molly Braun)

ter quarters there was the Lewis and Clark Expedition, on its way up the Missouri and across the Rockies to the Pacific Coast. The American explorers engaged Charbonneau as a guide and interpreter. At Charbonneau's request, Sacajawea was permitted to join the expedition. Before setting out on the historic journey, Sacajawea gave birth to a son, Jean Baptiste, whom she would carry on her back on the epic trek across the western half of North America.

Sacajawea proved to be of great service to Lewis and Clark throughout the expedition. Her knowledge of Indian sign language allowed them to communicate with the many Indian tribes they were to encounter, most of whom had never had any contact with white people. She had a good geographical knowledge of the territory through which they traveled, especially the lands around the Three Forks of the Missouri. It was her recommendation that the expedition take the westernmost fork—a stream they had named the Jefferson River—that brought them into the Bitterroot Valley and eventually into her native Shoshone homeland. There she was reunited with her brother, Cameahwait, now a Shoshone chief. He helped the explorers acquire the horses essential to continue their journey westward.

Sacajawea and Charbonneau spent the winter of 1805–06 with Lewis and Clark on the Oregon coast. In the spring, they accompanied Clark while he independently explored the Yellowstone River on the return journey eastward.

The details are not clear of what became of Sacajawea after she left the Lewis and Clark Expedition in North Dakota. She may have journeyed southward to St. Louis to deliver her infant son to the care of William Clark, then returned up the Missouri with one of Manuel Lisa's fur-trading expedition. Some accounts suggest she died soon after this from disease, although other stories relate she may have gone on to the Southwest to live with the Comanches, later settling on her people's Wind River Indian Reservation in Wyoming, where she lived until the early 1880s, reaching the age of 100.

William Clark (Photo courtesy of the Library of Congress)

By late April of 1805, Lewis and Clark had ascended the Missouri River to a point beyond the mouth of the Yellowstone. They continued up the Missouri as it swept westward, traveling through 1,200 miles of territory in which they encountered no Indians. On May 26, 1805, they caught their first glimpse of the distant Rocky Mountains. A week later, they came upon a fork in the river. Lewis named the stream flowing from the north the "Marias," after a cousin. While Clark and most of the party continued westward along the Missouri, Lewis explored up the Marias for 70 miles before it became unnavigable. He then returned to the Missouri, rejoining Clark and the rest of the group near the Great Falls of the Missouri in mid-June of 1805.

The Corps of Discovery came upon the Three Forks of the Missouri, the three branches of which they named the Jefferson, Madison and Gallatin (after secretary of the treasury Albert Gallatin). Sacajawea led them up the westernmost branch, the Jefferson, which took them towards the Continental Divide, and into the land of the Shoshones, Sacajawea's native people.

Still seeking a westward flowing river, the expedition resorted to carrying their canoes overland into the Bitterroot Valley in what is now western Montana. Here they encountered a band of Shoshones, headed by none other than Sacajawea's brother. From the Shoshones, the American explorers secured horses. With their canoes

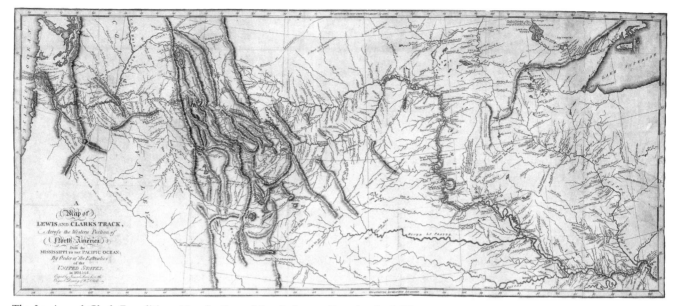

The Lewis and Clark Expedition, Map by Samuel Lewis from a Drawing by William Clark, 1806 (Photo courtesy of the Library of Congress)

cached for the return journey, they made their way through the Lemhi Pass and across the Continental Divide.

The Corps of Discovery next followed the Lolo Trail into the country of the Nez Perce Indians. With their help, they fashioned canoes and were guided to the Clearwater, a westward flowing stream that emptied into the Snake River.

On October 16, 1805, Lewis and Clark entered the Columbia, whose swift current through the Cascades brought them to the river's estuary on the Pacific Coast by November 7. Recording the event with his penchant for eccentric spelling, Lewis noted in his diary entry for that date: "Great joy in camp we are in view of the Ocian, the great Pacific Octean which we been so long anxious to See."

The expedition set up its winter quarters, Fort Clatsop, on the Pacific Coast, six miles south of the mouth of the Columbia in Chinook Indian country. In March of 1806, Lewis and Clark embarked on the return journey. Near the Continental Divide, the group split up. Lewis, still hoping to find a practical river route between the Upper Missouri and the Columbia, led a small contingent northward from the Great Falls of the Missouri and again surveyed the Marias River, hoping it might lead to the Saskatchewan. Meanwhile, Clark and the rest of the party followed a more southerly route through the Bozeman Pass and eastward along the Yellowstone River.

Lewis headed eastward through what is now known as the Lewis and Clark Pass. After a violent encounter at an encampment of Blackfoot Indians, in which two tribal members were killed, Lewis and his companions reached the mouth of the Yellowstone, where they soon rejoined Clark and the rest of the expedition. They made

a rapid downriver journey along the Missouri, arriving in St. Louis by September 23, 1806.

Lewis and Clark immediately went to Washington to present their report to President Jefferson. Their journey across thousands of miles of previously uncharted wilderness had yielded much information about the region's geography, as well its animal and plant life. It had also established the earliest American contacts with numerous Indian tribes. The explorers' descriptions of the country west of the Missouri was the first to characterize the region as "prairie" and "Great Plains." In their separate eastward explorations, they had traversed a wide arc of territory in present-day Wyoming and Montana, proving that no all-water route existed linking the Columbia and the Missouri. Their account of the overland accessibility into the rich beaver country of the Upper Missouri River region and Rocky Mountains revealed the economic potential of the region to a new generation of American pioneers—the fur traders.

ZEBULON PIKE EXPLORES THE UPPER MISSISSIPPI AND THE SOUTHWEST

While the Lewis and Clark Expedition was making its way westward, yet another group of army explorers had been dispatched to investigate the northern reaches of the newly acquired Louisiana country. In early August of 1805, a detachment of 20 soldiers, commanded by Lieutenant Zebulon Pike, headed northward from St. Louis by keelboat, intending to explore the upper Mississippi River, and if possible, determine its source. Unlike

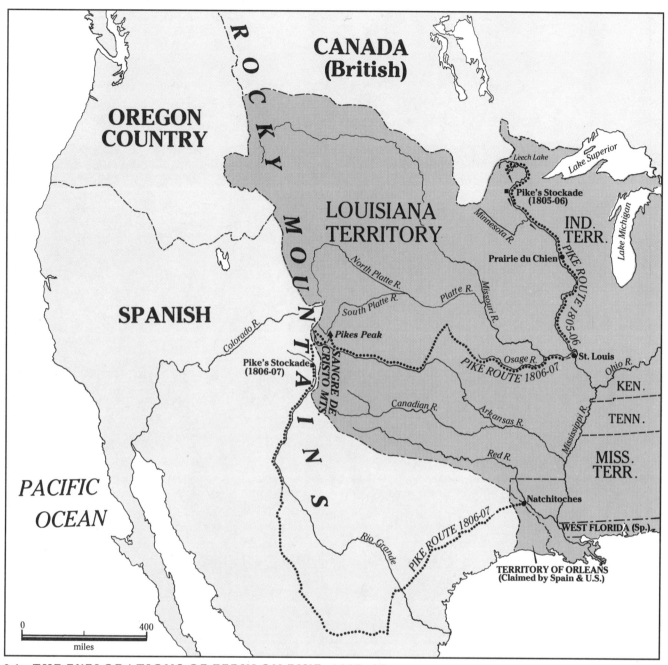

2.4 THE EXPLORATIONS OF ZEBULON PIKE: 1805–07

the Lewis and Clark Expedition, this one had not been ordered by Jefferson, but by General James Wilkinson, commanding general of the U.S. Army and at that time the Louisiana territorial governor out of St. Louis.

By the end of September, Pike and his men had ascended the Mississippi as far as the mouth of the Minnesota River. There he managed to purchase a military reservation from the local Sioux Indians around which later developed the city of St. Paul, Minnesota.

Over the following winter, with most of his command encamped near present-day Little Falls, Minnesota, Pike undertook an exploration farther northward. He reached northern Minnesota's Leech Lake, which he mistakenly

took to be the source of the Mississippi River. (The true source of the Mississippi, Lake Itasca, was discovered by Henry Rowe Schoolcraft in 1832.) Pike and his men arrived back in St. Louis at the end of April of 1806. Only two and a half months elapsed before Pike embarked on another exploration, this time into the southwestern regions of the Louisiana country. Again under orders from Wilkinson, he had been directed to explore the Red River and the Rio Grande in an effort to survey the southwestern boundaries of Louisiana. While the U.S. claimed that the Louisiana Purchase extended as far south as the Rio Grande, the Spanish, who still held the adjoining territory to the west and south, maintained

New Spain, Map by Zebulon Pike, 1810 (Photo courtesy of the Library of Congress)

that its true southwestern limits were hundreds of miles to the north, defined by the Red River, along the southern boundary of present-day Oklahoma.

Pike and his command followed the Missouri and Osage rivers across what is now Kansas and southern Nebraska, then traveled overland to the Arkansas River, ascending it as far as what is now Pueblo, Colorado, where they established a small stockade. At this point, Pike was clearly trespassing on Spanish territory. It was during this part of his explorations in the eastern Rockies that he sighted the mountain that now bears his name—Pikes Peak.

Pike and his men set out for the Red River in the spring of 1807. He led them southward across the Sangre

de Cristo Mountains and into the valley of the Rio Grande. They constructed a temporary stockade a few miles above the mouth of the Conejos River, a tributary of the upper Rio Grande. It was there, on February 26, 1807, that a Spanish patrol caught up with Pike and his expedition and arrested them.

Spanish authorities in New Mexico, learning of Pike's movements into their territory, had suspected he was leading an espionage mission. Pike and his men were taken to Santa Fe where they were interrogated, but no spying charges could be proven. After being detained for a short time, Pike and his party were escorted across northern Mexico and Texas to the American border settlement at Natchitoches, Louisiana. Although all his notes of the expedition had been confiscated by the Spanish, he was able to reconstruct from memory enough of what he had observed to publish one of the earliest non-Indian accounts of the territory now comprising the states of Kansas, Nebraska, Oklahoma, Colorado, New Mexico and Texas.

General James Wilkinson, who had ordered Pike's expedition, had long been involved in plots and intrigues with the Spanish or the French, and for many years had operated as a secret agent for the Spanish. After the Louisiana Purchase, he conspired with Aaron Burr, Jefferson's first vice president who had gained notoriety for his killing of Alexander Hamilton in a duel.

Wilkinson's involvement with Burr's secret plan to detach Louisiana from the United States and conquer Mexico with a private army cast a shadow on the motives behind Pike's explorations in the Southwest. Although implicated in the Burr-Wilkinson plot on his return, Pike was later exonerated of any wrongdoing.

In his report, Pike described a vast wasteland that would never develop along the pattern of agricultural settlement found in the lands east and west of the Appalachians. To Jefferson and others the territory held little value, except as a place to relocate Indian tribes displaced as white settlement pushed westward toward the Mississippi from the Ohio Valley and the southern states and territories.

THE FIRST AMERICAN FUR TRADERS

The Louisiana Purchase opened the Far West to the American fur trade. Lewis and Clark's reports of the region's bountiful beaver resources soon drew enterprising traders and trappers from St. Louis and the Mississippi Valley up the Missouri River and into the Rocky Mountains. One of the first of these was Manuel Lisa.

Manuel Lisa was born in New Orleans of Spanish parents; with the transfer of Louisiana to the United States in 1803, he became an American citizen. By then, he was well-established in the fur trade, operating out of St. Louis with an exclusive right to trade with the Indians along the Osage River in present-day Kansas.

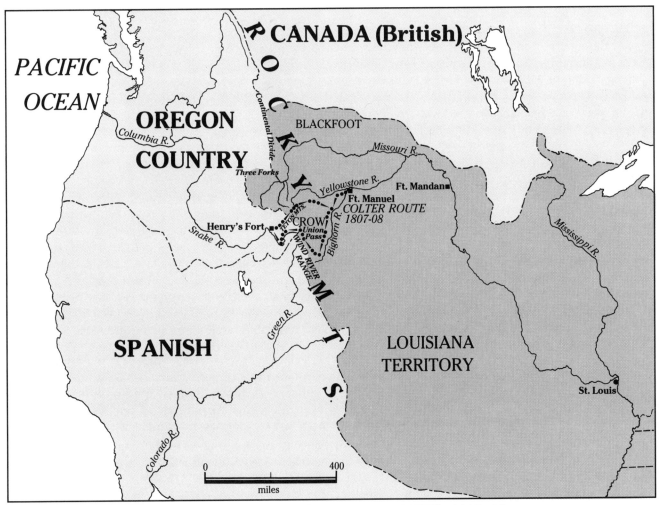

2.5   MANUEL LISA'S FUR EXPEDITIONS INTO THE ROCKIES: 1807–10

In the spring of 1807, Lisa led a party of about 40 men from St. Louis up the Missouri, then westward across present-day Montana by way of the Yellowstone River. One of his partners in the enterprise was George Drouilliard, who had crossed the Great Plains and Rockies with Lewis and Clark. At the junction of the Bighorn and Yellowstone rivers, Lisa established a trading post, Fort Manuel, the first known non-Indian settlement in what is now eastern Montana.

While Fort Manuel was under construction, one member of Lisa's party, John Colter—another veteran of the Lewis and Clark Expedition—headed westward on his own, seeking to open trade contacts with the Blackfeet. His travels took him through the Teton Mountains and the South Pass, and into the country now comprising Yellowstone National Park. He also explored the headwaters of the Green River as well as the Snake.

Lisa's next fur-trading expedition to the Rockies and upper Missouri was organized on a much larger scale as the St. Louis Missouri Fur Company, later becoming known as the Missouri Fur Company. He sent 150 men up the Missouri in the spring of 1809. Among his partners were William Clark, at that time governor of the Louisiana Territory, St. Louis merchant Pierre Chouteau and Andrew Henry. After establishing additional posts on the upper Missouri, the group reached Lisa's original post at the mouth of the Bighorn River where they engaged in a lucrative trade in furs with the Crow Indians.

In the spring of 1810, Andrew Henry led a party toward the Three Forks of the Missouri, establishing a trading post in what is now southwestern Montana. They were in the country of the Blackfeet, who still harbored a great animosity against whites because of the death of two of their people at the hands of the Lewis and Clark Expedition. Although Henry and his men began a profitable enough season of trading and trapping, they suffered a series of raids by Blackfoot war parties. Five of the traders were killed, and their furs and supplies were stolen.

The hostility of the Blackfeet drove off some of the traders. Andrew Henry, however, pushed westward across the Continental Divide to what became known as Henry's Fork of the Snake River, where he established a trading fort, Henry's Fort, near present-day Elgin, Idaho, returning to St. Louis in 1810. He later entered the lead-mining business with William Henry Ashley, with whom he would return to the fur trade after the War of 1812.

ASTORIA

The Lewis and Clark Expedition had shown there was a feasible river and overland route between the Mississippi and the coast of the Pacific Northwest, inspiring St.

John Jacob Astor (Photo courtesy of the Library of Congress)

Louis fur traders to embark up the Missouri and its tributaries to the eastern slopes of the Rockies. It was New York fur entrepreneur John Jacob Astor, however, who first envisioned using the Snake and Columbia River route to the Oregon coast as a gateway to the Orient. Like Captain Cook's sailors and John Ledyard before him, Astor considered the China trade as the real prize in the fur business. In the Chinese ports of Canton and Shanghai, a single ship carrying sea otter pelts from the Pacific Northwest coast and beaver pelts from the inland streams could bring a fortune far greater than an entire year's Rocky Mountain catch in St. Louis.

The Louisiana Purchase brought U.S. territory almost to the Pacific. All that stood in between was the Oregon Country, a region to which the United States, based on the explorations of Robert Gray and Lewis and Clark, now held a tenuous claim. Astor launched a great commercial enterprise to take advantage of both the newly gained access to Louisiana and American claims to the Oregon Country.

By 1810, Astor was a leading figure in the Great Lakes fur-trading business. His American Fur Company was ri-

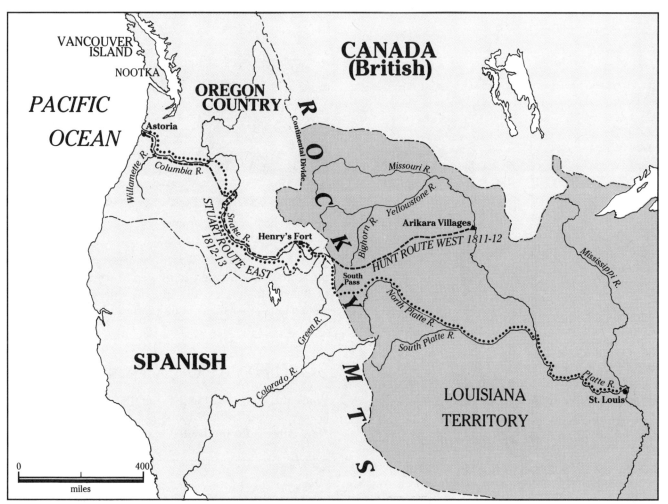

2.6 JOHN JACOB ASTOR'S FUR TRADERS IN THE FAR WEST: 1810–13

valed only by the Canadian-based Hudson's Bay Company and the North West Company.

For his enterprise in the Pacific Northwest, Astor formed a subsidiary firm, the Pacific Fur Company, with some of the principal personnel recruited in Montreal, many of them hired away from his competitors.

Astor planned a two-pronged effort: one by sea from New York and around Cape Horn to the Oregon coast, and the other up the Missouri River and overland across the Rockies to the mouth of the Columbia. His ship the *Tonquin* sailed from New York City on September 10, 1810, arriving at the mouth of the Columbia the following March. Soon afterward, the fur-trading settlement of Astoria was constructed six miles south of the river's estuary. Fur trading commenced at once, with expeditions sent deep into the interior of present-day Oregon, Washington and Idaho.

In June of 1810, the *Tonquin* cruised northward to trade with the tribes along the coast of present-day British Columbia. While stopping at Vancouver Island, a dispute erupted in which a Nootka chief was slapped in the face. In the ensuing fight, only one crew member survived. The lone survivor managed to ignite the vessel's store of gunpowder, blowing up the ship and killing himself and all the Indians aboard.

In late April of 1811, while Astoria was under construction, the landward portion of the enterprise, the "Overland Astorians," embarked by keelboat up the Missouri from St. Louis. They were led by Wilson Price Hunt, a New Jersey merchant who had settled in St. Louis. Although Hunt had originally planned to follow the Lewis and Clark route west, the Blackfoot bands of the Northern Plains were still a major threat to whites traveling through the region. To avoid Indian raids, the Astorians left the Missouri at the Arikara villages, south of Fort Mandan, acquired horses from the Indians, and headed westward toward the Bighorn Mountains and the Wind River. They then followed the Green River, the Snake and the Columbia, arriving at the Astoria settlement in mid-February of 1812.

Throughout that year, the traders at Astoria extended their operations inland, undertaking fur trapping on the Willamette and Okanagan rivers, as well as on the upper Columbia River in what is now eastern Washington.

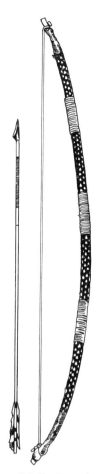

Blackfoot Bow and Arrow (Molly Braun)

Astoria (Photo courtesy of the New York Public Library)

Far West was slow to attract a great population. In the meantime, the vast land continued to remain the domain of the fur trader and the Indian, with few permanent settlements other than trading forts and military posts.

SOUTHWARD EXPANSION

While the Louisiana Purchase of 1803 had resolved the issue of access to the Mississippi River and the port of New Orleans for the United States, the adjoining region

In June of 1812, a small party of the Astorians, led by Robert Stuart, set out on an overland journey eastward to report on the enterprise's progress to John Jacob Astor. They wintered in what is now Wyoming, then crossed Nebraska and traveled down the Platte to the Missouri, arriving in St. Louis in April of 1813. Their eastward route from the Oregon coast, well to the south of the one taken by Lewis and Clark on their return journey in 1806, would years later become the important emigrant pathway—the Oregon Trail.

By December of 1812, word had reached Astoria that war had broken out between the United States and Great Britain. With a British warship on its way to take over the settlement, Astor's fur traders decided to sell Astoria to visiting traders of the North West Company to keep it from falling to the British as a prize of war. The sale, completed in October of 1813, marked the end of Astor's Pacific Northwest venture.

The onset of the War of 1812 imposed a hiatus on official U.S. exploring efforts and fur-trading activities in the Trans-Mississippi West. But the pattern for American occupation of its western lands had been established and would resume within a decade. Rather than a flood of emigrants pouring into the region to create replications of the agricultural communities of the East, America's

2.7 EXTENT OF U.S. SETTLEMENT, WITH PRINCIPAL POPULATION CENTERS, IN 1810

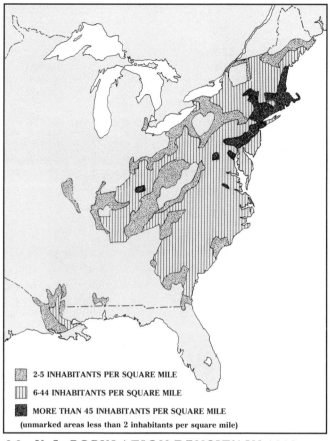

2-5 INHABITANTS PER SQUARE MILE

6-44 INHABITANTS PER SQUARE MILE

MORE THAN 45 INHABITANTS PER SQUARE MILE

(unmarked areas less than 2 inhabitants per square mile)

2.8 U.S. POPULATION DENSITY IN 1810

to the east still remained separated from the Gulf Coast by Spanish-held West Florida.

By 1810, the frontier inhabitants of the Old Southwest—Kentucky, Tennessee and present-day Alabama and Mississippi—were demanding access to the Flint, Chattahoochee, Coosa and Tombigbee rivers, the natural trade routes for the movement of goods southward to the Gulf of Mexico. Moreover, Americans from the adjoining U.S. states and territory who had settled in the region were clamoring for independence from Spain. Spanish West Florida had also become a haven for runaway slaves from Georgia and the Mississippi Territory, a factor that also served to irritate Americans in the adjoining U.S. territory.

With the support of influential Kentucky congressman Henry Clay, a group of frontier filibusterers organized an independent military expedition to seize Spanish West Florida. In September of 1810, they captured the Spanish outpost at Baton Rouge, and soon afterward, looked to the federal government to annex the region. With the support of Congress, President James Madison complied. He justified the action on the basis of a broad interpretation of the 1803 Louisiana Purchase Treaty, declaring that the territory France had ceded extended eastward to western Alabama's Perdido River, a region that then comprised most of Spanish West Florida.

In 1812, the western segment of the lands appropriated from Spanish West Florida were incorporated into the newly admitted state of Louisiana, and the eastern portion was assigned to the Mississippi Territory.

DIPLOMACY AND REAL ESTATE

Probably the greatest real estate deal in history, the Louisiana Purchase of 1803 more than doubled the size of the United States, stretching its western limits to the Rocky Mountains. Through diplomacy rather than war, the nation had made its first great thrust of territorial expansion.

In the succeeding decades, traders and government exploring expeditions probed the new western country. Yet unlike what had occurred in Kentucky and the Old Northwest, settlement into the region did not come on the heels of territorial acquisition and exploration. The region's Great Plains and the mountain ranges beyond would long be perceived by westbound emigrants as barriers that had to be traversed on their way to the more desirable lands of Oregon and California. As a result, settlement in much of the territory acquired by the Louisiana Purchase did not occur until the second half of the 19th century, when the region's agricultural potential was finally recognized.

America's purchase of Louisiana not only brought the nation a vast domain in which to expand, but it also established the legal and political precedents for the ensuing acquisitions of Florida, Texas, Oregon, California and Alaska.

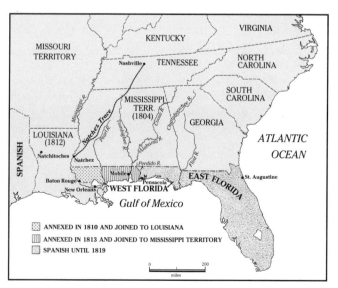

ANNEXED IN 1810 AND JOINED TO LOUISIANA

ANNEXED IN 1813 AND JOINED TO MISSISSIPPI TERRITORY

SPANISH UNTIL 1819

2.9 SPANISH FLORIDA AND ADJOINING U.S. TERRITORY: 1810–12

ELI WHITNEY AND THE COTTON GIN

In 1793, a young New Englander living in the South invented a machine that was to have a profound impact on the course of westward expansion.

Born in Westborough, Massachusetts, Eli Whitney (1765–1825) exhibited a penchant for inventing at an early age. As a boy he developed labor-saving devices for the manufacture of nails and hatpins.

In 1792, after graduating from Yale College, Whitney moved to Savannah, Georgia, where he studied law while working as a tutor at Mulberry Grove, the plantation owned by the widow of Revolutionary War hero Nathanael Green. Mrs. Green persuaded the young man to apply his talent for technological innovation to the problem faced by the region's cotton growers.

At that time, cotton production was limited mostly to a variety known as "sea island cotton," a type that could only be grown along the coast. Another type of cotton, known as "upland cotton" could be extensively raised on the abundant lands of the interior. Yet large-scale production of "upland cotton" had never been profitable because an entire day of labor was required to separate the seeds from a single pound of the short fibers.

Using tools he had fashioned himself, Whitney constructed a "cotton gin" ("gin" being short for engine) that dramatically reduced the amount of labor required to separate cotton seeds from the fiber. With the use of a rotating drum, cotton was drawn through a grating and over a series of circular saws,

Eli Whitney (Photo courtesy of the Library of Congress)

which automatically removed the seeds from the fiber.

The invention soon revolutionized the cotton industry. The cotton gin, when operated by an external power source, could process up to 1,000 pounds of cotton in a day, an amount equal to the hand labor of 1,000 slaves. The machine's impact on production was immediate as well as astounding. While in 1791, cotton exports from the South totaled only about 190,000 pounds, nine years later the amount had skyrocketed to 41 million pounds.

In England and New England, innovations in textile production brought about by the Industrial Revolution had greatly increased the demand for cotton. Spurred on by this new demand, and with a new way to profitably process "upland cotton," the plantation-based agriculture rapidly spread into the interior regions of Georgia, South Carolina, Louisiana and Arkansas.

The need for slaves to work these new cotton plantations also soared. Prior to Whitney's invention, slavery had begun to wane, outlawed in the North for moral reasons and on the decline in the South because it had become economically unprofitable. The advent of the cotton gin reversed this trend. Slavery was now essential for the spread of the newly infused cotton economy of the South. Even in the North, slavery won new supporters. The South's "peculiar institution" was now seen as vital not only for cotton production, but for the continued growth and prosperity of the newly developed textile industry of the northeastern states, an industry that thrived and depended on the availability of cheaply produced cotton.

Whitney himself had a difficult time realizing any gain from his invention. Before he could secure a patent, his cotton gin had already been copied and manufactured without his authorization. He litigated his cause in more than 50 costly lawsuits before he

The Cotton Gin (Photo courtesy of the Library of Congress)

saw any profit from his history-making invention. Eventually, the state of South Carolina awarded him $50,000, and the state of North Carolina arranged for royalty payments for his invention.

The introduction of the cotton gin led to a new surge of westward expansion in the South. Demand for more territory for cotton-growing brought about a migration of settlers inland from the Southeast Coast and the Gulf Coast as well as into the lower Mississippi Valley. Unlike the pioneers who settled the northern Trans-Appalachian West, these settlers did not establish small self-sufficient farms, but large plantations worked by slaves. With this expansion also came the strong sectional sentiments over the extension of slavery, an issue that would greatly influence the settlement of the West as well as the fate of the entire nation.

Chapter 3
CRISIS ON THE FRONTIER (1812–1820)

THE GREAT WESTERN DOMAIN acquired in the Louisiana Purchase of 1803 did little to satisfy America's hunger for new lands. Early 19th-century farmers and settlers viewed the unforested plains west of the Mississippi as an uninviting wasteland that lacked timber for building homes and towns, navigable rivers for shipping their goods to markets and adequate rainfall for the crops they raised.

Instead, throughout the first decade of the 19th century, the main thrust of western settlement was into the territories carved out of the Old Northwest, north of the Ohio River. Emigrants from the East and the Trans-Appalachian regions of Kentucky and Tennessee continued to push northward and westward into Ohio, Indiana and Illinois territories. In their wake they left depleted lands, rendered unproductive after only a few years by agricultural practices that paid little heed to crop rotation or the conservation of vital resources.

The perception of a limitless supply of fertile lands provided little motivation to alter this pattern. The relentless push westward continued. The advance of white settlement into areas reserved for the Indians under the 1795 Treaty of Fort Greenville caused a new struggle with the tribes north of the Ohio, a conflict that would help propel the United States into a second major war with Great Britain—the War of 1812.

INDIAN LAND CESSIONS AND A NEW INDIAN WAR IN THE OLD NORTHWEST

Soon after William Henry Harrison became governor of the newly organized Indiana Territory in 1800, he began an aggressive program of land acquisitions from the Indian tribes. His negotiating methods included plying tribal leaders with liquor, promising them military support in intertribal conflicts, offering them bribes, as well as threatening them with the use of armed force; he succeeded in winning Indian land cessions of tens of millions of acres in what is now southern Indiana and much of present-day Illinois.

In 1803, Harrison gained a huge chunk of the Illinois country from the Kaskaskias and other tribes of the Illinois Confederacy. In 1804, he met with representatives of the Delawares and other tribes at the Indiana territorial capital at Vincennes where he obtained the cession of a great crescent-shaped swatch of territory in southern Indiana. That same year, he obtained from the Sauk (Sac) and Fox tribes 15 million acres of Indian lands south of the Wisconsin River. At the same time, Michigan territorial governor William Hull was making similar arrangements for the cession of large tracts of Indian lands in what is now eastern Michigan.

The Indiana Territory was greatly diminished in size when the region to the west was organized as Illinois Territory in 1809. In response, Harrison sought to open more Indian lands to white settlement in Indiana; that year, he summoned representatives of the Delawares and Potawatomis to a conference at Fort Wayne. In September of 1809, in the ensuing Treaty of Fort Wayne, tribal leaders ceded 3 million acres of Indian lands along the lower Wabash River region to Indiana Territory. In return, the Indians received an increase in their annuities and a cash payment of $1,750, a price that amounted to less than a penny per acre.

Meanwhile, Indian resentment against these encroachments had begun to mount. Tecumseh, a leading Shawnee, was extremely outspoken about Harrison's land

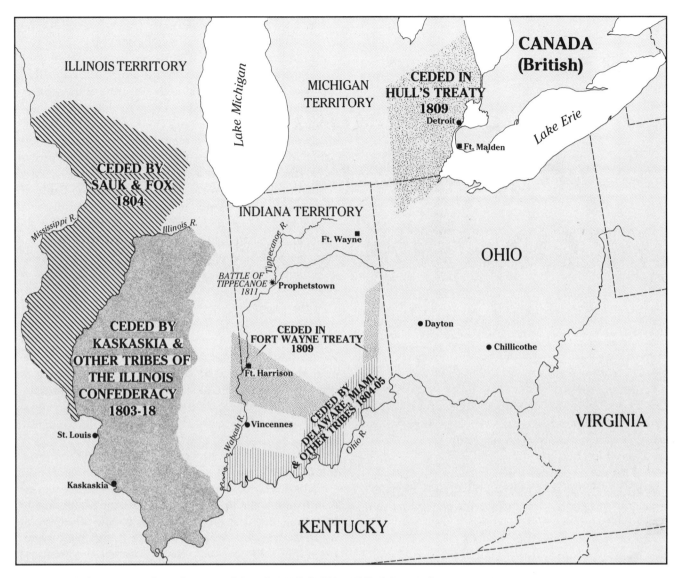

ILLINOIS TERRITORY

CEDED BY
SAUK & FOX
1804

Mississippi R.

Illinois R.

CEDED BY
KASKASKIA &
OTHER TRIBES OF
THE ILLINOIS
CONFEDERACY
1803-18

St. Louis●

Kaskaskia●

Lake Michigan

MICHIGAN
TERRITORY

INDIANA TERRITORY

Tippecanoe R.

Ft. Wayne■

BATTLE OF
TIPPECANOE ✱ Prophetstown
1811

CEDED IN
FORT WAYNE TREATY
1809

Ft. Harrison■

Wabash R.

Vincennes●

CEDED BY
DELAWARE, MIAMI
& OTHER TRIBES 1804-05

Ohio R.

KENTUCKY

CEDED IN
HULL'S TREATY
1809

Detroit●

■Ft. Malden

CANADA
(British)

Lake Erie

OHIO

●Dayton

●Chillicothe

VIRGINIA

3.1 APPROPRIATION OF INDIAN LANDS IN THE OLD NORTHWEST AND THE BATTLE OF TIPPECANOE: 1800–12

acquisition tactics. In his travels among the Ohio Valley tribes, the Iroquois of New York, as well as the Creeks, Choctaws and Cherokees in the South, he voiced strong opposition against these incursions upon territory reserved for the Indians. Tecumseh proclaimed that these lands were the common property of all the Indians, and no individual tribe or Indian leader had the right to bargain away territory without the consent of all Indians. He sought to unify all the tribes in a confederation that would resist further land cessions as well as repudiate past unauthorized transfers of Indian territory.

Tecumseh's brother, Tenkswatawa ("Loud Mouth"), a reformed alcoholic, had become something of a mystic in 1805, and afterward was known as the Prophet. He went about preaching to the Indians that their destruction could be averted if they rejected all contacts with whites, and renounced all trappings of white culture, including Christianity, tools and especially liquor. He

spread the word of his new Indian religion among the tribes throughout the Ohio Valley, the lower Missouri River region, as well in the South.

In 1808, Tecumseh and the Prophet established a new center for their Indian movement at the junction of the Tippecanoe River and the Wabash River. Known as Prophetstown, it drew Indians from near and far who accepted Tecumseh's plan to create a unified Indian nation.

Tecumseh also brought his protests directly to Harrison. At a meeting with the territorial governor at Vincennes in August of 1810, the Shawnee leader voiced his outrage over the recent Fort Wayne Treaty when he exclaimed, "Sell our country! Why not sell the air, the clouds, and the great sea, as well as the earth?"

When it became apparent that the Americans would not rescind the recent land cessions made by the Indians, Tecumseh sought the support of the British at Fort

Painting of Tecumseh and Tenskwatawa (Photo courtesy of the Library of Congress)

Malden in Upper Canada (present-day Ontario), near Detroit. British fur traders were still operating in U.S. territory around the Great Lakes and the upper Mississippi, despite the restrictions of the Jay Treaty of 1795. With growing Indian resentment against American settlement, the British saw an opportunity to further their own interests by supporting Tecumseh's concept of an Indian state. An independent Indian state, the British hoped, would serve as a buffer between the United States and British Canada, extending from the Ohio to the Mississippi.

Armed and encouraged by the British, Indian resistance against frontier settlements in Indiana and Illinois erupted when whites began moving into the lands ceded under the Fort Wayne Treaty. In the fall of 1811, Harrison used Tecumseh's absence as an opportunity to launch a sudden and decisive blow against the Indians of the upper Wabash River region. In command of a 1,000-man militia force, he moved up the Wabash toward Prophetstown, by then the designated capital of the proposed new Indian state. En route, Harrison established Fort Harrison on the site of what would become

Terre Haute, Indiana, and in early November of 1811, he advanced to a position near Prophetstown.

The Indians struck first, however, on the morning of November 7, 1811, incited by the Prophet's claim that they would be invulnerable to the firearms of the whites. Although at first caught by surprise, Harrison and his command repelled the attack, then moved on Prophetstown. Informed by his scouts that the Indian stronghold had been evacuated, Harrison had his men destroy the village.

The engagement later became known as the Battle of Tippecanoe, and although it was by no means a decisive victory for the Indiana militia, it won Harrison great acclaim as an Indian fighter. In his subsequent political career, Harrison's reputation as "Old Tippecanoe" would help him win the presidency of the United States in 1840.

In the meantime, however, rather than break Indian resistance, Harrison's destruction of Prophetstown only served to further inflame the frontier with heightened Indian hostilities. When Tecumseh returned to the region soon afterward, he directed his followers to seek British support for an all out war against the Americans.

THE WEST AND THE WAR OF 1812

British infringement on the rights of American ships to freely navigate the high seas, along with the impressment of American seamen into the British navy were, ostensibly, the primary issues prompting President James Madison and the U.S. Congress to declare war on Great Britain in June of 1812. Yet, enthusiasm for the war was not forthcoming from the coastal New England states, even though that region relied most heavily on shipping as a major industry. Instead, it was the land-locked Trans-Appalachian West and the predominantly agricultural South that had demanded and eventually brought about the war declaration.

The reasons underlying this paradox stemmed from economic conditions not directly related to the activities of the British fleet. In 1812 the West found itself in the grip of a severe economic downturn. Although partly brought about by the Napoleonic War and the British blockade of European and Caribbean ports, prices for the West's agricultural output plunged mainly as a result of overproduction, coupled with limited inland transportation routes to eastern markets and coastal ports.

Although the war in Europe had heightened demand for American agricultural exports, the oversupply of goods flooding the few centers of the West's export trade only served to drive prices down, a situation further aggravated by both the British blockade as well as by U.S.

Butter Churn (Molly Braun)

that war with Great Britain was the only honorable response to their infringement of American maritime rights led one of their critics, John Randolph of Virginia, to dub the group the "War Hawks."

Henry Clay, John C. Calhoun of South Carolina, Felix Grundy of Tennessee and other War Hawks in Congress laid the entire blame for the West's economic woes on Great Britain. Asserting that the British blockade was largely responsible for the depression, they sought to regain the nation's honor. Moreover, the War Hawks and their constituents blamed the recent Indian uprisings in the Old Northwest as having been instigated by the British to protect their fur-trading interests in Canada.

Southerners in Congress, led by Calhoun, also pushed for war with Great Britain as a way of acquiring the remainder of Spanish Florida. It was hoped that Spain, as a British ally, could be goaded into the war, and thereby justify an American seizure of Florida. While a large chunk of West Florida had already been annexed in 1810, the South still coveted Spanish East Florida. The acquisition of all of Florida would secure the rest of the Gulf Coast for southern and western trade interests. An added attraction for southern politicians was that U.S. expansion into Florida promised to bring with it new territory in which to extend slavery, thereby increasing the power and influence of the southern slave-holding states in Congress.

government-imposed trade embargoes. Producers of cotton, rice, wheat, corn and other raw materials of the Ohio and lower Mississippi valleys relied on the Mississippi River as the main outlet for their products. While the Louisiana Purchase of 1803 had assured access to the river and the port of New Orleans, goods shipped southward were all headed for the same place, engendering intense competition for buyers in a limited market.

The New England shipping business—although curtailed by losses arising from the British seizure of merchant vessels, and the restrictions imposed by the Embargo Act in 1807 and the Non-Intercourse Act in 1809—still managed to reap profits. As a result, there was little in the way of an outcry against the violation of America's "Neutral Rights" from the citizens of northeastern states or their representatives in Congress.

Even though the West's prosperity had been halted, its political influence in the federal government was on the rise. While it had once flirted with the idea of separatism, the West's loyalty to the Union was cemented with the Louisiana Purchase. The elections of 1810 had brought into office a powerful political faction of westerners and southerners who came to dominate Congress. The group was led by Henry Clay of Kentucky, who became prominent as Speaker of the House of Representatives. Clay's and his followers' virulent outcry

AN ATTEMPT TO CONQUER CANADA

With less than a dozen warships, America was no match for Britain, then the world's greatest naval power. Instead, prompted by the outbreak of renewed Indian conflicts on the Great Lakes frontier, America's war strategy centered on an attack on Canada. While some political leaders hoped to capture Canada and hold the colony hostage as a way of forcing Britain to relent in its aggressive maritime policies against U.S. shipping, others hoped to drive the British entirely out of North America. Such a move, it was thought, would end the Indian threat, open up the rich lands of the Ontario Peninsula to American settlement, and eliminate the British as competitors in the fur trade of the Great Lakes and the Far West.

William Hull, governor of the Michigan Territory, was named as commander of U.S. forces in the Old Northwest. Although a veteran officer of the Revolutionary War, Hull, at the age of 60, was reluctant to undertake the leadership of an American invasion of Canada. Meanwhile, Tecumseh brought his warriors to the British cause and he was eventually commissioned a brigadier general.

In late July of 1812, Hull led an expeditionary force of 1,600 men from Detroit and across the St. Clair River, hoping to capture Fort Malden, the main British garrison in Upper Canada. British troops to the west had captured the American base at Mackinac Island, thereby taking control of the upper Great Lakes. Soon afterward, Fort Dearborn, at the southern end of Lake Michigan (the site of present-day Chicago), also fell to the British, whose Indian allies wiped out an American force marching northward to join Hull.

Learning of these defeats to the West and South, Hull decided to call off his advance, withdrawing to Detroit. That garrison was soon surrounded by British and Indian forces, commanded by General Isaac Brock. Fearing the onslaught of the Indian troops, who often were encouraged by the British to spare no lives, Hull surrendered Detroit and his entire army to Brock without having fired a shot.

Other American reverses soon followed. An advance from Fort Niagara in western New York was repelled by the British. Another assault on eastern Canada from Lake Champlain failed in November of 1812, when New York militiamen, under General Henry Dearborn, refused to advance beyond the Canada-New York boundary.

William Henry Harrison succeeded Hull as commander of American forces in the West in the fall of 1812. Earlier, he had consolidated Kentucky militia and U.S. army forces in Indiana and Ohio, and had recaptured Fort Wayne from the British-allied Shawnees. He then prepared to retake Detroit and mount another assault on Fort Malden and Upper Canada.

A portion of Harrison's 10,000-man force, commanded by Brigadier General James Winchester, pushed northward to Frenchtown (present-day Monroe) at the mouth of the Raisin River in southeastern Michigan. There, on January 22, 1813, the Americans were defeated by an overwhelming force of British and Indians.

The American defeat at the River Raisin led Harrison to withdraw to the Maumee River in northern Ohio, where he established Fort Meigs. There, in April and May of 1813, he succeeded in fending off British and Indian attacks. Meanwhile, Harrison ordered a portion of his army to take up positions at Fort Seneca and Fort Stephenson in the Sandusky River region to the East, where ensuing British assaults were successfully repulsed.

Control of western Lake Erie was essential if the Americans were to retake Detroit and mount another offensive against Canada. To this end, Captain Oliver Hazard Perry of the U.S. Navy had directed the construction of a small fleet of fighting vessels near Presque Isle (present-day Erie, Pennsylvania), and in early September of 1813, he engaged the British warships at Put-in-Bay on the western end of Lake Erie. On September 10, 1813,

Perry's forces defeated the British in a naval victory that came to be known as the Battle of Lake Erie.

With Perry's victory, the British and their Indian allies, under Tecumseh, were cut off from supplies and reinforcements from eastern Canada. Harrison and his army were ferried across the lake and moved against Fort Malden. Colonel Proctor, believing that he could only save his army by withdrawing, retreated from Fort Malden eastward along the Thames River, with Harrison and his forces in pursuit. On the Thames River, near Moravian Town, the British made a stand against the Americans in October of 1813. But Harrison's army advanced, spearheaded by mounted Kentucky militia, and won a decisive victory in what later became known as the Battle of the Thames. In that conflict, Tecumseh was killed while covering the British retreat.

Elsewhere in the Old Northwest, American forces under General Benjamin Howard defeated the Indians throughout the Illinois country, breaking the last remnants of Tecumseh's confederation. The victory in the Battle of the Thames reestablished American sovereignty north of the Ohio, putting an end to overt British-backed Indian resistance to American expansion in the Old Northwest. In the years immediately following the end of hostilities in the region, emigration into Michigan Territory accelerated, pushing the frontier westward to the Mississippi.

Although the counter-offensive of 1813 restored America's hold on the Ohio Valley and the lower Great Lakes, the conquest of Canada proved elusive. The war still had to be waged in the South, and Britain soon began enlarging its forces in Canada, a factor that discouraged further U.S. invasion efforts and posed the threat of a new British attempt to cut off the Northeast from the rest of the nation with an offensive down Lake Champlain and the Hudson River Valley to New York.

THE WAR OF 1812 ON THE SOUTHERN FRONTIER

While Northern frontier interests looked upon the seizure of Canada as the primary aim of the war, the South viewed East Florida, then held by Spain, as the principal prize to be gained in the new conflict with Great Britain.

Even before the official declaration of war in June of 1812, U.S. efforts were underway to take Florida from Spain. In March of 1812, a combined land and naval force under General George Mathews occupied the St. Marys River region, with plans to march on St. Augustine. When it became apparent that Spain was not about to join Great Britain in the coming conflict, President James Madison ordered the expeditionary force to withdraw. One year later, however, in an effort to fore-

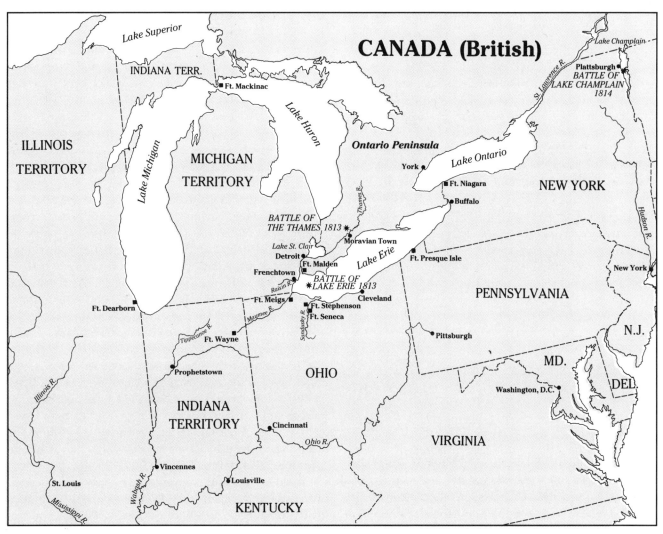

3.2 THE WAR OF 1812 NORTH OF THE OHIO RIVER

stall British advances in the region, American forces under General James Wilkinson moved against the last major Spanish stronghold in West Florida at Mobile, capturing that city in April of 1813.

Meanwhile, news of General William Hull's defeat at Detroit inspired the warrior faction of the Creeks, known as the Red Sticks, to revolt against American settlers along the frontier region of Mississippi Territory in what is now Alabama. Supplied by the British, they launched a series of raids on the southern frontier in the spring of 1813, driving frontier settlers to seek the safety of stockades and forts. On August 30, 1813, Fort Mims, at the confluence of the Alabama and Tombigbee rivers, suffered an attack in which more than 500 settlers were killed either in the flames or while trying to escape when the Creeks under Red Eagle (William Weatherford) set fire to the fort. More than 100 others were taken captive; the black slaves among the captives were freed.

To suppress the Creek uprising, a 5,000-man militia commanded by General Andrew Jackson—a former backwoods lawyer and judge from Tennessee—headed southward from Tennessee in October of 1813. After having fortified Huntsville, Jackson and his army advanced into the Creek homelands, destroying their villages at Tallushatchee and Talladega on the Tallapoosa River.

On March 27, 1814, Jackson won a decisive victory over the Creeks when he destroyed their stronghold at Tohopeka, located on the Horseshoe Bend of the Tallapoosa River. In what became known as the Battle of Horseshoe Bend, American forces—along with a faction of White Stick Creeks that were friendly to the American cause, plus Cherokees—destroyed the Red Stick fortifications in an engagement in which more than 800 Creeks were killed, many while trying to swim to safety.

Soon afterward, Jackson established Fort Jackson at the junction of the Coosa and Tallapoosa rivers, where he negotiated a peace settlement with the surviving members of the Red Stick Creeks. On August 9, 1814, he forced the defeated Indians to agree to the Treaty of Fort

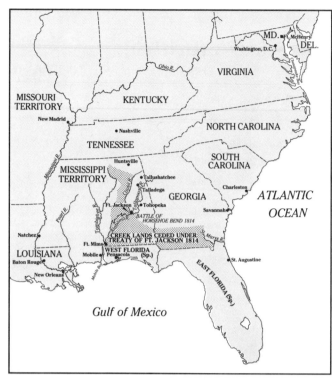

3.3 THE WAR OF 1812 SOUTH OF THE OHIO RIVER

fully repelled a British invasion force sent from Jamaica to New Orleans. The British forces, which numbered more than 10,000 men, suffered more than 2,000 losses, including the British commander, Sir Edward Pakenham. Jackson's effective defensive tactics kept American casualties to fewer than 100 men.

THE TREATY OF GHENT

Although a great military triumph, the American victory at New Orleans had no influence on the final outcome of the War of 1812. On December 24, 1814, at Ghent (in what is now Belgium), American peace negotiators John Quincy Adams, Albert Gallatin and Henry Clay had entered into a settlement with the British. With trans-Atlantic communications still dependent on sailing ships, word of the treaty did not reach American shores until several weeks after the Battle of New Orleans.

At the outset of peace negotiations in August of 1814, the British held to their demands for an independent buffer state controlled by the Indians south of the Great Lakes, which would have included much of Ohio, as well as present-day Indiana, Illinois, Michigan and Wisconsin. The American peace commissioners refused to even consider such a concession, which may have incited a rebellion in the West.

On the other hand, support for the continuance of the war was on the wane in England, where the populace had been beleaguered with the tax burdens of international conflict since 1793. As a result, in an effort to bring the war to a prompt conclusion, the British negotiators withdrew the idea of the proposed Indian buffer state. But the British still wanted each side to retain any territorial gains they had made up to that time, giving them the region around Fort Mackinac, and with it most of the upper Great Lakes, as well as the lands around Fort Niagara and nearly half of what is now the present state of Maine.

News of the British defeat on Lake Champlain bolstered the Americans' negotiating stance. Heartened by the victory, they refused to consider anything less than a reversion to the territorial status that existed prior to the outbreak of the war. When the Duke of Wellington—who had led the British in the defeat of Napoleon—not only declined to take command of the war effort in North America, but suggested to the British Foreign Office that its territorial demands would only forestall peace efforts, the British decided to relent.

In the end, the Treaty of Ghent did little else but end the War of 1812. The peace settlement made no provision for the prohibition of British impressment of American seamen on the high seas or the violation of U.S.

Jackson, under which they ceded 22 million acres of territory, an area that comprised about half of their tribal homeland. Even the White Stick Creeks, allies to Jackson, lost lands. Promoted to major general, Jackson then moved upon the Spanish positions at Pensacola, capturing that city in November of 1814.

By late 1814, Great Britain's victory over Napoleon in Europe had freed up its armed forces for a renewal of operations against the United States. A three-pronged attack was planned, including an invasion southward from Canada along Lake Champlain and the Hudson, an offensive into the mid-Atlantic region by way of Chesapeake Bay and a frontal assault against the lower Mississippi region aimed at New Orleans.

In August of 1814, British soldiers moved up the Potomac, capturing Washington, D.C., where they burned the Capitol and the White House. Yet they withdrew the land attack soon afterward when the British fleet, facing unyielding American resistance from the guns of Fort McHenry, failed to capture the vital port of Baltimore.

In September of 1814, the British advance from the north was halted in the Battle of Lake Champlain near Plattsburgh, when American forces under Captain Thomas McDonough defeated the British fleet.

The final battle of the War of 1812 occurred on January 8, 1815, when Andrew Jackson, in command of a combined force of Kentucky and Tennessee militia, success-

United States, 1814 (Photo courtesy of the Library of Congress)

neutral rights—the main reasons that had brought the U.S. to declare war. Yet these issues had become irrelevant by 1814, since with the end of the Napoleonic War in Europe, both impressment and interference with U.S. shipping had become unnecessary. No significant territorial gains were made by either side, and both the United States and Great Britain would peacefully settle boundary discrepancies along the U.S.–Canada border in the near future.

The War Hawks had brought the United States into the War of 1812 amid visions of a rapid conquest of Canada. Not only had their designs failed to materialize, but early in the war, a large portion of the Old Northwest was in jeopardy of being lost to the British. The only territorial gain to be realized by the United States in the conflict was Mobile on the Gulf Coast, occupied by General James Wilkinson in April of 1813. Wilkinson and a force of 600 men landed near the fort guarding the city. The Spanish defenders, seeing that they were far outnumbered, surrendered without firing a shot.

POST-WAR TREATIES AND TERRITORIAL ADJUSTMENTS

THE RUSH-BAGOT AGREEMENT

In April of 1817, the United States and Great Britain entered into a treaty to limit the number of warships each nation could deploy on the Great Lakes. Known as the Rush-Bagot Agreement, after British diplomat Charles Bagot and his American counterpart Richard Rush, the treaty provided that neither the United States nor Great Britain could maintain more than two major naval vessels on any one of the Great Lakes.

Remaining largely unmodified until World War II, when it was revised to allow for naval construction and naval training bases for the war effort against the Axis powers, the Rush-Bagot Agreement set the precedent for the unguarded frontier policy that evolved between the United States and Canada.

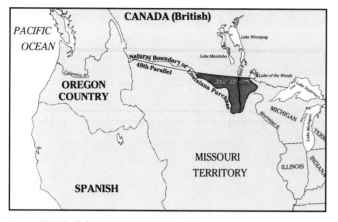

3.4   THE CONVENTION OF 1818

THE CONVENTION OF 1818

The second major international agreement that addressed issues left unresolved by the Treaty of Ghent was the Convention of 1818. In addition to allowing American fishing rights off the Newfoundland coast, it clarified the northernmost boundary of the Louisiana Purchase. In 1803, France had been vague in defining the northern limits of Louisiana. Under the Convention of 1818, a definite demarcation line was agreed upon, which gave the United States possession of the Red River Basin. The new boundary began at the southwesternmost corner of the Lake of the Woods and ran westward to the crest of the Rocky Mountains. Beyond that point, the Oregon Country was acknowledged to be occupied jointly by the United States and Great Britain, with the region open to both British and American settlers until 1828. After that, the agreement on Oregon was subject to renewal.

THE ADAMS–ONIS TREATY

In February of 1819, John Quincy Adams, acting U.S. secretary of state, and Luis de Onis, representing Spain, signed a treaty in Washington, D.C., under the terms of which Spain recognized America's prior claims to West Florida. Moreover, East Florida, the portion still in Spanish hands after the War of 1812, was ceded to the United States, thus extending U.S. ownership to the entire eastern rim of the Gulf of Mexico.

In return, the United States agreed to a settlement on the southwestern extent of the Louisiana Purchase, thereby redefining the southwestern border of the United States. The newly clarified boundary started from the mouth of the Sabine River in eastern Texas and, after zigzagging northwestward across the Southwest to the 42nd parallel, extended westward to the Pacific Coast. Spain also ceded its claims on the Oregon Country to the north of the 42nd parallel, thus defining the northern

3.5   THE ADAMS–ONIS TREATY OF 1819

limits of what would eventually become the state of California.

One result of the Adams–Onis Treaty, with long-range impact on the course of U.S. westward expansion, was that the U.S. had for the time yielded its claim to most of Texas. Having consented to accept Spain's position that the southern limits of the Louisiana Purchase were defined by the Red River, and not the Rio Grande as the U.S. had maintained since 1803, the U.S. had in effect agreed to shift its southern boundary hundreds of miles northward, along what is now the Oklahoma-Texas state line.

NEW STATES AND TERRITORIES IN THE WEST AND SOUTH

Domestic territorial changes also ensued in the aftermath of the War of 1812. Indiana Territory was admitted to the Union as the 19th state in 1816. The next year, Alabama Territory was created out of the eastern portion of Mississippi Territory, and that same year Mississippi was admitted to the Union as the 20th state.

By 1818, the population of Illinois Territory had grown to more than 40,000; that year, Illinois entered the Union as the 21st state. The northern region was incorporated into Michigan Territory, with the new state's northern boundary to reach only as far as the southern tip of Lake Michigan. Yet, in order to give the new state access to the Great Lakes, the boundary was adjusted 50 miles

3.6 TERRITORIAL CHANGES IN THE OLD NORTHWEST: INDIANA, 1816

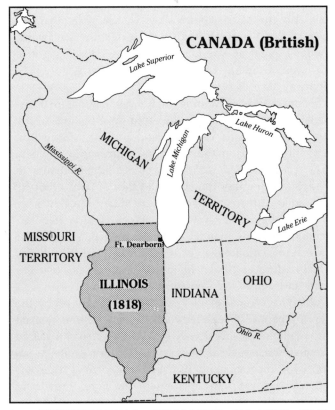

3.7 TERRITORIAL CHANGES IN THE OLD NORTHWEST: ILLINOIS, 1818

northward to provide Illinois with frontage on Lake Michigan, including Fort Dearborn, around which developed the city of Chicago. Under Illinois' original constitution, slaveholders were allowed to keep the slaves they had at the time of statehood; but no subsequent extension of slavery was permitted within the new state, a provision which in effect made Illinois a free state.

The end of British influence over the Indians enabled the U.S. government to assert its authority over the tribes of the Mississippi and Missouri frontier. In 1815, William Clark, governor of the Missouri Territory, negotiated the treaty of Portage de Sioux under which the territory's Sioux bands acknowledged American sovereignty.

Additional southwestern lands were opened for settlement in 1818, when the Quapaw Indians ceded their homelands between the Arkansas and Red rivers, then the southern part of the Missouri Territory, to the federal government. This region was soon incorporated into Arkansas Territory, which was organized as a slave territory in 1819.

THE GREAT MIGRATION

In the decade preceding the "Great Migration," a major economic depression had affected all parts of the nation. From 1805 to 1815, the economy of the Northeast, dependent on export trade, had been slowed by the Napoleonic Wars in Europe as well as by U.S. trade restrictions of the period. Likewise, the halt in overseas trade had a devastating effect on the economy of the South, whose prosperity greatly depended on the export of agricultural products to overseas markets.

Contrary to what might be assumed, hard times in the East did not spur a movement westward in search of greener economic pastures. Would-be settlers found themselves lacking the cash necessary to pick up and move from their homes in the East. Furthermore, the West's own economic woes, arising from overproduction and the lack of adequate transportation routes, had brought about a decline in prices for its output of agricultural and other raw materials. These factors, further aggravated by the outbreak of renewed Indian warfare in the Ohio Valley and in the lower Mississippi region, and the ensuing upheavals arising from the war with England, served only to discourage westward movement, reducing it to a fraction of what it had been in the years prior to 1805.

The situation greatly changed after 1815. The economy of the Northeast was revived, now relying more on manufacturing than on shipping for its prosperity. With the return of peace in Europe, the demand for American agricultural products accelerated. Prices rose, especially for cotton, spurring a demand for lands in the South for newer and bigger plantations, prompted in no small way by the introduction of Eli Whitney's cotton gin.

For their military service, war veterans received bonuses in the form of land grants. More often than not, these land certificates were resold and speculated rather than used to claim lands, resulting in an increased supply of available lands at much lower prices. William Henry Harrison's victorious campaigns against Tecumseh's confederation north of the Ohio, along with Andrew Jackson's triumph in the South over the Creeks, had displaced Indian peoples and opened millions of acres of lands to white settlement.

With more cash available to cover the costs of relocation, and spurred on by the attraction of cheaper lands, the inhabitants of the Piedmont region, as well as the now well-settled areas of western New York, Kentucky, Tennessee and eastern Ohio, began to move westward in large numbers after 1815. This period, at its peak in 1818–19, is known as the "Great Migration."

The young Abraham Lincoln's boyhood experiences characterize the frontier population's tendency to stay on the move during this period. Two years after he was born in Nolin Creek, Kentucky in 1809, Lincoln's family moved northward to a new farm at Knob Creek. In 1816, having lost title to his lands there, his father moved the family westward across the Ohio River to settle on government lands in Indiana Territory. When he was 21, Lincoln moved with his family once again, this time to settle on the prairies around Decatur, Illinois.

Improved transportation played a major role in bringing on the Great Migration. In 1818, the National Road, also known as the Cumberland Road, stretched from Cumberland, Maryland to Wheeling, in what is now West Virginia. Begun in 1811, with construction halted by the outbreak of the War of 1812, its eastern segment followed the route originally blazed by General Edward

Descending the Tennessee River in a Flatboat (Photo courtesy of the Library of Congress)

Braddock in 1755. Built at the expense of the federal government, it was 20 feet wide and paved with crushed stones. The National Road, along with other new and improved routes linking East and West, provided an all-weather pathway for west-bound emigrants, and served as an important route for the shipment of Ohio Valley farm products to markets in the East, as well as a major overland conduit for eastern manufactured goods headed for the West. From Pittsburgh and Wheeling—the National Road's major westernmost points—multitudes of emigrants took to flatboats, descending the Ohio River as they continued their westward movement into the newly opened farming country of Indiana, Illinois and the Mississippi Valley. In the years that followed, the National Road was extended westward, reaching as far as Vandalia, Illinois by 1850. Its right of way was eventually incorporated into what is now U.S. Highway 40.

Steamboats were another major innovation in transportation, helping to spur the rapid development of the region between the Appalachians and the Mississippi. First introduced on the Ohio and Mississippi rivers in 1811, they enabled frontier farmers and merchants to cheaply and rapidly transport all types of farm products and goods upstream in large quantities, quickly supplanting the much slower keelboats, which had depended on costly manual labor. Steamboats spurred the growth of commercial centers throughout the West, which before had been limited to the port of New Orleans and other Gulf Coast markets.

With the West's revived prosperity brought on by the development of diversified markets, new settlers flocked into regions that, previously ignored because of a lack of adequate access, were now linked to the rest of the nation with improvements in overland and river transportation. This was most evident in the rapid growth of settlement in the upper Wabash River region of Illinois, as well as in the Raisin River region of southern Michigan Territory.

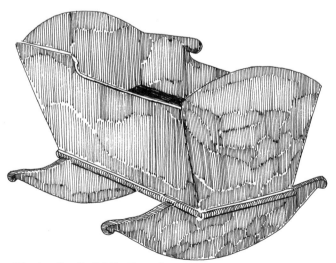

Wooden Cradle (Molly Braun)

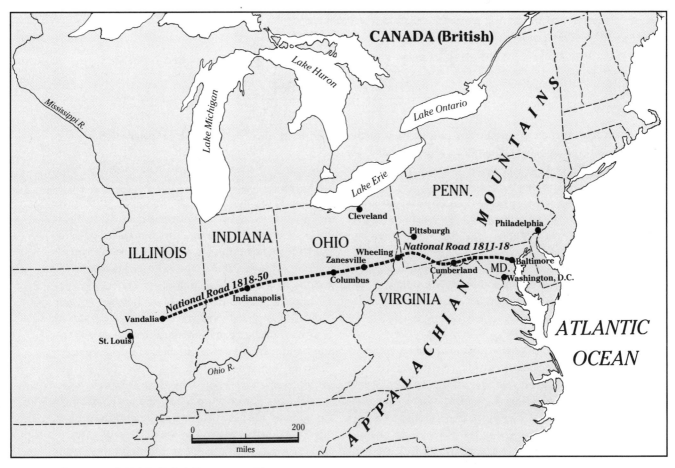

3.8   THE NATIONAL ROAD: 1811–50

The increase in land sales in this period also reflects the magnitude of the Great Migration. While in 1814, the government had sold one million acres of public lands, the annual figures for both 1818 and 1819 exceeded three million acres.

The impact of the Great Migration was also felt in the region south of the Ohio River. From Kentucky and Tennessee, new settlers flooded into the country around the Great Bend of the Alabama River, into the country along the southern Mississippi River region, and as far westward as western Mississippi and eastern Arkansas Territory. Louisiana also saw a great influx of newcomers, most of them wealthier than their northern counterparts, who poured into Louisiana to found new plantations and spread the slave economy of the Southeast.

Agricultural expansion was not the only result of the Great Migration in the North. With the growth in population and the improvement in transportation, manufacturing centers began to develop in western cities that, only a few decades before, had been nonexistent or only served as frontier outposts. Pittsburgh, formerly Fort Pitt, developed such diversified industries as iron, glass and rope manufacturing. Cincinnati, formerly Fort Washington, became so dominant as a center for the pork-packing industry that it came to be known as "Por-

kopolis." St. Louis, once seen as the most distant settlement on the western frontier, mushroomed into the focal point of the booming fur trade of the Far West.

The Panic of 1819 brought a sudden end to the Great Migration. This financial downturn came about partly as a result of Europe's recovery from nearly three decades of warfare on the Continent. With the revival of European industry and agriculture, the demand for American goods overseas declined, bringing with it a downturn in prices for both manufactured goods and raw materials. A more immediate cause, and one that had a dire impact on the West in particular, was the "hard money" policy adopted in 1819 by the Second Bank of the United States. Debts arising from the sale of public lands were now payable only in hard currency, a medium of exchange then in short supply west of the Appalachians. As a result, many newcomers on western lands found themselves facing eviction. The decline in the export trade, and the resulting fall in prices for flax, wheat, corn, cotton and other crops caused more financial ruin. Moreover, the decline in prices brought with it a devaluation in the value of lands. With available money depreciated by federal monetary policies, many western farmers saw their savings virtually wiped out overnight, and creditors forced them off their farms. Overproduc-

THE COMING OF THE STEAMBOAT

The introduction of steamboats to the rivers of the West revolutionized the region's commerce and accelerated westward settlement south of the Ohio River.

With few roads in the Old Northwest and lower Mississippi Valley, the principal means of transporting people and goods was by way of the Ohio and Mississippi rivers and their tributaries. Large quantities of bulky goods, such as flour, salt, rum, potatoes, brandy, pork and cordage products, could be shipped fairly inexpensively downstream to New Orleans by flatboats, propelled along by the river's current.

Transporting products upstream was a different matter. The keelboat, a sturdily constructed, barge-like craft with a keel, was the principal type of vessel used. Large crews were required to row the keelboats upstream where the water was deep or pole along the bottom where the water was shallow enough. Upstream travel through difficult parts of the river required the keelboats to be towed from shore. All of these methods depended on manual labor, making the transportation of goods by keelboat both expensive and time-consuming. Moreover, keelboats could transport only relatively small loads of merchandise, and the time it took to reach upriver destinations limited the type of goods shipped to less perishable, more profitable items such as molasses, sugar and coffee.

On August 11, 1807, Robert Fulton of New York successfully demonstrated the first practical steamboat. His *Clermont* traveled up the Hudson River from New York to Albany in 32 hours, making the downriver return voyage in 30 hours. In association with Robert Livingston, Fulton soon obtained a monopoly for steamboat service not only in New York but along the rivers of the Louisiana Territory as well.

Realizing the great potential his innovation could have in the West, Fulton sent an associate, Nicholas Roosevelt, to Pittsburgh in May of 1809. From there he was to tour the downriver region to evaluate what interest there might be for steam-powered river transport on the Ohio and Mississippi rivers.

Roosevelt's favorable reports soon prompted Fulton to direct the construction of a steamboat at Pittsburgh; the *New Orleans* was built there at a cost of $38,000, completed in March of 1811. Equipped with a wood-burning steam engine, it measured 138 feet long and 26½ feet wide. It set out down the Ohio River on its maiden voyage in October of 1811, and within a few days, had arrived in Louisville. After an elaborate official reception by the town's commercial leaders, the *New Orleans* undertook a demonstration of its upstream capabilities, successfully forging its way against the current and through the Falls of the Ohio. Although slowed to an upstream speed of only three miles per hour, the citizens of Louisville and other trade centers along the Ohio were sufficiently impressed, and promised to utilize this new mode of river commerce should it come into regular service.

From Louisville, the *New Orleans* headed downstream to its namesake city at the mouth of the Mississippi, arriving there on January 10, 1812. Within a short time, the vessel was engaged in regular traffic between New Orleans and Natchez.

Although the career of the *New Orleans* was short-lived (it was wrecked on a snag near Baton Rouge and sank on July 14, 1814), its appearance on the Mississippi and Ohio rivers marked the beginning of a new era. Farmers, artisans and plantation opera-

tion was still a problem, and the glut of farm output drove down prices even further, spreading economic hardship to many more westerners.

Unable to pay their debts, and with the U.S. government holding mortgages on their lands, the small farmers that had built up the West in such a short time now faced economic devastation.

Nevertheless, the Great Migration had made tremendous changes in the distribution of the nation's population. According to the Census of 1820, there were 1,140,000 more people living west of the Appalachians than had lived there in 1810. Ohio, with 600,000 inhabitants, was the most populous of the Trans-Appalachian states. By 1820, roughly one-quarter of the nation's pop-

The Warrior *Firing on Fleeing Sauk and Fox Indians at the Battle of Bad Axe in 1832* (Photo courtesy of the Library of Congress)

tors could now transport their products upstream at only a slightly higher cost than that of downstream shipments. In 1815, the potential of steamboat service on the rivers of the West was fully realized when the *Enterprise* traveled from New Orleans against the currents of the Mississippi and Ohio rivers as far as Louisville.

The burgeoning cotton plantations in the Old Southwest benefited the most from the introduction of the steamboat. It now made economic sense to ship massive quantities of cotton to coastal ports and trade centers, prompting the spread of cotton plantations farther inland in Louisiana, Alabama and Mississippi.

Communication between distant points along the river was also greatly improved, and the transportation opportunities the steamboat afforded brought isolated settlements along the rivers closer together,

helping to forge cultural and social links throughout the lower Mississippi Valley.

In 1824, Fulton's monopoly over steam navigation came to end when the United States Supreme Court decided against his company in *Gibbons v. Ogden*. In that case the court ruled that only the federal government had exclusive control over interstate commerce, including navigation on inland waterways. The breaking of the monopoly led to increased competition among steamboat operators on the western rivers, giving rise to improved designs and faster craft. The revolution in water transportation was introduced farther north in 1818, when *Walk-In-The-Water* made its maiden voyage as the first steam-powered vessel on the Great Lakes, extending the West's revolution in trade and transportation into the region north of the Ohio.

ulation was living in the West, greatly increasing the region's influence and power in the U.S. Congress and in other branches of the federal government.

The West's newly founded political clout was soon felt in Congress, prompting the enactment of the economic relief measures that came to be known as the Land Law of 1820. Under this legislation, debt payments were post-

poned, and reductions were made in the amounts of lands that had been allocated, thus making it possible for farmers to retain smaller tracts of land to which their prior payments had been credited. Reforms were also made in the sale of public lands, with the minimum purchase reduced from 160 acres to 80 acres. The price per acre was also reduced retroactively, thereby shrinking

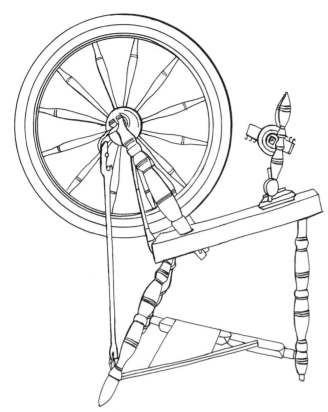

Spinning Wheel (Molly Braun)

Log Cabin in the Early 19th Century (Photo courtesy of the New York Library)

the debt burdens of westerners who had settled on public lands.

The Land Law of 1820 helped stave off the economic catastrophe threatening settlers in the West. At the same time, it established a governmental policy favoring individuals of modest means in their acquisition of public lands, a factor that would, over the next 70 years, set the pattern of settlement of the Trans-Mississippi West.

THE MISSOURI COMPROMISE

From 1815 to 1820, the great population shift brought about by the Great Migration led to the creation of a number of new states and territories. With the admission of Alabama in 1819, there were 11 free and 11 slave states in the Union. Missouri's application for admission as a slave state threatened to upset this balance, however, bringing about the first great sectional dispute in the nation's history.

Southern leaders strongly supported the admission of Missouri as a slave state, while northern political interests opposed it with equal vigor, fearing that the slave states would have a majority in Congress.

In February of 1820, a settlement was reached, largely through the efforts of Henry Clay. Passed into law as the Missouri Compromise, it allowed Missouri to enter the Union as a slave state, with the provision that slavery would not be permitted in any state to be formed from the remaining territory of the Louisiana Purchase north of latitude 36°30′ (the southern boundary of Missouri).

In the meantime, Maine, recently separated from Massachusetts, was admitted as a free state in 1820. The balance of free and slave states was re-established, however, when Missouri entered the Union as a slave state on August 10, 1821. The 24th state, Missouri, was also the first to be admitted west of the Mississippi.

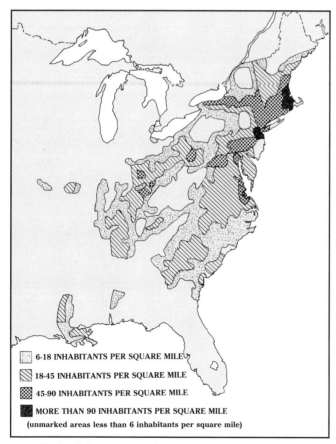

☐ 6-18 INHABITANTS PER SQUARE MILE

▨ 18-45 INHABITANTS PER SQUARE MILE

▦ 45-90 INHABITANTS PER SQUARE MILE

■ MORE THAN 90 INHABITANTS PER SQUARE MILE

(unmarked areas less than 6 inhabitants per square mile)

3.9 U.S. POPULATION DENSITY IN 1820

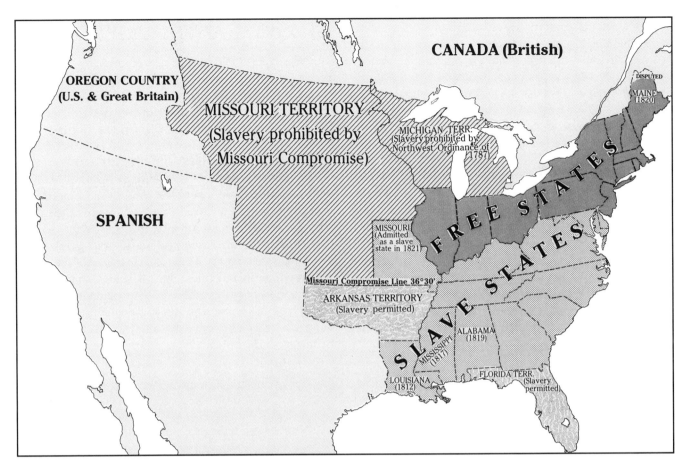

3.10 THE MISSOURI COMPROMISE: 1820–21

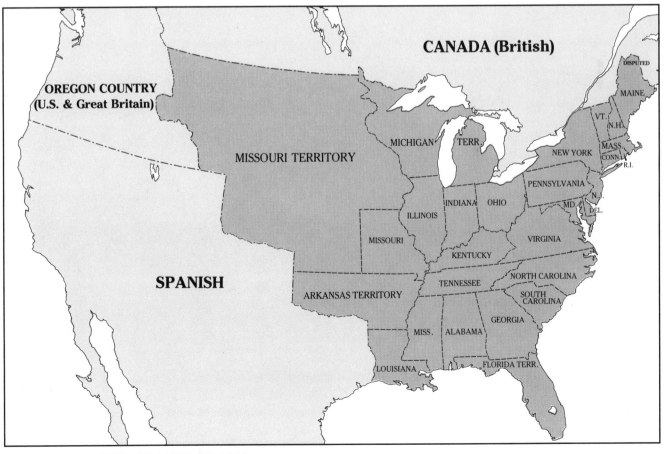

3.11 THE UNITED STATES IN 1821

The Missouri Compromise of 1820 resolved, for a time, both the North's and the South's concerns over the future of territorial expansion and the extension of slavery.

For the North, the precedent established by the Northwest Ordinance of 1787—that Congress could outlaw slavery in newly organized territories—had been reaffirmed. Northern interests felt assured that the remaining unsettled areas of the West would eventually be organized as free territories and states. The South had not only retained slavery in Missouri, but could now count on the future admissions of Arkansas and Florida as slave states. Despite the temporary accord, the Missouri Compromise set the stage for future North–South conflict.

The Missouri Compromise marked the first time the slavery issue had been debated on the floor of Congress. Commenting on the coming crisis that he saw arising out of the Missouri controversy, former president Thomas Jefferson wrote, "This momentous question, like a fire-bell in the night, awakened and filled me with terror."

GROWTH AND COMPROMISE

The War of 1812 had been a near-disaster for the United States. What was envisioned as a campaign of conquest ended with the nation negotiating to preserve its pre-war territorial boundaries. Following the war, international agreements firmly established the northern and southwestern limits of the country, and resolved, for the time, the Oregon question.

Native Americans east of the Mississippi, in both the North and the South, were left without the support of a foreign power, thus weakening their efforts to resist white settlement. Emigration within the nation accelerated, leading to increased settlement in all parts of the Trans-Appalachian West, the development of roads and the growth of inland cities. The Missouri Compromise of 1820 had temporarily resolved the question of slavery in new states and territories. It also signaled the beginning of an era in which westward expansion would be intertwined with the issues arising out of the sectional differences between the North and South.

Chapter 4

AN EXPANDING NATION (1821–1845)

IN THE FOLLOWING DECADE, the national government—with its prestige bolstered by its stand against Great Britain in the War of 1812—shaped a new international policy. It also began dealing with long-standing domestic problems. In the meantime, canals became an essential part of the nation's economic development. And scattered bands of mountain men and traders threaded their way across the Great Plains and Rocky Mountains toward the Pacific coast of Oregon and California.

THE MONROE DOCTRINE

A new balance of power in Europe had emerged with the defeat of Napoleon in 1815. Spain, allied with the restored monarchist government of France, was making plans to retake her former colonies in Central and South America. In the Pacific Northwest, Russian expansion threatened to compromise the U.S. and British joint claim on the Oregon Country. On September 4, 1821, Czar Alexander I of Russia issued a *ukase* (an imperial decree) announcing that Russia had extended its claim to Alaska southward from the 55th parallel to the 51st, in effect closing the northern portion of the Oregon Country to American and British fur traders. Moreover, the Russian government banned foreign ships from entering within 100 miles of the coastline of Russian territory on the Pacific coast of North America, thereby barring American whalers from operating in the Bering Sea and the waters around the Aleutian Islands.

At first, the British government sought to join with the United States in preventing the designs of European powers on the Americas. But the United States turned down Great Britain's offer so as not to foreclose on its own expansionist ambitions in regard to Cuba and Texas. Instead, in December 1823, as part of his annual address to Congress, President James Monroe expressed the nation's unilateral opposition to European interference in the affairs of the Western Hemisphere, and stated that any attempt by a European power to oppress or control the new republics of Latin America would be viewed as a hostile act against the United States.

The Monroe Doctrine, as this warning against colonial expansion came to be known, was a bold admonition from a fledgling republic that lacked the military might to enforce it. If Monroe's remarks apparently discouraged Spanish plans in the Western Hemisphere, it was Great Britain that provided strength to his pronouncements. With Mexican independence in 1821 and the overthrow of Spanish colonial rule, new markets had opened in the Americas for the British; to maintain them, it was imperative for Great Britain to discourage Spain from attempting to retake her former colonies. A few months before President Monroe had officially voiced his warning against foreign intervention, Great Britain had informed France and Spain that any attempt to interfere with the affairs of the newly independent Latin American countries would be opposed by the force of the British fleet.

The problem posed by Russian expansion southward from Alaska was resolved by international agreement. Again prompted by the threat of British military force, Russia withdrew its previous claim and agreed that its North American territory extended only as far south as 54°40' south latitude, thus recognizing the U.S. and British claims on the northern extent of the Oregon Coun-

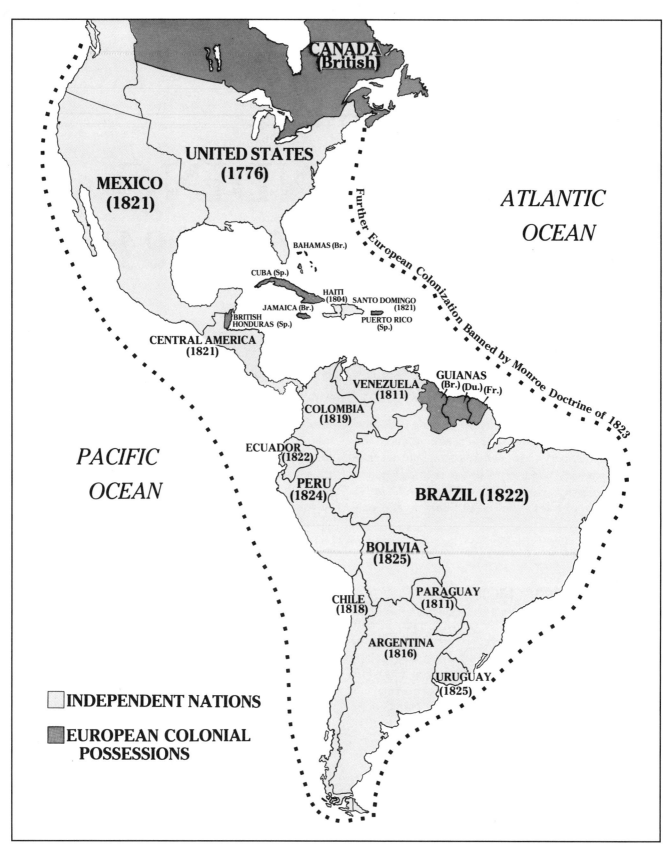

CANADA
(British)

UNITED STATES
(1776)

MEXICO
(1821)

*ATLANTIC
OCEAN*

BAHAMAS (Br.)

CUBA (Sp.)

HAITI
(1804)   SANTO DOMINGO
(1821)

JAMAICA (Br.)

BRITISH
HONDURAS (Sp.)   PUERTO RICO
(Sp.)

CENTRAL AMERICA
(1821)

VENEZUELA
(1811)   GUIANAS
(Br.) (Du.) (Fr.)

COLOMBIA
(1819)

*PACIFIC

OCEAN*

ECUADOR
(1822)

PERU
(1824)   BRAZIL (1822)

BOLIVIA
(1825)

CHILE
(1818)   PARAGUAY
(1811)

ARGENTINA
(1816)

URUGUAY
(1825)

Further European Colonization Banned by Monroe Doctrine of 1823

☐ INDEPENDENT NATIONS

▨ EUROPEAN COLONIAL
   POSSESSIONS

4.1   THE AMERICAS AND THE MONROE DOCTRINE: 1823–25

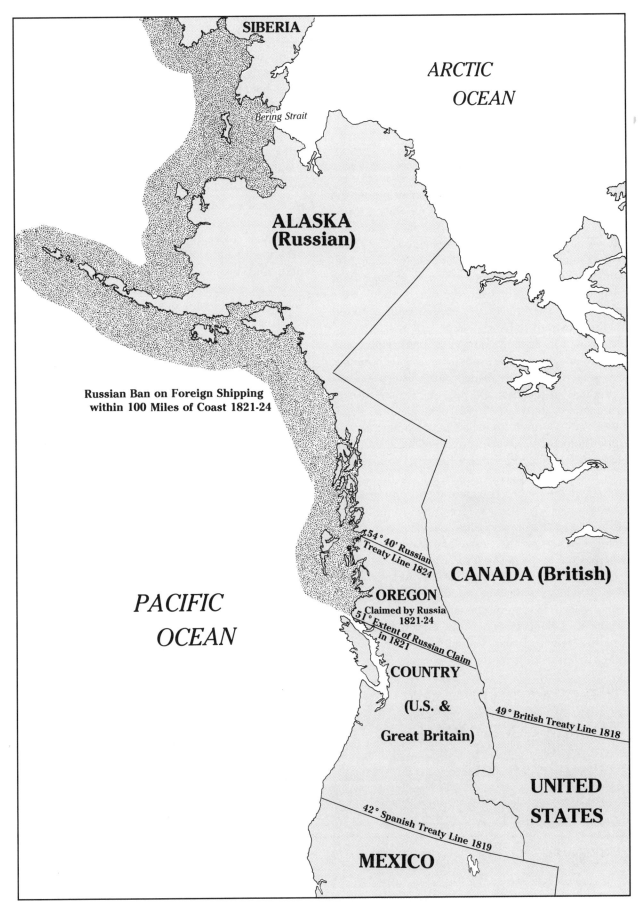

Russian Ban on Foreign Shipping
within 100 Miles of Coast 1821-24

54° 40' Russian
Treaty Line 1824

OREGON
Claimed by Russia
1821-24

51° Extent of Russian Claim
in 1821

COUNTRY

(U.S. &

Great Britain)

49° British Treaty Line 1818

42° Spanish Treaty Line 1819

4.2   THE RUSSIAN CHALLENGE IN THE PACIFIC NORTHWEST: 1821–24

try. Under the terms of the treaty signed on April 17, 1824, the Russians also withdrew its 100-mile offshore limit to foreign shipping, and allowed American vessels to enter the rivers of Russian Alaska, which emptied into the Pacific.

THE CANAL BOOM

The need for practical and cheap transportation links between the East and the West became evident during the War of 1812. Overland routes suitable for wagon traffic across the Appalachian Mountains were almost nonexistent. River transportation in the West served only points along the Ohio and Mississippi river system, leaving remote inland areas with no practical way to send farm products to markets. Moreover, the introduction of the steamboat on western rivers only tended to funnel western trade southward to New Orleans.

Businessmen in Boston, New York, Philadelphia and Charleston sought federal support for transportation projects that would open markets for western agricultural products in the East and provide a route to ship eastern goods to the West. By 1817, the National Road, built with federal funds, stretched from Cumberland on the upper Potomac to Wheeling on the Ohio River. This development caused concern among New Yorkers that western trade would now be diverted to Baltimore and make that city the leading commercial port on the Atlantic Coast.

Yet despite road improvements, overland transportation by wagon was still expensive and slow. A call for a canal across the low-lying valleys of western New York was proposed as an alternative, but Congress, dominated by Virginia's and other southern states' representatives, declined to approve federal funding. Instead, under the leadership of New York Governor De Witt Clinton, the New York State legislature voted to provide financing, with additional money coming from New

The Building of the Erie Canal (Photo courtesy of the New York Public Library)

York City banks and some financiers, including John Jacob Astor.

Construction of the Erie Canal began at Rome, New York, on July 4, 1817. Proposed as early as 1808, the project had been delayed by the onset of the War of 1812. Most of the hard work was performed by Irish immigrants, and the engineering was done by amateurs who improvised methods and machinery for the job. Forty feet wide at its top and 28 feet wide at the bottom, the Erie Canal extended 363 miles westward across New York, joining the Hudson River at Troy and Albany with Lake Erie at Buffalo.

The Hudson River connected the water route with the port of New York. Eighty-three locks raised westbound vessels to a height of over 560 feet above sea level at Buffalo and lowered them on the eastward journey. A series of aqueducts was constructed to carry the artificial waterway across rivers and valleys. Unlike many earlier and subsequent canal projects, the original route of the Erie Canal was entirely man-made. Streams and lakes were not incorporated into the waterway, freeing it from the problems that could arise from floods or low water levels caused by droughts.

At the time, the Erie Canal was one of the longest canals in the world, and it was hailed as the greatest publicly-funded engineering project in history. Critics, however, saw little use in building a waterway through the thinly settled western part of New York State and they derided the canal project as "Clinton's Ditch."

On October 25, 1825, after eight years of construction, the Erie Canal was officially opened. Governor De Witt Clinton and a party of dignitaries traveled the entire length of the canal eastward from Buffalo. The event was heralded by the boom of cannons fired along every 12 miles of the route. On November 4, after traveling down the Hudson River from Albany, Governor Clinton, aboard the *Seneca Chief*, was towed out into New York Harbor. Off Sandy Hook, New Jersey, he emptied a keg of Lake Erie water into the Atlantic, signifying "the wedding of the waters." A keg of Atlantic water was then transported westward to Buffalo and emptied into Lake Erie.

The canal had cost about $7 million to build, but within its first decade of operation, revenue from tolls would more than exceed that amount. The Erie Canal would soon have a profound impact not only on New York City and state, but also on the Trans-Appalachian West and the future course of westward settlement.

The immediate impact of the canal was the rapid rise of cities along its route in western New York. Utica, Syracuse, Rochester and Lockport grew overnight into important trade centers and shipping points. Buffalo became the gateway to the West for a stream of settlers from New England and the Middle Atlantic states, as well as for newly arrived immigrants from Western Eu-

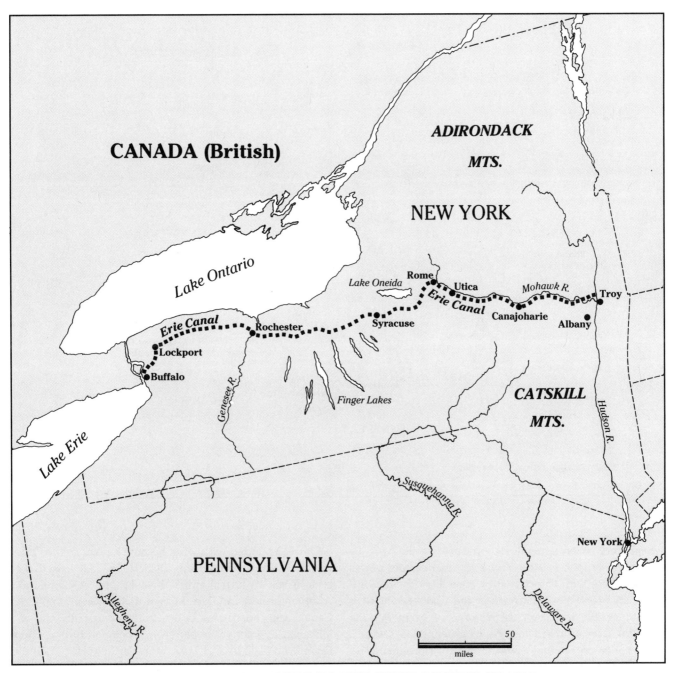

4.3 THE ERIE CANAL: MAN-MADE RIVER TO THE WEST OPENED IN 1825

rope. Scandinavians and Germans seeking fertile lands soon poured into the Lake Plains region around the Great Lakes and north of the Ohio River. That area had been recently opened to settlers as a result of the government's Indian removal measures of the late 1820s and early 1830s.

Along the Erie Canal's towpath, teams of horses and mules hauled barges laden with farm products from the Ohio and Mississippi valleys east to Albany. Hudson River steamboats then carried western goods downriver to New York City. Freight costs had been dramatically reduced. Transporting freight by wagons over the Appalachians could cost as much as $100 per ton; the canal

boats could now ship the same cargoes for as little as five dollars a ton. Likewise, eastern manufactured goods were carried to the West at a fraction of the former cost. The travel time between Buffalo and New York was reduced from 20 days to less than a week. New York City rapidly became the foremost Atlantic port, the nation's largest city and the focal point of trade between the East coast and the Trans-Appalachian West.

From New England to the western Great Lakes, the Erie Canal brought great changes in agricultural production. Western farmers, no longer dependent on the Ohio and Mississippi rivers, could choose between markets in the East and the lower Mississippi Valley. Western

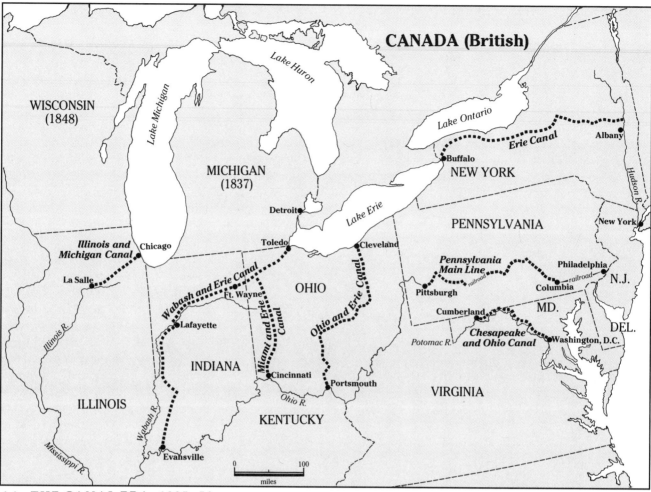

4.4 THE CANAL ERA: 1825–50

wheat and other agricultural products could now be profitably shipped to New York and other eastern points and compete with the output of producers in New England and New York. Farmers in the Connecticut River Valley, unable to match the volume of grain flowing from the West, turned to tobacco growing. In western New York—once a major wheat and corn producing region—agriculture became diversified and eventually centered on dairy farming.

The tremendous success of the Erie Canal soon prompted a flurry of canal building projects in other states. In Pennsylvania, the Main Line was constructed between Philadelphia and the Ohio River at Pittsburgh. This route combined artificial waterways, existing rivers and a system of inclined planes that hauled freight over the mountains by cable and a railroad in which cars were drawn by horses.

Maryland and Virginia undertook the construction of the Chesapeake and Ohio Canal, which had first been proposed in the 1790s by a company headed by George Washington. Construction began in 1828, and by 1850 the waterway extended along the Potomac River as far as Cumberland, Maryland.

Ohio responded with what became known as the Ohio and Erie Canal. Built from 1825 to 1832, it linked the Ohio River at Portsmouth with Lake Erie at Cleveland. Another project in Ohio, known as the Miami and Erie Canal, was constructed between 1825 and 1845, and established a water route between Cincinnati on the Ohio River with Toledo and Lake Erie. Farther west, in Indiana, the canal-building boom took hold in 1832, and construction began on the Wabash and Erie Canal, which by 1842 extended between Toledo, Ohio, and Lafayette, Indiana, on the Wabash River; within a few years it reached the Ohio River at Evansville. In Illinois, the Illinois and Michigan Canal, built between and 1836 and 1848, linked Lake Michigan at Chicago with the Illinois River.

The canals built in Ohio, Indiana and Illinois during this period were financed by state bond issues bought by eastern investors. The federal government also lent support by granting tracts of public lands along the right of ways. These and similar projects were delayed by the economic crisis brought on by the Panic of 1837. In some cases, the national depression brought the building of canals to a halt when the states defaulted on their bond obligations. Some of the canals were then taken over by private interests, while other projects were abandoned in the face of stiff competition from the railroads beginning in the late 1830s and early 1840s.

While the impact of western canals on commerce never approached that of the Erie Canal, their construction brought about the transference of huge tracts of public lands in the West to state and private ownership under the federal government's policy of granting liberal land grants for canal right of ways. The practice carried over to the construction of the transcontinental railroads in the years after the Civil War, establishing a pattern for the disposition of the public domain lands of the Great Plains.

Although a relatively brief period, the canal-building era wrought enormous changes on the Trans-Appalachian West. Canal building spurred the growth of cities like Cleveland and Chicago. The projects brought in hordes of workers who settled in the previously uninhabited areas adjacent to the canal routes, giving rise to the development of towns such as Fort Wayne and Evansville in Indiana. The resulting influx of capital to the Ohio and upper Mississippi valleys and the surge of industrial growth led to a de-emphasis of an economy based on agriculture alone.

The shift in trade patterns also brought about cultural and political changes throughout the nation. The West, which in earlier years had been closely tied to the development of the South, now identified with the East. Its population, once primarily made up of settlers with roots in the South, came to be dominated by immigrants from the Northeast and Europe. The new westerners had little reason to support the free-trade and pro-slavery policies of the southern states, and instead identified with the Northeast. The future of the West was now tied to the North, leaving the South—traditionally a champion of western interests—to become both economically and politically isolated.

THE GREAT AMERICAN DESERT

An expedition led by Major Stephen H. Long across the Southern Plains and into the Southern Rockies in 1820 marked the resumption of official U.S. exploring efforts into the Trans-Missouri West since the War of 1812 had halted army explorations. Long's mission grew out of Secretary of War John C. Calhoun's plan to create a line of forts along the nation's western frontier.

By that time, the nation's settled areas extended to the eastern edge of the Great Plains in what is now the eastern portions of Arkansas, Missouri and Iowa. The Great Plains and the mountains beyond provided a natural barrier against an invasion from a foreign power from the west; Calhoun's inner line of defense was designed to counter Indian tribes. He also recommended that American fur-trading interests in the upper Mississippi River region and the Great Lakes be protected from unlawful encroachments of the British-owned Hudson's Bay Company and the North West Company. These two commercial giants, which were to merge in 1821, threatened to dominate the field if the government did not take steps to curtail their operations on American territory. Accordingly, the proposed U.S. forts were to include government trading houses to regulate commerce with the Indians and assert U.S. authority over unlicensed British fur traders from Canada.

Major Long was an officer with the army's Corps of Topographical Engineers, a unit that would play a major role in all government-sponsored exploring efforts into the American West until the outbreak of the Civil War. In 1817, he surveyed the lower Arkansas River and selected a site at the mouth of the Poteau River on which Fort Smith was soon constructed. That same year, he led an expedition up the Mississippi River into present-day Minnesota during which he chose the site for Fort St. Anthony (later renamed Fort Snelling), and around which eventually grew the cities of Minneapolis and St. Paul. Fort Smith and Fort St. Anthony were to be the southern and northern ends of the government's line of defense along the western frontier.

In 1818, Calhoun enlarged his plans to include the establishment of a military post on the upper Missouri River, either at the Mandan villages near present-day Bismarck, North Dakota (the site of the Lewis and Clark Expedition's 1804–05 winter quarters), or upriver at the mouth of the Yellowstone. What came to known as the "Yellowstone Expedition" was organized to carry out the project, with funding provided by Congress. An additional purpose was to gather scientific information about the West.

The project began inauspiciously when the five steamboats engaged to transport the troops up the Missouri from St. Louis failed to navigate beyond the mouth of the Kansas River. By September of 1819, the 1,100-man force under Colonel Henry Atkinson had only managed to reach as far as Council Bluffs; there the group established Fort Atkinson, several miles north of present-day Omaha, Nebraska. At the time, it was the nation's westernmost official outpost.

A sixth steam-powered vessel, the *Western Engineer*, carrying the scientific segment of the expedition under Long's command, did manage to reach Council Bluffs. Specially designed for the expedition with stern-mounted paddle wheels and a very shallow draft to negotiate areas of low water, the *Western Engineer* was the first steamboat to ascend that far up the Missouri River. As a decorative touch, the form of a huge serpent had

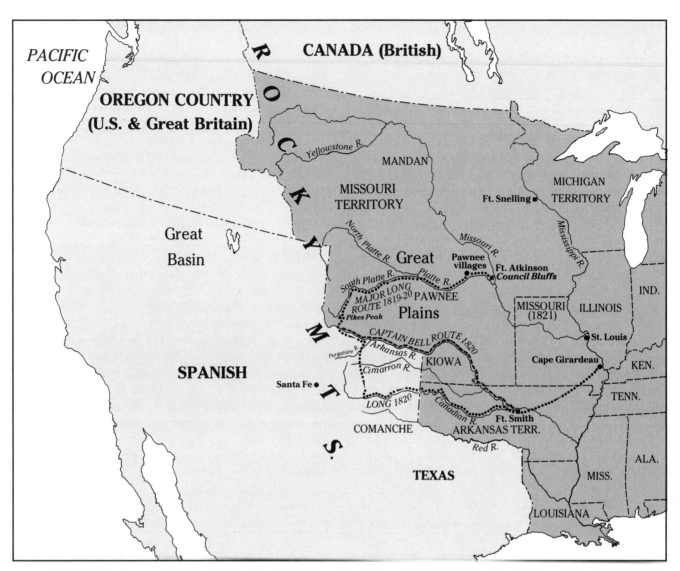

PACIFIC OCEAN

CANADA (British)

OREGON COUNTRY
(U.S. & Great Britain)

Great Basin

SPANISH

Santa Fe

TEXAS

COMANCHE

MANDAN

MISSOURI TERRITORY

Yellowstone R.

North Platte R.

Great Plains

South Platte R.

MAJOR LONG ROUTE 1819-20

Pikes Peak

PAWNEE

Platte R.

Pawnee villages

Missouri R.

Ft. Snelling

Ft. Atkinson
Council Bluffs

MICHIGAN TERRITORY

Mississippi R.

MISSOURI (1821)

ILLINOIS

IND.

CAPTAIN BELL ROUTE 1820

Arkansas R.

Purgatoire R.

Cimarron R.

KIOWA

LONG 1820

Canadian R.

Red R.

Ft. Smith

ARKANSAS TERR.

St. Louis

Cape Girardeau

KEN.

TENN.

ALA.

MISS.

LOUISIANA

4.5 STEPHEN H. LONG'S EXPLORATIONS OF THE SOUTHERN PLAINS AND EASTERN ROCKIES IN 1820

been mounted on its bow, and the smoke streaming from the creature's mouth created a strange and sometimes startling spectacle, especially for Indians who had never seen a steamboat before.

Leaving his men at Fort Atkinson, Long traveled east to Washington, D.C. to report to Congress and receive additional orders. Congress reacted negatively to the news that the Yellowstone Expedition had fallen far short of reaching the upper Missouri as planned. Moreover, over the winter of 1819–20, 100 of Atkinson's men had died of scurvy at Council Bluffs. Charging waste and mismanagement by the War Department, Congress voted against providing additional funds to carry out the project. Instead, a much smaller expedition to explore the Rocky Mountains was authorized, with Long in command. The aim of this scaled-down version of the Yellowstone Expedition was to find the sources of the Platte, Arkansas and Red rivers, and gather scientific data about the Southwest.

Long returned to Fort Atkinson in the spring of 1820. In early June, he set out westward from the Missouri River post in command of a party of 19 men, including botanist and geologist Dr. Edwin James, and Philadelphia landscape artist Samuel Seymour. Traveling on horseback, Long and his expedition followed the Loup river into present-day central Nebraska. Their first stop was at the Pawnee villages along the river, where they distributed gifts among the Indian inhabitants as a gesture of the government's good will. They then crossed southward to the Platte River, which they followed westward across the plains.

On June 30, Long and his men came within sight of the eastern slopes of the Rocky Mountains. Within a week, they arrived at the site of what is now Denver, Colorado; the next day, they explored the upper reaches of the South Platte in the nearby mountains. Turning southward from that point, they reached the future site of Colorado Springs, and while the expedition was encamped there, Dr. James and two soldiers set out on what proved to be the first known ascent by whites to the top of nearby Pikes Peak.

By late July of 1820, Long and his men had reached the Arkansas River at a point near present-day Pueblo, Colorado. A small party explored up the Arkansas as far as the Royal Gorge, where the rough terrain forced them back. Soon afterward, Long divided the expedition into two groups. While one detachment under the command of a Captain Bell followed the Arkansas downstream to the southeast, Long and the rest of the expedition headed southward hoping to find the Red River, which they planned to trace to its lower course.

Long and his group crossed the Purgatoire and Cimarron rivers; they eventually came upon a southeastward flowing stream that Long believed was the Red River. Proceeding downstream, the men suffered from the extreme heat of summer; they also ran short of food supplies. Adding to their difficulties were skirmishes with bands of Comanches and Kiowas. It was not until they found that the river flowed into the Arkansas instead of the Mississippi did Long realize that he had been following the Canadian River and not the Red River.

On September 13, Long joined up with Bell and the rest of his men at Fort Smith. From there, the entire expedition made its way down the Arkansas River for a short distance before turning northeastward. On Octo-ber 12, 1820, after having traveled overland across northeastern Arkansas, Long and his men reached the Mississippi River at Cape Girardeau in southeastern Missouri, where the expedition came to an end.

In his subsequent report, Long echoed Pike's earlier impressions, describing the Great Plains as a barren region, "unfit for cultivation, and of course uninhabitable by a people depending upon agriculture for their subsistence." On his accompanying map, he identified the area extending westward from the 95th meridian to the Rocky Mountains as the "Great American Desert," a designation that, over the next 50 years, would appear on maps of the United States.

Long also put forth the idea that the nation's western sections might "prevent too great an extension of our population westward" and thereby forestall the spread of settled areas over an area too large for the national government to administer effectively.

Samuel Seymour, the expedition's artist, produced some of the first sketches and paintings of the Plains Indians as well as the earliest known picture of the Rocky Mountains made from firsthand observation.

Dr. James's report on the plant life of what is now Kansas, Oklahoma and eastern Colorado mainly dealt with what vegetation he saw growing there, and did not take into account the potential the region's soil had for sustaining crops. Together with Long's account, this description of the Great Plains would discourage settlement for more than 40 years. Yet, with later innovations in agricultural production and the introduction of new strains of wheat and other adaptable crops, the Great Plains—once dismissed as a wasteland—would by the end of the 19th century develop into one of the greatest food-producing regions in the world.

The so-called Great American Desert, having been confirmed as unfit for white settlement, became attractive to the government as a place to relocate the Indian tribes remaining east of the Mississippi River. As a result, within five years of Major Stephen H. Long's expedition, a national policy to remove the eastern tribes to the lands west of the Mississippi had been formulated by Calhoun and President James Monroe.

FUR TRADERS AND MOUNTAIN MEN EXPLORE THE WEST

As the edge of the frontier progressed westward through the first three decades of the 19th century, the pattern of settlement was repeated: Lands appropriated from Native American tribes were organized into territories; government surveying teams divided newly-opened regions

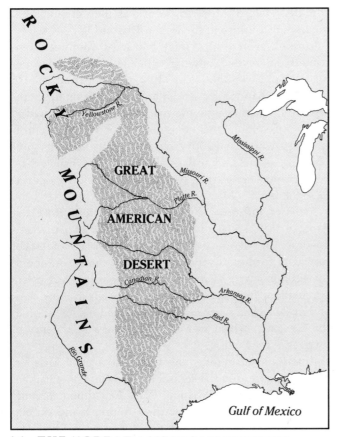

4.6   THE "GREAT AMERICAN DESERT"

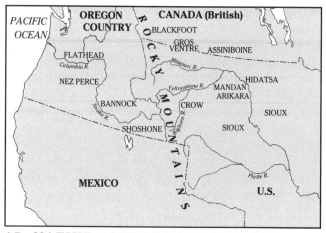

OREGON CANADA (British)
COUNTRY
PACIFIC OCEAN
BLACKFOOT
GROS VENTRE ASSINIBOINE
FLATHEAD
Columbia R.
Missouri R.
NEZ PERCE
HIDATSA
Yellowstone R. MANDAN ARIKARA
BANNOCK CROW
Snake R.
SIOUX
SHOSHONE SIOUX
MEXICO
Platte R.
U.S.

4.7 NATIVE AMERICAN TRIBES AND THE FUR TRADE ON THE UPPER MISSOURI AND IN THE NORTHERN ROCKIES

into townships and sections; and the lands of the public domain were sold to settlers and speculators.

By 1821, a continuous band of settled areas extended from the Appalachians to the western fringes of the Mississippi Valley. But to the west, the treeless Great Plains and the eastern slopes of the Rocky Mountains beyond had little appeal to the type of pioneer whose efforts had led to the rapid peopling of the Trans-Appalachian West. With its few scattered military outposts along the frontier, the United States could claim only nominal sovereignty over this vast area. The tribes of the Great Plains and Rocky Mountains still considered the land as their own.

Yet, just as the prospect of lands newly opened to cultivation had propelled the movement of farmers westward—drawing a multitude of emigrants into Tennessee, Kentucky and the Ohio and Mississippi valleys—the rugged terrain of the Rocky Mountains promised opportunities for another kind of pioneer: the fur trader and trapper. The myriad streams and rivers that flowed down the eastern and western slopes of the Rocky

Beaver Hat (Molly Braun)

Mountains teemed with beaver, a resource as valuable to these "mountain men," as they came to be known, as fertile land was to an earlier generation of pioneers. The naturally waterproof underfur of the beaver was highly valued because it could be matted into felt and shaped into hats. Clothing fashions of the 1820s and early 1830s also made wide use of beaver fur. The resulting high demand for pelts in the East and in Europe inspired a renewed interest in finding new sources of beaver in the West, and provided the impetus for the next phase of the nation's westward movement.

On February 13, 1822, a St. Louis newspaper, the *Missouri Gazette*, published the following advertisement:

TO Enterprising Young Men: The subscriber wishes to engage ONE HUNDRED MEN, to ascend the river Missouri to its source, there to be employed for one, two or three years. For particulars enquire of Major Andrew Henry, near the Lead Mines, in the County of Washington, (who will ascend with, and command the party) or to the subscriber at St. Louis.

—William H. Ashley.

The subscriber, William Henry Ashley, was a St. Louis businessman and the lieutenant governor of the newly admitted state of Missouri, who was then organizing a fur-trading venture to the upper Missouri.

In the War of 1812, Ashley had led a volunteer company that defended outlying settlements along the upper Mississippi River and lower Missouri River frontiers. He had also expanded his lead-mining operations in southern Missouri to include the manufacture of gunpowder, which he sold to the government for the war effort. After the war, Ashley invested the profits from his gunpowder business in real estate and had prospered by buying and selling tracts of Missouri land newly opened to settlement.

Ashley's business shrewdness saved him from the Panic of 1819. Having been elected in 1820 as lieutenant-governor of Missouri, he was now seeking additional capital to further advance his political career. Although the economic crisis had ended the boom in real estate speculation, fur prices had remained high in New York and in European markets. Ashley turned his attention to the fur trade, which was then drawing a resurgence of interest in St. Louis.

American fur-trading efforts in the upper Missouri River region and in the central Rocky Mountains had begun soon after the Lewis and Clark Expedition. Manuel Lisa and Andrew Henry had led trapping and trading parties up the Missouri into the Yellowstone River and Bighorn River regions, and John Jacob Astor had mounted a major fur-trading expedition to the Pacific Northwest.

Before the War of 1812 brought it to a halt, the American fur trade in the Rocky Mountains and the upper Missouri River region had relied mainly on trading forts, strategically located at river junctions where Indians would come to trade furs for merchandise, and from which small parties of trappers employed by the fur companies would venture out to trap beaver. Since the high cost of employing large numbers of white trappers would have made these operations impractical, the participation of native peoples was essential. But the Indians, with their own tribal and individual needs, proved to be independently minded partners, and the furs gathered by hired trappers failed to make sufficient profits.

Some of the most attractive trapping lands were in the heart of Blackfoot country, around the Three Forks of the Missouri in present-day southwestern Montana. Although the Blackfeet engaged in the fur trade with whites, they preferred to deal with the Canadian and British traders of the Hudson's Bay Company, who operated out of bases around Flathead Lake to the north and the Columbia River Basin to the west.

Ashley's plan involved a new method of operation. Instead of depending on the Indians, he intended to bring "free trappers" into the field. These men would work for themselves, operating in small brigades over a wide area for long periods of time. At the conclusion of the winter trapping season, they would bring their catch to central collecting points and sell it to Ashley and his partners for cash and supplies for the next year's fur harvest.

Among those answering Ashley's call for trappers in 1822 and 1823 would be men who would become legendary as explorers of the Far West: Jedediah Smith, James Bridger, Thomas Fitzpatrick and James Beckwourth.

Ashley's enterprise of 1822 was not the only fur-trading expedition to venture up the Missouri River and into the Rocky Mountains that year, but it proved to be the most successful. His working partner, Andrew Henry, was a veteran of Manuel Lisa's fur-trading expeditions to the Big Horn and Yellowstone river region in the years preceding the War of 1812.

On April 3, 1822, a small advance party, led by Andrew Henry, set out up the Missouri River from St. Louis with a single boat and a small overland party traveling on horseback. Within a few months, they had reached the mouth of the Yellowstone River in what is now western North Dakota, where Henry established Fort Henry. A month after Henry's departure from St. Louis, the main body of the expedition—about 80 men—set out aboard the keelboat Enterprize. Just 300 miles into the 2,000-mile journey to the mouth of the Yellowstone, near what is now the town of Sibley in western Missouri, a mishap with an overhanging tree caused the vessel to capsize and sink, sending $10,000 worth of supplies to the bottom of the Missouri River. The men survived and made their way to nearby Fort Osage to await further instructions from Ashley.

In less than three weeks, Ashley had secured another keelboat. Taking personal command, he embarked up the Missouri, accompanied by 46 more men. He picked up the rest of his men at Fort Osage; in October of 1822, the expedition reached Fort Henry at the mouth of the Yellowstone. Soon afterward, with the furs that had been obtained up until then, Ashley returned downriver to St. Louis where he made preparations for a second expedition the following spring.

Over the winter of 1822–23, while Ashley recruited more men and obtained additional supplies in St. Louis, Henry dispatched trapping parties up the Yellowstone and Missouri rivers toward the eastern slopes of the Rockies. The more abundant beaver trapping grounds were located along the streams flowing into the Yellowstone, including the Powder, Tongue and Big Horn rivers. These rivers were for the most part unnavigable, making horses essential to transport men into the region and to carry the beaver pelts out. Since Henry and his men had lost most of their 50 horses to Assiniboine raiders on the overland journey to the Yellowstone, the trappers were unable to range very far beyond the region around the fort.

In the spring of 1823, one of Henry's men, Jedediah Smith, descended the Missouri in a canoe to contact Ashley and inform him of the need for more horses. By then, Ashley was on his way up river with the second expedition; they met up at Fort Atkinson, near Council Bluffs. Ashley and his party, traveling in two keelboats—the Yellowstone Packet and the Rocky Mountains—included about 50 new recruits, including James Clyman, Edward Rose and Thomas Fitzpatrick.

Learning of Henry's situation, Ashley stopped at the Arikara villages at the mouth of the Grand River, where he hoped to purchase the needed horses from the Indians. The Arikaras, alarmed that Ashley's activities would threaten their role as middlemen in the trade with the Plains tribes, were at first reluctant to comply. In a meeting with Arikara chiefs Little Soldier and Gray Eyes, Ashley seemed to allay their concerns when he assured the Indians that he only intended to trap and would therefore pose no threat to Arikara trade interests. He succeeded in obtaining 19 horses in exchange for guns and ammunition.

The next morning, the Indians, apparently having second thoughts about Ashley's intentions, attacked the 40 men he had left on shore with the horses. Fourteen were killed, while the rest fled to the keelboats on the river. Fearful of another attack, the men refused to proceed farther upriver. Faced with choosing between a threatened mutiny and an Arikara raid, Ashley was compelled to withdraw downstream to the safety of Fort Atkinson.

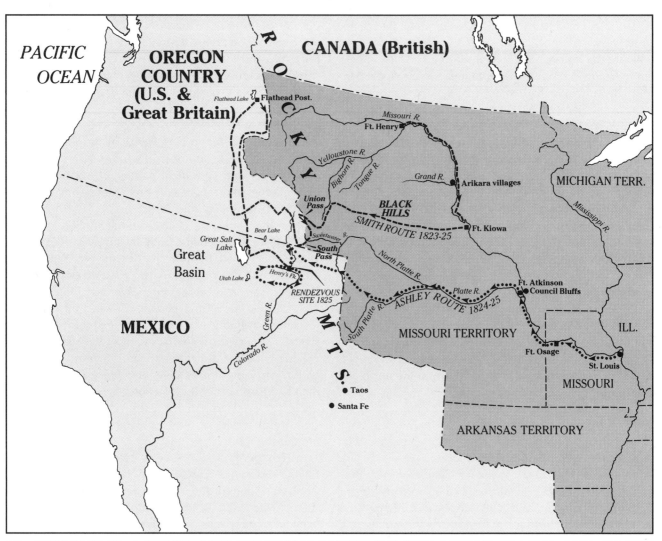

PACIFIC OCEAN

OREGON COUNTRY (U.S. & Great Britain)

CANADA (British)

ROCKY

Flathead Lake — Flathead Post.

Missouri R.

Ft. Henry

Yellowstone R.

Bighorn R.

Tongue R.

Grand R. — Arikara villages

MICHIGAN TERR.

Union Pass

BLACK HILLS

SMITH ROUTE 1823-25

Ft. Kiowa

Mississippi R.

Bear Lake

Great Salt Lake

Sweetwater R.

South Pass

Great Basin

Utah Lake

Henry's Fk.

RENDEZVOUS SITE 1825

North Platte R.

Green R.

ASHLEY ROUTE 1824-25

Platte R.

Ft. Atkinson
Council Bluffs

MEXICO

South Platte R.

MISSOURI TERRITORY

Colorado R.

ILL.

Ft. Osage

St. Louis

MISSOURI

MTS.

Taos

Santa Fe

ARKANSAS TERRITORY

48 WILLIAM H. ASHLEY AND JEDEDIAH SMITH ON THE GREAT PLAINS AND IN THE CENTRAL ROCKIES: 1823–25

Word reached Ashley that the Blackfeet had attacked some of Henry's men on the Yellowstone and those of a rival fur company on the Big Horn; he took it as a further indication that Indian resistance would thwart any American attempts to penetrate the Rockies by way of the Missouri River. In Washington, D.C., officials voiced suspicions that the British, represented by the Hudson's Bay Company, had instigated the Indian attacks in an effort to forestall American occupation of territory under supposed U.S. sovereignty. At Fort Atkinson, a punitive military expedition against the Arikaras was organized under the command of Colonel Henry Leavenworth for that summer.

The endeavor was sanctioned by Indian superintendent of the Missouri region, William Clark, as well as by Secretary of War John C. Calhoun. Accompanying Leavensworth's 230 officers and men up the river was a contingent of mountain men drawn from Ashley's company as well as other St. Louis fur-trading firms. Also taking part was a group that had come down river with An-

drew Henry. The volunteers became known as the "Missouri Legion," and were commanded by Ashley, who at that time held the rank of general in the Missouri militia.

The combined force reached the Arikara villages on August 9, 1823. Seven hundred and fifty mounted Sioux warriors also took part in the American offensive. The Sioux also traded in furs and had long resented the Arikaras' practice of serving as middlemen in the upper Missouri fur trade. A preliminary artillery assault on the palisaded villages of the Arikaras killed many of the inhabitants, including Chief Gray Eyes. The Arikara leader Little Soldier then sought to negotiate a cease-fire, an offer that Leavenworth accepted. In the ensuing meeting, the Indians agreed to return the horses Ashley had purchased from them earlier, and to desist from further raids. The negotiations stalled when the Arikaras refused to provide Leavenworth with hostages to take back to Fort Atkinson as a guarantee of the peace agreement; when Leavenworth relented, the Arikaras agreed to a treaty.

Just as Leavenworth and his command were departing, Edward Rose and another member of the Missouri Legion visited one of the Arikara villages, possibly in search of the companionship of an Indian woman. An altercation ensued in which Rose's companion was killed. As Rose escaped back to the keelboats, the village erupted in flames; the fire was probably set by Rose, who believed Leavenworth had been too lenient in dealing with the Indians. As a result, the Arikaras fled northward to seek refuge among the Mandans. This incident, the first U.S. military offensive against the Indians west of the Mississippi, served to further inflame Indian animosity against whites on the upper Missouri River.

With the Missouri River route to the Rocky Mountains now effectively closed by the threat of more Indian resistance, Ashley and Henry had to alter their plans. They sponsored a small overland party westward across the Plains from Fort Kiowa, a fur-trading post on the Missouri, below the site of the battle with the Arikaras. This group, which included Jedediah Smith, Thomas Fitzpatrick, William Sublette and James Clyman, planned to carry out trapping operations along the western slopes of the Rockies, a region that had not been explored by Americans since before the War of 1812. Henry would return overland to the Yellowstone, then proceed westward into the Rockies to trap in the Crow country around the Bighorn River and hopefully meet up with Smith and his party. Ashley would return to St. Louis to resume his duties as lieutenant governor and await the results of the trapping expeditions.

Smith and his companions, traveling on horseback, followed the White River southwestward across present-day South Dakota. After having skirted the southern edge of the Black Hills, they made their way through what is now central Wyoming, traversed the Owl Creek Mountains, reached the valley of the Bighorn River and then proceeded westward to the Wind River. There they met up with men from Henry's contingent.

In February of 1824, seeking to reach the western slopes of the Rockies, Smith and his men tried to cross the Wind River Range by way of Union Pass, the route used in 1811 by Astor's men under Wilson Price Hunt. Encountering heavy snows, they took the advice of Crow Indians that a way westward might be found to the south, and headed southward around the southern end of the Wind River Range. They then followed the Sweetwater River westward into South Pass. This wide depression in the mountains was open to travel, taking them across the Continental Divide. Crossing it in March of 1824, Smith and his men became the first non-Indians to locate the pass' eastern approach, although another Astorian, Robert Stuart, had used the route on his eastbound trek 10 years earlier.

Smith and his men set out to trap in the Green River country of what is now southwestern Wyoming and northeastern Utah, reaping a rich harvest of furs in a region that had never before been trapped by Americans. The next summer, Fitzpatrick traveled eastward to Fort Atkinson. His route took him along the Platte River to the Missouri, thus pioneering an overland route between the Missouri and the western slopes of the Rocky Mountains. From Fort Atkinson, Fitzpatrick sent news to Ashley in St. Louis of the successful trapping season in the Green River Valley.

In November of 1824, Ashley himself set out for the mountains from Fort Atkinson, intending to deliver supplies to his trappers. His expedition of 25 men and 50 pack horses retraced part of the route Stephen H. Long had followed in 1820 along the north bank of the Platte River. After having wintered with the Pawnees at their villages at the forks of the Platte, near the site of present-day North Platte, Nebraska, he continued westward into the eastern Colorado Rockies. He traversed the Front Range, then headed northward across Wyoming's Laramie Plains. Pushing westward, he reached the Green River on April 19, 1825.

While his trapping parties fanned out into the upper Green River region and around Bear Lake, Ashley and some of his men explored the lower course of the Green River in boats made of buffalo skins. His downriver trip took him through the turbulent waters of the Green's Flaming Gorge and into a valley later known as Brown's Hole. He eventually reached the Uinta Mountains where he met up with French-Canadian trapper Etienne Provost, who had penetrated the area from Taos to the South.

Ashley accompanied Provost in an exploration of the Uinta Mountains, then headed for Henrys Fork of the Green River, where a meeting with his trappers had been prearranged for the summer. On July 1, 1825, Ashley met up with all 120 of the men he had sent into the mountains. He bought their year's catch, trading ammunition, guns, traps and other necessary supplies for the furs they had gathered. This proved to be the first of the annual trappers' rendezvous that would be convened at various locations in the Central Rockies every year until 1840.

On his return journey eastward, Ashley followed the Bighorn River into the Yellowstone. At the confluence of the Yellowstone and the Missouri, he encountered Henry Atkinson, now a general in command of an 1,100-man military expedition that had been sent up the Missouri to demonstrate American sovereignty and to enter into treaties with the region's tribes. Guarded by Atkinson's forces, Ashley safely descended the Missouri and brought his first large haul of Rocky Mountain furs to St. Louis.

Before attending the 1825 rendezvous at Henrys Fork, Smith and his men had traveled northward into what is now southern Idaho, where they had met a Hudson's

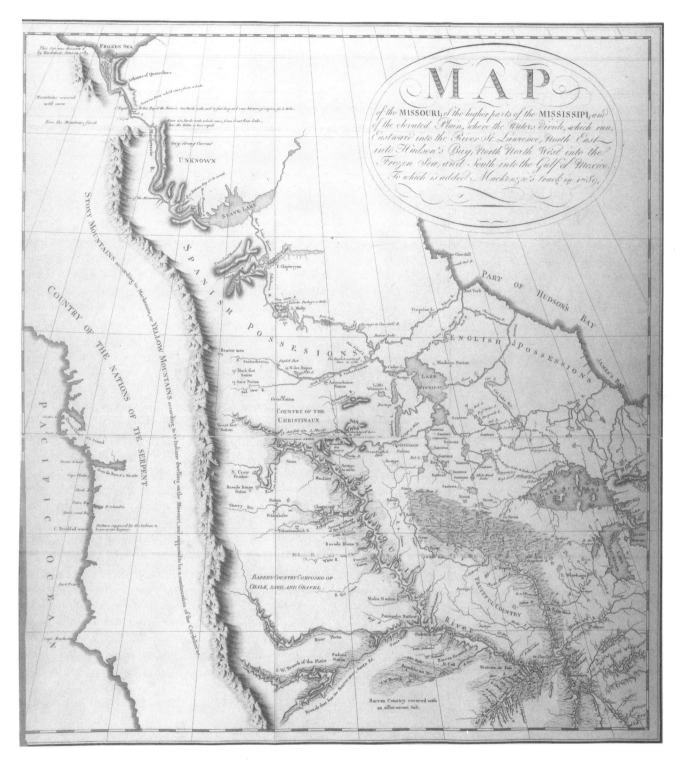

Missouri River Country, 1826 (Photo courtesy of the Library of Congress)

Bay Company trapping party, which they followed back to Flathead Lake. Between Ashley's explorations to the south, and Smith's probes to the north, a large area of the mountains and streams west of the Continental Divide had now been thoroughly explored by non-Indians.

The presence of Smith and other American trappers in the Northwest did not go unnoticed by the directors of the Hudson's Bay Company. Concerned that Americans might soon begin extensive trapping in the Oregon Country—present-day Oregon, Washington and British Columbia—the company responded by ordering its men to exhaust the sources of beaver south of the Columbia River. They hoped to create a zone barren of beaver between the Central Rockies and the Oregon coast and thereby discourage American movement into the Pacific Northwest.

James Bridger (Photo courtesy of the Library of Congress)

Later in 1825, Smith succeeded Henry as Ashley's partner. That year, Ashley led a supply caravan of 70 men and 160 pack animals along the now-familiar Platte River route into the mountains and through the South Pass to Cache Valley in the Green River region. From there, small parties dispersed to trap along the upper Snake and Bear River region, as well as along the Green.

In 1826, at the summer rendezvous in Cache Valley, Ashley sold his interest in the fur business to Jedediah Smith, William Sublette and David Jackson. From then on, Ashley would concentrate his efforts on supplying fur-trading expeditions and furthering his career in Missouri politics.

Smith meanwhile, ever in search of untapped beaver sources, set out southwestward and entered the arid regions of the Great Basin. He was seeking the fabled Buenaventura River, believed to be an upper tributary of the Sacramento flowing into San Francisco Bay. If found, it would provide a western outlet for the American fur trade in the Central Rockies.

In the winter of 1824–25, another one of Ashley's men, James Bridger, led an expedition to the lower course of the Bear River and came upon the Great Salt Lake, marking one of the earliest non-Indian discoveries of the body of water. Because of its great expanse and the salt taste of its water, Bridger at first believed he had found an inland arm of the Pacific Ocean. Several months later, however, four other trappers for Ashley circumnavigated the lake in small boats and found no stream flowing out of it, thus revealing that the Great Salt Lake was landlocked without an outlet to the Pacific.

In the fall of 1826, Smith and his men traveled south of Utah Lake and came upon the Colorado River, which he determined to be the southern extension of the Green River. Continuing southward across the Great Basin, he reached the Mojave villages in what is now southwestern Arizona. From there, guided by Indians, he and his small party crossed the Mojave Desert and, after making their way through the San Bernardino Mountains, reached San Gabriel Mission near present-day Los Angeles.

Mexican authorities interpreted the presence of the American party in California as the start of U.S. encroachment from the east. At first they threatened to arrest Smith and his men for illegally entering Mexican territory, but in the end the group was allowed to depart along the same route by which they had come.

Instead of obeying the order, Smith and his men headed northward along California's San Joaquin Valley, hoping to find the lower Buenaventura and trace it back to the Great Salt Lake. They were stopped by heavy snows in the mountains near the Stanislaus River. Leaving most of his companions there, Smith and a small party sought a route through the Sierra Nevada, planning to return for the rest of his men the following year.

Smith managed an eastward crossing of the Sierra, then recrossed the Great Basin of present-day northern Nevada and Utah to arrive at the annual rendezvous at northeastern Utah's Bear Lake in early July of 1827. In less than two weeks, he set out with a party of 18 men to locate the group he had left in California.

Smith retraced his previous route to the lower Colorado River. The Mojaves had recently suffered depredations inflicted by American fur traders out of Taos; they attacked Smith's group while they crossed the Colorado River on rafts. Smith lost 10 men before reaching the safety of the west bank. The survivors crossed the Mojave Desert, and on reaching the San Bernardino Mountains, headed northward back to the Stanislaus, where Smith was reunited with his earlier party in September of 1827.

In need of supplies, Smith sought the help of Mexican authorities in Monterey. Again threatened with imprisonment, Smith and his men were aided by a visiting American sea captain, who bought their cache of furs. The Mexicans eventually relented and allowed Smith and his men to leave California. They headed northward, circled around San Francisco Bay, and explored the Sacramento River, only to learn that it did not lead to the Great Salt Lake, but extended only to its source west of the Sierra Nevada. From there, Smith led his men northward into southern Oregon. On the Umpqua River, while Smith and two others were scouting

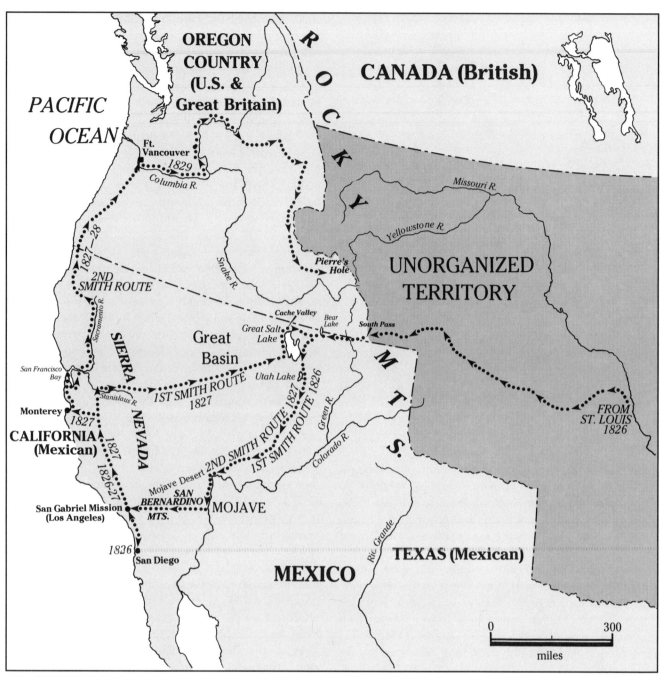

4.9 JEDEDIAH SMITH IN THE GREAT BASIN, CALIFORNIA, AND THE OREGON COUNTRY: 1826–29

ahead, the rest of the party was attacked by Umpqua Indians.

Smith and three survivors headed northward to seek help at Fort Vancouver, the Hudson's Bay Company post on the Columbia River near present-day Portland, Oregon. The company's chief director, Dr. John McLoughlin, provided them with aid and assisted in retrieving the furs and horses that had been taken in the Indian attack. McLoughlin then purchased Smith's furs and equipped him for a return journey eastward. In the spring of 1829, Smith and one of his original party ca-

noed up the Columbia and Snake rivers, managing to reach the 1829 trappers' rendezvous at Pierre's Hole in present-day Idaho.

Smith spent his last year as a trapper along the headwaters of the Missouri River. At the 1830 rendezvous at the Popo Agie River in the Wind River region, Smith, Jackson and Sublette sold their company to Thomas Fitzpatrick, James Bridger and their partners. The firm became known as the Rocky Mountain Fur Company. In bringing supplies to the 1830 rendezvous site, William Sublette had made use of 10 wagons rather than the customary caravan of pack animals. These wagons were the first ever to cross the Great Plains to the eastern slopes of the Rocky Mountains and marked the beginning of regular wagon traffic on the eastern leg of what would later become known as the Oregon Trail.

After Smith's return from the 1830 rendezvous, he settled for a short time in St. Louis. Within a year, he again turned his attention westward by investing in a trading venture that would follow the Santa Fe Trail from Missouri into New Mexico. With his former trading partners David Jackson and William Sublette, he set out in the spring of 1831 from Independence, Missouri, leading a 24-wagon caravan. On May 19, 1831, while scouting ahead for water in the Cimarron Desert of what is now southwestern Kansas, he was killed in an ambush by a Comanche hunting party.

The potential for profits in the fur trade continued to attract eastern business interests. John Jacob Astor, whose attempt to establish a large-scale fur-trading operation in the Pacific Northwest had ended unsuccessfully in 1813, had then turned his attention to the upper Missouri River and the Rocky Mountains. Starting in 1822, his American Fur Company had begun operations on the

upper Missouri River, and within a few years had absorbed most of his competitors.

In 1828, the company's regional director, Kenneth McKenzie, had established Fort Union, a new post at the mouth of the Yellowstone that soon came to dominate the fur trade of the Upper Missouri River Region. Other posts were soon established farther up the Yellowstone and into the Rockies, including Fort McKenzie, at the mouth of the Marias River, and Fort Cass at the mouth of the Bighorn.

The American Fur Company's steamboat, the *Yellowstone,* arrived at Fort Union in 1832, the first steamboat to ascend that far up the Missouri. The great improvement in transportation into the region brought about a rapid expansion of trade with the Indians of the upper Missouri. As the sources of beaver tapered out in the Rockies, the upper Missouri trade turned to the commerce in buffalo robes, starting the depletion of that animal as a resource for native peoples. The increased white presence in the upper Missouri also brought white diseases into the region, especially smallpox, which in the mid–1830s would decimate the Mandans and other Indian nations.

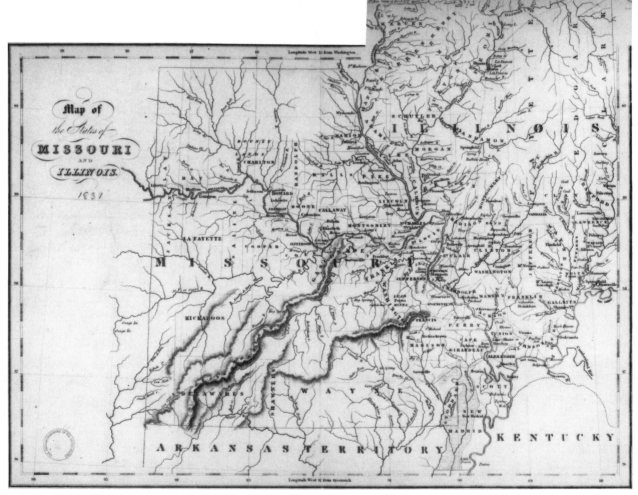

Illinois and Missouri, 1831 (Photo courtesy of the National Archives)

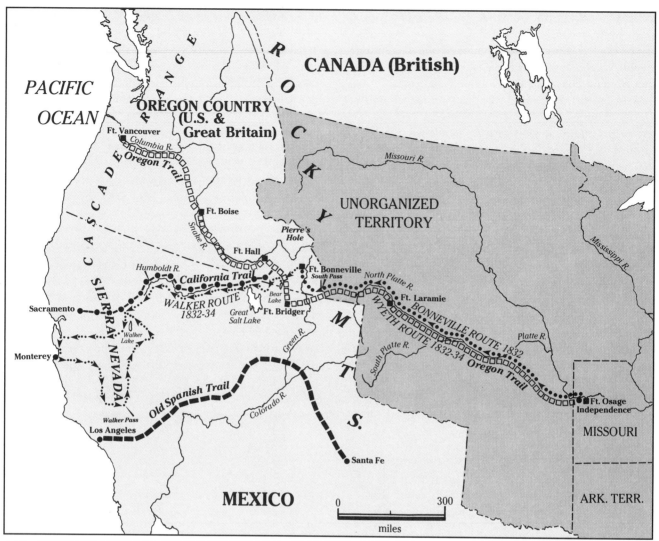

Also in 1832, Captain Benjamin Louis Eulalie de Bonneville, on extended leave from the U.S. Army, launched a major fur trading effort into the Rocky Mountains and Great Basin region, backed by New York financier Alfred Seton, a former Astor associate. Bonneville's overland expedition left Fort Osage on the Missouri, and followed the Platte River westward. The 28 wagons in his caravan became the first wheeled vehicles to traverse the Continental Divide by way of South Pass. On the west bank of the Green River, he established Fort Bonneville from where he dispatched trapping expeditions into the surrounding territory. One group, under Joseph Reddeford Walker, made an extended foray into the country beyond the Great Salt Lake.

Walker's party made its way westward along the Humboldt River of present-day northern Nevada and crossed the Sierra Nevada into the Yosemite region of central California, then continuing on to San Francisco Bay. From there they visited the settlements at Monterey and San Juan Bautista and explored the San Joaquin Valley. On his return journey eastward, Walker pioneered a route through a pass in the Sierra Nevada that now bears his name, and which brought him to the western edge of the Mojave Desert. Walker and his men retraced their route along the Humboldt River to the Great Salt Lake, then headed northward to the Snake River in present-day southern Idaho. Soon afterward, he rejoined Bonneville at his encampment on the Bear River in present-day northern Utah. Although Walker did not locate streams rich in beaver as he had hoped, his 1833–34 expedition across the Great Basin laid the basis for a viable wagon route through the Sierra Nevada by way of Walker Pass and provided additional geographic information about the Southwest.

In 1832, still another fur-trading venture helped bring about American expansion into the Far West. Inspired by New England schoolteacher Hall Jackson Kelley's call for an American colonization effort to the Oregon Country, Boston ice merchant Nathaniel J. Wyeth headed westward that year with a company of 18 men, intending to establish a fur-trading post at the mouth of the Columbia River.

Wyeth's plan resembled that of John Jacob Astor's scheme of 20 years before. A ship with supplies and trade goods was dispatched from Boston on a trip around Cape Horn to the Oregon coast. At the same time, Wyeth and a party of 20 men headed overland to Independence, Missouri. Joining up with William Sublette's annual trade caravan there, they traveled up the Platte River route and crossed the Continental Divide by way of the South Pass, arriving in time to attend the 1832 fur traders' rendezvous at Pierre's Hole in what is now southwestern Wyoming. At that point, the difficulties of the journey had caused half the men to drop out of the expedition and return to the East. Soon afterward, Wyeth and his remaining men took part in a skirmish with a band of Gros Ventres that became known as the Battle of Pierre's Hole.

Wyeth and his companions continued overland to the Snake and Columbia rivers, and in late October they arrived at Fort Vancouver, the Hudson's Bay Company post near present-day Portland, Oregon. He learned that his supply ship had been wrecked in the South Pacific, putting an end to his plan to trade on the Oregon coast that year. Wyeth and his men spent the winter at Fort Vancouver, then set out for the East in the spring. En route, they stopped at the 1833 summer rendezvous on the Green River where Wyeth entered into an agreement with the Rocky Mountain Fur Company to provide trade goods and supplies for the next annual gathering of trappers.

Soon after his return to Boston, Wyeth organized a second expedition, and in the spring of 1834 he again set out for the West. In commercial terms, this venture was to prove no more successful than Wyeth's first. When he reached the summer 1834 rendezvous on Ham's Fork of the Green River, Wyeth found that William Sublette had arrived before him with his own shipment of supplies and trade goods and had already bought out the year's beaver catch.

In the face of this setback, Wyeth constructed Fort Hall on the Snake River near present-day Pocatello, Idaho. Wyeth hoped to buy furs with his unsold goods as well as divert independent trappers away from trading with the Rocky Mountain Fur Company.

More bad luck was awaiting him at Fort Vancouver. Again he had sent a supply ship around Cape Horn, but it arrived too late in the season to carry on the salmon-fishing operations he had planned. Moreover, he soon found that Fort Hall was unable to seriously compete with Fort Boise, the Hudson's Bay Company post to the west. Seeing no future for himself in the fur trade, Wyeth returned to his ice business in Boston in 1836, and the following year he sold Fort Hall to the Hudson's Bay Company.

Although Wyeth's ventures in the West did not bring him financial gain, his exploits did influence the future movement of American settlers into the Far West. In his 1832 overland journey from Boston to the Oregon coast, Wyeth and his companions had made the first continuous crossing of the continent from the Atlantic to the Pacific. On their trip from the lower Missouri River to the Willamette Valley of Oregon, they had demonstrated the feasibility of a route that would soon become a major pathway for westbound emigrants—the Oregon Trail. Fort Hall, the post Wyeth had established on the Snake River in 1834, was the first American settlement west of the Continental Divide, and within a few years would become an important stopping point on the Oregon and California trails.

In 1834, William Sublette and fellow mountain man Robert Campbell established Fort Laramie at the junction of the North Platte and Laramie rivers in present-day southeastern Wyoming. Nine years later, James Bridger and his partner Louis Vasquez established Fort Bridger on Black's Fork of the Green River in what is now southwestern Wyoming.

The heyday of the Rocky Mountain fur trade came to an end in the late 1830s. By that time, the demand for furs had declined as hat and clothing manufacturers, yielding to the dictates of fashion, had turned to other materials. Meanwhile, most of the sources of furs had been depleted, with the beaver of the Rocky Mountains having been hunted to near extinction. The mountain men of the Rocky Mountain fur trade would go on to play significant roles in the next phase of westward migration: the movement of settlers across the Great Plains and Rocky Mountains to California and Oregon. The western outposts became important way-stations for overland emigrants bound for California and Oregon.

Jedediah Smith and his partners David Jackson and William Sublette had written to President Andrew Jackson's secretary of war, John Eaton, in 1830, informing him of the great extent of British activity in Oregon. While the Convention of 1818 had provided for joint British and American occupation of the Oregon Country, the United States had made little progress in settling the region. In their letter, the mountain men urged the use of the overland route they had pioneered to take American settlers to the Far West, and warned that if such steps were not taken, the region would fall under British domination.

In 1841, Thomas Fitzpatrick, who had begun his career as a mountain man with Ashley in the early 1820s, guided the first Oregon-bound wagon train through the

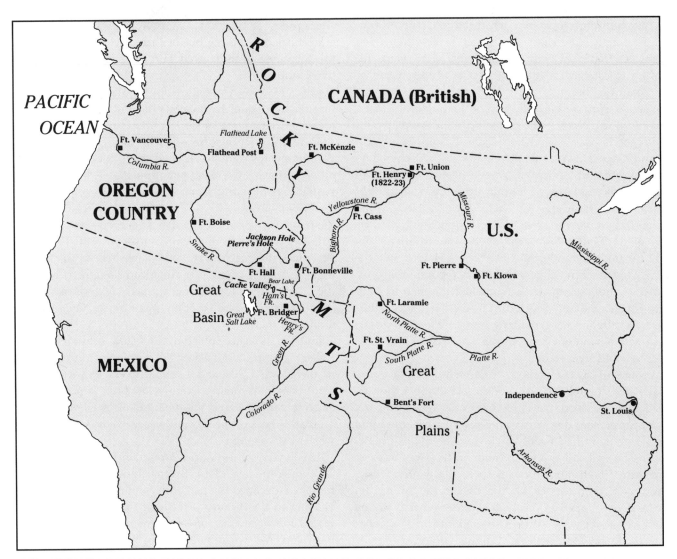

4.11 RENDEZVOUS SITES AND FUR-TRADING POSTS OF THE WEST: 1822–43

Rockies to Fort Hall as it traveled along the Oregon Trail to the Willamette Valley.

OPENING THE SANTA FE TRAIL

In the early 1820s, the prospect of wealth from buffalo robes and beaver pelts also attracted frontier traders and trappers to the Southern Plains and Southern Rockies.

After his explorations south of the Arkansas River in 1806–07, Zebulon Pike had reported the presence of huge buffalo herds on the Southern Plains, sparking interest among traders and hunters from St. Louis and other settlements along the lower Missouri River. American frontiersmen venturing into the region sometimes ranged across the international boundary into New Mexico, then a colonial province of Spain. They faced the ever-present threat of arrest and imprisonment by Span-

ish authorities who, ever since Pike's expedition, regarded Americans entering the region from the east with suspicion, fearing that they were the vanguard of a foreign invasion.

Some Americans did trap for beaver in the streams that flowed down the slopes of the Sangre de Cristo and San Juan mountains north of Taos, but more often American traders and hunters limited their forays into the Southwest to the region within U.S. territory, north of the Arkansas River. They traded with the Indians for mules, taken in raids from outlying Mexican settlements along the upper Rio Grande, and resold them for a large profit in Missouri, where they were in short supply. Missouri soon became a primary source of mules in the West.

Pike had also described Santa Fe, New Mexico's provincial capital, as a place where cloth, hardware and other imported manufactured goods were exorbitantly priced in comparison to what these same items cost in the United States, due to the Spanish policy of imposing high taxes on all foreign imports to its colonies. Moreover, U.S. goods were allowed to enter Mexico only through the port of Veracruz. The high cost of transportation from that point 1,500 miles northward to Santa Fe added to the selling price of merchandise when it finally reached New Mexico.

William Becknell, a trader presently operating out of Franklin on the Missouri frontier, was among the first to benefit from the establishment of direct trade links with New Mexico. In the summer of 1821, he advertised in the *Missouri Intelligencer* for men to join him in a venture to the Southern Plains in which he intended to trade with the Comanches for mules and horses and to capture "wild Animals of every description." Accompanied by a small party of men leading a train of pack animals loaded with trade goods, Becknell set out westward along the Missouri River, following it as far as its great bend to the north. At that point, he crossed the river and headed across the Southern Plains to the great bend of the Arkansas River near present-day Dodge City, Kansas. From there, Becknell and his men proceeded westward along the Arkansas into the foothills of the southern Colorado Rockies.

When Becknell and his party reached the site of what is now La Junta, Colorado, they turned southwestward along the Purgatoire River and entered Spanish territory. Still seeking Comanches to trade with, they made their way through the narrow chasms of Raton Pass and soon afterward encountered a detachment of Mexican soldiers. They now expected to be arrested for trespassing on Spanish territory. Instead, the soldiers informed them that Mexico had gained its independence from Spain in a revolution. With the end of Spain's harsh restrictions against foreigners and imported goods, they and their wares would now be welcomed in Santa Fe.

Becknell and his companions arrived in Santa Fe on November 16, 1821. The goods he had intended for the Indian trade were sold at a fantastic profit. After a month in Santa Fe, Becknell and a few of his men headed back to Franklin with their saddlebags loaded with a small fortune in Spanish silver coins. They made the 870-mile journey in 48 days. The rest of the Missouri traders remained behind in Santa Fe to reap further riches by trapping beaver in the mountains to the north.

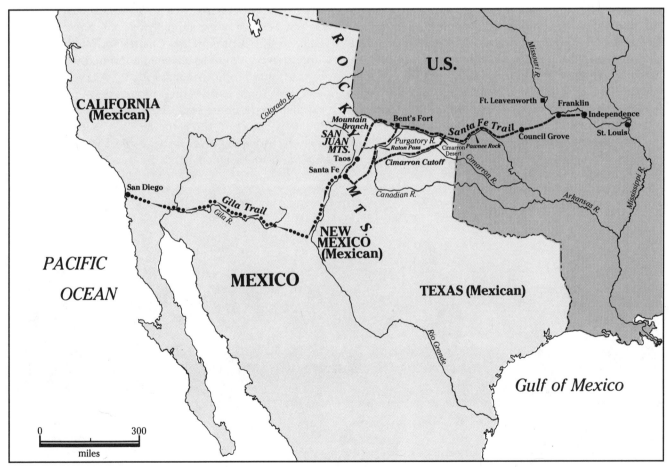

4.12 PATHWAYS INTO THE SOUTHWEST: THE SANTA FE TRAIL AND THE GILA TRAIL, 1821–35

News of Becknell's success in Santa Fe soon reached other merchants in Franklin, St. Louis and other settlements along the lower Missouri. On his return to Franklin, Becknell organized an even larger expedition to follow up his earlier venture. He set out again for Santa Fe with a group of other merchants on May 22, 1822.

This time, Becknell and his associates carried their merchandise westward in three wagons, marking the first use of wheeled vehicles for travel westward from the Missouri. His route across the plains of present-day Kansas at first retraced the one he had taken the previous year. But beyond the great bend of the Arkansas River, instead of following the river westward as he had on his earlier trip, he turned southwestward across the waterless wastes of the Cimarron Desert, a more direct route to Santa Fe by 100 miles. He may have learned of this alternate route through trading contacts with the Comanches. The main reason for the change, however, was that the Raton Pass to the west would have been impassable for his wagons.

Becknell led his caravan across the trackless Cimarron Desert, navigating by the stars. He and his men became so desperate from thirst that they slit the ears of their mules for the blood. At one point, a buffalo approached from the east. When it was shot, it was discovered that its stomach contained water, and its legs were covered with undried mud, revealing a water source not far off. They followed the animal's track, which led Becknell and his men to the Cimarron River, where they dug holes in the dried riverbed and found water. From there, they made their way southward to the upper reaches of the Canadian River, and after skirting around the southern end of the Sangre de Cristo Mountains, arrived in Santa Fe. This shorter route to Santa Fe that Becknell had blazed would later be known as the Cimarron Cutoff.

Becknell's second trip to Santa Fe proved to be even more profitable than his first. Over the next several years, annual trade caravans would follow in his wake, establishing the trail as a well-marked thoroughfare from the Missouri frontier into the Southwest. In 1825, Senator Thomas Hart Benton of Missouri, who sought to further the interests of his Missouri constituents, succeeded in convincing Congress to enact legislation providing for a survey of the Santa Fe Trail. Money was also allocated to pay the Indians for the rights of way along the route. On August 10, 1825, at a site 50 miles southwest of present-day Topeka, Kansas, a U.S. government delegation met with leaders of the Osage tribe who agreed to allow safe passage of trade caravans through their hunting grounds in return for $800 in trade goods. In honor of this occasion, the place was later known as Council Grove, and it soon became the central gathering point for subsequent trade expeditions to Santa Fe.

In 1827, the government established Fort Leavenworth to protect travel on the Santa Fe Trail; the post also served as a base for later exploring expeditions into the West. Repeated raids by Comanches, whose territory straddled the western segment of the Santa Fe Trail, led the government to provide military escorts for the Santa Fe trade starting in 1829.

By 1831, over a quarter of a million dollars in merchandise was being shipped annually over the Santa Fe Trail. That year, the Bent brothers, Charles and William, along with Ceran St. Vrain, established a fortified trading post near La Junta on the Arkansas River. Becknell's Cimarron Cutoff route had by then proven to be too hazardous, and a safer route was later adopted. Known as the Mountain Branch of the Santa Fe Trail, it led westward along the Arkansas River to Bent's Fort where it turned southward to Taos and Santa Fe. The new route made

Caravan Arriving at Santa Fe (Photo courtesy of the Library of Congress)

Bent's Fort the principal stopover point on the Santa Fe Trail as well as a center for the trade in buffalo robes in the American Southwest.

While the trade with Santa Fe was extremely profitable for the merchants of St. Louis and other towns along the lower Missouri River, it had little impact on the national economy. Yet the commerce of the Santa Fe Trail helped extend America's southwestern frontier, leading to the establishment of additional settlements. Independence, Missouri, soon replaced Franklin as the westernmost U.S. settlement and became the starting point for trade caravans headed for Santa Fe. Later it also served as the staging point for emigrant wagon trains headed for Oregon and California along the Oregon and California trails. William Becknell became known as the "Father of the Santa Fe Trail."

Sylvester Pattie and his son James Ohio Pattie were two other American frontiersmen whose travels in the Mexican-held Southwest preceded the westward extension of the nation's territorial limits. Originally from Kentucky, they moved from there to Missouri in 1812 where they worked as fur trappers. By the mid–1820s, they had moved west to New Mexico to trap in the mountains around Taos. In 1828, they headed into present-day southern Arizona and trapped along the Gila River, then traveled to the mouth of the Colorado and across the desert to San Diego, making them the first Americans to reach the Pacific Coast along what became known as the Gila Trail. It was along this route that Kit Carson, who had also been a mountain man in New Mexico in the 1820s, led American forces westward in their march to California in 1846.

THE QUESTION OF TEXAS

The northeastern Mexican provinces that now comprise the present state of Texas had been claimed by the United States as part of the Louisiana Purchase in 1803. Spain, which at that time ruled Mexico, not only questioned the validity of the Louisiana Purchase itself, but insisted that the territory France had sold to the United States extended southwestward only as far as the Sabine River (the western boundary of the present-day state of Louisiana), and therefore did not include Texas.

From the U.S. point of view, the southwestern limit of the Louisiana Purchase was hundreds of miles to the south at the Rio Grande. The dispute persisted more or less peaceably over the next 15 years.

The Texas country itself was at first of little concern to either Spain or the United States; the Spanish had not made a serious effort to populate Texas, and in the United States, there was still more than ample room for new settlement in the lands east of the Mississippi River.

Still, American adventurers, or "filibusters," tried several abortive schemes to occupy Texas. A "private" conquest of Texas was supposedly one of the major goals of the conspiracy hatched by General James Wilkinson and Aaron Burr in 1807.

In 1819, the Adams–Onis Treaty between the U.S. and Spain offered a resolution of the Texas question. Under its terms, the United States renounced its claim to Texas by recognizing the southwestern border of the Louisiana Purchase as the Sabine and Red rivers, and not the Rio Grande. In return, Spain turned over its remaining territory in Florida. The arrangement enlarged the southeastern United States and resolved a border dispute on the southwestern frontier that from time to time had brought the U.S. to the brink of war with Spain.

The treaty was not without opponents in Congress who, led by Henry Clay of Kentucky and Thomas Hart Benton of Missouri, descried it as an unneccesary cession of territory to a nonbelligerent power. These views echoed the sectional sentiments of southerners who saw the loss of Texas as a constraint on the spread of slavery. The Missouri Compromise of 1820 added fuel to their concerns, and made Texas even more attractive as a source of new slave territories.

News of the impending treaty inspired yet another independent American attempt to take Texas by force. In 1819, Dr. James Long, who had served with Andrew Jackson in the Battle of New Orleans four years before, led a force of 300 men from the Louisiana border country into Texas, hoping to establish an independent state. He occupied the area around Nacogdoches and there proclaimed an independent republic. A provisional government was organized and Long was elected as its head. Land was distributed to his followers and within a few months there were more than 1,000 settlers. Long then forged an alliance with the notorious Gulf Coast pirate Jean Laffite who controlled the Galveston Bay area. Before the year had ended, however, a Spanish military expedition had succeeded in driving Long's American settlers out of Texas.

Ratification of the Adams–Onis Treaty was delayed for two years as Congress debated the Texas question. Western and southern newspapers protested the U.S. plan to give up its claim to Texas, crying out against the "shame of dismembering the valley of the Mississippi . . ."

The promising opportunity that Texas held for American settlement came to the attention of Moses Austin of Potosi, Missouri. He had heard favorable reports about the coastal region of eastern Texas from friends in New Orleans, and by 1820 he was sorely in need of a promising new opportunity of his own. As Congress deliberated in Washington over the Adams–Onis Treaty, the full force of the Panic of 1819 was being felt in the West. Speculative land sales coupled with a more conservative government policy toward the sale of public lands had caused a financial chain reaction of foreclosures and bank failures. When the Bank of St. Louis failed in 1819, Moses Austin, its principal stockholder, was financially ruined.

Moses Austin was born in Durham, Connecticut, in 1761. He had been a merchant in Philadelphia and later entered the lead–mining business in Wythe County, Virginia. In 1798, business setbacks prompted him to move west to Spanish territory in present-day southeastern Missouri. He became a naturalized Spanish citizen, obtained a land grant from the Spanish colonial government, established another lead mining operation and founded the settlement of Potosi. His business prospered over the next 20 years, and he became an active participant in government affairs after the region had become a U.S. territory in 1803.

Austin, although nearing the age of 60 in 1820, sought to remake his fortune by establishing a colony in Texas. Unlike earlier American attempts to settle Texas, his plan was to have the complete approval of the Spanish colonial government. In November of 1820, he set out from Little Rock, Arkansas for Texas, arriving at the provincial capital at San Antonio late the next month. The local governor, Colonel Antonio Maria Martinez, at first rejected his plan to bring several hundred settler families into Texas and ordered Austin out of Spanish territory. But through the influence of Baron de Bastrop, a Dutch adventurer who had settled in Texas, Austin succeeded in obtaining Spanish support for his idea from Martinez's superiors in Monterey. Austin's status as a Spanish citizen of Louisiana helped convince the Spanish authorities in Texas that he would remain a loyal colonial administrator.

Austin was permitted to settle 300 families on 200,000 acres of Texas land. The Spanish colonial authorities had become concerned that eastern Texas, sparsely populated and remote from the center of government in Mexico City, could all too easily fall to the expansionist ambitions of the United States or be taken over by another foreign power. Over the preceding two centuries, Spanish attempts to populate the region by establishing missions had attracted few Mexican settlers. The Comanches, Kiowas and other regional tribes were yet to be pacified, and with the government in Mexico City reluctant to provide military protection, Indian attacks remained a constant threat. It was hoped that Austin's colony would not only impose order and establish a government in the region, but also create an effective buffer between the United States and Mexico's northeastern frontier.

In the spring of 1821, Austin headed back northward to Missouri to recruit settlers for his Texas colony. The rigors of the trip proved too much for him, however, and en route he contracted pneumonia and died near Nacogdoches. His son, Stephen Fuller Austin, who was traveling to join his father in the colonization attempt, learned of his father's death soon after leaving Natchitoches, Louisiana. On his deathbed, the elder Austin had bequeathed the grant for the Texas colony to his son, and Stephen proceeded to San Antonio to carry out his father's project.

Stephen Austin had managed his father's banking and mining businesses and had been a territorial legislator in Missouri. Twenty-seven years old in 1821, he had been studying law in New Orleans and had been serving as a circuit judge in the Arkansas Territory. In San Antonio, Governor Martinez recognized the younger Austin as heir to his father's land grant and directed him to choose a site for his colony. He selected the lands between the Brazos and Colorado rivers on the Texas coastal plain, then returned to New Orleans to gather the first party of colonists.

There was an abundant number of applicants, many of them lower Mississippi Valley settlers who had lost their lands in the Panic of 1819. Austin's offer to new home-seekers was highly attractive: The U.S. government was still selling public land at $1.25 per acre while Austin offered huge tracts of Texas land at only twelve-and-a-half cents per acre.

While Stephen Austin was installing his first 300 families at his colony of San Felipe de Austin, Mexico became independent from Spain. As a result, he had to seek reconfirmation of his grant from the new republican government in Mexico City. After a long delay caused by the unsettled state of the government, Austin managed to work out an agreement with the Congress of Mexico. The terms permitted his granting up to 4,605 acres to each household of settlers he could bring to the colony. For every 200 families, he received a bonus of 67,000 acres. He also obtained additional grants for more colonies on which to settle as many as 800 families. He was given complete control of the administration of the colonies. In addition, tariffs and taxes were suspended for his colonists. Although the Mexican government was moving toward the abolition of slavery, he managed to obtain an exemption that allowed his colonists to bring slaves with them, provided that any slaves born in Texas were to be freed at the age of 14. Mexico's generosity stemmed from a concern that if Texas were not sufficiently colonized it could easily fall prey to absorption by the United States.

The Mexican government also approved plans for additional immigration into Texas by other colonial organizers, known as "empresarios." Among them was Haden Edwards, who established his colony around Nacogdoches. In 1826, he came into conflict with former Mexican settlers on his land grant who protested his unauthorized demand for a fee to transfer their land titles. Their objections reached the Mexican regional authorities, who responded by nullifying Haden's grant and expelling him from Texas. Edwards, together with his brother Benjamin, reacted by leading a band of followers into Nacogdoches in December of 1826 and declaring himself leader of a new independent republic that he called "Fredonia." The Fredonian Rebellion was soon suppressed when Mexican forces, aided by the loyal Stephen Austin and his followers, helped drive Edwards and the rebels out.

Although unsuccessful, the Fredonian Rebellion was seen by the Mexican government as an omen of future troubles with American immigrants in Texas. Attempts by the United States to buy Texas—first by President John Quincy Adams who offered $1 million and later by President Andrew Jackson who increased the offer to $5 million—were declined, and they underscored Mexican concerns over U.S. expansionist designs on Texas. In response, a new Mexican immigration law was enacted in 1830 forbidding foreigners from settling on lands adjacent to their home country, in effect precluding any more American immigration. The government also annulled all empresario contracts that had not been fulfilled by then, causing more than a few colonization schemes to disintegrate overnight.

Austin went to Mexico City to seek relief from these measures and to obtain greater autonomy for the American colonies in eastern Texas. In December of 1833, he succeeded in getting a repeal of most of the objectionable parts of the 1830 immigration law. He was unable, however, to convince the Mexican government to separate Texas from the adjoining Mexican province of Coahuila, which would have created an American-dominated state in the Mexican confederation. In January of 1834, while traveling back to the Texas colony, Austin was arrested when letters revealing his sentiments for Texas independence were intercepted by government officials. He remained in custody in Mexico City for more than a year, and was not able to return to Texas until July 1835. By that time, support was growing around San Felipe de Austin and the other Anglo–American settlements for an independent Texas.

In 1835, General Antonio Lopez de Santa Anna took over the Mexican government and declared himself dictator of Mexico. He renounced the constitution of 1824 and brought the states of Mexico under the direct control of his centralized authority. Anglo–American settlers in Texas, totaling more than 30,000, greatly outnumbered the less than 4,000 Mexican inhabitants. On November 3, 1835, the American Texans, at a convention in San Felipe de Austin known as the "Consultation," voted to restore the 1824 Mexican constitution and re-establish the state government.

Santa Anna reacted by dispatching troops to suppress the rebellion. At the port of Anahuac, a Mexican garrison established to collect tariffs, the troops were forced

The Alamo (Photo courtesy of the New York Public Library)

out by a band of Texan militants under William B. Travis. More armed resistance erupted at the town of Gonzales when Mexican cavalrymen, sent to retrieve a cannon that had been given to the colonists for protection against the Indians, were driven back to San Antonio after a battle with the Texan colonists.

General Martin Perfecto de Cos, brother-in-law of Santa Anna, occupied San Antonio and disbanded the Coahuila y Texas state legislature. In December of 1835, the Texans launched a counterattack led by American empresario leader Benjamin Milan. In the assault, Milam was killed, but the Texans—after fierce house-to-house fighting—recaptured San Antonio. Cos surrendered his forces and agreed to leave Texas. Yet after withdrawing to the Rio Grande, he turned back, and joined by Santa Anna's 5,000-man army from northern Mexico, marched on San Antonio. Outnumbered, the Texans withdrew to the outskirts of San Antonio to take up fortified positions at a mission known as the Alamo. On March 6, 1836, after a 12-day siege, Santa Anna and his army attacked the Alamo and killed all 187 of the Texan defenders. Among those who lost their lives at the Alamo were legendary American frontier heroes Davy Crockett and Jim Bowie.

Meanwhile, at the settlement of Washington-on-the-Brazos, a convention of Texas leaders had met and declared their independence as the Republic of Texas on March 2, 1836. David Burnet was made provisional president and Sam Houston, a former governor of Tennessee and friend of President Andrew Jackson, was named commander of the Texas armed forces. On March 27, a force of 300 Texans was captured by Mexican troops at Goliad and all were executed as rebels.

The defeats at the Alamo and Goliad only served to inspire support among Texans for an independent nation. The provisional government and the army at first retreated northward in the face of Santa Anna's advance. American colonists fled their homes in a disorganized

Bowie Knife (Molly Braun)

flight that became known as the "Runaway Scrape." On April 21, 1836, however, Houston stood against the Mexican army at the San Jacinto River, near the site of the city that now bears his name. In a battle lasting less than 20 minutes, the Texas forces—spurred on by the cry of "Remember the Alamo"—overwhelmed the Mexican army. Santa Anna, disguised as a private, was captured.

Although there was a call to execute the Mexican dictator, Houston spared his life and elicited a pledge from Santa Anna to recognize the independence of the new Texas Republic. He sent Santa Anna to Washington, D.C., to seek similar recognition from the United States. U.S. authorities, however, refused to meet with him and sent him back to Mexico aboard a warship. In an effort to preserve his position as Mexico's leader, Santa Anna soon repudiated the promise he had made under duress. Nevertheless, for the time being, his defeat at the Battle of San Jacinto had caused him to fall from power.

The leaders of Texas now sought to have their republic annexed by the United States. Their proposal was resisted by northerners in Congress who feared annexation would provoke a war with Mexico and that as many as five slave states would be formed from Texas, upsetting the balance between slave and free states. Former president John Quincy Adams, presently a leading voice in Congress, opposed the move throughout the congressional session of 1836.

Texans, meanwhile, had chosen Sam Houston as their first elected president. Stephen Austin was made secretary of state, but he died later in 1836. In the face of unrelenting congressional opposition, Texas withdrew its proposal for annexation. On March 3, 1837, as his last official act as president, Andrew Jackson extended U.S. recognition to the Republic of Texas.

During the next several years, immigration from the United States accelerated, spurred on by the Texas government's offer of generous land grants to newcomers. The westward movement of settlers had been deflected southward by the creation of the Indian Country in the early 1830s, and the economic pressures of the Panic of 1837 had caused a renewed demand for new and cheaper lands by displaced frontier settlers. Thousands arrived by steamboat from New Orleans, while even more came overland across the Sabine River. Settlers poured into Texas from Europe as well, with many new arrivals coming from the German states, Ireland and France. By 1842, the population exceeded more than 140,000. The Republic of Texas soon established diplomatic ties with France, Great Britain, the Netherlands and Belgium.

A major goal of Texas' foreign policy was to gain Mexico's recognition of an independent Texas. The Texas–Mexico border was a point of major dispute. The Mexican government maintained that the Nueces River was the boundary and refused to negotiate, insisting that neither Texas nor Coahuila—the state to which it had been joined—had ever extended to the Rio Grande, as Texans now claimed. Border friction was continuous; in 1842, Santa Anna, now reinstated as head of Mexico, again invaded Texas. He withdrew after briefly occupying San Antonio.

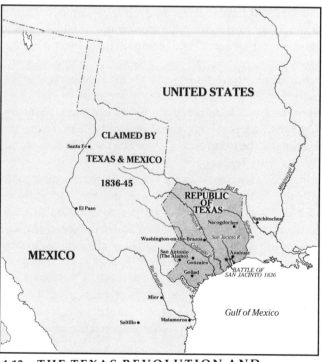

4.13   THE TEXAS REVOLUTION AND REPUBLIC: 1835–45

Texas, under the leadership of its second president, Mirabeau Buonaparte Lamar, attempted to take over the adjoining Mexican provinces of New Mexico, with hopes of expanding the infant republic as far westward as the Pacific. In June 1841, a Texas military expedition, under the guise of a trade caravan, marched against Santa Fe only to be driven back by forces under New Mexico governor Manuel Armijo. The following year, an independent Texas expedition moved southward against the Mexican town of Mier on the Rio Grande. The attempt ended with the capture of 300 Texans. One hundred and seventy-five of them managed to escape, but they were eventually retaken.

Sam Houston, who had become president of Texas again in 1841, now made another attempt to have Texas joined to the United States. He invited the British to mediate the border dispute between Texas and Mexico, possibly hoping to play on U.S. fears concerning the establishment of a British protectorate over Texas against anti-annexation sentiments in the U.S. Congress. The British readily accepted the offer; closer ties with the new republic could benefit the British textile industry with cheaper imports of Texas cotton.

At that time, Great Britain was engaged in a crusade to abolish slavery throughout the world, and the new British interest in Texas sparked fears in the United States that under British influence an independent Texas might end slavery. The possibility sparked fears among southerners that there would be a haven for runaway slaves on the nation's doorstep. Northerners became alarmed that a British foothold in Texas would compromise the nation's sovereignty and present a formidable obstacle to U.S. expansion.

The annexation of Texas became a central issue in the U.S. presidential race of 1844. Democratic candidate James Knox Polk made it a major goal of his campaign. His call for the "re-annexation" of Texas to correct the earlier diplomatic blunders of the Adams–Onis Treaty played a large part in his victory over his Whig opponent, Henry Clay, who had declined to make a strong stand on the question.

The outgoing president, John Tyler, seeing that the addition of Texas to the Union was now inevitable, took the matter up as one of his last acts as president. Congress, still divided on the issue, could not be counted on for the two-thirds vote needed in both houses to approve annexation by treaty. Instead, with the help of his secretary of state, John C. Calhoun, Tyler pushed through a joint congressional resolution for Texas annexation, which he obtained by a simple majority in the House and the Senate.

Texas readily agreed to the resolution, which provided the option that Texas, if it chose, could divide itself into as many as five states. Texas had other plans, however,

and refused to be divided. On December 29, 1845, the Republic of Texas came to an end and Texas entered the Union as the 28th state. In keeping with the terms of the Missouri Compromise of 1820, slavery was to be permitted south of the 36°30' line, thus allowing it to continue within the entire area.

The Mexican government, which by now thought an independent Texas was preferable to having the area absorbed by the United States, saw the annexation of Texas as a hostile act. As soon as Texas entry into the Union became imminent, Mexico broke off diplomatic relations with the United States and prepared for war.

The annexation of Texas increased the territory of the United States by one-third. Texans saw their new state as encompassing all the lands adjacent to the former state of Texas y Coahuila lying north and east of the Rio Grande in present-day New Mexico and Colorado, in addition to the territory that had made up their former republic. Texas also claimed all of the panhandle of present-day Oklahoma, the southwestern corner of present-day Kansas and a portion of present-day south-central Wyoming. Although most of this territory was also claimed by Mexico, the issue was obscured by the outbreak of the Mexican War in 1846.

At the conclusion of that conflict in 1848, the Texas state government attempted to organize the newly conquered territory of New Mexico and Colorado into counties, planning to use the sale of those lands to settle the immense debts incurred during 10 years of independence. But the federal government refused to recognize the Texas claims, and under the Compromise of 1850, organized the area into New Mexico and Colorado territories. Texas, reduced to its present boundaries, received $10 million in compensation, which it used to pay off the huge debts the Texas government had incurred during its decade as an independent republic.

THE INDIAN REMOVAL POLICY

As an expression of foreign policy, the Monroe Doctrine was little more than a "No Trespassing" sign requiring the watchdog of Great Britain to enforce it. On the domestic front, however, the Monroe administration acted decisively in dealing with the problems posed by the presence of a people most of the nation regarded as an alien power living within its midst—the Native Americans inhabiting lands east of the Mississippi River.

By the mid–1820s, white settlers were advancing in great numbers into the Lake Plains of the Old Northwest. Settlers from Kentucky and the Northeast sought the fertile lands of northern Illinois and present-day

SAMUEL COLT AND THE
SIX-SHOOTER

Hartford Connecticut native Samuel Colt was 16 years old in 1830 when he went to sea on a merchant ship. On the long voyage from Boston to India, he spent his free time whittling away at pieces of wood. Out of one of his carvings—a model of a pistol with a rotating cylinder—he developed a tool that would leave its mark on the history of the American West.

Colt patented his pistol design in England in 1835, then in the United States the next year. In 1838, he founded the Patent Arms Company, with a factory in Patterson, New Jersey, and began manufacturing his new type of revolver. This weapon could fire six rounds before it had to be reloaded; most pistols and rifles in use at the time were capable of firing only a single shot, with reloading requiring up to a minute.

Colt had hoped to sell his revolvers to the army and navy, but the high manufacturing costs made them too expensive for the U.S. government to consider. Yet there was another government to the south, the newly formed Republic of Texas, which needed a weapon that could be used to defend against the raids of Comanche warriors on their northwestern frontier and the incursions of the Mexican army from the southwest.

The American settlers of Texas were among the first to realize the demands of combat on the Great Plains. In their struggle for independence from Mexico in 1835–36, they had fought with single-shot, muzzle-loading rifles that had long-range accuracy but were only effective when fired while on foot. For fighting on horseback, they had used pistols that were also limited to a single shot before they had to be reloaded. The Mexican army, well-adapted to mounted warfare, fought effectively with lances and swords in cavalry assaults.

The Comanches were even more adept at mounted warfare than the Mexicans. Although lacking firearms, they proved to be formidable opponents with their great skill as horsemen and their use of the bow and arrow. In the minute it took a frontiersman to reload an ordinary weapon, an Indian warrior could launch as many as 20 arrows from a charging horse. An Indian could then pursue his retreating enemy and come in for the kill with a 12-foot long lance.

In 1835, the Texas Rangers was organized as a small elite force to protect the outlying settlements from the Comanches. In about 1839, soon after Colt had begun turning out his revolving pistols, the guns came into use on the Texas frontier. They may have been introduced by a prominent merchant and cattleman named S. M. Swenson who brought them to the attention of Texas government officials. Colt soon received orders for his revolvers from Texas, and the guns played a key role in the victories of the Texas Rangers over the Comanches in the battles of Council House, Plum Creek and the Perdanales River in 1840.

The demand from the Lone Star Republic for Colt's revolvers was so great that he called his first model the "Texas." On the recommendations of Samuel H. Walker, commander of the Texas Rangers, Colt made several modifications to his gun. He added a trigger guard and made the gun heavier so that it also could be used as a club. A disadvantage of the "Texas" was that to reload, it had to be disas-

southern Michigan and Wisconsin. Indian homelands were engulfed by the white tide of migration, and conflicts arose between Indians who feared encroachment and whites who coveted Indian land and were prepared to grab it without regard to prior government treaties.

Migration into the Lake Plains also came from the South. Farmers of smaller holdings in Georgia, Alabama and Mississippi, unable to compete with the expanding plantation economy, poured into the region, attracted by the more affordable lands of the public domain. In the South itself, Native Americans—in particular the Chero-kee, Chickasaw, Choctaw, Creek and Seminole tribes—found themselves encircled by whites as settlement in that region advanced into the remaining open lands of western Georgia, Florida, Alabama and Mississippi.

The usual practice of forcing tribal leaders to cede their ancestral homelands in exchange for reservations in adjacent areas only pushed the Indians in advance of white settlement and left them to fall prey to unscrupulous traders and whiskey peddlers. Moreover, such measures only forestalled inevitable new conflicts that arose when whites appropriated Indian lands and homes.

sembled into three pieces, a procedure that could cause a man on horseback to easily lose one of the parts. To remedy this problem, Colt redesigned his revolver with a loading lever. The new model, which first appeared in about 1842, was called the Walker Colt in honor of the Texas Ranger commander.

The Republic of Texas, now faced with a shortage of funds and a mounting public debt, was able to maintain only a small force of fighting men, and likewise could purchase only small quantities of six–shooters; Colt's firm fell into bankruptcy in 1842. The United States government, influenced by unfavorable reports of military experts, remained unimpressed by the revolver and declined to give Colt a contract. Western settlement had not yet advanced much beyond the Mississippi, and there was little demand among frontiersmen for a weapon designed mainly for Indian-fighting on the Great Plains.

The outbreak of the Mexican War in 1846 turned things around for Colt. The Texas Rangers, under John Coffee Hays, had formed a regiment that joined General Zachary Taylor's forces on the Rio Grande. These men, who furnished their own equipment and arms, mainly used Colt revolvers. Taylor was so impressed by the Rangers and their use of Colt's revolving pistols in their engagements with the Mexicans that he requested that the federal government provide the Texas volunteers with 1,000 of the guns.

By that time, Colt was out of business and did not even have one of his own guns to use as a model. Starting from scratch, he created an improved design. Lacking the resources to manufacture the guns himself, he entered into a partnership with the Whitney Company, a firm established a generation before by cotton gin inventor Eli Whitney. Although he lost money on his first government contract, Colt later became a millionaire and established Colt's Patent Fire–Arms Manufacturing Company. Located in his hometown of Hartford, it endured as a major American industrial enterprise for many years. His six-shooter was so popular that in time the name Colt became synonymous with the revolving-breech pistol.

Samuel Colt's revolvers became standard equipment for the multitudes headed for Oregon and the California goldfields. The six-shooter also came to be an indispensable tool of the cowboys of the Great Plains and a prevalent symbol in the mythology of the American West.

Samuel Colt (Photo courtesy of the Library of Congress)

The Indian policy formulated by the Monroe administration called for relocating Indian tribes of the Old Northwest and the Old Southwest to territory west of the Mississippi. Zebulon Pike and Stephen Long had characterized it as unfit for white habitation. The "Great American Desert," it was argued, would be the most suitable place to move the remaining eastern tribes. There it was hoped the native peoples could adapt themselves to agriculture and white civilization in an environment isolated from the corrupting influence of white frontier society.

Establishing a permanent Indian frontier would not only protect the Indians from encroachment but also check the westward spread of the white population. It was feared that the rapid rate of western settlement was making the nation too spread out to effectively administer from a central government in the East. The nation was entering into an era when internal improvements were being promoted to connect the eastern seaboard with the the Ohio and Mississippi valleys. Under Henry Clay's plan for an "American System," roads and canals were planned to help consolidate the nation's economic

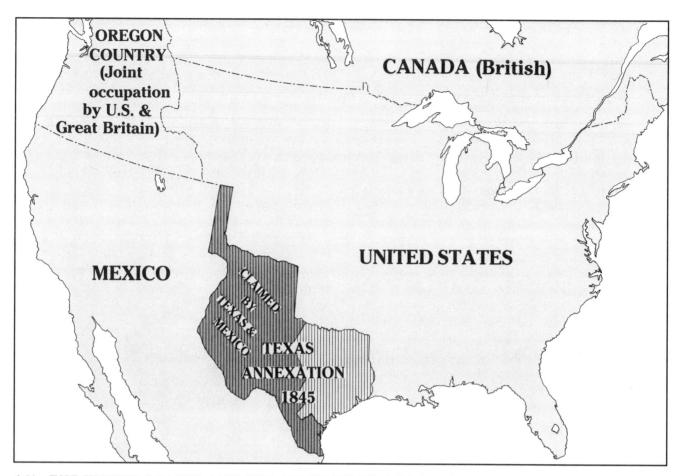

4.14 THE UNITED STATES AND THE ANNEXATION OF TEXAS: 1845

life and make it less dependent on imports from Europe. These plans were centered upon the development of the Trans-Appalachian West, and did not include the development of the Plains region, then considered a natural barrier to the nation's westward expansion.

Compelling the Indians to migrate to the West was not a new idea. In 1803, President Thomas Jefferson had proposed using the western lands acquired in the Louisiana Purchase for this very purpose. After the Revolutionary War and the War of 1812, some tribes, faced with the unrelenting advance of white encroachment, had voluntarily given up their lands in the East to settle on lands west of the Mississippi.

Early in 1825, President James Monroe announced his new Indian policy as part of his last annual address to Congress. It had been developed by his secretary of war, John C. Calhoun. Under his direction, New England missionary and geographer Jedediah Morse had traveled throughout the lands of the eastern and western Indians in 1819–23, surveying their situation and estimating their numbers. Based on Morse's 1823 report, Calhoun recommended that the Indians remaining east of the Mississippi cede their lands in exchange for new and permanent homelands in the West.

A permanent Indian frontier was proposed beyond which white settlement would be prohibited. The line first ran west from the mouth of Green Bay on the western shore of Lake Michigan, then crossed present-day northern Wisconsin to the Mississippi. Upper Wisconsin was to be left to the Indians who lived there. From there, the line followed the Mississippi River south through eastern Iowa to the northern border of Missouri and turned west as far as the Missouri River. Then it turned southward again, along the western boundaries of Missouri and Arkansas to the Red River border with Texas. The lands north of the Platte were to be reserved for tribes who then inhabited that region. The area between the Platte and the Red River was earmarked as the new homelands for the tribes to be relocated from the East.

To implement the plan, a series of treaties was required in order to determine exactly which lands each eastern tribe claimed. By establishing these tribal boundaries, the government could then negotiate for the cession of these lands and proceed with relocating the individual tribes. In August of 1825, a major conference was held with leaders of the Potawatomi, Chippewa, Sauk, Fox and Winnebago Indians at Prairie du Chien in present-day Wisconsin. The government was repre-

The Treaty Gathering at Prairie du Chien in 1825 (Photo courtesy of the New York Public Library)

sented by Governor Lewis Cass of the Michigan Territory and General William Clark of Missouri. Within a few years, these tribes had ceded their lands in Indiana and Wisconsin in exchange for cash payments and the promise of annuities. Other tribes still residing north of the Ohio River followed suit so that by 1827, most of the Indians of the Old Northwest had relocated to lands west of the Mississippi or had agreed to move within a given time.

The removal of the Indians of the Old Northwest was not accomplished without some resistance. In 1827, a band of Winnebagos under Chief Red Bird made a stand against the growing numbers of farmers and lead miners in their ancestral homeland, conducting a number of raids in the vicinity of Prairie du Chien. The uprising failed to attract the support of neighboring tribes. Federal troops under General Henry Atkinson, as well as Illinois volunteers and a contingent of miners out of Galena, converged on Red Bird's followers, isolating them and forcing additional land cessions from the tribe.

The Black Hawk War of 1832 also resulted from the shrinking Indian domain. Twenty-eight years earlier, some leaders of Sauk and Fox bands had entered into a treaty with Indiana territorial governor William Henry Harrison in which they agreed to give up their lands on the eastern side of the Mississippi between the mouths of the Wisconsin and Illinois rivers. They were permitted to retain the use of these lands until such time that they were to be opened to white settlement. The time came in 1831 when white settlers began streaming into their

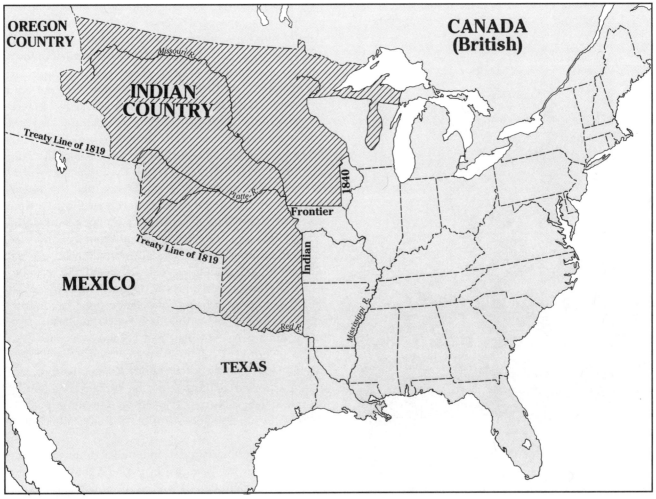

4.15 "THE PERMANENT INDIAN FRONTIER": 1825–40

tribal domain around the mouth of the Rock River in western Illinois.

One of the principal chiefs, Keokuk, believed that resisting white encroachment was hopeless; after negotiating with white officials for his own power and profit, he led his people west across the Mississippi into lands allocated to the Indians in present-day Iowa. But his followers had arrived on their Iowa lands too late in the season to plant a crop of corn for the winter. During the winter of 1830–31, with game scarce, they faced starvation. Another Sauk chief, Black Hawk, decided to lead a band of his people back across the Mississippi to where he hoped to join with the Winnebagos and plant corn to support his people. At 60 years of age, Black Hawk was a veteran of the War of 1812 in which he had fought alongside the British. He believed that he might be able to gain the support of the British in Canada to regain his people's original lands.

In the spring of 1832, Black Hawk and a group of 400 warriors and 600 women and children crossed back into Illinois. The move was viewed by Illinois settlers as an Indian invasion. The militia and federal troops under General Atkinson were called out. Black Hawk and his people defied orders to return to Iowa. Instead, he headed eastward up the Rock River with a large force of federal troops and frontier militia in pursuit. When he

Black Hawk (Photo courtesy of the Library of Congress)

failed to win the alliance of the Winnebagos, Potawatomis and Kickapoos, Black Hawk decided to surrender to the American forces. His emissaries, carrying a flag of truce, were fired upon, and some of them were killed. Black Hawk saw no other alternative but to counterattack. Over the next three months, his warriors managed minor victories. But with the women and children among his band suffering from disease and starvation, he chose to return to the rest of the tribe on the Iowa side of the Mississippi.

Black Hawk's retreat westward took him down the Wisconsin River. Along the way, federal troops and frontier militia fired on the women and children as they descended the river on rafts. At the mouth of the Bad Axe River on the Mississippi, Black Hawk again attempted to obtain a cease-fire, hoping to lead his followers across the river to Iowa. But the soldiers ignored his white flag of truce and fired on his people.

Only 150 of those who had started out with Black Hawk survived. Most of these, including Black Hawk, eventually surrendered. Taken to Washington, D.C., he was received by President Andrew Jackson who presented him with a medal and a ceremonial sword. Despite his defeat, his futile stand against overwhelming odds had made him the embodiment of Indian bravery in the eyes of the public, and crowds flocked to catch sight of him when he toured eastern cities.

Released in June of 1833, Black Hawk returned to Iowa where he spent the rest of his days with his people. To the nation that had taken away his lands, he reportedly remarked, "Rock River was a beautiful country. I loved my towns, my cornfields, and the home of my people. I fought for it. It is now yours. Keep it as we did "

The government entered into a new treaty with Sauk and Fox representatives, in which the Indians agreed to remain on the west side of the Mississippi. As reparations for the hostilities of 1832, the two tribes were forced to cede a 50-mile strip along the west bank of the Mississippi, extending from the northern boundary of Missouri to Prairie du Chien. In return the Indians received a $20,000 annuity, a cash payment of $40,000 and a quantity of tobacco and salt. Opened to white settlement soon afterward, the Iowa lands along the Mississippi became known as the Black Hawk Purchase.

The Indian removal plan had become a major aspect of the government's domestic policy. While slowed during the presidency of John Quincy Adams, who considered the forced relocation of the Indians immoral, it became a major feature of Andrew Jackson's political platform in his first successful bid for the White House in 1828.

Jackson's enthusiasm for the Indian removal policy stemmed from his years as an Indian fighter and from his role as a champion of southern frontier interests. In his first year as president, he journeyed among the

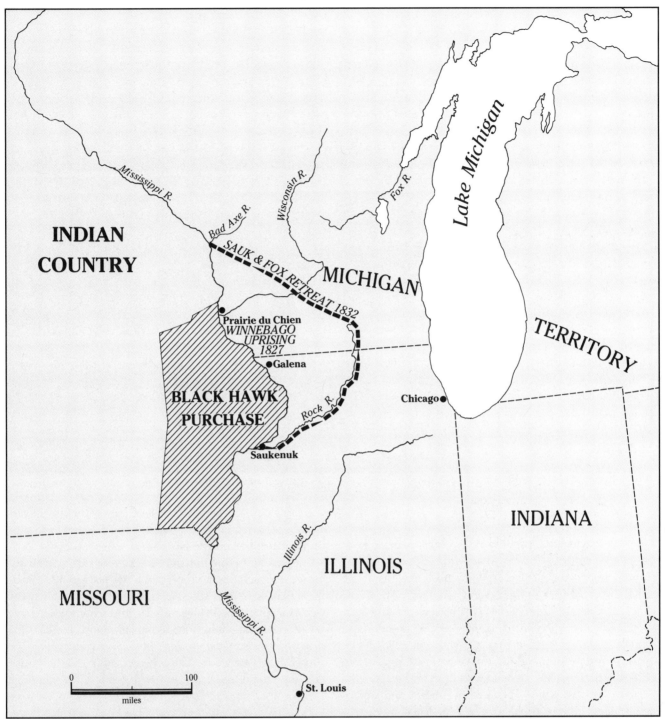

4.16 THE WINNEBAGO UPRISING OF 1827 AND THE BLACK HAWK WAR OF 1832

southern tribes—some of them former allies in the War of 1812—to persuade them to give up their lands peacefully and move to the West. In an address to the Creeks, he assured the Indians of the new security they would find in the West, promising: "Your white brothers will . . . have no claim to the land and you can live upon it, you and all your children, as long as the grass grows or the water runs, in peace and plenty. It will be yours forever."

Earlier, in 1802, Georgia had agreed to give up its claim to its western lands in return for the federal government's promise to extinguish the land titles of the Creeks and Cherokees within the state. It was not until Jackson took office in 1829, however, that the Georgia state government acted to take over these Indian lands. The area inhabited by the Indians was annexed and organized into counties, and the Indian lands were then distributed to white settlers by lottery.

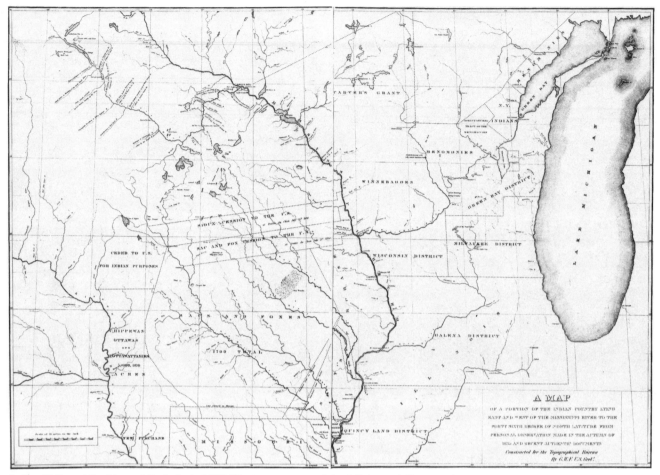

Indian Tribes of the Upper Mississippi, 1835 (Photo courtesy of the Library of Congress)

Certain Southeast tribes—in particular the Cherokee, Chickasaw, Choctaw, Creek and Seminole, referred to as the "Five Civilized Tribes"—had adopted many of the cultural traits of white society and used their lands in much the same way as their white neighbors. The Cherokees of Georgia, Tennessee, North Carolina and Alabama had established farms, plantations, workshops and schools. One of their members, Sequoyah, had developed a written alphabet for the Cherokee language. In 1828, the tribe began publishing its own newspaper, the *Cherokee Phoenix*, which appeared in English and Cherokee editions. Many tribal members had become Christians and, with the help of missionaries, maintained churches. Their resistance to the removal plan was to be carried out in the courts.

On July 26, 1827, the Cherokees declared themselves a sovereign nation and adopted a constitution modeled after that of the United States. As an independent nation, the Cherokees held that the state of Georgia had no authority over them. The discovery of gold on Cherokee territory gave the Georgia state government added incentive to remove the Indians. With the support of President Jackson, the Indian Removal Bill of 1830 was enacted, giving the federal government the authority to allocate western lands to Indians who consented to give up their territory in the East.

Spurred on by the apparent backing of the Jackson administration, Georgia proceeded in its plan to dispossess the Cherokees. The Cherokees brought suit against the Georgia government, seeking an injunction against the execution of the state's action against them. In 1831, the case of *Cherokee Nation v. State of Georgia* went before the United Supreme Court. Chief Justice John Marshall ruled that the Cherokees could not be considered a sovereign

Cherokee Dance Wand (Molly Braun)

nation, but were in fact a "domestic dependent nation," and therefore did not have the standing of a foreign nation to sue Georgia.

In a related case the following year, *Worcester v. State of Georgia*, the Cherokees held that Georgia laws had violated federal treaties with their tribe. This time, Marshall and the Supreme Court concurred with the Cherokees' contention, but President Jackson refused to provide federal backing to enforce the finding. He reportedly proclaimed: "John Marshall has made his decision; now let him enforce it."

In the end, the Cherokees and other tribes of the South were forced to comply with the Indian Removal Act of 1830. By 1835, a treaty was signed by a minority faction of the tribe in which their Georgia lands were ceded and opened to white settlement. Over the next three years, the Cherokees were transported westward by the government in overland caravans and by steamboat to new reservations in what is now Oklahoma.

Of the southern tribes, only the Seminoles mounted any significant armed resistance to their forced removals. They fled into the Florida Everglades, where from 1835 to 1842 they waged a fierce struggle against U.S. Army efforts to round them up and ship them to the West. In 1838, their leader, Osceola, had been taken captive at a supposed peace conference. He died as a prisoner of war. Over the next few years, with one army after another mounted against them, the Seminole resistance was gradually broken. Many of their people were relocated, but others managed to stay in their homeland. Most soon joined the other southern tribes in a forced removal to the West.

The hardships of the Five Civilized Tribes did not end with their eviction from their ancestral territories. As they were transported to the West they suffered from hunger, exposure, disease and steamboat accidents. Of the tens of thousands of southern Indians who were removed, nearly one-quarter perished while making the journey. The route of their forced exodus has since been characterized as the "Trail of Tears."

By 1840, most of the territory west of the Mississippi River—excluding the states of Louisiana, Missouri and Arkansas—had been designated as Indian Country. In land cessions from the relocated Indian tribes, the United States had expended more than $30 million and given some 54 million acres of western lands to the Indi-

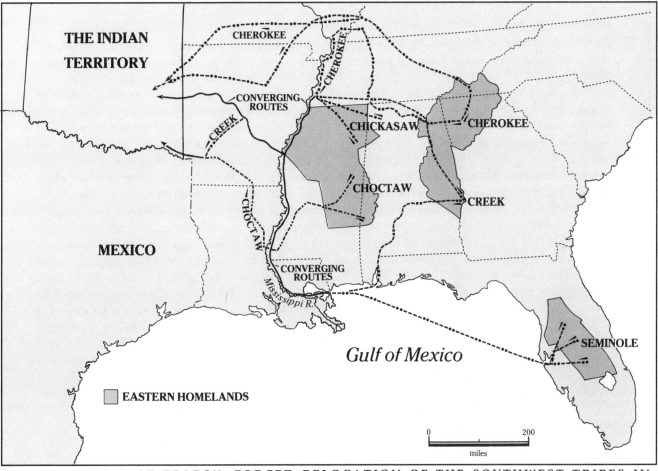

4.17 "THE TRAIL OF TEARS": FORCED RELOCATION OF THE SOUTHWEST TRIBES IN THE 1830s

SEQUOYAH AND THE
CHEROKEE ALPHABET

The Cherokees became unwilling pioneers when they were compelled to leave their homelands in the southeastern states for reservations in present-day Arkansas and Oklahoma. Their forced migration, which occurred over a period of more than 20 years, could have destroyed their identity as a people were it not for an invention by a Cherokee silversmith and trader known as Sequoyah.

Sequoyah was the son of a Cherokee woman, Wurteh (the sister of a chief) and probably a white trader and explorer named Nathaniel Gist. He was born in about 1770 at a Cherokee village in what is now Loudon County, Tennessee. A short time before his birth his white father disappeared, and he was raised by his Indian mother.

When he was 12, the young Sequoyah and Wurteh went to live among the Cherokees near present-day Willstown, Alabama. His mother, emulating the ways of the neighboring white settlers, began raising dairy cows and planting corn. Although it was not the custom for males of his tribe to do so, Sequoyah helped in tending the herd and assisted his mother in raising crops.

As a young man, Sequoyah engaged in trade with whites. With the silver coins he earned, he fashioned jewelry and ornaments. In his contacts with whites, he observed that they wrote down ideas on paper, using what the Indians called "talking leaves" to store information that could later be transmitted. He realized the great benefit a written language could bring to his people and sought to learn this skill for himself.

Sequoyah first tried to learn to read and write from the white missionaries who worked among his people. But they taught these skills in English, a language that he had never mastered. Undaunted, he set about developing a written form of Cherokee. In about 1809, he began experimenting with pictographs, symbols that represented words and ideas of the Cherokee language. When he found that this approach would require over 1,000 such characters—far too many to commit to memory and be of practical use—he turned to developing a system based on the sounds of basic Cherokee syllables.

In 1818, Sequoyah and a group of Cherokees agreed to a removal treaty and migrated to a reservation in what is now Pope County, Arkansas. In the new Cherokee lands, he continued his efforts to develop a written form of Cherokee, and by 1821 he had designed an alphabet of 86 letters that phonetically represented all the syllables of the Cherokee language.

In 1821–22, Sequoyah visited with the Cherokees who had remained in the East, bringing with him letters from their Arkansas relatives written in his new alphabet. The Cherokee leaders were quick to realize the great benefit his invention could provide and officially adopted it as the written form of their language. Within a short time, his alphabet or syllabary brought literacy to most of the Cherokees. In 1828, the Cherokees drafted a constitution in their own language and began publishing a newspaper in Cherokee, the *Cherokee Phoenix*, the first Native American newspaper on the continent.

Over the next decade, Sequoyah's alphabet enabled the eastern and western segments of the Cherokee nation to remain in contact even though separated by hundreds of miles. Sequoyah and his family resettled in what is now Sallisaw, Oklahoma in 1829. The remaining eastern Cherokees arrived there in 1839. By then, he had become the president of the Western Cherokees; in that role he worked to ease the problems faced by the influx of newcomers from the East. His invention enabled the Cherokees to record land titles, codify laws and communicate ideas. Being a unified people helped them adapt to the demands of a modern mode of life in their new homes on the eastern edge of the Great Plains.

In 1825, in recognition of his contributions to the tribe, the Cherokee ruling council presented him with a silver medal. Three years later, while in Washington, D.C. as part of an official Cherokee delegation, he was acclaimed for his work by scholars and government leaders. A statue of him now stands in the U.S. Capitol, and a county in Oklahoma was named in his honor. His name was later immortalized by the Hungarian naturalist Stephen Endlicher who gave the name "sequoia" to the genus of giant California redwood trees.

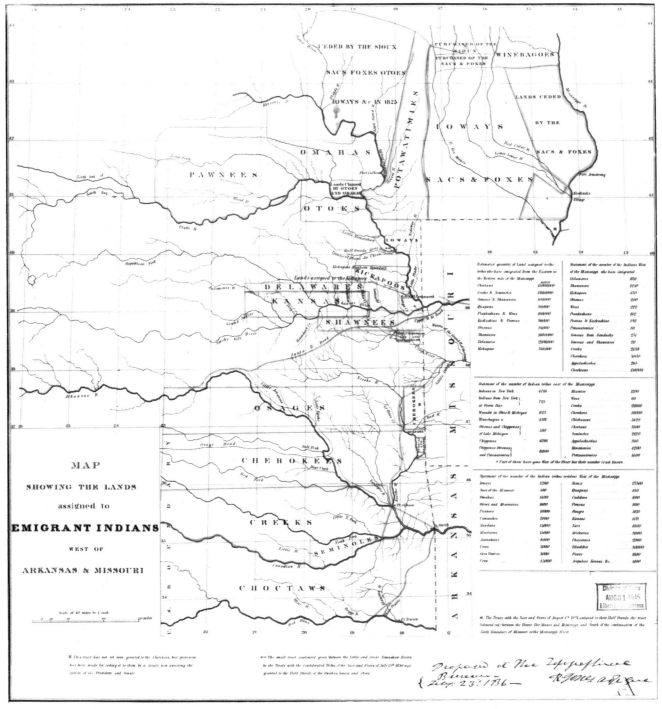

Original Western Homelands Assigned to Eastern Indians, 1836 (Photo courtesy of the Library of Congress)

ans. The lands the eastern tribes had ceded amounted to more than 400 million acres.

In terms of real estate, the United States had also fared well with its Indian removal policy, in which the cost of securing the lands of the eastern tribes amounted to 10 cents per acre (almost matching the price paid in the Louisiana Purchase, at 8 cents per acre). The government was soon able to sell most of the newly enlarged public domain to settlers at $1.25 per acre. The enor-

mous profit realized by the sale of the former lands of the eastern tribes eliminated the national debt and created a surplus in the government treasury that helped bolster the national economy and finance federally funded road and canal projects.

Contrary to the government's intentions, the establishment of an Indian Country west of the Mississippi did little to stem the nation's rapid westward movement. Instead, it created a two-pronged advance, with the stream of migrating settlers deflected northwestward to the Oregon Country and southwestward into Texas.

As for the eastern Indians who had been resettled in present-day eastern Oklahoma, Kansas and Iowa, they found themselves undersupplied by the government and frequently at odds with their Plains Indians neighbors, who regarded the newcomers with as much as hostility as they would white intruders in their midst. Within a generation, the eastern tribes again found their lands in demand for white settlement, and many were compelled by the government to relocate once more.

MANIFEST DESTINY FOR SOME

The Monroe Doctrine enabled the United States to assert itself as a power to be reckoned with in the Western Hemisphere. The Indian removal policy begun in the 1820s and 1830s had cleared the way for the nation's surge of growth westward. The ensuing development of roads and canals in the Trans–Appalachian West had cemented economic ties between the West and the North, bringing about a new alignment of sectional interests that ultimately left the South isolated.

In the meantime, the fur trade of the upper Missouri River and the Rocky Mountains had opened the way for American occupation of the Far West. It introduced American business into the region, and together with the military, established a U.S. presence over a vast area that would otherwise have remained remote and isolated from the rest of the nation. Reports describing the unsettled fertile country of California and Oregon inspired a new generation of eastern land–seekers.

The annexation of Texas had marked the beginning of a new era in the westward growth of the United States. It was the first time that an entire sovereign nation, rather than the colonial possessions of a European power, had been joined to the United States. And Texas had entered the Union as a result of the self-determination of its people, a development that was expressed in a July of 1845 editorial by John L. O'Sullivan in the *United States Magazine and Democratic Review.* Chiding the nation's hesitation to antagonize Mexico while in the process of annexing Texas, O'Sullivan proclaimed that it was the nation's "Manifest Destiny . . . to overspread the continent allotted by Providence for the free development of our yearly multiplying millions."

"Manifest Destiny" soon became the catch phrase for supporters of expansionism, a policy that had been openly adopted in 1845 by the newly elected president, James K. Polk. The idea that the United States was destined to occupy the entire North American continent, although later modified, served to justify the nation's appropriation of more and more Indian lands and its headlong rush into a war with Mexico that, although begun as a border dispute, quickly grew into a campaign of conquest.

Chapter 5
A TRANSCONTINENTAL REPUBLIC (1846–1853)

THE UNITED STATES ENTERED the 1840s with most of its western frontier defined by the Rocky Mountains and the Continental Divide. The legal limits of white settlement extended only as far as the single vertical tier of states and settled territories that bordered the western bank of the Mississippi River. The lands beyond had been reserved for the Indians.

Yet within three years of the middle of the decade, 1845–48, the nation broke beyond its borders to encompass the Oregon Country, California and the rest of Mexico's northern territory in the Great Basin region of the American Southwest.

The annexation of Texas in 1845 had whetted the nation's appetite for unbridled territorial growth. The concept of Manifest Destiny sprang from the public debate over the Texas issue and brought with it sentiments that ignited a patriotic fervor in support of an aggressive foreign policy of unabashed expansionism. Whether motivated by economic or political necessity, the nation's commitment to the cause of liberty was now wedded to a drive to push the nation's boundaries as far as the natural limits of geography would allow, or at least to the extent that diplomatic efforts or the fortunes of war would permit.

THE OREGON COUNTRY

At the beginning of the 19th century, the area of North America we now call the Pacific Northwest was known as the Oregon Country. Stretching between the Continental Divide and the Pacific Coast, it extended northward to the southern tip of Russian Alaska; on the south it was bounded by California and the adjoining Spanish (and later Mexican) territory to the east. The name derived from the legendary river, the "Oregon," which was thought to flow westward through the region and empty into the Pacific. Jonathan Carver, a colonial militiaman from Connecticut, had learned of the legend from the Indians while exploring the western Great Lakes in 1767–68, and the name was later applied to the entire region.

The U.S. claim to the Oregon Country stemmed from private and government explorations. In 1792, Boston sea-captain Robert Gray's navigations along the Oregon coast had revealed the mouth of the Columbia River. The Lewis and Clark Expedition had traversed the region from the East and wintered on the Pacific Coast in 1805–06. Employees of American entrepreneur John Jacob Astor's western fur-trading operation had explored inland to the Snake River; they maintained a trading post, Astoria, near the Columbia River's mouth for more than two years before it was sold to the British-owned North West Company in 1813.

Americans were not the first to claim the Oregon Country on the basis of exploration. Spanish navigators had surveyed the Oregon coast beginning with the voyage of Sebastian de Vizcaino in 1603. Spanish naval commander Juan Perez had explored Nootka Sound on the coast of present-day British Columbia in 1774. Soon afterward, other Spanish naval expeditions under Bruno Hecete and Juan Francisco Bodega y Quadra made a series of landings along the Pacific Northwest coast between present-day Gray's Harbor, Oregon and the Gulf of Alaska.

The British also claimed sovereignty over the region based on the work of the great navigator Captain James Cook who, in 1778, had examined the coast of present-day British Columbia and Alaska while searching for the fabled Northwest Passage. The reports brought back from that voyage sparked the lucrative trade in sea otter pelts between the Pacific Northwest and China. In 1792, at the same time that Gray was in the area, Captain George Vancouver of the British navy carried out extensive explorations along the Pacific Northwest coast; a group from his expedition traveled 100 miles up the Columbia River. During the 1790s and early 1800s, British fur traders Sir Alexander Mackenzie and Simon Fraser had undertaken extensive overland explorations between the Canadian Rockies and the Pacific Coast.

Russia was the fourth nation with a claim on the Oregon Country. Since the 1790s, the Russian American Company had been extending its fur-trading operations southward from the Gulf of Alaska into northern California.

By 1825, international treaties left only Great Britain and the United States in control of the region. The Convention of 1818, which had established the Canada–U.S. boundary along the 49th Parallel east of the Rocky Mountains, also had provided for joint British–U.S. occupation of the Oregon Country. With the Adams–Onis Treaty of 1819, Spain had bowed out of the disputed area by agreeing to the 42nd Parallel as the northern limit of California and its other possessions in the American West. Russia, in separate treaties with the United States and Great Britain in 1824 and 1825, had withdrawn its claim to the Pacific Northwest south of 54°40′.

No sooner was the joint occupation agreement ratified than Congress began to reconsider the prospect of sharing the Oregon Country with Great Britain. In 1820, at the urging of Representative John Floyd of Virginia, a Congressional committee was set up to study the feasibility of establishing American settlements in Oregon. Floyd, as the committee's chairman, warned that if efforts were not made to expand the American presence there, Oregon would soon fall under British domination by default. His knowledge and interest in the region came through his friendship with fellow Virginian and Oregon explorer William Clark, and from his cousin, Charles Floyd, who had also been a member of the Lewis and Clark Expedition.

In his report to Congress, Floyd emphasized how vital the Oregon Country was to both the western fur trade and to New England whaling efforts in the North Pacific; he also stressed its potential value as a source of lumber for export, and its possibilities for agricultural development. In this way he tried to gain the support of each of the major sectional interests: westerners, northerners and southerners. Based on his committee's recommendations, he presented a bill calling for the annexation of Oregon. It did not pass because a majority in Congress deemed the region too remote and wild for American occupation. The bill's opponents feared that a government-sponsored colony in Oregon would eventually become a separate state, independent of the rest of the nation. Moreover, any move to annex the region would most certainly bring about a confrontation with Great Britain, and at that time few in Congress thought the Oregon Country was worth going to war over.

Next Floyd introduced legislation providing for the organization of Oregon as a U.S. territory when its population reached 2,000, a measure that also failed to pass. In all, between 1821 and 1827, Floyd introduced four bills on the Oregon issue. In 1824, he declared that "Oregon is destined to be the great place of North America . . . he who can go, and grow with the country, will, and must, in three or four years, possess wealth and influence . . ." Although he had been unable to prod Congress to action, he nevertheless succeeded in directing the public's attention to the forested and fertile lands of the Pacific Northwest. In his public statements on the issue, he had fired the imagination of individuals who

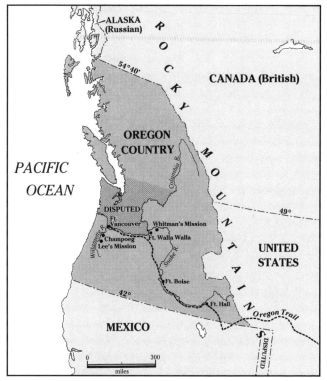

5.1 THE OREGON COUNTRY

went on to spearhead the American occupation of Oregon.

During the same period that John Floyd was beseeching Congress to support an American takeover of the Oregon Country, John Quincy Adams—first as secretary of state, and later as president—made four attempts to negotiate a final settlement of the Oregon question. He proposed to the British that the 49th Parallel boundary be extended westward to the Pacific. The British, however, wanted to make the Columbia River the boundary, thereby retaining most of present-day Washington State and British Columbia, a region that was still vital to the fur trade. Yet this arrangement would have cost the United States Puget Sound, which was coveted as a vital Pacific Coast port.

Congressional concerns over the Oregon question faded after 1827, when the joint-occupancy arrangement was renewed. The revised treaty allowed either Great Britain or the United States to terminate unilaterally the agreement on one year's notice to the other nation. That provision gave the two claiming nations flexibility in adopting their respective Oregon policies to the subsequent course of events.

Meanwhile, by 1825 the British, through the Hudson's Bay Company, had come to dominate the Oregon Country. That year, the company established Fort Vancouver on the north bank of the Columbia River, opposite present-day Portland, Oregon. To remain profitable, the post had to become self-sufficient in terms of food production. Under the management of Fort Vancouver director Dr. John McLoughlin, company employees cleared lands around the fort and planted wheat and corn. They also imported herds of cattle and pigs from California and the Hawaiian Islands and established a gristmill and a sawmill. These agricultural projects were so successful that within a few years Fort Vancouver was exporting surpluses to Mexican California and Russian Alaska.

While the public debate over Oregon in the halls of Congress and other branches of government lay dormant, private Oregon boosters began to make their message heard. One of the most vocal of these was Hall Jackson Kelley, a Boston textbook writer and schoolteacher, who had paid close attention to congressional representative John Floyd's rhapsodizing on the Oregon Country in Congress.

Kelley's interest in the Oregon Country began with his reading of the accounts of the Lewis and Clark Expedition. Leaving his teaching position in 1823, he devoted himself to promoting his plan for a New England-type farming community on the lower Columbia River. In 1828, he submitted a "Memorial" to Congress calling for government support for his colonizing plans for Oregon. In letters to newspapers and government leaders, and in pamphlets, he called for a permanent American settlement in the Oregon Country. To carry out his Oregon colonization plan, he organized the American Society for Encouraging the Settlement of the Oregon Territory, hoping to attract enough followers to induce governmental financing of a mass American migration to the Pacific Northwest.

When Congress declined to embrace his plan, Kelley undertook a journey on his own to the Oregon Country. In 1833, he sailed from New Orleans to Veracruz, then traveled overland across Mexico into southern California. In San Diego, he joined up with frontiersman Ewing Young, who was headed northward with a herd of horses to sell at Fort Vancouver. Along the way, they were joined by a small party of men who, unknown to Young and Kelley, were fugitive horse thieves. When they arrived at Fort Vancouver, Dr. John McLoughlin, having received word of the desperadoes from California authorities, assumed the entire group to be outlaws and withheld the hospitality he usually extended to American visitors.

Young, who had been barred from trading at the fort, established a ranch a few miles to the south in the Willamette Valley. Kelley, at that time ill with malaria, was permitted to stay in a hut outside Fort Vancouver's walls. He eventually cleared his name, and with money borrowed from the Hudson's Bay company, he sailed back to Boston in the spring of 1835.

While Hall Jackson Kelley's propagandizing efforts did not materialize into a permanent American foothold in the Oregon Country, they did inspire fur-trader Nathaniel Wyeth to lead two commercial ventures to the region. On his second expedition in 1834, Wyeth was accompanied by Jason Lee and his nephew Daniel Lee, both Methodist missionaries from New York State, who had been sent by their church to minister to the Indians of the Pacific Northwest. Although they had originally planned to establish their mission in the Flathead country of present-day western Montana, while stopping at Fort Vancouver, Dr. McLoughlin advised them that the region was too close to militant Blackfeet and convinced them to set up their mission in the nearby Willamette Valley instead.

Within a few years, more missionaries and support staff arrived, and developed what would one day become the city of Salem, Oregon, around Lee's mission. At about the same time, Presbyterian and Congregationalist missionaries, sponsored by the American Board of Commissioners for Foreign Missions, had begun to enter the field. In 1835, the Reverend Samuel Parker and medical missionary Marcus Whitman made a preliminary tour of the region. The next year, Whitman and his wife Narcissa—accompanied by missionary Henry Spalding, along with his wife Eliza—made the overland journey from St. Louis by way of the Oregon Trail. This journey marked the first time white women had crossed the Rockies, and it was also the first time a wheeled vehicle had been used to travel as far west as Fort Boise.

The Whitmans established their mission near Fort Walla Walla, while the Spaldings established theirs to the east at Lapwai. As with the Lees before them, their efforts were more successful at attracting additional American settlers to the region than they were at introducing Christianity to the Native Americans.

In 1836, President Andrew Jackson sent William A. Slacum to check on the progress of the American settlements in the Oregon Country. While there, he helped the settlers organize the Willamette Cattle Company to import much needed stock. Ewing Young was sent to California and returned with 600 head of cattle. Ten years after the joint occupation agreement had been renewed, Slacum's favorable report aroused a renewed interest in Oregon.

News of the prosperity of the Willamette Valley settlements spread to the Ohio and Mississippi valleys just when the Panic of 1837 had caused farm prices and land values to plummet. Within a few years, large parties of emigrants were heading westward in organized wagon trains—most for the Oregon Country, and others for California. In 1843, the largest group to date, numbering almost 1,000 men, women and children, with more than 100 wagons and 5,000 head of cattle, left Independence, Missouri. The party followed the Platte River westward to Fort Laramie, the first leg of the Oregon Trail. From there, they crossed the Continental Divide by way of the South Pass, then headed southwestward to Fort Bridger.

A circuitous route around the Wasatch Mountains took them northwestward to Fort Hall, the post estab-

lished by Nathaniel Wyeth in 1834. Beyond that point, some of the emigrants broke off from the main group for the Humboldt River route across the northern edge of the Great Basin to the Sierra Nevada and California's San Joaquin Valley. Most of the wagon train continued along the by now well-established route to Fort Boise and Fort Walla Walla. Marcus Whitman, who accompanied the 1843 expedition, guided the wagons to the Columbia, and beyond to the Willamette Valley.

By 1845, the American population of the Oregon Country, most of it centered in the Willamette Valley, had mushroomed to more than 6,000. Even before that time, American settlers had felt an urgent need for some kind of formal governmental authority to assure title to their lands and to provide for the transfer of property. This problem was underscored when Ewing Young died in 1841, leaving an estate of some 600 cattle and no will. In 1843, the Americans organized a provisional government at Champoeg and proclaimed the region as the "Oregon Territory."

The Hudson's Bay Company, which had been as benevolent to the American newcomers as business would allow, now felt threatened by the large number of emigrants living in the vicinity of Fort Vancouver. By 1845, the beaver trade south of the Columbia had declined to such an extent that Fort Vancouver was only marginally profitable. That year, the company moved its Pacific Northwest headquarters north to Fort Victoria on the southern end of Vancouver Island.

Meanwhile, James Polk had been elected as U.S. president on a platform that called for the "re-annexation of Texas" and the "re-occupation of Oregon." In December of 1845, his call for the end of the joint occupation of

Covered Wagons on the Oregon Trail (Photo courtesy of the Library of Congress)

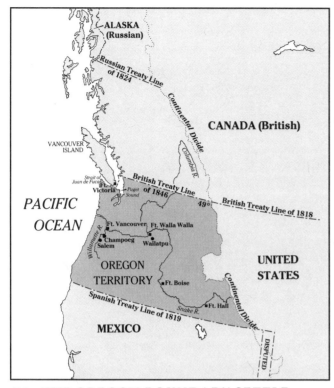

**5.2 THE OREGON BOUNDARY SETTLE-
MENT OF 1846**

Oregon was approved by Congress. He then opened negotiations to settle the Oregon question with Great Britain.

Polk ostensibly held to a hard line policy that demanded "Fifty-four Forty or Fight," implying that the United States claimed all of the Oregon Country as far north as the border with Russian Alaska. Yet with hostilities about to erupt on the Mexico–Texas border, he was not prepared to risk the outbreak of an additional war with Great Britain. Instead, he agreed to a British proposal that embraced the earlier American plan to extend the 49th Parallel boundary to the Pacific Coast, with the provision that the line run through the Strait of Juan de Fuca. At the time the British were more concerned with trade than territory and hoped a softer position on the Oregon question would encourage Polk's low tariff policy.

Under the Oregon Treaty of 1846, Great Britain gained control of all of Vancouver Island, and the United States secured its access to the harbors of Puget Sound. The agreement was finalized in June of 1846, just weeks after the outbreak of the Mexican War. With the resolution of the Oregon question, the United States achieved total domain over more than 280,000 square miles of territory in the Pacific Northwest.

The formal organization of Oregon as a territory was delayed for two years by the slavery issue. Although the settlers' provisional government had banned slavery, the pro-slavery faction in Congress opposed the admission of Oregon as a free territory.

Circumstances finally hastened the decision over whether Oregon should be made a territory. In 1847, a measles epidemic brought by westbound emigrants flared up at Marcus Whitman's Mission. A medical doctor, Whitman treated both the Cayuse and white children who had come down with the ailment. The white children—with their natural immunity—recovered, while the Indian children died.

The Cayuse, suspecting that Whitman's medicine was poisoning their children, rose up against the missionary, killing him and his wife Narcissa as well a number of other whites. News of the incident prompted Congress to immediate action, and in August of 1848, the bill authorizing the creation of the Oregon Territory was passed.

Five years later, the area north of the Columbia was organized as Washington Territory, and in 1863 the area to the east was designated as Idaho Territory. At the time, Idaho Territory included all of present-day Montana and much of what is now Wyoming.

THE MORMONS SETTLE THE GREAT BASIN

South of the Oregon Country and bounded on the east by the Rocky Mountains and on the west by the Sierra Nevada, lie the arid plains and valleys of the Great Basin. At the beginning of the 1840s, the region was nominally under Mexican sovereignty. The first Europeans to explore it were Spanish missionaries Silvestre Velez de Escalante and Atanasio Dominguez in 1776. In later years, the surrounding mountains became well-known to Canadian and American fur traders and mountain men.

Isolated from the main overland routes, and with sparse annual rainfall, the area remained the domain of the Bannock, Shoshone, Ute and Paiute bands, who managed to eke out a subsistence level of survival amid that harsh environment. The wagon trains of westbound emigrants heading for the lush valleys of California and Oregon avoided the area altogether or made their way across its waterless expanse as quickly as possible. Yet it was this remoteness and seeming lack of promise for agricultural development that ultimately brought about its rapid occupation by a unique group of American settlers—the Mormons.

The westward exodus of the Mormons, as the followers of the Church of Jesus Christ of Latter-day Saints came to be known, began soon after the church was established in 1830. Founder Joseph Smith was the son of

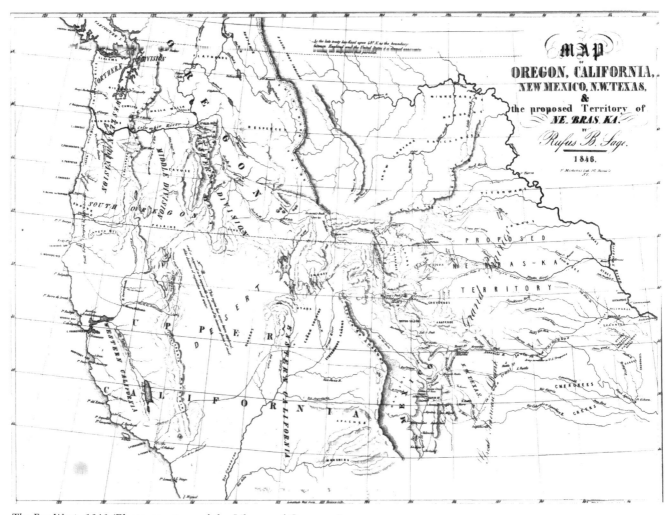

The Far West, 1846 (Photo courtesy of the Library of Congress)

a New England farm family that had settled in the central New York State town of Palmyra, near Rochester. Starting in 1820 at the age of 14, he reported having a series of a mystical experiences in which angels of the Lord had informed him that he was destined to found the one true Christian church.

In 1830, Smith published his beliefs in the *Book of Mormon* and before long had won a small number of converts from the surrounding area who recognized him as their prophet and leader. Among them was Brigham Young who would rise to prominence in the newly established church. Through divine revelations, Smith decreed that the property of his followers was to be owned by the church. The fledging church soon drew the ire of the area's non-Mormons (or Gentiles, as Mormons referred to them), who resented the Mormons' attitude of superiority as "God's chosen people" and viewed their unorthodox beliefs as blasphemous. To escape persecution, in 1831 Smith led his followers to the town of Kirtland in northeastern Ohio, near Cleveland, where he established the first Mormon community. Soon afterward, groups of Mormons headed westward to establish

a new Zion on the Missouri frontier, while missionaries sent to England and Scandinavia won thousands of converts who immigrated to America to join the Mormon communities at Kirtland and in the West.

The Mormon community at Kirtland prospered for the next few years. Yet within a short time, anti-Mormon feelings in the surrounding towns erupted, fermented in no small way by Mormon business and banking practices that were viewed as unfair to Gentiles. When the Panic of 1837 brought about the collapse of a bank that had been founded by Smith and the Mormon Church, Smith and many of the Latter-day Saints left Kirtland to join the Mormons who had preceded them to Far West, north of Independence, Missouri. Yet within a year, anti-Mormon mobs in Missouri—enraged by the Mormons' anti-slavery stand, as well by their commercial clannishness—soon made conditions intolerable for them. At the time, the Permanent Indian Frontier precluded their moving on to adjoining territory to the west, and so in 1839, escorted by state militia troops, the Saints fled their Missouri settlements and crossed the Mississippi River eastward into Illinois. Near the Mississippi River town of Quincy, Smith and his church purchased the lands of a failed communal town called Commerce and obtained a city charter from the Illinois state government, which gave the Mormons virtual autonomy over their own affairs.

The Mormons called their new settlement "Nauvoo," derived from a Hebrew expression meaning "place of beauty." By 1844, the town had become the largest city in Illinois, its population swelling to more than 14,000 by a steady stream of converts from the industrial cities of the eastern United States and England. It had its own state militia unit, the Nauvoo Legion, numbering 1,500 men, with Joseph Smith as commander. Yet the same antagonisms that had dogged the Mormons from the beginning emerged again when Smith, in 1843, announced that he had had a divine revelation to allow Mormon men to enter into polygamous marriages. The news not only incensed the non-Mormons around Nauvoo but brought protests within the Mormon community. In June of 1844, Mormon dissidents who opposed Smith's

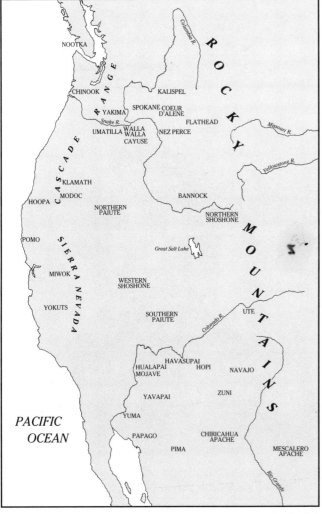

5.3 ANCESTRAL HOMELANDS OF THE TRIBES OF THE FAR WEST

autocratic rule and espousal of plural marriage voiced their protest in a newspaper, the Nauvoo *Expositor*.

Smith acted swiftly against the insurgents. Proclaiming that the opposition newspaper was a public nuisance, he had all copies of the offending paper and the presses that printed it destroyed. Leaders of the anti-Smith faction then fled to nearby Carthage, Illinois, where they lodged complaints against Smith and the Mormon leaders, charging they had violated their constitutional right to freedom of the press and accusing them of the unlawful practice of polygamy. Earlier that year, anti-Mormon sentiments had been aroused by Smith's announcement that he planned to run for U.S. president on an anti-slavery platform. The huge block of Illinois voters he controlled in Nauvoo could have brought the state under Mormon domination. The accusations of polygamy and dictatorship further inflamed the hostilities of the region's non-Mormon residents who now openly threatened violence against the Mormons of Nauvoo.

To quell this volatile situation, Joseph Smith and his brother Hyrum, also a Mormon leader, surrendered to Illinois state authorities in Carthage. On June 27, 1844, a band of Illinois militia broke into the jailhouse and shot Smith and his brother to death. The murder of the Mormon prophet shocked both the Mormon and non-Mormon communities and brought a temporary halt to the turmoil, but popular feelings against the Mormons still ran high.

Brigham Young, who succeeded Smith as head of the Mormon Church, decided that the only salvation for his people was to remove them to a place beyond the jurisdiction of the United States. Over the next year, he studied John C. Fremont's published report of his 1843–44 expedition to the Great Basin. He learned that although the Great Salt Lake Valley appeared desert-like, its soil could support vegetation and might be made agriculturally viable by diverting water from surrounding mountain streams. The natural mountain and desert barriers would discourage settlement by Gentiles. Moreover, settling outside of U.S. territory—and with no other white settlements for hundreds of miles in any direction—the Mormons could re-establish their religious community without fear of persecution.

In February of 1846, the first leg of the great Mormon trek across the plains began with the evacuation of Nauvoo. Nearly 2,000 Mormons crossed the frozen Mississippi River to Sugar Grove, Iowa. Soon afterward, the rest of the population of Nauvoo followed them. During the next year, encampments were established westward across Iowa, and by the spring of 1846, 12,000 of the Saints were amassed at a base they called Winter Quarters on the west bank of the Missouri River, near what is now Omaha, Nebraska.

When war erupted between the United States and Mexico in April of 1846, Young organized 500 Mormon

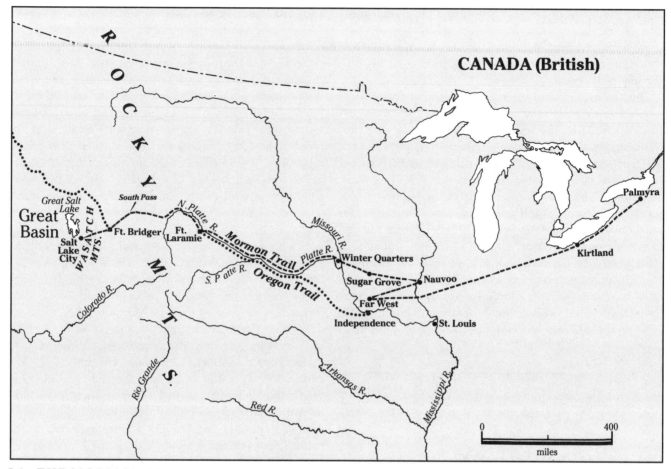

5.4   THE MORMON EXODUS TO THE WEST: 1830-50

volunteers into the Mormon Battalion to serve with American forces in California. This gesture was meant to ensure U.S. protection for the Mormons for their intended settlement in the Great Basin, then still Mexican territory. As it turned out, California fell to American forces before the Mormon Battalion arrived there. Yet they contributed to the war effort by blazing a wagon road between Santa Fe, New Mexico and San Diego, California.

Over the winter of 1846-47, the Mormons prepared for the planned migration to the West. On April 16, 1847, the first advance party set out. Known as the Pioneer Band, and led by Brigham Young, the group consisted of 143 men and three women, traveling westward with 73 wagons and a herd of livestock. Although the now well-traveled Oregon Trail followed the south bank of the Platte River, Young decided to blaze a new wagon route along the Platte's north bank instead, hoping to avoid hostile encounters with non-Mormon emigrants along the way.

Young and the Pioneer Band crossed the Platte near present-day Casper, Wyoming and traversed the Continental Divide along the usual South Pass route. After traveling southwestward to Fort Bridger, they continued south into the Wasatch Mountains along a trail that had

Brigham Young (Photo courtesy of the New York State Library)

been blazed the year before by the ill-fated Donner party. The route through the mountains was nearly impassable for wagons, but the Mormons persisted in their efforts and found their way into the Great Salt Lake Valley by way of a passage that they called Emigration Canyon. Upon first viewing the valley on July 24, 1847, Young reportedly proclaimed it as the Mormon's promised land with the words, "This is the place."

No sooner had the first Mormons arrived in the valley of the Great Salt Lake then they set about cultivating the land. They established an irrigation system in which water was diverted from the mountain streams, allotted lands to families according to needs and laid out the streets of a settlement that would soon burgeon into Salt Lake City.

Before long, Young returned eastward along his outbound route, subsequently named the Mormon Trail, to supervise the overland migration of the thousands of Mormons who were making their way westward from Iowa and Nebraska. By the end of 1847, the Mormon settlement next to the Great Salt Lake had grown to 1,800, and within a few years, nearly all of the 12,000 Mormons who had fled Nauvoo had settled in there. A "Perpetual Emigration Fund," established in 1849, provided financing for thousands of more Mormon converts who had been recruited in Europe and would stream into the new Mormon settlement over the next few years.

Although Brigham Young had planned to carve an independent Mormon nation out of the Great Basin, the lands the Mormons had settled became part of the United States at the conclusion of the Mexican War. Yet he still hoped to create a government for his people that would leave them free to follow the doctrines of the Mormon church without interference from federal authorities.

In March of 1849, a convention was held in which the Mormon settlements around the Great Salt Lake were organized into what was named the State of Deseret, in honor of the Mormon name for the honeybee, whose industry and communal effort symbolized the Mormon philosophy of hard work and cooperation. The boundaries of the proposed new state extended westward to the California coast to San Diego, and included all the land between the Sierra Nevada and the Rocky Mountains south of the Oregon Country, comprising all of what is now Utah and Nevada, and portions of Oregon, Idaho, southern California, Wyoming and Colorado.

By the time the Mormons' request for admission to the Union arrived in Washington, D.C., Congress was embroiled in the debate over the disposition of the vast territory that had been acquired in the Mexican Cession. As part of the Compromise of 1850, the area the Mormons had hoped would form their new state was pared down to an area comprising Utah and Nevada and parts of

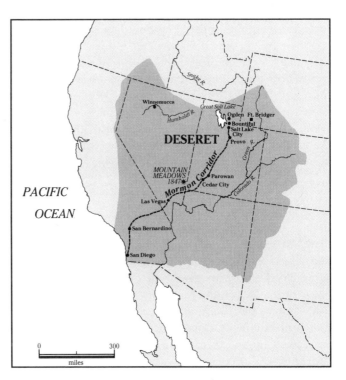

5.5 THE PROPOSED STATE OF DESERET: 1849

Colorado and northern Arizona. It was to be called Utah Territory, after the Ute Indians. Still, Young was appointed as the territory's first governor, and for a time he ruled the territory as head of a Mormon-dominated theocracy.

In the early 1850s, Young dispatched colonizing expeditions to the north, south and west of Salt Lake City. Among the additional settlements established between 1847 and 1850 were Bountiful, Centerville and Ogden. At the same time, Mormon cadres were sent northward to establish communities in what is now southern Idaho. Starting in 1850, additional Mormon settlements were founded to the southwest of Salt Lake City, including Parowan and Cedar City. More Mormon colonies were established across present-day Nevada at Winnemucca and Las Vegas, and in southern California at San Bernardino. The string of settlements between Salt Lake and San Diego became known as the Mormon Corridor.

The isolation that the Mormons hoped to find in the Great Basin was short-lived. In 1849, with the onset of the California Gold Rush, thousands of non-Mormon emigrants began to cross Utah Territory on their way to the California goldfields. The Mormons at first prospered by selling much-needed supplies to westbound travelers, but clashes with non-Mormons were inevitable.

A conflict between the Mormon establishment and the federal government erupted in 1856–57. Known as the Mormon War, it began when federally appointed judges claimed that their authority was being circumvented by local Mormon authorities. President James Buchanan responded by sending 1,500 federal troops to march on Salt Lake City to enforce federal authority and to install a newly appointed non-Mormon territorial governor. The Mormons viewed this development with alarm, believing it was the first step of a campaign to exterminate them. They fought a guerrilla war against U.S. troops in the mountain approaches to the Great Basin and managed to stop their advance at Fort Bridger.

In September of 1857, at a place called Mountain Meadows, a wagon train of settlers from Arkansas and Missouri was besieged by Indians. They had treated the Indians abusively and had also made disparaging remarks to Mormon women. A militant local Mormon faction joined the Indians in the attack on the wagon train and helped massacre nearly all of the 120 emigrants. News of the "Mountain Meadows Massacre" only fueled fears among the Mormons that massive federal retaliation was imminent. Young ordered the evacuation of Salt Lake City and threatened to destroy it if it were occupied by U.S. troops.

An all-out war with the federal government was avoided when President James Buchanan reached a compromise with Young and the Mormons. Although Young agreed to accept the presence of a non-Mormon territorial governor, actual governmental authority still remained vested in the church under Young's leadership.

In the wake of the troubles of 1857–58, the Mormons had withdrawn from the western portion of Utah Territory. In 1859, the gold and silver mining boom resulting from discovery of the Comstock Lode near Virginia City brought a great influx of non-Mormons into the area, and in 1861 Congress set aside the region as Nevada Territory.

The Mormon's adherence to the practice of polygamy continued to be a point of contention in relations between the Mormon community and the federal government. Brigham Young himself had 27 wives in 1877, the year he died. Thirteen years later, the Mormon Church banned polygamy, the last obstacle to statehood. In 1896 Utah—reduced to its present boundaries—was admitted to the Union.

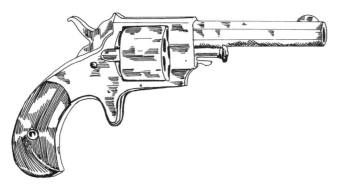

Early Six-Shooter (Molly Braun)

The American settlement of the Trans-Appalachian West, Oregon and California grew out of the individual efforts of pioneers driven by the desire to acquire lands in the West at little or no cost. By contrast, the Mormon settlement of Utah and the Great Basin resembled the early settlement of New England by the Puritans in the 17th century, carried out by a highly organized people impelled more by the fervor of religion than the prospect of personal gain.

WAR WITH MEXICO

In March of 1845, Mexico broke off diplomatic relations with the United States in protest over the impending annexation of Texas. Mexico had never formally recognized the independence of the Lone Star Republic and had long suspected that the United States, hoping to absorb what was clearly Mexican territory, had instigated and aided the 1836 Texas revolution.

The Mexican government was further outraged when the United States government took up the Texas cause in its long-simmering dispute with Mexico over its southwestern boundary. Prior to gaining its independence, Texas had been part of the Mexican state of Texas–Coahuila, the southern boundary of which extended only as far as the Nueces River. Yet under the terms of the treaty extracted from General Antonio Lopez de Santa Anna after his defeat at San Jacinto in 1836, the Texas Republic proclaimed its southwestern boundary to be the Rio Grande, 150 miles to the south. Although the Mexican government promptly repudiated the agreement, Texas maintained a tenuous claim to the region between the Nueces and the Rio Grande and brought the dispute with it on joining the Union in December of 1845.

U.S.–Mexican relations were also strained over the issue of monetary claims that Mexico owed to American citizens. In 1839, an international commission had ruled that Mexico had to pay more than $2 million for harm done to Americans and their property in the course of the nation's many political upheavals since 1821. Although five annual installment payments were specified, Mexico was unable to make payments after the third year.

Hoping to avert war yet still advance his program of territorial expansion, President James Polk sent special envoy John Slidell to Mexico City to seek a peaceful settlement of the Texas border dispute. In this regard, Slidell had been instructed to propose that the U.S. assume responsibility for the balance of the damage claims and offer $5 million for the province of New Mexico and $25 million for California, provided that the Mexicans accept the Rio Grande as the southern and western boundaries of Texas.

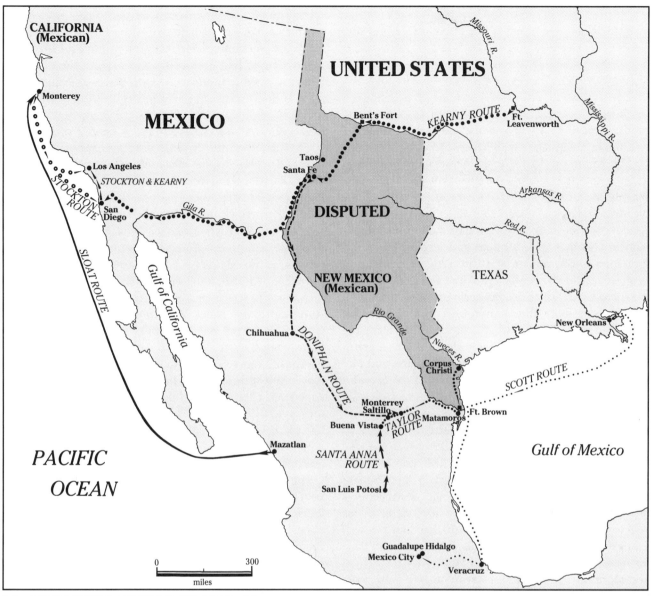

5.6 THE MEXICAN WAR OF 1846–48

When Slidell reached Mexico City in December of 1845, he found that although the Mexican government under President Herrera may have been willing to negotiate, Mexican public opinion strongly opposed any surrender of territory to the United States. Later that month, just two days after Texas' formal admission into the Union, the Herrera government was overthrown by General Mariano Paredes. The new Mexican regime not only refused to discuss the Texas boundary issue, but vowed to reclaim all of Texas for Mexico even if it meant going to war with the United States.

When President Polk learned of the failure of Slidell's mission, he ordered General Zachary Taylor and his force of 4,000 men to advance into the disputed area and take up positions on the Rio Grande. Technically, American troops were already on territory claimed by Mexico. Since June of 1845, Taylor and his command had been waiting at Corpus Christi on the Texas coast just south of the mouth of the Nueces, but the Mexicans did not express any protest.

By early April of 1846, Taylor and his men were installed at what would become known as Fort Brown (later the site of Brownsville, Texas) on the north bank of the Rio Grande, opposite the Mexican town of Matamoros. On April 24, a large Mexican cavalry force crossed the Rio Grande and attacked a small American patrol. Some of the Americans were killed and the rest were taken prisoner. Within a week, Fort Brown was under attack and Taylor was soon involved in two major battles. On May 8 and 9, at Palo Alto and Resaca de la Palma, his severely outnumbered forces, with the aid of superior artillery, defeated the Mexicans and drove them back across the Rio Grande. Taylor and his men then occupied Matamoros.

A TRANSCONTINENTAL REPUBLIC (1846–1853) 107

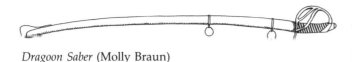

Dragoon Saber (Molly Braun)

Back in Washington, D.C., Polk and his cabinet had already decided that war was inevitable in order to resolve the ongoing crisis with Mexico. When news came that Mexican troops had crossed the Rio Grande and had attacked American troops, the president had the provocation he needed to justify a request for a war declaration from Congress.

Within two days, Congress produced the formal declaration of war that Polk wanted, and authorized an appropriation of $10 million and the recruitment of up to 50,000 troops for the conflict. In August of 1846, General Taylor began an advance into northern Mexico. After a fierce four-day siege, the Mexican town of Monterrey fell to U.S. forces on September 25. Although defeated, the Mexican army was allowed to withdraw. After an eight-week truce, Taylor resumed his advance and by mid-November had captured Saltillo, the capital of the Mexican state of Coahuila.

By that time, Mexican forces were massing for a counteroffensive at San Luis Potosi, between Taylor's troops and Mexico City. Commanding this force was General Antonio Lopez de Santa Anna, who had returned from exile in Cuba. He had been aided by U.S. government officials, who hoped his presence would bring about a quick negotiated peace. Santa Anna had plans of his own, however, and soon raised a 20,000-man army to advance northward from San Luis Potosi and halt Taylor's march into the Mexican heartland.

Learning of a large Mexican army approaching from the south, Taylor fell back to defensive positions near Buena Vista ranch. There, in late February of 1847, although outnumbered five-to-one, his well-entrenched command managed to repel the Mexican forces. With Taylor's defensive victory at Buena Vista, the United States was in control of all of northeastern Mexico south of the Rio Grande.

THE CONQUEST OF NEW MEXICO

On the day that Congress issued the war declaration against Mexico, President Polk expressed his expansionist ambitions for the war's outcome when he confided to cabinet members that "in making peace with our adversary, we shall acquire California, New Mexico, and other further territory, as an indemnity for this war, if we can."

In June of 1846, the "Army of the West," under the command of General Stephen Watts Kearny, began its westward march from Fort Leavenworth on the Missouri River. Kearny had been instructed to seize the northern Mexican province of New Mexico, then continue westward to join American naval forces on the Pacific Coast (under Commodore John D. Sloat and Commodore Robert F. Stockton) and complete the American conquest of California. His force of three thousand men, consisting of regular army troops, Missouri frontier volunteers and about 500 Mormons recruited from their winter encampment on the Missouri, followed the Santa Fe Trail to Bent's Fort, which they reached by late July.

Awaiting Kearny's army in Santa Fe was a force of 3,000 Mexican troops under the command of New Mexico's governor Manuel Armijo. Rather than engage the enemy in a headlong assault, Kearny chose to rely on diplomacy to win New Mexico. From Bent's Fort he sent American trader James Magoffin and Captain Philip St. George Cooke into the New Mexican capital to negotiate with Armijo. Soon afterward, Armijo brought his troops to Apache Canyon, near Raton Pass, but as Kearny and his forces approached, the Mexicans withdrew. The Americans then advanced unopposed into Santa Fe, and on August 19, 1846, Kearny accepted the formal surrender of New Mexico. He established a civilian government, and named Charles Bent, co-founder of Bent's Fort, as the territory's new American governor.

The ease with which New Mexico fell to the American advance may have been due to the province's divided loyalty. Since 1821, New Mexicans relied on the United States as its main trading partner and had come to resent the taxes imposed on them from the distant government in Mexico City. The fact that Kearny took Santa Fe without firing a shot may also have stemmed more from the Mexican governor's willingness to accept a bribe for his cooperation than from Kearny's diplomatic skill.

Kearny established a civilian government for New Mexico, declaring its 80,000 inhabitants to be American citizens. Leaving Colonel Sterling Price in command at Santa Fe, he then headed westward with part of his command to aid in the American campaign in California. At the same time, the Missouri volunteers, under the leadership of Colonel Alexander W. Doniphan, marched southward against the northwestern Mexican province of Chihuahua. "Doniphan's Thousand," as his force of Missouri frontiersmen was known, first took El Paso, then captured Chihuahua in February of 1847. He next led his men deep into Mexico, and in May joined up with General Taylor's forces at Monterrey.

The American occupation of New Mexico did not go smoothly after the departure of Kearny and Doniphan. Abusive conduct by the American garrison at Taos and Santa Fe instigated an insurrection by the Mexican and Indian inhabitants. On January 19, 1847, Governor

Charles Bent and several other local government officials were killed by rebels in Taos. The outbreak of violence that ensued against the occupying American forces was soon countered by Colonel Sterling Price, who laid siege to Taos and was able to quell the "Taos Rebellion" by early February.

THE TREATY OF GUADALUPE HIDALGO

Although California, New Mexico and most of the northern Mexican provinces had fallen to the Americans by November of 1846, the Mexican government refused to come to terms with the United States over the issues that had prompted the war. Polk and his advisors came to the conclusion that only the capture of Mexico City would bring the Mexican leaders to the negotiating table.

Polk was also faced with mounting opposition to the war at home. His Whig opponents viewed the war as a plot by the South to gain more territory for the spread of slavery and thereby gain an advantage in the Congress. Moreover, "Old Rough and Ready" Taylor, a Whig, had

become extremely popular after his series of victories and Polk feared the general could become a formidable opponent in the upcoming presidential election. Rather than have Taylor advance southward on the Mexican capital—a doubtful prospect given the desert-like terrain of central Mexico—Polk decided on an invasion of Mexico from the Gulf Coast.

Polk commissioned General Winfield Scott to command the amphibious forces dispatched from New Orleans. In early March of 1847, Scott conducted a successful amphibious landing south of the port of Veracruz in which 12,000 men armed with artillery landed on the beaches south of the city. After a fierce artillery siege, Veracruz was taken. From there, he undertook a westward march into the interior. His route retraced the one taken by Hernando Cortés and the conquistadors in the Spanish conquest of Mexico of 1519–21. Despite strong resistance all along the way, Scott and his army reached Mexico City by September of 1847, and, after three days of fighting, elicited a surrender of the Mexican capital on September 17, 1847.

Soon afterward, General Santa Anna abdicated the presidency and fled the country. Traveling with Scott's forces was the chief clerk of the State Department, Nich-

American Troops Attacking Mexico City, September 13, 1847 (Photo courtesy of the New York Public Library)

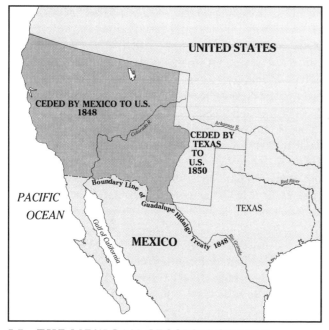

5.7   THE MEXICAN CESSION OF 1848

olas P. Trist, whom Polk had sent to seek a negotiated peace with the Mexican government. On February 2, 1848, a peace accord was finally reached at the town of Guadalupe Hidalgo, near Mexico City. Under the terms of the treaty, Mexico consented to the Rio Grande as the boundary of Texas and agreed to cede all of California and New Mexico in return for a payment of $15 million; the United States also agreed to assume $3.25 million in damage claims still outstanding against the Mexican government.

THE TAKING OF CALIFORNIA

California's rapid transformation from Mexico's sparsely populated northern province in 1847 to its incorporation into the United States in 1850 marked the culmination of half a century of American interest and settlement, accelerated by the events of the Mexican War of 1846–48.

The earliest recorded European discovery of California dates back to the voyage of Spanish navigators Juan Rodriguez Cabrillo and Bartolome Ferrelo in 1542–43. (It is possible, however, that southeastern California may have been visited in the early 1530s by Álvar Núñez Cabeza de Vaca in the course of his wanderings in the American Southwest.) These explorations were not followed up until the beginning of the 17th century with the discovery of Monterey Bay by another Spanish seafarer, Sebastien Vizcaino, in 1602.

More than 150 years elapsed before the Spanish made their first efforts to establish permanent settlements in California. Beginning in the 1770s, Franciscan missionar-

ies, led by Father Junipero Serra and supported by military leader Gaspar de Portola, began setting up missions along the coast between San Diego and San Francisco. Colonists from the Mexican provinces of Sonora and New Mexico also began arriving in expeditions organized and commanded by Juan Bautista de Anza.

The Spanish missions and settlements at San Diego, Los Angeles, Monterey and San Francisco had been founded mainly to counter Russian and British expansion southward from Alaska and the Pacific Northwest. They remained isolated from the major cities and towns of New Mexico and Mexico by the lack of a viable overland route across the harsh deserts and nearly impassable mountain ranges to the south and east. Since the main trade and communication links between California and the rest of Spain's North American empire were by sea, ties were dependent on fair weather and favorable winds. As a result, by the beginning of the 19th century, Spanish settlement in California had developed to only a fraction of the level as that of the more populous provinces to the south. Yet California's relatively small European population (less than 10,000 people when Mexico achieved its independence from Spain in 1821) developed a prosperous economy centered around cattle production along the coastal region between Sonoma and San Diego.

The first direct American contacts with California began in the first decades of the 19th century with the rise of New England shipping and whaling enterprises in the North Pacific. American ships from New Bedford, Boston and New York regularly put in at Monterey and San Francisco for reprovisioning during their long whaling voyages. American seafarers engaged in the lucrative trade of seal and sea otter furs between the Pacific Coast and China also took part in the commerce in hides and tallow, the main products of California's cattle-raising industry. Demand was high for these products, especially with the rapid development of the New England shoe and boot manufacturing industry, which provided a ready market for California leather.

American sea captains and other Yankee traders soon brought back reports of California's idyllic climate and fertile land. American settlers began to trickle in as early as 1814 when John Gilroy was granted a large tract of land near present-day San Jose by the Spanish colonial government.

Following the maritime traders, the next Americans to enter California were the mountain men in the 1820s and 1830s. Progressing westward in their search for new sources of beaver pelts, frontiersmen such as Jedediah Smith, Ewing Young, Kit Carson, James Ohio Pattie and Joseph Reddeford Walker blazed new trails across the Southern Rockies and the Great Basin, foreshadowing the great waves of overland emigrants during the next decades.

Emigrants to California on the Platte River (Photo courtesy of the New York Public Library)

One of the earliest non-Spanish settlers in California was the German–Swiss Johann Augustus Sutter, who arrived in Monterey in 1839, and soon afterward convinced provincial governor Juan Bautista Alvarado to grant him nearly 50,000 acres of land on the American River near Sacramento. In the early 1840s, Sutter's enterprise attracted more American settlers, who streamed into the region along the California and Oregon Trail—the newly developed wagon route across the Northern Plains and through the Rocky Mountains.

Official U.S. government interest in acquiring California was first expressed during the Texas war of independence after the Battle of San Jacinto in 1836. In mediating the peace treaty, President Andrew Jackson offered Mexico's leader Antonio Lopez de Santa Anna $3.5 million for all of California north of the 38th parallel, but the Mexicans declined. Subsequent diplomatic overtures to purchase California generated by Secretary of State Daniel Webster during the Tyler administration in the early 1840s were also turned down by the Mexicans.

The first hint that the United States was willing to take California by military force came in the fall of 1842. While on patrol in the waters off the coast of Peru, Commodore Thomas Ap Catesby Jones of the U.S. Navy received unconfirmed reports that war had broken out between Mexico and the United States. He immediately sailed his naval force northward and, without resistance from Mexican provincial authorities, occupied Monterey. After it became apparent that Mexico and the United States were not at war, Jones withdrew with elaborate apologies.

In 1845 James K. Polk became president of the United States. He was a staunch adherent of Manifest Destiny, the belief that the United States should occupy the entire North American continent from the Atlantic to the Pacific. At that time, it was feared that Mexico might transfer California to Great Britain in an effort to keep the region out of American hands in the event of war over increasing tensions regarding the U.S.–Mexican border in Texas. Amid this background, Captain John Charles Fremont of the U.S. Army Corps of Topographical Engineers entered the historical scene; his decisive actions during the next two years would play a critical part in the ultimate U.S. acquisition of California.

Fremont, a career army officer, was a native of Savannah, Georgia. His father was a French emigre and his mother was a member of the prominent Whiting family of Richmond, Virginia. In the late 1830s he had taken part in government surveys on the upper Mississippi River, and these had been followed by an expedition across the Northern Plains and into the South Pass region of the Wind River Range of present-day Wyoming in 1842. His next exploration into the American West took him along a wide sweep from the Great Salt Lake into the Oregon Country, then southward to California's Sacramento River Valley and Sutter's settlement.

In 1845, Fremont set out on his third western expedition from Bent's Fort on the Arkansas River in present-day Colorado. He had been commissioned to survey the upper reaches of the Arkansas and Red rivers and complete his earlier investigation of the Great Salt Lake, then continue into California, ostensibly seeking a new and shorter route from the Rocky Mountains to the mouth of the Columbia River. On his arrival at Monterey in the fall of 1845, Mexican authorities became suspicious of his intentions, and ordered him and his party out of California.

John C. Fremont (Photo courtesy of the Library of Congress)

THE DONNER PARTY

By 1845, about 10,000 emigrants had made the trek across the Great Plains and the Rocky Mountains to Oregon and California. Although the overland trails were well known by then, there was always room for improvement, or so thought California settlement promoter Lansford W. Hastings. That year, he published his *Emigrants' Guide to Oregon and California* in which he described a shortcut that would save California-bound pioneers 400 miles on the westward journey between Fort Bridger and the final mountain barrier of the Sierra Nevada. Actually, Hastings had never taken the route himself but in his guidebook he insisted that:

> The most direct route, for the California emigrants, would be to leave the Oregon route, about two hundred miles east from Fort Hall; thence bearing west southwest, to the Salt Lake; and thence continuing down to the bay of St. Francisco [San Francisco Bay].

George and Jacob Donner were in their sixties when they decided to pull up stakes in Illinois and seek a brighter future in the milder climate of California. They had read the account of the "Hastings Cutoff" and were convinced that it would provide a quicker

and easier route across the Great Basin and the Sierra Nevada to the Sacramento Valley.

In April of 1846, the Donner brothers and their extended families left Independence, Missouri and followed the Platte River route across the Kansas and Nebraska plains, joining up with other parties of emigrants along the way. Near Fort Laramie, they met up with former mountain man and frontier guide James Clyman who warned them to keep to the usual route by way of Fort Hall. Earlier that year, he had traveled eastward with Hastings through the untested "Hastings Cutoff" and determined that the route through the Wasatch Mountains and the deserts beyond was impractical for wagons since they had to cross the Sierra before the first snows closed the passes for the winter.

Some members of the group decided to heed Clyman's advice and broke off from the rest near the Big Sandy River and made for Fort Hall. They eventually reached California without undue hardship. Such was not the case for the Donners and the others who opted to try the Hastings Cutoff.

The Donner party, by now consisting of 87 people and 23 wagons, left Fort Bridger in early August. A few days ahead of them, Hastings himself was lead-

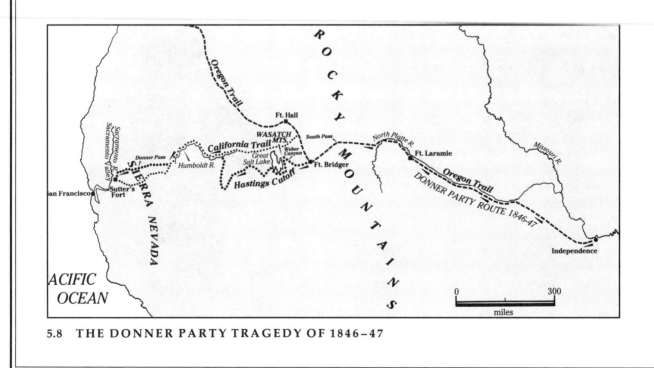

5.8 THE DONNER PARTY TRAGEDY OF 1846–47

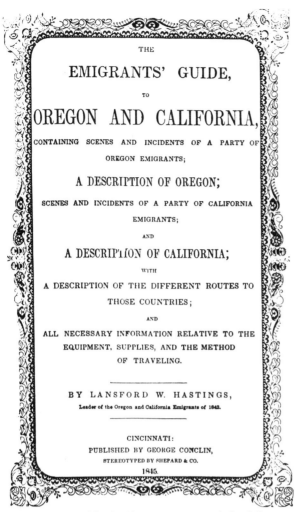

Hastings' Guidebook (Photo courtesy of the Library of Congress)

ing another group of emigrants along his untried route through the Wasatch Mountains and was leaving markers to indicate the trail. At Weber Canyon, the Donner party found a note from Hastings attached to a forked stick telling them to send someone ahead so that he could point out the way through the mountains to the valley of the Great Salt Lake.

Donner Party member James Reed returned with news from Hastings after five days. As it turned out, the route Hastings had indicated proved to be strewn with boulders and ran through narrow canyons that were at times so impassable that the wagons had to be hoisted up the steep walls with winches. The delays cost them valuable time and they did not reach the valley of the Great Salt Lake until the end of August. By this time, supplies of food, water and fodder for the draft animals were running low.

More hardships were encountered in crossing the Great Salt Lake Desert. Hastings had instructed them to take water and grass for the animals for two days and two nights. Actually, it was to take six days for the entire Donner party to cross, and by that time they had lost many of their animals, slowing their progress even more. Tensions among the family groups became strained as water and food became scarce. A dispute over tangled harnesses ended with James Reed stabbing another settler to death. Banished from the group for his action, he rode on ahead to obtain additional supplies at Sutter's Fort across the Sierra.

The Donner party finally reached the eastern slopes of the Sierra Nevada in mid-October, dangerously late in the season. They had hoped to follow the Truckee Pass recommended by Hastings, but an early snowfall made the steep granite slopes impassable, even after they abandoned their wagons and tried to make the ascent with what few possessions they could lash to their oxen. Their animals were soon lost in a blizzard and the passes ahead became choked with snowdrifts.

The emigrants were forced to winter east of Truckee Pass. One group of about 20 found an abandoned cabin at Truckee Lake. About five miles back down the trail, at Alder Creek, the Donner brothers and the other 60 emigrants improvised rude shelters out of wagon canvas and tree limbs. The food situation became so desperate that the stranded pioneers resorted to eating oxhides that had been boiled down to a glue-like substance.

In mid-December of 1846, a group of 15 men and women that came to be known as the "Forlorn Hope" left the encampment at Truckee Lake with rations for six days in an attempt to force their way across the Sierra Nevada and obtain help at Sutter's Fort. Within a short time, they were caught in a fierce storm, and when it was over, four of them had died of exposure and starvation. Faced with certain death, the survivors cut strips of flesh from their fallen companions, roasted them over a fire and ate them. What they didn't consume, they wrapped for the rest of the journey, carefully marking each piece so no one would unwittingly eat a relative.

It was not until mid-January, over a month after leaving Truckee Lake, that the Forlorn Hope group managed to reach help at a settlement in the Sacra-

THE DONNER PARTY (*Continued*)

mento Valley. By then, there were only seven left, two men and five women. Several attempts were made to reach the Donner party but it was not until February 4 that the first rescuers reached the emigrants stranded at Alder Creek. James Reed was not able to return to his family in the mountains until mid-March. He found the survivors in a terrible state, with clear evidence that, like the Forlorn Hope group, they too had been driven to cannibalism.

Rescue efforts continued until April 17, 1847. By that time, George and Jacob Donner had both died, their bodies cut up and eaten by the those still cling-

ing to life. Of the 82 people of the Donner Party who reached the Sierra Nevada, 35 had died.

Those who lived resumed their quest for a new life in California. Truckee Lake and Truckee Pass were soon renamed Donner Lake and Donner Pass to commemorate one of the most harrowing ordeals in the history of the overland migrations to the Far West. Recounting the experience in a letter to a cousin in Illinois, Donner party survivor Virginia Reed, daughter of James Reed, advised would-be pioneers to "Never take no cut ofs and hury along as fast you can."

Although Fremont at first defied the Mexican authorities by establishing a temporary base at Hawk's Peak near Salinas in the San Joaquin Valley, he soon withdrew northward to the region around Klamath Lake in the Oregon County. There, in May of 1846, he was contacted by an American secret agent, Lieutenant Archibald Gillespie of the U.S. Marine Corps, who instructed him to return to northern California and lend his assistance if hostilities broke out between the United States and Mexico.

At Sonoma, California, American settlers under Ezekiel Merritt and William B. Ide organized an uprising against the Mexican government, fueled in part by a simmering personal vendetta against the Vallejo family, who wielded Mexican authority in the north. Added to this was the rivalry between the Mexican military commandant of California at Monterey, General Jose Castro, and the civilian governor in Los Angeles, Pio Pico. On June 14, 1846, Merritt, Ide and the American settlers at Sonoma declared themselves independent of Mexico in what was later called the "Bear Flag Revolt," after the crude flag the Americans fashioned as their symbol. Fremont arrived at Sonoma soon afterward, and on July 5, 1846, in a meeting with the American rebels, was declared the leader of a hastily-organized Bear Flag Republic.

Unknown to both the Mexicans and Americans in California, open conflict between the United States and Mexico had erupted over the Texas border issue, with the U.S. Congress officially declaring war against Mexico on May 13, 1846. Three weeks later, a U.S. naval force under Commodore John D. Sloat landed troops at Monterey and occupied the port. News of the outbreak of the Mexican War finally reached Fremont and his supporters

in Sonoma on July 9, 1846. They organized themselves into the California Battalion and headed southward to aid U.S. troops at San Francisco and Monterey.

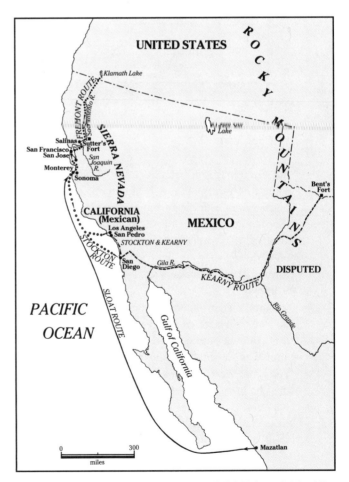

5.9 **THE TAKING OF CALIFORNIA: 1846–47**

By August 13, 1846, Fremont had succeeded in taking Los Angeles with very little resistance, and most of California fell under U.S. military control. Sloat's successor, Commodore Robert F. Stockton, appointed Gillespie as military governor in the south, based at Los Angeles, and Fremont as commander of U.S. forces in the north at Monterey.

The next month, Mexican Californians, resentful of U.S. military rule, staged a counter-revolution against Gillespie in Los Angeles, driving him from the settlement. On his withdrawal to San Pedro, he was met by U.S. naval vessels with reinforcements. Additional troops, led by General Stephen Watts Kearny, arrived overland following a successful campaign in New Mexico, and with their help the uprising was soon suppressed. On January 13, 1847, at a ceremony at a farmhouse in Cahuenga Canyon near Los Angeles, Fremont formally accepted Mexico's cession of California to the United States.

Fremont later faced a court-martial for his alleged unauthorized actions in the California revolt. Although found guilty, he was offered reinstatement and promotion to the rank of lieutenant colonel, an arrangement he refused. He later undertook additional privately funded explorations for a proposed railroad route through the Southern Rockies. In 1856, he unsuccessfully ran for president as the Republican Party's first presidential candidate.

On January 24, 1848, gold was discovered at Sutter's Creek on Johann Sutter's settlement in the lower Sacramento Valley. Just over a week later, the United States and Mexico entered into the treaty of Guadalupe Hidalgo, ending the Mexican War. Under its terms, California and present-day Arizona, Nevada and New Mexico were officially ceded to the United States.

Shovel (Molly Braun)

CALIFORNIA GOLD FEVER

When Johann Augustus Sutter decided to expand his enterprise in California's Sacramento Valley with a sawmill, he touched off a chain of events that not only dramatically altered the course of history of the American West, but also led to his ruination.

By 1847, Sutter's 49,000-acre land grant on the American River near present-day Sacramento had drawn a number of American settlers, and his gristmill, tannery and stores had begun to prosper from the growing population. To meet the increased demand for lumber, he directed John W. Marshall, a carpenter and mechanic from New Jersey, to dig a millrace and construct a sawmill 45 miles up the American River from his fort.

On January 24, 1848, after letting the stream run through the newly dug channel, Marshall noticed some yellowish metallic flakes clinging to the bedrock. Suspecting that it might be gold, he took some of the material to Sutter. The two men made some basic tests outlined in an encyclopedia and confirmed that Marshall had found gold.

Sutter hoped to keep the discovery secret at least until the sawmill was completed. But news of the find reached some of the laborers, members of the Mormon Battalion who were working for him. They went upstream on their own and found more gold deposits. In early May, they were visited by Samuel Brannan, head of the Mormon community in California. Brannan, who owned businesses in San Francisco as well as a store near Sutter's Fort, hurried to San Francisco with news of the discovery.

Brannan knew the gold strike at Sutter's Mill was bound to draw hordes of fortune-seekers. The demand for picks, shovels, pans, flour, coffee and other essential supplies would bring a tremendous amount of business to his store. On May 12, 1848, he walked along the streets of San Francisco displaying a quinine bottle full of gold dust, proclaiming "Gold! Gold! Gold from the American River!"

Although rumors of the discovery had begun to trickle into town weeks before and had been reported in the

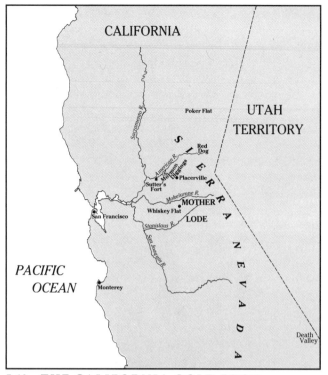

5.10 THE CALIFORNIA GOLD RUSH: 1848–52

his stores at San Francisco and Sutter's Fort, as gold-seekers poured in willing to pay exorbitant prices for supplies. In the first year of the gold rush, the diggings were yielding fantastic daily profits for some. Yields worth $1,000 a day were not unheard of, and most miners were scraping out about an ounce of gold a day, worth $20, many times the prevailing daily wage for labor.

The California Gold Rush made fortunes for others not directly involved in the mining. Collis P. Huntington, later one of the founding partners of the Southern Pacific Railroad, began his fortune by realizing a thousand percent profit when he shipped iron bars costing $20 a ton that he then sold to miners at $1 a pound. Levi Strauss, a clothing manufacturer from the East, made a fortune by selling durable trousers to the miners.

Reports had filtered East as early as September of 1848, but the news was not confirmed in the public's mind until President James Polk commented on the California gold find in his December 5th message to Congress. Several days later, 230 ounces of pure gold arrived in Washington—sent by California's provisional governor, Richard B. Mason—and were displayed at the War Department. The fever soon spread to the Atlantic Coast states. Thousands sought passage by ship to California. Demand was so great for berths on California-bound vessels that the New England whaling fleet turned to taking passengers on the six-month voyage around Cape Horn. Some of the "argonauts," as the gold–seekers were dubbed, opted to go by way of Panama. They sailed to the east coast of Panama at Chagres, then made their way across the isthmus by riverboat and mule train to the Pacific port of Panama City, hoping to obtain passage there on a coastal vessel bound for San Francisco. Although the Panama route was the shortest—taking about six weeks if all went well—once on the Pacific side, travelers typically faced a long wait for a berth on a northbound ship.

The real surge for California gold began when the news reached the Ohio and Mississippi valleys. In the spring of 1849, thousands joined the annual wagon train emigration at St. Joseph, Independence and Council Bluffs on the Missouri River. Most headed westward along the Oregon Trail; on reaching Fort Hall or Fort Bridger, they took a variety of routes across the Sierra Nevada. Some tried to circumvent the mountains by skirting to the south, often meeting disaster in Death Valley. Others tried their luck with a southern route from Fort Smith, Arkansas, to Santa Fe, New Mexico, and from there made their way along the Gila River to California. More than thirty-five thousand "Forty-Niners" crossed the Great Plains and Rocky Mountains to California that spring. In the course of that period of mass exodus, a cholera epidemic struck the wagon trains of the overland argonauts, taking a toll of thousands,

local press, few people had taken the news seriously. But Brannan's excited announcement and the actual gold dust in his hands were enough to touch off the greatest gold rush in history: Workers abandoned their jobs; merchants left their businesses; scores of sailors from the U.S. Navy's Pacific Squadron anchored in San Francisco Bay jumped ship; soldiers deserted nearby garrisons; and hundreds quit their jobs or sold their businesses to take advantage of the gold fields on the American River.

Before long, more gold deposits were found near other streams north and south of the American, comprising a region that came to be known as the "Mother Lode." The news had an electrifying effect as it spread to other towns along the coast. By mid-June, Monterey was half-deserted as most of the town's male population streamed northward, stricken with "gold fever." The impact was the same at Los Angeles, San Diego and other coastal settlements. Thousands of Mexicans from the northern province of Sonora heard the news and streamed northward to make their fortune in the Sacramento Valley. Settlers in Oregon also received word of the gold discovery; hundreds headed southward for the American River.

Word was first carried out of California by ship to Hawaii, attracting more gold-seekers from planters, merchants, sailors and a number of native Kanakas. From there, the news reached Australia, drawing thousands more to California.

Brannan's publicity efforts succeeded beyond his wildest expectations. He raked in tremendous profits at

who ended up buried in unmarked graves along the trail.

The influx of population to California had a dramatic effect, especially in San Francisco, which became the principal port of entry for the seaward argonauts. Within the first few weeks of Samuel Brannan's public cry heralding the gold strike in the Sierra Nevada foothills, San Francisco turned into a virtual ghost town when most of the 900 or so inhabitants left for the riches promised on the American River. Yet within a few months, ships had brought thousands of gold-seekers from the East Coast, Australia, the Pacific islands, China and Europe. By 1850, the city had a population of 30,000 and had become a mecca for miners seeking to spend their new-found fortunes on fun and frolic. San Francisco was quick to oblige them as scores of saloons, gambling houses and brothels sprang up almost overnight. Labor and materials for new construction were scarce. To meet the demand, ships, which had been abandoned by their crews for the gold diggings, were deliberately run aground along the waterfront and served as quarters for these new enterprises.

During the first year of the Gold Rush, California was still under a military government. Local officials were hard pressed to maintain law and order. In San Francisco, the "Sydney Ducks"—gangs of former convicts who had arrived from Australia's penal colonies—inflicted a crime wave on the city that was only checked with the institution of vigilante groups and the lynch law.

By the end of 1849, the population of California had exploded from 20,000 to 100,000. Within three years, the steady stream of new arrivals, mostly overlanders, would more than double that figure.

The first wave of gold-seekers found abundant deposits of placer gold in the eastern foothills of the Sierra Nevada, consisting of fragments of the precious metal that had worked its way through veins in the earth's crust and had been washed down into stream beds and rocky crevices by erosion. Miners could wash out the gold by rinsing gold-bearing gravel in pans. A device called a "cradle" was soon introduced that could process even larger amounts of "paydirt." The "long-tom" was even more effective, consisting of a long wooden chute through which water was run over the gravel, filtering out the gold at its end. Within the first few years, most placer deposits were exhausted, and mining became more of a large-scale operation, requiring large capital outlays and more sophisticated techniques and machinery. It is estimated, however, that by 1852 the individual efforts of the first argonauts had yielded more than a quarter of a billion dollars worth of gold.

Until the California Gold Rush, the primary lure of the West had been the promise of cheap or free lands for farming. But easterners now headed westward with dreams of acquiring quick wealth. The early pioneers were primarily family groups seeking to recreate the pastoral societies of the Northeast and the Mississippi and Ohio Valleys; the Gold Rush brought in a different type of pioneer, more adventurer than settler. These pioneers of the mining frontier would introduce a new kind of economy to the region, based on large-scale capital investment. Mining thus spurred the rapid peopling of the West; within 10 years of the initial gold strike at Sutter's Mill, the mining frontier would push eastward across the mountains into what is now Nevada.

A convention met at Monterey in the fall of 1849 and drew up a proposed state constitution. After much Congressional wrangling and as one of the principal outcomes of the Compromise of 1850, on September 9, 1850, California was admitted to the Union as the 31st state. California's tremendous rise in population from 1849 to 1850, amid the period's great sectional differences over slavery, had rapidly hurled it into statehood, bypassing a transitional period as a U.S. territory—a process characteristic of most other states admitted since 1789.

Although Johann Sutter sparked the Gold Rush, the event was to mark the beginning of his downfall. His lands were quickly overrun with gold-seekers heedless of his property rights. His workers left him for the diggings, and his businesses fell idle. Within four years of the initial gold strike, he was bankrupt.

The final blow for Sutter fell soon after California achieved statehood. He lost title to his vast estate when the new state government refused to recognize his original Mexican land grants. In 1864, however, the state of California did award him a $250-a-month pension. He spent the rest of his life fruitlessly petitioning the state and federal government for compensation for his losses. Ultimately, the U.S. Supreme Court ruled that his claims were invalid.

From some of the precious metal recovered at his California mill, Sutter had a ring made, engraved with his family's coat of arms and the inscription:

THE FIRST GOLD DISCOVERED IN CALIFORNIA IN JANUARY, 1848

EXPANSION AND SLAVERY

Even as the Mexican War was in its initial phase, the question of slavery in territories that might be taken from Mexico came to the forefront of national debate. In August of 1846, Congressman David Wilmot, a Pennsylvania Democrat, proposed an amendment to a $2 million war appropriations bill that would have banned slavery in any new lands obtained from Mexico. Southern Whigs and Democrats alike were opposed to the measure, while northern anti-slavery Whigs and Democrats supported it. Wilmot based his proposal on the language of the Northwest Ordinance of 1787, which declared that "neither slavery nor involuntary servitude shall exist . . . in the said territory."

The debate that ensued divided Congressional leaders along sectional rather than party lines. Although passed by the House, the bill that ultimately became law did not include the Wilmot Proviso. Yet the question of slavery in new territories re-emerged from the debate over the issue.

The lands of the Mexican Cession remained without governments for two years because of the slavery issue. Some moderate southerners in Congress proposed extending the Missouri Compromise line of 36°30' to the Pacific Coast, a solution that would have allowed slavery in most of the new territory.

Anti-slavery northerners wanted to have slavery outlawed in the Mexican Cession lands by act of Congress. Southern pro-slavery interests in Congress rejected this idea, insisting that the federal government did not own the lands; rather, they were held jointly by the states, and the central government only administered the western territories for the states as a lawyer might administer the property of a group of partners.

Less extreme congressmen on both sides of the slavery issue proposed that the controversy be left to the judgment of the Supreme Court. Westerners, on the other hand, favored popular sovereignty to settle the issue; settlers in each of the new territories would decide for themselves whether slavery would be allowed or banned.

The need to organize the new western territories gained new impetus after the onset of the California Gold Rush in 1849. The sudden influx of population made it imperative that some form of local government be established for California. In 1850, Congress debated over the admission of California as a free or slave state. From this grew what would be known as the Compromise of 1850. Put together by Senator Henry Clay of Kentucky and later promoted by Senator Stephen Douglas of Illinois, the proposed legislation called for the admission of California as a free state. The remaining lands of the Mexican Cession would be organized into the territories of Utah and New Mexico with no prohibition of slavery, but with the provision that each territorial legislature could allow or bar slavery, and would be admitted as free or slave states according to the state constitutions they eventually would adopt.

Extremists on both sides of the slavery issue resisted passage of the compromise measures. Senator John C. Calhoun of South Carolina led the pro-slavery opposition, rejecting Clay's proposal because it could ultimately lead to the southern slave states being outnumbered in both the House, the Senate and the Electoral College, thereby "irretrievably destroy[ing] the equilibrium which existed when the government commenced."

Senator Daniel Webster of Massachusetts, although from the anti-slavery Northeast, strongly favored the Compromise in his speech on the Senate floor of March 7th, 1850. He stressed that a federal ban on slavery in Utah and New Mexico would be unnecessary since the new western territories were geographically unsuitable for the type of agricultural economy that made slavery profitable in the South.

President Zachary Taylor, whose efforts in the war had swept him into the White House in 1848, died on July 9, 1850. While Taylor did not endorse Clay's measures, his successor Millard Fillmore did, and with his support the Compromise of 1850 was passed by Congress and signed into law on September 20, 1850. In addition to the provisions for California and the rest of the newly-acquired Mexican territory, the law provided for the federal government to assume the debts incurred by Texas while it was a republic. Also in regard to Texas, it fixed that state's western boundary so as to exclude its claim on eastern New Mexico Territory. Texas' claim would have complicated the issue of slavery in the newly won territory since Texas allowed slavery, but the issue was still to be decided in New Mexico.

As a concession to southern slave interests, however, the Compromise of 1850 included the Fugitive Slave Act, which required local officials to assist slave owners in the recapture of escaped slaves. Anti-slavery interests succeeded in attaching a provision outlawing the slave trade from the nation's capital.

THE GADSDEN PURCHASE

The acquisition of the Southwest and California propelled the idea of a transcontinental railroad from a visionary scheme to a practical necessity. Southern interests naturally favored a route across the Southwest to the Pacific Coast, but the most suitable right of way west of Texas was south of the Gila River, an area that was still part of Mexico.

In 1853, Secretary of War Jefferson Davis, who oversaw the surveys carried out by the army for the proposed railroad, instructed the U.S. ambassador to Mexico, James Gadsden, to meet with then-Mexican president Santa Anna. He was to attempt to buy the 30,000 square mile wedge of territory lying south of the Gila River, between western Texas and southern California.

The Mexican government, sorely pressed financially as a result of the recent war with the United States, readily

ALASKA (Russian)

CANADA (British)

OREGON
COUNTRY
1846

MEXICAN CESSION
1848

UNITED STATES

GADSDEN
PURCHASE
1853

TEXAS
ANNEXATION
1845

MEXICO

5.11 THE UNITED STATES AND THE COLONIZATION OF THE WEST UNDER THE COMPRO-MISE OF 1850

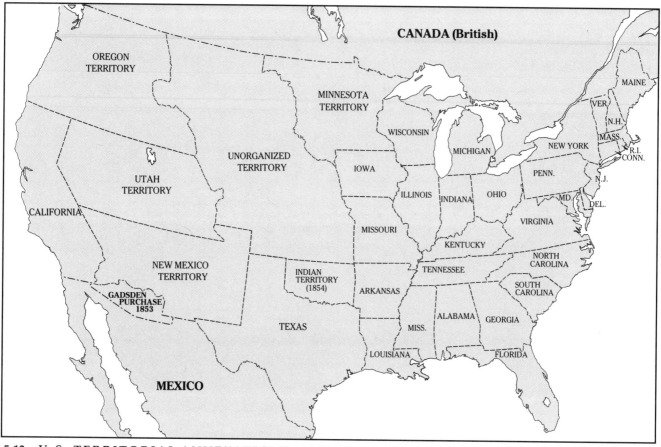

5.12 U.S. TERRITORIAL ANNEXATIONS: 1845–53

accepted the offer of $10 million for the land in what is now southern New Mexico and Arizona. The two nations agreed to the treaty on December 30, 1853, and it was ratified by the Senate the following June and signed into law by President Franklin Pierce.

NEW LAND, NEW CONFLICT

The expansionist fervor of Manifest Destiny that brought about the annexation of Texas in 1845 ended eight years later with the Gadsden Purchase. Within that time, the United States gained sole control of the Oregon Country south of the 49th Parallel and, after a 17-month war with Mexico, acquired California and the Southwest. With the

exception of the Alaska Purchase of 1867, the continental boundaries of the United States were now complete.

From these spectacular gains, however, re-emerged the national controversy over the extension of slavery into newly acquired territory. Even though the institution of slavery itself was not threatened, the South nonetheless faced the prospect of losing equal standing in Congress should it become outnumbered by newly organized free territories and newly admitted free states.

The "popular sovereignty" doctrine embraced by the Compromise of 1850 settled the issue for the time being. But the great surge of territorial growth that occurred in the late 1840s reshaped the nation, and made inevitable a future conflict that no compromise could peaceably resolve.

Chapter 6
WEALTH OF THE WEST (1854–1860)

PROPELLED BY THE SPIRIT of Manifest Destiny, the United States had, through both diplomatic and military success, achieved a rapid course of territorial expansion. More farmlands had become available and new resources were discovered, in particular mineral wealth.

Growth had its price in human terms. With California, Oregon and the Southwest as part of the United States, the Permanent Indian Frontier came to be ignored as a geographic boundary; the peoples it protected were viewed as an inconvenient obstacle.

There was a political price to pay as well. Although overland migrations across the Great Plains continued, all pioneers were not headed for the Far West. Public lands newly opened for settlement and available at low cost drew thousands of settlers into the eastern prairie regions between the Mississippi and Missouri rivers. Territories were created to meet the needs of the new population in these areas and also to prepare the way for transportation links intended to straddle the continent.

The creation of new territorial governments in what was now the nation's midsection would re-ignite the controversy over the spread of slavery. The issue would grow to threaten the survival of the Union. By the end of the 1850s, Thomas Jefferson's dreaded "Firebell in the Night" would begin to toll louder and louder.

THE END OF
THE PERMANENT
INDIAN FRONTIER

When the American mountain men and traders of the 1820s and 1830s set out to tap the fur sources of the Rocky Mountains and the commerce of Santa Fe, they first had to cross the domain of the Plains Indians. These frontiersmen—many from the Ohio and Mississippi valleys—were familiar with the eastern woodland tribes who typically made permanent homes along rivers, but on the Great Plains they encountered Indians with a nomadic way of life.

The Plains Indians did not yet know the destruction that the advance of white settlement had inflicted on eastern tribes. They had not been caught up in the colonial struggle for North America. Their numbers had not yet been decimated by the ravages of diseases such as smallpox, typhus, syphilis and tuberculosis. And thus far they had not faced the relentless tide of white settlers eager to transform their ancestral homelands into farmlands and towns.

While each of the Plains tribes was distinguished by language and lifeways, they shared one major aspect: They all had mastered the horse, and in so doing, had become masters of their environment. In the mid- and late-1600s, the Southern Plains tribes first acquired horses in raids on Spanish settlements in the outlying Mexican provinces in what is now New Mexico and Texas. Over the next two centuries, the horse was introduced to other native peoples throughout the Great Plains as a result of intertribal trade and warfare.

Horses enabled the Plains Indians to adopt a mode of life in which existence was not dependent on the meager subsistence afforded by agriculture on the semi-arid grasslands of the plains. They could now hunt buffalo with ease and much greater effectiveness from horseback. In the past, the movement of a buffalo herd could have meant starvation. With horses, they could follow the herds across hundreds of miles. The buffalo became a source of seemingly infinite wealth. The buffalo pro-

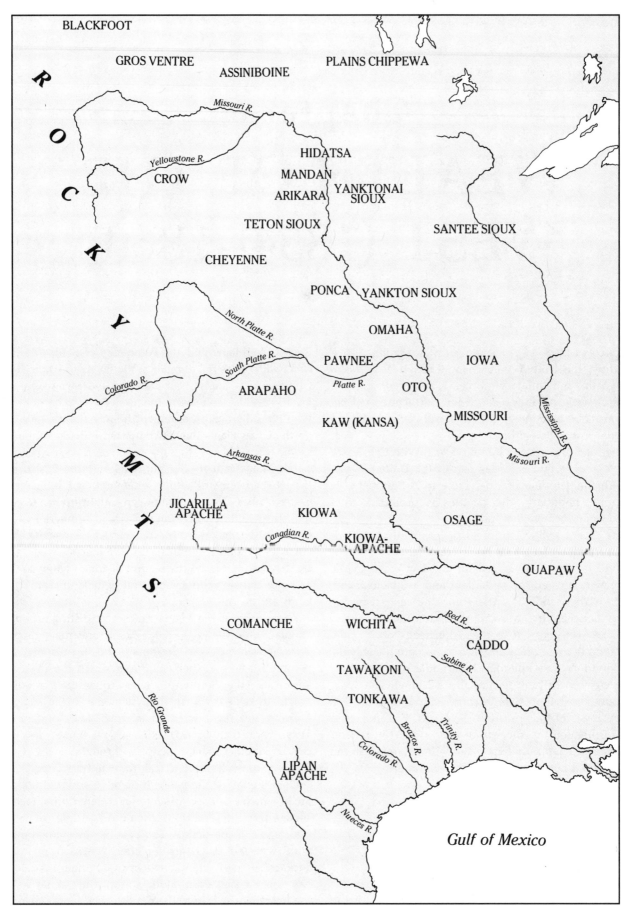

6.1   ANCESTRAL HOMELANDS OF THE PLAINS INDIAN TRIBES

vided almost every necessity, from food and clothing to materials with which to make shelters as well as jewelry and other adornments. Plains Indians came to take great pride in the athletic prowess necessary to hunt buffalo from horseback, readily adapting these abilities to mounted warfare.

The whites these Indians encountered did not arrive as conquering armies but as individual traders. The Indians viewed them more as curiosities rather than threats, and on more than one occasion, adopted them into tribes. Jim Beckwourth, a black mountain man from St. Louis, grew to prominence as a chief among the Crows.

While the Plains Indians were far less numerous than Woodland Indians, they still greatly outnumbered the whites who visited their lands. The American traders operating within their midst during the peak years of the fur trade had less of an impact on the life of the Indians than vice-versa. Many mountain men who engaged in trapping and trading in the Northern Rockies and upper Missouri River region took Indian wives and adopted Indian lifestyles.

The Mandans, Arikaras and Hidatsas, who lived in villages along the banks of the Missouri River in present-day North and South Dakota, were the first of the Plains Indians to come into regular contact with European fur traders. Although living 1,600 miles from the closest white settlement, their proximity to the Missouri River made them accessible to French and British traders from Canada and later to American traders and explorers from St. Louis and the lower Mississippi Valley. Like many tribes on the eastern edge of the Great Plains, they raised corn, squash and beans around their permanent settlements of large earthwork lodges. But they also regularly roamed westward onto the Plains in pursuit of buffalo to supplement their existence. On these extended forays, they became nomads, living in portable structures, tepees, which their horses pulled behind them on sled-like travois.

The Missouri River tribes experienced the ill-effects of extensive trade contact with whites before other Plains Indians. Alcoholism and disease rapidly engulfed them. A smallpox epidemic brought up river by white traders in 1837 all but exterminated the Mandans. Of the 1,600 members of the major band that lived around Fort Union and the mouth of the Yellowstone, only 125 survived the outbreak.

The semi-agricultural Pawnees who dwelled on the lower Platte River undertook extensive buffalo hunts and raids on other tribes, which took them westward to the Rockies, northward to the upper Cheyenne River in Wyoming and as far southward as the Pecos River in western Texas.

The Comanches and Kiowas of the Southern Plains, whose homelands were adjacent to the early Spanish settlements, were probably among the first of the Plains tribes to adopt the horse as an integral part of their culture. The horse had such a great impact on the Comanches that their entire society came to revolve around it. While buffalo hunting provided for their basic needs, acquiring large numbers of horses became their main preoccupation. In the early 1820s, when the first American traders ventured into their lands in present-day western Oklahoma, southwestern Kansas and southeastern Colorado, they came upon bands of Comanches and Kiowas who bred huge herds of horses for trade as well as for their own use.

West of the Missouri, the Plains Indians were exclusively nomadic. This was the land of the Sioux, Cheyennes, Arapahos and the Blackfeet, who followed the buffalo herds with their mobile villages. They had become horse Indians by the mid-1700s, several generations before Lewis and Clark ventured through their lands on the northwestern edge of the Great Plains in 1805. Within that span of time, their culture had been transformed by the horse.

The horse had been an unintentional gift to the Indians from the Europeans. Ironically, both the self-sufficiency and the military advantage that the Plains Indians gained from the European introduction of the horse not only allowed them to live independently from whites in a state of natural prosperity, but enabled them to resist American efforts to contain them on reservations until well into the latter half of the 19th century.

Since the early 1830s, keeping the Great Plains as "one big reservation" for the Indians who lived there had been a major tenet of United States Indian policy. Indian Country, the remaining unorganized territory left over

Plains Indian Tepee (Molly Braun)

from the Louisiana Purchase, had for years been thought of as the "Great American Desert." Lacking sufficient rainfall and with scant timber, the region had been deemed unsuitable for white settlement and left as a preserve for the Plains Indians. It was to be a homeland in which they could roam unhindered and carry on their hunting-based tribal way of life, and live free of the corrupting influences of white contact. Government authorities thought 50 years would be sufficient time for the Plains tribes to turn away from hunting and adopt the agriculture-based frontier life of white settlers, just as the Cherokees and other southern tribes had done many years before.

At the close of the Mexican War in 1848, Indian Country was still colonial territory, lying outside the organized United States and administered directly by the federal government in Washington, D.C. Yet with the rapid expansion of the nation's boundaries from the Missouri Valley to the Pacific Coast of California and Oregon, the Permanent Indian Frontier no longer defined the country's western limits.

The nation's security had once called for keeping the Great Plains unsettled so it could effectively serve as a buffer against possible aggression from Great Britain or Mexico. With the settlement of the Oregon boundary in 1846 and the victory over Mexico in 1848, a buffer was no longer necessary. Indian Country had been viewed as a wasteland on the nation's western fringe and fit only for wild Indians. But by 1850, it was surrounded by states and organized territories to the east, west and south. Indian Country now loomed as a glaring gap on the map, a great chasm of unorganized territory in the nation's newly defined heartland that separated the nation's settled eastern sections from the newly taken possessions in the Far West.

The series of events that brought an end to the Permanent Indian Frontier and the "one big reservation" concept did not grow out of expansionist-driven land hunger, but stemmed from concern for the plight of the Indians. Starting in the early 1840s, increasing numbers of emigrants ventured out into Indian Country as they traveled along the western trails, bound for Oregon and California. The tens of thousands of draft animals that hauled the pioneers' prairie schooners across the Great Plains—along with the large herds of cattle that many of them brought along for their new homes in the West— left in their wake a great band of depleted grasslands north and south of the Oregon Trail. The buffalo herds had to roam farther and farther to find adequate grazing lands and they began to decrease in numbers.

Since the buffalo had to range over a wider area to find adequate grass, the Indians had to search farther to hunt them. One tribe would inevitably trespass upon the traditional hunting grounds of another, leading to intertribal warfare. The buffalo herds were further de-

pleted by pioneer hunters, who had quickly found the abundant game of the Great Plains to be a convenient, mobile source of fresh meat for the journey westward.

The stream of emigrants increased dramatically in 1849, spurred on by the California Gold Rush. The despoliation of the Great Plains accelerated, impoverishing the Indians and driving some to attack the problem at its source by harassing travelers along the western trails.

One of the first government officials to voice concern over the dire impact that the overland migrations was having on the Indians of the Great Plains was Thomas Fitzpatrick, U.S. Indian Agent at Fort Laramie in what is now southeastern Wyoming. After a gun accident injury in his early years, he was known among the Indians as Broken Hand. A native of Ireland, his 30-year career on the western frontier had begun in the early 1820s as a fur trapper on the upper Missouri River for William Henry Ashley. He went on to explore the Great Plains and the Rocky Mountains with Jedediah Smith; in the 1830s, he was a trader on the Santa Fe Trail, and later became a guide for the first emigrant wagon trains on the Oregon Trail. Since 1845, he had been an Indian agent, first for the Cheyennes and Arapahos on the upper Arkansas River, and a few years later for the Sioux, Northern Cheyenne and Northern Arapaho bands of the Platte River area around Fort Laramie.

In 1849–50, Fitzpatrick had witnessed one of the greatest mass-movements of people in history as more than 50,000 emigrants passed by his Oregon Trail post at Fort Laramie, most bound for the gold diggings of California and some headed for the lush valleys of Oregon. At that point, the Oregon Trail followed the Platte River, skirting the southern edge of Sioux country. It wasn't long before the Sioux complained that whites passing through their lands were shooting thousands of buffalo and that the animals of emigrant wagon trains had depleted the grasslands, forcing the diminishing buffalo herds to wander far from traditional Sioux hunting grounds.

Yet the Sioux tribes showed forbearance, even in the face of a crisis that threatened to undermine their way of life. Fitzpatrick knew that something had to be done soon to offset an impending disaster. Realizing that there would be no effective way to restrict the stream of emigrants passing through Indian lands, he considered the best solution would be to arrange for annual payments to compensate the Plains Indians for their losses in grass and game.

Cheyenne Pipe (Molly Braun)

Such an idea was not new. In 1825, the federal government had entered into treaties with Cheyennes and Comanches to allow safe passage along the Santa Fe Trail. In that case, however, the damage inflicted by trade caravans hardly approached the extent of devastation wrought by the wagon trains now streaming along the Oregon Trail in increasing numbers. Yet Fitzpatrick saw such a measure as the only hope for bringing peace and justice to the Plains tribes. In 1849, Fitzpatrick took his plan to Washington and presented it to his superiors in the Bureau of Indian Affairs. Not long before, the Bureau of Indian Affairs had been transferred from the War Department to the newly created Department of the Interior. The move reflected the government's changing view of the Indians. No longer were they considered a quasi-foreign power to be dealt with by the military. With U.S. sovereignty achieved over the Far West in 1848, the Indians who inhabited the Great Plains no longer lived outside the U.S. proper. They had clearly become a domestic concern, and as such were relegated to a civilian authority.

With the support of both the Commissioner of Indian Affairs and the Secretary of the Interior, Fitzpatrick's plan won the approval of President Millard Fillmore, and a bill passed the Senate authorizing a great conference of the Plains tribes for the purpose of drawing up a general treaty. There was some initial opposition in the House of Representatives, that in 1850 voted down a bill providing money for "The Big Talk" as the conference came to be known by the Indians. In response, Fitzpatrick expressed his frustration to Colonel David Mitchell, superintendent of all the Indians between the Missouri River and the Rocky Mountains, warning of dire consequences if the Indians turned hostile. His outspokenness cost him his job—at least briefly. But with the influence of the Missouri congressional delegation, most notably Senator Thomas Hart Benton, he won reinstatement a year later in 1851. Not coincidentally, the Missourians favored the proposed treaty plan, hoping it would clear the way for a proposed central route for the planned transcontinental railroad. Later that year, Congress authorized $100,000 for the treaty council, which was scheduled to take place in September of 1851.

Agents, subagents and traders sent the word out to the Plains tribes announcing the big powwow that was to be held near Fort Laramie. Teton Sioux, Cheyennes, Arapahos, Crows, Assiniboines, Gros Ventres, Mandans and Arikaras were represented. In September of 1851, at a place called Horse Creek—36 miles from Fort Laramie—gathered the largest assemblage of Indians ever seen by white officials, numbering more than 10,000 tribal members. The Indians themselves were not sure what to expect, except that they had been promised presents if they attended. But their mounting concerns over the loss of buffalo, and their eagerness to solve the crisis, were underscored by the fact that the Crows were convinced to encamp peacefully next to their traditional enemies—the Sioux.

Attending the conference as interpreter to the Shoshones was legendary frontiersman Jim Bridger. Also serving as an interpreter was former mountain man and one-time Crow Chief, the black frontiersmen Jim Beckwourth. Father Jean De Smet, who had spent years as a missionary to the Indians of what is now central and western Montana, was also in attendance.

Superintendent Mitchell told the assembled tribal leaders that "the Great Father" in Washington was well aware of their plight. But the treaty, which had originally been intended to specify only the amount of compensation, had grown to include provisions that would ultimately hasten the demise of the Plains Indians' way of life. Under the terms proposed by Mitchell, the tribes had to promise to cease warring among themselves; to facilitate this, he required the Indian nations to agree upon the boundaries of their territories. Furthermore, the Indians had to agree to allow safe passage for emigrants passing through their country and to permit the federal government to develop roads and construct forts within their tribal domains.

In effect, the Indians had surrendered a large degree of their sovereignty. They were no longer able to range where they wished; they were restricted to defined areas. As the buffalo continued to dwindle, the Indians would become more and more dependent on government handouts for survival.

To the Sioux went the region north of the Platte River, an area encompassing much of what is now North and South Dakota. Crow territory was to be the area west of the Powder River in present-day eastern Montana and Wyoming. The Cheyennes and Arapahos were relegated to the foothills of the Colorado Rockies between the North Platte and the Arkansas rivers. Similar territorial assignments were agreed upon for the Mandans, Blackfeet, Shoshones and Assiniboines.

In return for these concessions, the U.S. government agreed to make annual payments to the individual tribes totaling $50,000 in food and trade goods for a period of 50 years (later pared down to 15 years but with the annual amount increased to $70,000). Again the government projected that by the time the treaty expired, the Plains Indians would have abandoned their dependence on the buffalo and turned to agriculture.

The treaties were carried out over the next few years, resulting in the removal of most of the Indians from what was to become Kansas and Nebraska territories. By the end of the 1850s, the Indians of the Great Plains were to be relegated to two major areas to the north and south of their original territory. All that remained of Indian Country was a portion of present-day Oklahoma that became known as Indian Territory.

Other land cessions followed on the Southern Plains. In 1853, Fitzpatrick made similar treaties with Comanche, Kiowa and Kiowa–Apache bands at Fort Atkinson in present-day southwestern Kansas. Then in 1854, former eastern tribes that had been removed to Indian Country in the 1830s—the Omaha, Shawnee, Ottawa, Sauk, Fox, Iowa, Kickapoo, Delaware, Kaskaskia (Illinois), Peoria (Illinois) and Miami—were compelled to cede up to 13 million acres. In exchange for annuities, and for allowing the passage of a proposed railroad route through their lands, they gave up their territory for small reservations in present-day Oklahoma.

The U.S. government viewed the Fort Laramie Treaty of 1851—and the ones that followed—as agreements with foreign nations who just happened to reside in lands the U.S. had already acquired in the Louisiana Purchase of 1803.

From the Indians' vantage point, the Fort Laramie Treaty and the ensuing agreements provided a quick fix for the impoverishment they suffered as result of the devastation of their homeland by the overland migrations of whites. Moreover, by permitting roads and forts to be constructed within their lands, they hastened the demise of their hunting culture.

With the Fort Laramie Treaty of 1851, the "one big reservation" concept had been supplanted by an Indian policy based on the idea of "concentration." Instead of alleviating Indian poverty and ushering in a new era of peace, the practice of confining the Indians to small reservations led to their falling prey to the corrupt administration of the Indian Bureau. More often than not, their annuities were stolen or mismanaged. The buffalo herds diminished more rapidly as emigrant wagon trains, and later the railroads, took their toll on the natural environment of the Great Plains.

NEW MINING FRONTIERS: THE WEST MOVES EAST

The quest for riches in the West knew no fixed direction. In the past, the frontier had gradually edged westward from the settled states and territories of the East. But new discoveries of mineral wealth now lured tens of thousands of fortune-seekers to the Colorado Rockies, to what would become western Nevada, and to other unsettled parts of the West. They came not only from the East, but also included a fair number of "yonder siders" from regions west of the Rocky Mountains in the Southwest, California and the Pacific Northwest.

Far-flung mining settlements began to dot the map of the West like a chain of islands that stretched from the border towns of Missouri and Kansas, across the Great Plains and Rocky Mountains to the Sierra Nevada and California. New transportation links would have to be strung across the continent to join these isolated areas with the rest of the nation, and to make it possible for the East to gain full access to the wealth of the newly won West.

For years, travel across the unsettled regions of the West had been a hazardous affair, undertaken by individuals willing to risk the perils and challenges of the trail. But the western mining centers had to be joined with the rest of the nation, and spurred by this economic and political necessity, overland western travel rapidly evolved from the realm of pioneer adventure into the sphere of big business enterprise.

Henry Tompkins Paige Comstock was known as "Old Pancake" by his friends in the mining camps of the Washoe Mountains. The nickname grew out of his reputation as the most shiftless man at the diggings; he was even too lazy to bake bread. Yet despite his laziness as a prospector, his name would be forever associated with one of the richest mineral finds in U.S. history—a discovery that for a time reversed the direction of westward expansion.

Comstock was one of the hundred or so gold prospectors who, by the mid–1850s, had drifted eastward from California's Mother Lode Country to try their luck on the eastern slopes of the Sierra Nevada. By then, the day of the prospector had ended in California; most of the easy pickings had already been washed from the stream beds and rocky outcroppings of the Mother Lode.

Independent prospectors, working alone or in small groups with only washing pans and crude mining devices, had given way to large industrial mining operations. There was still plenty of gold to be mined, but most of what remained was bound up in ore-bearing rocks that had to be blasted out of the ground or dug from deep beneath the surface. Profitable gold-mining now required extensive excavation as well as expensive machinery to crush and refine the ore.

The huge outlays of capital this type of mining demanded far exceeded the means of most Forty-Niners. Many of the original gold-seekers returned to their homes in the East, enriched only with rip-roaring tales of their experiences in the California Gold Rush of 1849. Some remained in California to prosper in other types of endeavors, while many others, still holding on to the dream of some day striking it rich, found the free and easy life of the prospector too attractive to give up.

There were other gold rushes. In 1858, reports of gold strikes lured thousands of California prospectors, along with the merchants who supplied them, to the Columbia River region of western Washington Territory and to the lower Fraser River Valley of western British Columbia. But these booms were short-lived; the strikes were limited to a few rich veins of surface gold that were quickly exhausted or taken over by large mining companies, and

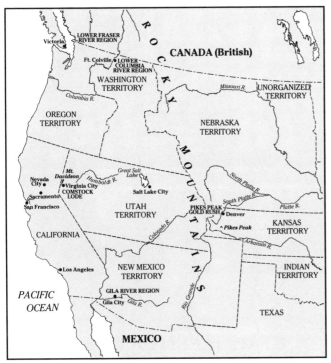

6.2 NEW MINING BOOMS IN THE WEST: 1855–59

soon all but a few of the gold-rushers went back to California.

The Washoe Mountains, which stood in front of the eastern slopes of the Sierra Nevada, northeast of Lake Tahoe, presented still another opportunity for fortune-seekers. Some traces of gold had been found by members of the Mormon Battalion returning eastward from California in 1848, but not enough to attract the hordes that were then descending on the goldfields of the Mother Lode on the other side of the Sierra Nevada. Still, the region seemed promising enough to keep a few die-hards digging away along the streams and exposed rocks of the range's foothills. A few mining camps were established along the slopes of Mount Davidson—the highest peak of the Washoe range—and a small settlement called Johntown grew around nearby Dutch Nick's saloon.

In June of 1859, two Irish miners, Patrick McLaughlin and Peter O'Riley, discovered gold dust at a site on the northern slope of Mount Davidson, known as Six Mile Canyon. At the time, Comstock and a few others were prospecting at Gold Hill on the southern slope of Mount Davidson. Comstock convinced McLaughlin and O'Riley that they were working a claim that he and two friends had already staked out. To settle the matter, they agreed to a five-man partnership with Comstock and his friends Manny Penrod and James Fennimore (who was known as "Old Virginny," after his native state).

They called the Six Mile Canyon diggings the Ophir Mine, after the biblical reference to the site of King Solo-

mon's mines. During the next few weeks, Comstock and his partners were able to extract two to three hundred dollars worth of gold a day. But then the vein appeared to run deeper, and the work became more difficult since what precious metal there was now had to be separated from a vein of bluish quartz rock. At first they discarded the cumbersome "blue stuff" as worthless, but one of the partners, Manny Penrod, decided it might be valuable and he sent some of it across the Sierra to Nevada City, California to be analyzed. The results were astounding: An assay of the ore sample revealed that it came from a vein of quartz containing three-fourths pure silver and one-fourth pure gold, and was estimated to be worth close to $4,000 a ton.

Word of the fabulous strike leaked out to a handful of Nevada City businessmen and others at nearby Placerville. Some of them wasted no time in rushing off to the Washoe diggings. George Hearst, a mine owner from Nevada City (whose son was to found the famous newspaper empire), arrived at the site even before the good news reached Comstock and his partners. He persuaded McLaughlin to sell his interest in the Ophir Mine for $3,500. Other Californians soon appeared on the scene. Instead of washing pans and pickaxes, they brought cash and managed to buy out the other partners for sums that would seem insignificant compared to the vast wealth that the mine eventually gave up. Comstock received $10,000, while O'Riley held out for $40,000. Comstock and the others had no way of knowing what they were giving up, and they were happy to accept what seemed to be huge sums for shares in a mine that appeared to have already seen its best days.

Not nearly as lucky was "Old Virginny" Fennimore who sold his share in the mine to Comstock for a blind horse and a bottle of whiskey. Yet he was to gain in fame what he had missed in wealth. One night after a round of drinking, he stumbled and broke his whiskey bottle while returning to his quarters in the mining camp that had quickly sprung up near the Ophir Mine. He picked up the broken bottle, and whimsically sprinkling the last drops on the ground, proclaimed, "I baptize this ground Virginia City!" Henry Comstock, or "Old Pancake," gained fame as well; he had done less digging and more self-promoting as the "discoverer" of the rich vein, and as a result, the entire mining district became known as the Comstock Lode.

Before the end of the year, 4,000 hopeful prospectors descended on the Washoe District. By the following spring, the rush intensified and Virginia City rapidly grew to a population of more than 10,000, most of the newcomers having come eastward from California. Soon the town could boast over 150 businesses, including a theater, law offices, 8 hotels, 38 stores, 9 restaurants, 25 saloons and a generous number of other recreational establishments.

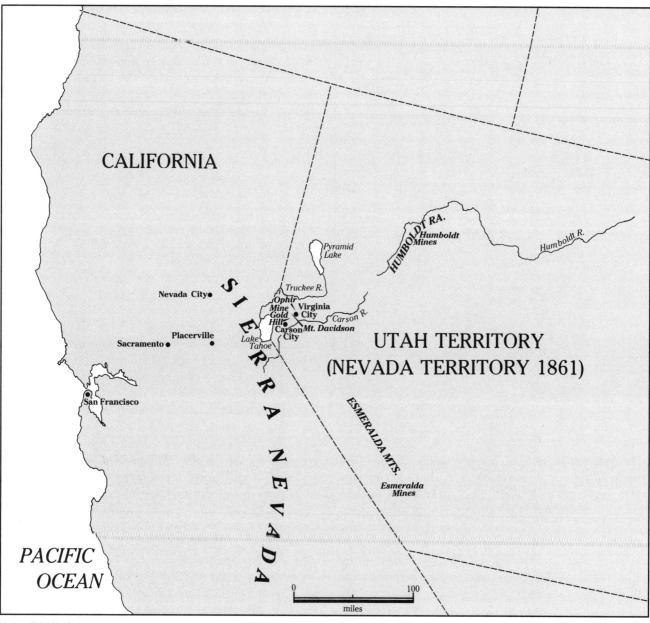

CALIFORNIA

PACIFIC
OCEAN

Nevada City●

Sacramento●   Placerville●

San Francisco●

Pyramid
Lake

Truckee R.

Ophir
Mine   Virginia
Gold   ● City
Hill   Carson● Mt. Davidson
Lake   City
Tahoe

Carson R.

SIERRA NEVADA

HUMBOLDT RA.
Humboldt
Mines

Humboldt R.

UTAH TERRITORY
(NEVADA TERRITORY 1861)

ESMERALDA MTS.

Esmeralda
Mines

0   100
miles

6.3   THE COMSTOCK LODE AND VIRGINIA CITY: 1859–61

Yet amid this flurry of business activity, little mining was actually done. Most of the prospectors had neither the experience nor the financial wherewithal to begin to exploit the rich silver ore of the Comstock Lode. The Ophir Mine at Six Mile Canyon was the northern outcropping of the lode, and Comstock's original claim at Gold Hill marked the southern end. Although the major vein was five-miles long and at some places close to a half-mile wide, most of it was buried deep within the eastern side of Mount Davidson. Between the outcroppings at the Ophir Mine and at Gold Hill, there were few places where independent prospectors could get at the gold and silver of the Comstock Lode without a considerable investment of money and equipment.

The first prospectors on the scene nonetheless quickly staked out claims all along the Comstock Lode. Others fanned out to promising sites to the northeast in the Humboldt Range and to the southwest in the Esmeralda Mountains.

Although actual mining was impractical for most of the earliest arrivals, money could be made by speculating in unproven claims. Prospectors, storekeepers and workers bought and sold both entire claims as well as shares and stocks in undeveloped mining ventures with such wistful names as the "Wake-Up-Jake," the "Let-Her-Rip," the "Root-Hog-Or-Die," the "Treasure Trove" and the "Grand Mogul."

Nearly 17,000 claims were staked out, but only the Ophir Mine, the diggings at Gold Hill and a few other sites were actually yielding any gold-and-silver-bearing ore. The speculative fever nonetheless raged on in Virginia City and soon spread westward over the mountains to San Francisco.

The Washoe District lay along the northwestern edge of the Great Basin, in western Utah Territory. But Utah's territorial government could never exercise effective control over the area, and grass-roots movements for independence from Utah had gained momentum in 1851, 1857 and 1859. Moreover, since the Mormon conflict with federal authorities in 1857, most of the Mormon settlers had abandoned their settlements in western Utah Territory and returned eastward to the Salt Lake City area. On the heels of the mining boom of 1859, the Comstock Lode region's population rapidly swelled from a few hundred to more than 15,000. Although the number of new settlers was still not large enough for territorial status, the federal government nonetheless anticipated that the region's great potential wealth would no doubt soon attract an even greater population. Moreover, there was now an urgent need to impose law and order over the Comstock Lode's wild and wide-open mining communities that had seemed to spring up overnight.

To meet these needs, in March of 1861 Congress created a new territory out of the western half of Utah Territory. The new Territory of Nevada comprised the area west of the 113th meridian and south of the southern boundary of Oregon and Washington Territory. On the west and southwest it was bounded by the former border between what had been Utah Territory and California. Within a year, Nevada's eastern boundary was extended another degree of longitude eastward, at the expense of Utah Territory.

The first territorial governor was James W. Nye of New York, and the first territorial secretary was a young Missourian named Orin Clemens. Accompanying him was his younger brother, Samuel Clemens who, as Mark Twain, would later record the colorful mining-boom days in Virginia City and the Comstock Lode region in his classic account, *Roughing It* (1872).

Although by 1864 Nevada held hardly enough of a population to warrant statehood, it was nevertheless admitted to the Union that year. What propelled Nevada so rapidly from territory to state was the desire of Republican leaders in Congress to win the new state's electoral votes and thereby assure the reelection of their candidate, President Abraham Lincoln.

Over the next 20 years, the mines of the Comstock Lode would yield $300 million in silver and gold. Deep-shaft mining was the rule, with miners tunneling wherever the veins could be traced, even deep beneath the houses and streets of Virginia City. As was the case in

The Comstock Mine in the Late 1860s (Photo courtesy of the National Archives)

California, mining became a major industrial undertaking with little room for independent operators or inexperienced amateurs without large sums to invest.

Prior to the 1859 rush to the Comstock Lode, the advance of the frontier had been a westward push, either a gradual movement from the Ohio and Mississippi valleys by settlers in search of new farmlands, or a leapfrogging across the Great Plains by emigrants lured to Oregon and California. But the settlement of western Nevada showed that the frontier of the miner knew no fixed direction, but could rapidly shift to encompass any place where wealth was to be found.

THE PIKES PEAK GOLD RUSH

In 1859, gold lured thousands of fortune-seekers into the mountains of what was then western Kansas Territory. It was a stampede that grew in scope to rival the California Gold Rush of a decade earlier. Before the initial surge ended, the region—once only sparsely inhabited by a few scattered Indian tribes and a handful of white traders and mountain men—quickly filled with a large population of pioneers who before long had carved a new territory out of the Rocky Mountain West.

The Front Range of the Rocky Mountains, extending north-to-south between present-day southern Wyoming and the Arkansas River, had become known as the "Pikes Peak Country," after the area's most prominent natural landmark. Zebulon Pike had explored the region in 1806 and had heard reports of gold in the mountains from a trader he met in Santa Fe. For years afterward, mountain men spun tales of lost gold mines and Indian legends spoke of bullets forged from the precious metal. But such tales were not taken seriously until after the California gold strikes in 1849.

In 1850, a group of Cherokees from Georgia, traveling westward to try their luck in the California goldfields, paused to pan for gold in the streams that flowed down the Front Range into the upper reaches of the South Platte River. They managed to wash out some hints of gold, but not enough to keep them from their journey to the Mother Lode Country.

After they had returned to the East, William Green Russell, a white Georgian farmer married to a Cherokee—who also had tried his hand at prospecting in California—learned of the meager find in the Front Range and decided to investigate further. In the spring of 1858, he led a party of about 60 men, comprised of Cherokees and whites from Georgia and the Indian Territory (present-day Oklahoma), up the Arkansas River to Bent's Fort, then northward into Pikes Peak Country.

They prospected along the upper South Platte but did not find any gold. By early July, most of them had given up and headed homeward, leaving only Russell and 12 others. Several days later, however, the remaining prospectors washed some gold flakes out of the riverbed near the mouth of Cherry Creek. They managed to sift a few ounces of gold from the area, but it was soon apparent that this was no major discovery. Having panned what little they could, Russell and the others left to try their luck farther northward along the eastern slopes of the Front Range.

When Russell and his companions returned to the Cherry Creek site several weeks later, they met up with about a hundred men from Lawrence, Kansas, picking away at the exposed rock and washing gravel from the stream. Some months earlier, two Indian scouts had arrived in Lawrence carrying a few gold flakes they said they had found in the mountains to the south and west of Pikes Peak. It was hardly enough to inspire a gold rush, yet the news came in the midst of the hard times wrought by the Panic of 1857.

A year before, a major financial failure in Cincinnati had triggered a nationwide economic depression. The initial prosperity brought about by the California Gold Rush had caused investments to be overextended. When the bottom inevitably fell out, banks failed, businesses were ruined, farmers faced foreclosure and eviction, and thousands were thrown out of work. The economic downturn rapidly spread throughout the Ohio and Mississippi Valleys, and by 1858 it had reached the frontier settlements at Omaha and Council Bluffs, Missouri, and in eastern Kansas.

When the rumor of gold reached Lawrence, men eager to seize any opportunity that might bring a reversal of fortune hastily set out in 11 covered wagons to seek riches in the Rocky Mountains. Failing to find any paydirt in the southern mountains, they headed northward to the South Platte, where they had encountered Russell and his group.

Although there was still no significant gold to be had, the prospectors were confident that a large strike would soon be made. Anticipating the kind of massive influx that had occurred in California, Russell and his men, along with the newcomers from Lawrence, promptly staked out townsites they thought would be in great demand once the rush began in earnest.

Two principal settlements were established near the junction of Cherry Creek and the South Platte. They soon merged into one, called Denver, after James W. Denver, a recent governor of Kansas Territory. In the meantime, a trader had carried exaggerated news of the strike eastward to Kansas City, Missouri. In the fall of 1858, close to a thousand people hit the trail for the Pikes Peak Country. The news spread rapidly through the Midwest and thousands more made plans to head west for the new bonanza in the Rocky Mountains as soon as spring made travel across the Plains practical.

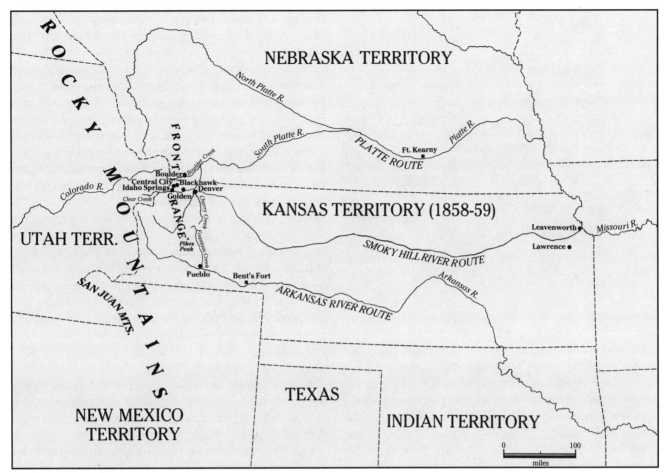

6.4   THE PIKES PEAK GOLD RUSH IN THE COLORADO ROCKIES: 1858–59

On the Missouri frontier, towns saw the coming gold rush as an opportunity to prosper as jumping-off places for the thousands of hopeful gold-seekers. Newspapers played up unfounded reports with such headlines heralding "Kansas Gold Fever" and "Gold! Gold! Gold!! Hard to Get and Heavy to Hold!! Come to Kansas!!"

Entrepreneurs churned out guidebooks to the Pikes Peak Country, each promoting the advantages of one of three major routes to the supposed goldfields. One was the Platte Route, located along the Platte and South Platte rivers. Another was the Arkansas River and Fountain Creek Route, which Russell and his companions had taken. The third was the largely untried Smoky Hill River Route through the arid plains of western Kansas. Highly touted as the best and shortest route by unscrupulous merchants at its eastern terminus in Leavenworth, Kansas, this last route proved to be a disaster for many inexperienced travelers who became lost and died of thirst and starvation.

A few hundred men and a few dozen women spent the winter of 1858–59 in the collection of makeshift cabins that comprised the new "city" of Denver. Scarcely any gold had been found, yet it was hoped that spring would bring a tide of settlers with money for supplies

and townsites. (Whether or not a gold strike was to be made was another matter.) And come they did. Even before there was grass enough to support draft animals on the plains, thousands headed west from Missouri River ports such as Kansas City, Independence and Omaha. The initial rush at least proved to be a boom for these towns, where merchants raked in profits selling "Pike's Peak boots, Pike's Peak shovels, and Pike's Peak goodness-knows-what-all" as one Missouri newspaper described it.

Yet by late spring, many of the newcomers came to realize that the gold strike in the Pikes Peak Country was more exaggeration than Eldorado, more ballyhoo than bonanza. Most of the promising sites along the South Platte had been staked out before they had arrived, and they found merchants charging outrageous prices for bare necessities. Still more gold-seekers came across the plains, only to be met by a reverse exodus of the disappointed. The negative reports spread eastward along the trail, and the bitterness became infectious. While as many as one hundred thousand hopefuls had set out across the plains of Kansas with banners reading "Pikes Peak or Bust" displayed across their wagons, about half that number or more were on their way back, their dis-

Pikes Peak or Bust (Photo courtesy of the New York Public Library)

appointment expressed in signs that said: "Busted, By God."

Many declared that the hoopla over Pikes Peak had been a great "humbug," a commercially generated hoax perpetuated by Missouri frontier merchants with excess goods to unload on the unwary, and by unscrupulous land speculators with overpriced townsites to sell in the fraudulently-touted "goldfields" around Denver, Clear Creek, Golden and Arapahoe. Dozens of other settlements existed more on paper than as actual communities. One local wit remarked that "before spring there were perhaps 20 cities in the country as large as New York, minus the wealth, population and buildings."

In the spring of 1859, a trio of eastern newspapermen headed west by stagecoach to determine the truth about the Pikes Peak Gold Rush. One was Henry Villard of the *Cincinnati Daily Commercial;* another was A.D. Richardson of the *Boston Morning Journal;* the third was none other than the famous Horace Greeley, the esteemed editor of the *New York Herald Tribune,* immortalized by his advice to "Go West, young man." Soon after the journalists arrived, a small strike of placer gold was discovered by George A. Jackson, a prospector from Missouri. His find at Chicago Creek was not particularly rich, but it fueled the hopes of many of the gold-seekers who were determined to hang on for the real thing. In a joint report issued that summer, the three newspapermen confirmed that the gold strikes in the Pikes Peak Country were genuine.

In May of 1859, John H. Gregory, who had previous experience seeking gold in Georgia as well as in California, came upon a significant vein of gold mixed with quartz. The site of his find was at Clear Creek, at a place that quickly came to be known as Gregory Gulch. The news sent tremors of excitement through Denver. Out on the trails to the east, thousands of "Go-Backs" heard that at last a real strike had been made. Over the next few weeks, thousands poured into the Gregory Gulch area, and a new settlement quickly sprang up there called Central City.

Within a few months, more strikes were made to the west at Golden and Idaho Springs, to the northwest at Boulder, and to the south at Pueblo on the Arkansas River. Prospectors soon inundated every creek and canyon of the Central Rockies, some making significant gold discoveries to the west of the Continental Divide, causing more settlements to come into existence almost overnight at California Gulch and along other streams that emptied into the Colorado River.

Nearly 700 miles west of any organized government, the problem of law and order, not to mention the protection of claims, was an early concern of the Fifty-Niners. As early as the winter of 1858–59, the miners around Cherry Creek organized themselves first into mining districts, then opted to create unilaterally a territorial government. Although there were less than a few hundred settlers in the region at the time, they held a constitutional convention and elected a delegate to Congress.

But the federal government declined to recognize the self-proclaimed Territory of Jefferson. Undaunted, the settlers in the Pikes Peak Country then opted to declare themselves as the "State of Jefferson."

Still, Congress failed to act, since the issue quickly became enmeshed in the sectional controversy over slavery. The movement for statehood was short-lived, nonetheless, since a majority of the settlers voted against it, thinking that as a territory, they would not be as heavily taxed. Territorial status was also preferable, since it would require the federal government to foot the bill for many essential expenses of governmental administration.

In February of 1861, after most of the southern states had seceded from the Union, the way was clear for the Pikes Peak Country and the adjoining area to the west to be organized into a new territory. Known as the Territory of Colorado, it included all of what had been western Kansas Territory west of the 102nd meridian, as well as a strip of eastern Utah Territory, the southeasternmost corner of Nebraska Territory and part of northern New Mexico Territory.

By then, the new territory had reached a stable population of about 35,000, despite the rapid fluctuations caused by the early boom and bust periods that characterized the heyday of the Pikes Peak Gold Rush. In other mining areas throughout the West, many settlements were abandoned as ghost towns as soon as the mineral wealth was exhausted. But this would not be the case for Colorado, which would continue to thrive throughout the rest of the 19th century, and well into the 20th century, as a result of subsequent strikes of silver, lead, oil, coal, natural gas and uranium.

The successive mining booms attracted farmers and ranchers to the region for the new market in agricultural products. Extensive agricultural development would be further spurred by massive irrigation projects that would transform the arid plains of eastern Colorado into thousands of square miles of newly fertile lands.

Colorado spanned the great mountain barrier at the western edge of the so-called "Great American Desert." Once deemed worthless for white settlement and left to the Indians who lived there, the sudden influx of population would soon cause problems for the Cheyenne, Arapaho and Ute tribes, who found themselves engulfed by settlers of a rich new mining frontier in the West.

STAGECOACH LINES AND THE PONY EXPRESS

The tens of thousands of Americans who had poured into California during the Gold Rush years relied on the mail as their only link with friends and relatives left behind in the East. The growth of banking and commerce in the Far West also required regular mail service, since vital commercial information needed to be sent between the East and West. There was also a growing demand for eastern merchandise in the new boom towns that had sprung up in the Far West. Moreover, for the mining enterprises of the Far West to prosper, mineral wealth once taken from the ground and refined had to be transported to the East.

The new population centers of the Far West were widely scattered between the Mississippi Valley and the Pacific Coast. The mining boom areas of California and what would soon be Nevada were a half a continent away from the settled areas of the East. Farther eastward, on the western edge of the Great Plains, 700 miles separated the Pikes Peak Country of the Colorado Rockies from the nearest towns of eastern Kansas and western Missouri. News of the latest developments in the East had to reach these far-flung settlements in order to keep them within the sphere of American social and political life.

To meet the needs of westerners, the federal government had subsidized ocean mail service to California by way of Panama. Starting in 1849, mail was carried by ships of the United States Steamship Company from New York to Panama, transported across the isthmus, then loaded aboard vessels of the Pacific Mail Steamship Company and shipped northward to San Francisco. Even with government support, the cost of this roundabout route was high, up to 80 cents an ounce, and the trip between New York and San Francisco could take longer than a month. Within a few years, Californians and others in the Far West were clamoring for a cheaper and faster way to keep in contact with the rest of the nation.

A railroad to the Pacific would solve the problem, but that massive undertaking was still a long way off. Besides the tremendous technical challenges that had to be surmounted, such a project could not even progress beyond the planning stage as long as North and South were deadlocked over the selection of the proposed route. In the meantime, a ready solution would be a stagecoach line to the Far West.

In May of 1856, Senator John B. Weller of California presented Congress with a petition signed by 75,000 of his constituents calling for the government to subsidize an overland mail service. A year later, Congress responded by authorizing Postmaster General Aaron V. Brown to award a contract for overland stagecoach service to carry mail and passengers from the Mississippi River to San Francisco.

Although the contract did not specify the route the stagecoach line should take, Brown, who was a southerner, well knew that it was likely to become "the pioneer route for the first great railroad that may be constructed to the Pacific." Driven by sectional sympathies, he therefore granted the $600,000 subsidy to John Butterfield, who had readily agreed to develop a southern express route to the West.

A long-time stagecoach line operator in the East, and one of the founding partners of the American Express Company, Butterfield offered a plan for service from two points in the East: Memphis in Tennessee (Postmaster General Brown's home state) and Tipton, Missouri, the western terminus of the railroad from St. Louis. The two branches would then meet at Fort Smith, Arkansas. From there, stagecoaches would travel southwestward across Texas to El Paso, through southern New Mexico Territory to Fort Yuma, and across the passes of the southern Sierra Nevada to Los Angeles, then northward through California to San Francisco.

On the map, the route appeared as a great semi-circle, and seemed anything but direct. Northern critics, who supported a stagecoach line across the well-traveled Platte River route and through South Pass, derided it as the "Oxbow Route," claiming that it ran "from no place through nothing to nowhere." Nonetheless, it was up to Postmaster General Brown alone to decide, and it was the Oxbow route that he chose. To justify his decision, Brown argued that "there was no other all-the-year-route between the Mississippi and the Pacific."

During the next year, Butterfield invested $1 million in the project. Some improvements were made to the wagon road west, and along the route nearly 200 stations were constructed at 10- or 15-mile intervals where teams of horses would be changed and where passengers could rest during brief stops.

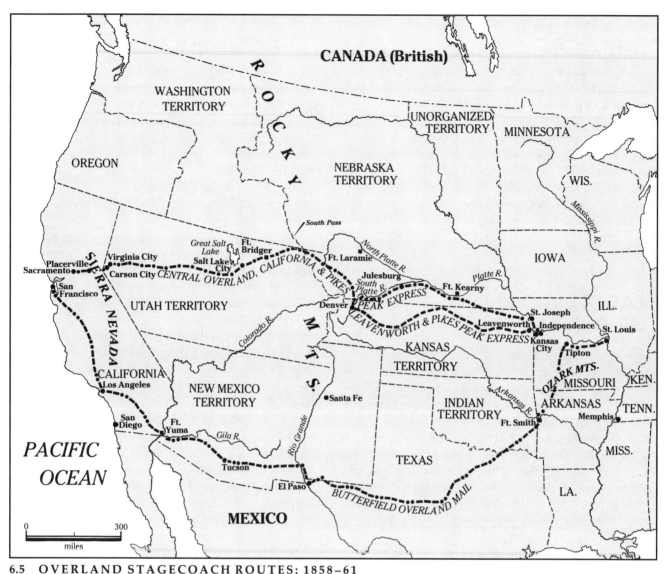

6.5 OVERLAND STAGECOACH ROUTES: 1858–61

Along the 2,800-mile route between Tipton and San Francisco, the Butterfield Overland Mail used Concord coaches, so named from their place of manufacture in Concord, New Hampshire. These were the coaches later immortalized in the hundreds of motion picture and television depictions of overland travel in the Old West. They were fitted with steel rimmed wheels, and could carry up to nine passengers. Mail and light freight were carried in a triangular-shaped "boot" in the rear. Hundreds of drivers, wranglers, station masters, blacksmiths and other support personnel were hired.

On September 16, 1858, all was ready for the first run of the Butterfield Overland Mail. At the reins of the first westbound coach was Butterfield's son, John, Jr. A day before, the first eastbound stagecoach had rolled out of San Francisco. Butterfield himself accompanied the mail as far as Fort Smith, then waited there for the arrival of the first coach from the west. Twenty-three days and 23 hours later, the first westbound coach arrived in San Francisco, well within the time allowed by the government contract. The eastbound coach reached Tipton, Missouri right on schedule, after a journey of 24 days and 18 hours out of San Francisco. This linking of the East and West was hailed by President James Buchanan in a telegram to Butterfield, declaring it to be "a glorious triumph for civilization and the Union."

The Butterfield Overland Mail followed the longest stagecoach route in history. There were dangers along the way: Comanches and Apaches sometimes attacked the coaches as they sped through western Texas and southern New Mexico Territory, and the coaches had to contend with floods on the plains and with blizzards that blocked the mountain passes. Under Butterfield's management, the coaches rarely failed to get through, his men driven by their devotion to duty and inspired by Butterfield, who constantly reminded them that "Nothing on God's earth must stop the United States mail!"

As efficient as the Butterfield Overland Mail was, other operators thought they could do better with the shorter central route to the north, along the well-established Oregon and California trails. One of them was William H. Russell, a partner in the freighting firm of Russell, Majors & Waddell.

Since 1854, the company had been under contract from the army to supply western military posts. Russell, Majors & Waddell wagon trains, pulled by teams of oxen, and manned by "bullwhackers," came to dominate the overland freighting business in the West. In 1857, the firm suffered a severe setback when the army ordered them to send shipments to Salt Lake City to support a military expedition against the Mormons. Near Fort Bridger, in northern Utah Territory, several of their wagon trains were attacked and destroyed by Mormon raiders. With the army unable to cover these losses, the firm tottered near bankruptcy. In response, Russell turned to stagecoaching, hoping that a line along the central route to the West would win a government mail contract that would put his business enterprises back on the track to financial recovery.

Russell's stagecoach line, the Leavenworth & Pikes Peak Express, began operations in April of 1859 with service between Leavenworth and Denver, the newly established settlement in the Pikes Peak Country. Inspired by news of gold strikes in the eastern Rockies, Russell was confident that his enterprise would reap immense profits from the inevitable gold rush. But as it turned out, the Pikes Peak Gold Rush rapidly fizzled into a "bust," and no government mail contracts were forthcoming.

Although the Leavenworth & Pikes Peak Express continued to operate, without a government subsidy it incurred heavy losses. Undaunted, Russell decided to expand the service, hoping to win government support by demonstrating the superiority of the central route to the West. He bought out a stage line that had been carrying the mail from Independence, Missouri, to Salt Lake City, and with financial backing from his freighting business partners, added a line between Salt Lake City and Placerville, California.

Re-christened the Central Overland, California & Pikes Peak Express, and heavily in debt, the reorganized operation had to gain a government subsidy for the entire route or perish. To this end, Russell seized upon a bold idea to promote the central route. His plan, which would cut the time it took for a letter to reach California by more than half, would no doubt convince the government to use the central route and thereby save his company.

In early January of 1860, Russell announced the scheme to his son in a brief telegram from Washington, D.C.: "Have determined to establish a Pony Express to Sacramento, California, commencing the 3rd of April. Time ten days."

Over the next few months, Russell recruited hundreds of riders. In San Francisco and along the Missouri frontier, he ran advertisements in newspapers calling for:

YOUNG SKINNY WIRY FELLOWS
not over eighteen. Must be expert riders
and willing to risk death daily.
Orphans preferred. WAGES: $25 per week.--

Russell set up 190 stations at 10 or 15 miles along the route where his riders would quickly change horses. In this way, the mail could be carried at a constant gallop over the entire distance between the eastern terminus at St. Joseph, Missouri and its western end in San Francisco. The work was dangerous and would test the stamina of the hardiest of young men. They would have to ride at high speeds over the roughest terrain and brave Indian attacks, scorching deserts in summer and frigid winter weather on the Plains.

To finance the bold new venture, Russell and his partners went deeper into debt, purchasing 500 semi-tamed horses, chosen more for their speed and stamina than for their manageability. Each rider would cover up to 75 miles in 10 hours, changing horses every 10 hours. Sometimes a rider would have to cover a greater distance if no other rider was ready to take over at the next way station. Young William F. Cody, later to earn fame as the great western showman "Buffalo Bill," once rode 380 miles non-stop while serving with the Pony Express.

The Pony Express charged five dollars an ounce for letters. At even that high a price, Russell and his partners still lost money. But less concerned with profits and more interested in the publicity the Pony Express would generate in support of the central route, they nonetheless continued to pour money into the venture.

At the same time that Pony Express riders were speeding across the West, a telegraph line was rapidly progressing across the Great Plains and mountains from both directions, eastward from California and westward from Nebraska. As the gap narrowed between the ends of the telegraph line, the days of the Pony Express came closer to an end. On October 24, 1861, the wires were joined at Salt Lake City, and soon afterward—after having been in operation just 18 months—the Pony Express was no longer necessary and it went out of business.

The earlier outbreak of the Civil War closed down U.S. mail service along Butterfield's southern Oxbow route after Texas and Arkansas seceded from the Union. As for Russell and his partners, whose stagecoach service was now well-established along the central route to the north, other events would propel their firm into scandal and ultimately bankruptcy.

While his Pony Express riders were galloping back and forth across the Far West, Russell remained in Washing-

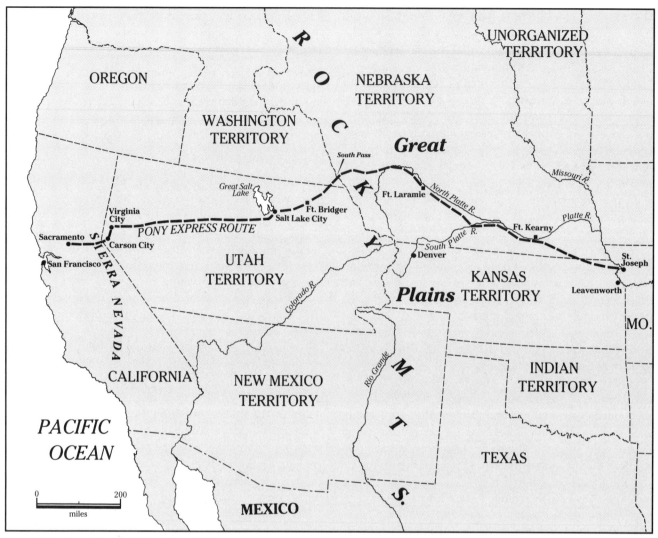

OREGON

WASHINGTON TERRITORY

NEBRASKA TERRITORY

UNORGANIZED TERRITORY

Great

South Pass

Great Salt Lake

Virginia City

Ft. Bridger
Salt Lake City

Ft. Laramie

North Platte R.

Missouri R.

Platte R.

Sacramento

Carson City

PONY EXPRESS ROUTE

South Platte R.

Ft. Kearny

St. Joseph

San Francisco

UTAH TERRITORY

Denver

Colorado R.

KANSAS

Plains TERRITORY

Leavenworth

MO.

CALIFORNIA

NEW MEXICO TERRITORY

Rio Grande

INDIAN TERRITORY

PACIFIC OCEAN

TEXAS

0   200
miles

MEXICO

6.6   THE PONY EXPRESS: 1860–61

ton, still lobbying Congress for the mail subsidy. The Pony Express, while it lasted, had been a spectacular success as a mail service, yet it was quickly draining the financial resources of its parent company. In dire need of additional funding while awaiting support from the government, Russell began accepting government bonds from a corrupt official of the Department of the Interior. At first Russell thought the man was a legitimate bond dealer, but he soon found out that he was actually embezzling bonds from a trust fund set up for the Indians. He nevertheless continued to borrow money against the pilfered securities until the scheme was exposed.

Russell was arrested, jailed briefly, then managed to escape government prosecution through the help of his able lawyers. But the scandal had tainted his reputation and that of Russell, Major & Waddell. As a result, when the government moved its mail service northward in 1861, the contract was not awarded to his Central Overland, California and Pikes Peak Express, but to John Butterfield's company. As a small consolation, Russell,

Majors & Waddell managed to get a subcontract from Butterfield for stagecoach and mail service between Independence and Salt Lake City.

By 1862, the company of Russell, Majors & Waddell had become heavily indebted to Ben Holladay, a man whose reputation for coarseness was only exceeded by his reputation as a major force in the overland transportation business. He purchased Russell, Majors & Waddell in a bankruptcy auction for a mere fraction of the worth of its assets.

Four years later, in 1866, Holladay sold out his interest to another giant in western transportation, Wells Fargo & Company. By then, Holladay could see that the end of the era of the animal-powered freight and stagecoach business was in sight. The first transcontinental railroad was then nearing completion. Both the ox-drawn wagon trains of overland freighters and the horse and mule-driven stagecoaches that had dominated overland transportation between the East and the West were soon to be supplanted by the Iron Horse.

IN SEARCH OF A RAILROAD ROUTE TO THE PACIFIC

In 1832, a decade before the first emigrant wagon trains made their way west along the Oregon Trail, *The Emigrant*, an Ann Arbor, Michigan weekly newspaper, ran an editorial calling for the construction of a transcontinental railroad. The route proposed would run from New York along the southern shores of Lake Erie and Lake Michigan to the Missouri River, and then along the Platte River and across the Rockies to the mouth of the Columbia River on the Oregon coast.

At the time, the idea was considered visionary; California and the Southwest were then northern provinces of Mexico, and the United States still shared sovereignty over the Oregon Country with Great Britain. Moreover, American railroading was then in its infancy; the first steam locomotives had begun rolling on the rails of the Baltimore & Ohio and Charleston & Hamburg lines only two years before, and there were not more than 200 miles of track in the entire country.

Yet the idea persisted, and in the early 1840s, it found its most outspoken voice in Asa Whitney, a New York merchant who had amassed a fortune in the China trade. Whitney stressed that with a railroad to the Pacific, the long ocean voyage to the Orient would be dramatically shortened. The riches of the Orient would be brought to the nation's doorstep, and the United States would become a dominant force in international trade between Europe and the Far East. Financing for this massive construction project, Whitney proposed, would be raised through grants of land along a 60-mile-wide right of way. The cost of labor would be met by paying workers with land along the route and additional money would come from the sale of land to settlers.

In January of 1845, Whitney presented his plan to the U.S. Congress. Meanwhile, interest for a transcontinental railroad had begun to mount, fueled in no small way by the expansionist philosophy and fervor of Manifest Destiny. Although the federal government did not immediately act on Whitney's plan, it sparked interest among businessmen. At conventions held in Chicago, St. Louis, Memphis, Philadelphia, Iowa City, New Orleans and Little Rock, supporters gathered to discuss and promote the idea. By 1852, railroad mileage had increased considerably in the eastern part of the nation, and every major city in the North and South now vied to be the terminus of the proposed railroad to the Pacific.

Asa Whitney's idea called for a railroad to be constructed along a northern route from Lake Michigan, through the South Pass, then on to the Oregon coast. Prior to 1848, a southern route seemed unfeasible since west of Texas it would have to be built across Mexican territory. Yet with the acquisition of California and the Southwest in 1848, followed by the admission of California as a state and the organization of the territories of New Mexico and Utah in 1850, a southern route quickly gained favor, predictably among southerners. They argued that only a route across Texas and New Mexico would be practical, since it alone would pass through organized territory. A route farther north would have to cross through Indian Country, in violation of treaties with the Plains tribes. But this obstacle was removed after 1851 when the government negotiated new treaties with the Indians in which they consented to allow the building of roads across the Great Plains. Moreover, by then a movement was already afoot to bring territorial government to the unorganized region between the Missouri River and the Rocky Mountains.

Whitney's efforts to convince Congress to underwrite his railroad plan inevitably ran headlong into the great sectional dispute over the extension of slavery in the new western territories. The West would be economically tied to the section through which the proposed railroad passed. No matter whether it was to be the North or the South, the outcome would upset the delicate balance of slave and non-slave influence in Congress after the new western territories achieved statehood. The impact would be greatest in the Senate, where representation was based on statehood alone, and not population.

Between 1845 and 1852, both houses of Congress attempted to enact legislation for the building of a transcontinental railroad.

By then, several other routes were being promoted. Senator Thomas Hart Benton of Missouri was a major proponent of a route along the 38th parallel that would link St. Louis with San Francisco. In 1848–49, he had sent his son-in-law, the western explorer John C. Fremont, to evaluate it. Although Fremont's expedition met with disaster when it became lost in a blinding snowstorm in the Southern Rockies of present-day northern New Mexico, he later proclaimed that he had found an all-weather route through the mountains suitable for a railroad.

In 1853, a bill introduced by Senators William Gwin of California and Richard Brodhead of Pennsylvania was passed into law allocating $150,000 for a government study of the potential routes for a transcontinental railroad. It was hoped that the issue would be resolved by determining which route was the most practical solely from an engineering standpoint.

The War Department directed the surveys. It was one of the first undertakings of the newly installed administration of President Franklin Pierce and was carried out under the supervision of Secretary of War Jefferson Davis. Born in Kentucky and raised in Mississippi, Davis was a champion of states' rights and he supported the expansion of slavery into the western territories. A West Point graduate, he had frontier experience at army posts

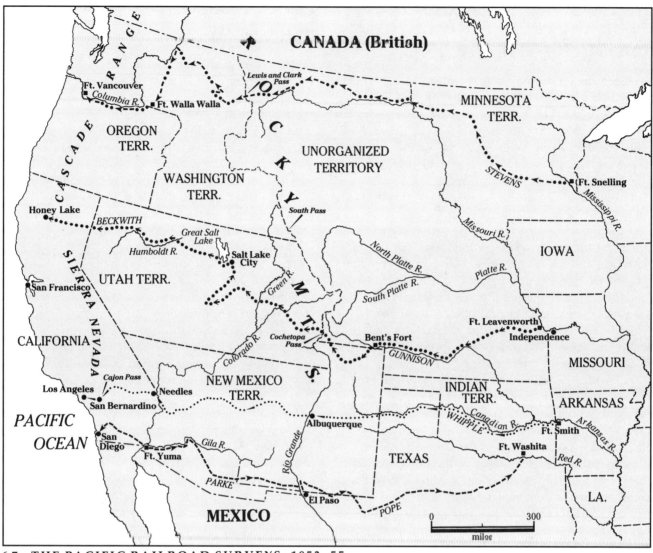

6.7 THE PACIFIC RAILROAD SURVEYS: 1853-55

throughout the Old Northwest and he was a veteran of the Black Hawk War. He married the daughter of Zachary Taylor in 1835, but she died three months after their wedding. Soon afterward, Davis left the military for the life of a Mississippi plantation owner. In 1845, he was elected to the House of Representatives but resigned the next year to serve under his one-time father-in-law in the Mexican War. He then served in the U.S. Senate until 1851, when he left to run for governor of Mississippi, an election that he lost by a narrow margin. Two years later, Pierce named him as Secretary of War.

Davis saw the railroad to the Pacific as more of a military necessity than a political issue. He viewed the Great Plains as the "Great American Desert" and could not imagine the region ever attracting settlement. For him, the primary reason for building the railroad was to enable the rapid deployment of troops to the West to control the Indians. Up until then, small frontier garrisons had been largely ineffective in this regard, having to de-

pend on long lines of supplies from the East. Instead, he proposed that the bulk of the frontier army be stationed at large installations on the fringe of the cultivated regions of the East, where they could obtain supplies from the surrounding country. From there, military expeditions could be dispatched when necessary, facilitated by the new railroad.

Of the surveys that were dispatched, the major ones involved explorations of the northernmost route between St. Paul, Minnesota and Puget Sound in Washington Territory; of Senator Benton's "Buffalo Trail"; and of two southern routes—one along the 35th Parallel between Fort Smith, Arkansas and Los Angeles, and the other from central Texas to San Diego.

Isaac Stevens, who President Pierce had just appointed as governor of the newly organized Washington Territory, commanded the survey of the northern route. In the spring of 1853, he led his team of topographical engineers westward from Fort Snelling near St. Paul.

Captain George B. McClellan was in charge of a second group of surveyors of the northern route, who headed eastward from the Puget Sound region. Stevens later reported favorably on the northern route in hopes of convincing the government that the projected Pacific railroad should pass through the Northern Plains of present-day Montana and terminate in Washington Territory. But McClellan was more candid about the problems of potential railroad construction in the Pacific Northwest. There were few suitable passes through the Cascade Range, and the difficulties involved in constructing a railroad through the region would make any such project too expensive to be practical.

That same spring, Captain John Williams Gunnison undertook a survey of the 38th Parallel route along Senator Benton's much touted "Buffalo Trail." From Fort Leavenworth in present-day western Kansas, he led his team westward to the upper Arkansas River to Bent's Fort. He then proceeded into the Sangre de Cristo Mountains and through Cochetopa Pass, retracing part of Fremont's earlier explorations of 1848–49. He managed to find a pass leading westward through the Wasatch Mountains that brought him to a point near Utah Lake in the Great Basin. From there, he followed the Sevier River southwestward, but in an attack by Ute Indians, Gunnison was killed along with nine other team members.

The survey of the 38th Parallel route was resumed in the spring of 1854 under the command of Lieutenant Edward G. Beckwith, who completed it from Salt Lake City, through the Sierra Nevada, to Honey Lake in northern California. Although the "Buffalo Trail" had proven practical from a topographical standpoint, the "Gunnison Massacre" underscored that the Indians could pose a greater problem than any mountain barrier, and the government soon lost interest in a railroad route through that part of the West.

A survey of a route across the Southern Plains, along the 35th Parallel, between Fort Smith, Arkansas, and Los Angeles, was more successful. Under Lieutenant Amiel W. Whipple's command, a team of topographical engineers followed the Canadian River westward to Albuquerque and beyond to the Colorado River at Needles, California. Although the route from there along the Old Spanish Trail to San Bernardino and Los Angeles was already well known, Whipple found that Cajon Pass, which led through the southern Sierra Nevada, would not be suitable for railroad construction.

Still farther south, a route along the 32nd Parallel was surveyed in various stages by teams commanded by Lieutenant John G. Pope and Lieutenant John G. Parke under him. They explored the region between Fort Yuma on the Gila River in present-day Arizona, El Paso in western Texas and Fort Washita on the Red River in

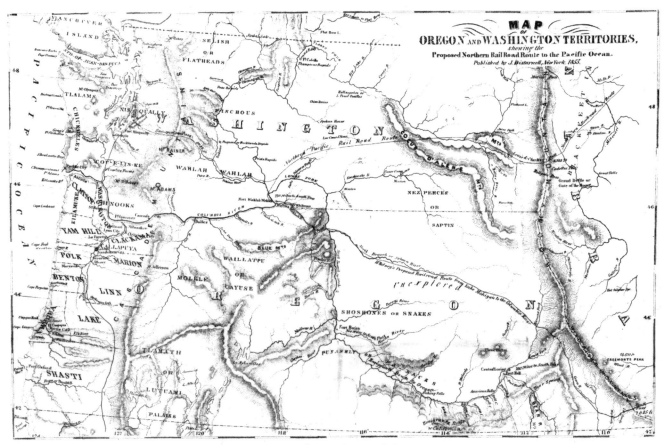

Proposed Northern Railroad Route, 1855 (Photo courtesy of the Library of Congress)

THE FIRST AND LAST U.S. ARMY CAMEL BRIGADE

One day in early August of 1857, a brightly painted red wagon approached an Indian village near Albuquerque, New Mexico. Trotting alongside it was a small group of animals, the likes of which had never before been seen in those parts. A crowd of Native Americans soon gathered around to take a closer look at these strange-looking beasts. One of the Indians approached and asked the white man driving the red wagon if this were a show wagon.

It was not. There was no circus coming to town, no monkeys and certainly no performing horses. What's more, the man in the red wagon was no showman. He was Edward Fitzgerald Beale, formerly a lieutenant in the United States Navy, and most recently Superintendent of Indian Affairs in California and Nevada. At the time, he was in command of a unique wagon road survey, the first to employ camels to traverse the "Great American Desert."

The project was the brainchild of Secretary of War Jefferson Davis. In 1848, Davis, then serving as senator from Mississippi, got the idea from an army officer, Major Henry C. Wayne, who was visiting Washington, D.C. Camels had been used by the French army in desert regions of North Africa for years. Why not employ them to carry supplies to military outposts in the remote southwestern regions of the newly acquired Mexican cession? That area had long been thought of as part of The Great American Desert. Camels could travel farther in that arid climate, and make do with less water than the mules then in use.

In 1853, soon after his appointment as Secretary of War to President Franklin Pierce, Davis immediately began promoting the scheme. It was not until March of 1855 that Congress took up Davis' suggestion. An appropriation of $30,000 was added to the annual allotment for military spending, and earmarked for "the purchase and importation of camels." Two months later, a U.S. Navy vessel, the *Supply,* sailed to Europe and the Middle East to carry out the plan. In charge of the expedition was Major Wayne, who first stopped in England to study camels at the London Zoo, went to Tunis where he obtained three camels, then sailed on to Turkey. The Crimean War was then raging, and Wayne learned that the British forces involved relied on camels as both draft animals as well as for cavalry mounts.

Edward F. Beale (Photo courtesy of the Library of Congress)

In Alexandria, Egypt, Wayne obtained a special permit to export camels, and in January of 1856 the *Supply* sailed back to the United States carrying 33 camels. One of them was so big that a hole had to be cut in the ceiling of the camel stable to provide enough room for the animal's hump.

Three months later, the ship landed at the port of Indianola, Texas, near Galveston, and the camels were then taken inland to Camp Verde, outside of San Antonio. A second shipment of camels arrived a few months later, bringing the total to 76. At Camp Verde, some observers expressed doubts about the strength of the camels. In response, Wayne showed some skeptics that the animals could carry loads weighing as much as 1,200 pounds.

In June of 1857, the War Department ordered that a survey be made of the wagon route across the southwestern desert from Fort Defiance in present-day Arizona, westward to the Colorado River and California. In addition to the survey, the expedition was to test the usefulness of the camels as pack animals in the Southwest. Edward F. Beale was in charge of the undertaking. Some years before, while exploring Death Valley with frontiersman Kit Carson, Beale had also hit upon the idea of using camels

The Landing of the Camels (Photo courtesy of the Library of Congress)

in the waterless tracts of the western deserts. His interest had come from the travel accounts of French explorer Abbe Huc, who had described the extensive use of camels for travel and commerce in the deserts of Asia in his book *Travels in China and Tartary*.

Soon after the start of the expedition, some of the camels became sick. But by the time the expedition had reached the Pecos River region of western Texas, the camels had recovered, carrying out their tasks with remarkable efficiency. They could travel up to 26 hours without water, and could live on local vegetation and thrive.

Beale and his "Camel Corps" then proceeded northward up the Rio Grande into central New Mexico.

The entire trip to the Colorado River was completed without any difficulties, thanks in large part to the splendid performance of the camels.

Once across the Colorado River, Beale took the camels to Los Angeles, where he paraded them through the streets, to the delight of the local inhabitants. He then brought them to Fort Tejon, 90 miles to the north near present-day Bakersfield, California. The camels remained there for the next few months, during which time Beale brought some of them high up into the Sierra Nevada to test their abilities in winter weather. They performed quite well in snows two- and three-feet deep, and were able to retrieve a snowbound supply wagon—a task that had stymied the efforts of a team of six mules.

The next spring, the camels were used on an east-bound expedition to the Colorado, during which they helped transport the first mail along the 35th Parallel route.

Despite the great praise that Beale and others had for the performance of the camels, their use did not catch on. They tended to frighten horses and mules, and western wranglers could never accustom themselves to handling these exotic beasts. The improvement of stagecoach service across the Southwest further discouraged continued use of camels.

With the outbreak of the Civil War in 1861, the government's interest turned away from developing overland transportation routes across the West. Moreover, the introduction of camels was too much identified with Jefferson Davis, and no project inspired by the man who had become the president of the Confederacy could continue to receive much support from the federal government.

After the war, the army sold its camels to circuses and zoos in the West. In the course of their use in the wagon route survey, however, some of the camels had wandered away and lived on for years in the isolated canyons of the western deserts. Indian and cowboy tales continued to speak of camel sightings for years to come, although none of the stories were confirmed. As recently as 1907, however, a Nevada newspaper reported that a prospector had come upon several camels wandering about in the desert, perhaps descendants of animals from the government's brief experiment with camels in the Great American Desert.

central Texas, as well as between Fort Yuma and San Diego in California. Although the 32nd Parallel route seemed feasible, the lack of water posed a serious problem for any projected railroad. But Davis later recommended this route in his 1855 report to Congress.

As a southerner with strong sectional ties, Jefferson Davis supported any route that would favor the South. To counter charges that he was forsaking practicality for the sake of sectional loyalty, he undertook several projects to prove the viability of the route. He sent teams out to drill artesian wells, hoping that would overcome the problem of the scarcity of water. When this project met with no success, he imported camels from the Middle East and introduced them along the southern route to demonstrate that these animals, who required much less water than mules or horses, could be employed to haul supplies for a railroad construction project through the southwestern desert. Neither artesian wells nor camels would win the support of northerners or the powerful Missouri and Illinois delegations in Congress. By the time the Pacific railroad surveys had been completed, all of Davis' efforts to win approval for the southern route had been derailed by the passage of the Kansas–Nebraska Act of 1854. With the establishment of organized territory in the Great Plains, the major objections to a central railroad route had been removed. At the same time, the Kansas–Nebraska Act allowed the spread of slavery into the new western territories and thereby threatened to increase the power of the South in Congress. Northerners would never approve government support for a railroad that would tie the West economically to the South.

As it turned out, the debate over which route would be used for the first transcontinental railroad was resolved only after the southern states seceded from the Union in 1861. With southern opposition removed, the central route easily won approval in Congress.

STEPHEN DOUGLAS AND THE KANSAS–NEBRASKA ACT

On January 23, 1854, Senator Stephen A. Douglas of Illinois introduced a bill that would provide territorial government to the unorganized region west of the Missouri River and north of the 37th Parallel. The proposed law promised to resolve the sectional controversy over the extension of slavery in the West and open the way for the construction of a transcontinental railroad. But as it turned out, Douglas' plan only exacerbated the issue, tore party loyalties asunder and set the stage for a bloody conflict that proved to be a prelude to the Civil War.

Stephen Arnold Douglas was a native of Vermont. After having studied law in upstate New York, he headed westward to Illinois in 1833, where he launched his political career. A Democrat in the tradition of Andrew Jackson, Douglas was a politician of unflagging energy, a trait that earned him the nickname of "Steam Engine in Britches." A man of modest physical stature (he was five feet four inches tall), his prodigious efforts nonetheless also made him known as "The Little Giant."

Douglas won election to the House of Representatives in 1843, and four years later he was elected to the Senate. A staunch adherent to the policy of Manifest Destiny, he advocated U.S. sovereignty over Oregon and the annexation of Texas. In the wake of the Mexican War of 1846–48, which Douglas supported, he promoted the doctrine of Popular Sovereignty, maintaining that the question of slavery be resolved by the people of new territories and states, without interference by the federal government. In this regard, he was a leading sponsor of the Compromise of 1850, which resulted in the admission of California as a free state, and left the slavery issue to be determined by the people of the newly organized territories of Utah and New Mexico.

Another major piece of legislation that Douglas was instrumental in engineering through Congress in 1850 was a land grant bill for the building of a railroad linking Lake Michigan at Chicago with the Gulf Coast at Mobile, Alabama. As a result of his efforts, the states of Illinois, Mississippi and Alabama were able to obtain from the federal government a six-mile-wide right-of-way in alternate sections along the route, an area comprising more than 2.5 million acres. This enactment set the precedent for later railroad land grants that would ultimately make possible the building of the first transcontinental railroad in the late 1860s.

Douglas was keenly interested in the development of railroads, not only to encourage national expansion, but to further his own financial interests. He owned extensive real estate holdings around Chicago and knew that their value would rise with the building of railroads through the area. When Congress began to seriously consider a route for a railroad to the Pacific in the early 1850s, Douglas turned his efforts to promoting a central route whose eastern terminus would be Chicago.

Before Jefferson Davis was able to present the results of the Pacific Railroad Surveys before Congress, Douglas was already working to clear the way for the approval of the central route. During his first term in Congress, in 1844, he had campaigned to transform the region west of Iowa and Missouri, the remaining lands of the Louisiana Purchase, into the proposed territory of Nebraska. Such a step would be a prerequisite for any railroad project, since private investors would require local freight business and settlers along the route to make the project profitable. Such conditions could arise only if the area came under a territorial government.

In 1851, midway through Douglas' first term in the Senate, the Treaty of Fort Laramie marked the beginning of the end of the government's policy of maintaining the Great Plains as a preserve for the Indians. But the way was still not clear for the territorial organization of the Great Plains. Under the terms of the Missouri Compromise of 1820, the region north of 36°30′, the southern boundary of the state of Missouri, was still closed to the spread of slavery. Any new territory to the west of Missouri would have to comply with this provision. As it stood, the North would block any legislation that added slave territory, and the South would stand in the way of any move that extended free territory.

As chairman of the Senate's Committee on Territories, Douglas was in an advantageous position to end the deadlock with a radical proposal. His Kansas–Nebraska Bill would provide for the creation of not one, but two new territories: Kansas, the area between the 37th and 40th parallels and westward to the Rocky Mountains (comprising all of present-day Kansas and part of central Colorado); and Nebraska, an area extending northward from the 40th Parallel to the Canadian border and westward to the eastern edge of Washington and Utah territories (comprising all of present-day Nebraska, most of present-day North and South Dakota and Montana, and portions of what would become Wyoming and eastern Colorado).

To appease both the North and South, Douglas attached the provision that the slavery issue in the new territories would be determined by the principle of Popular Sovereignty when these territories were ready to seek admission to the Union as states. As an extra added attraction to the South, a rider was added to the bill that explicitly repealed the Missouri Compromise.

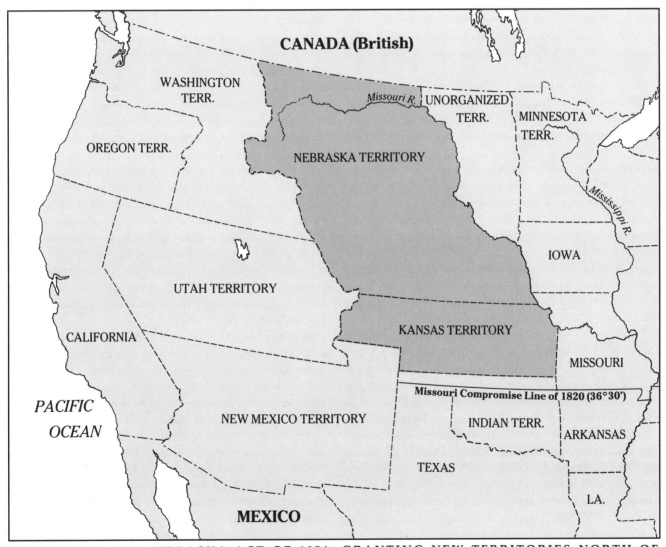

6.8 THE KANSAS–NEBRASKA ACT OF 1854, GRANTING NEW TERRITORIES NORTH OF THE MISSOURI COMPROMISE LINE THE OPTION OF CHOOSING OR BANNING SLAVERY

Although the measure ostensibly opened up a large area of the nation to slavery where it had once been forbidden by the Missouri Compromise (causing no small outrage among anti-slavery interests in the North), Douglas felt sure that the proposed law would ultimately satisfy both the North and the South. While the new territory of Kansas would no doubt attract settlers from adjoining pro-slavery Missouri, Nebraska to the north would be settled by immigrants from the free states of Iowa and the Old Northwest. In this way both the North and the South could look forward to the addition of one slave and one free state, thus maintaining the balance of slave and free states in Congress.

For his part, Douglas hoped to gain the gratitude of his home state of Illinois. He had opened the way for approval of a central route for the proposed railroad to the Pacific, the eastern terminus of which could be located in that state, hopefully at Chicago. The South would happily give up its support for the southern route now that it had won more territory for the extension of slavery. Moreover, for bringing about a peaceful resolution to the great sectional debate over slavery, Douglas hoped to gain national support for a run for the White House.

With the endorsement of President Franklin Pierce and the support of southern Democrats, the Kansas–Nebraska bill was passed into law in May of 1854. Yet rather than settle the great sectional controversy over the extension of slavery, the new law only widened the gulf between North and South. Although hailed in the South as a victory for states' rights and southern interests, the Kansas–Nebraska Act was condemned in the North for permitting the spread of slavery into an area that for 34 years had been deemed inviolate of any incursion of that "peculiar institution."

Contrary to what Douglas may have hoped, his efforts won him more scorn than praise. As an advocate of national expansion, he saw the slavery question as the chief obstacle to the realization of the nation's full potential. But anti-slavery Whigs (the political descendants of the party of Thomas Jefferson, John-Quincy Adams and Henry Clay) and free-soil Democrats recoiled at the prospect of the spread of slavery and left their respective parties to form a new coalition. Known as the Republican Party, it originated at an anti–Kansas–Nebraska rally held at Ripon, Wisconsin, while the controversial bill was still under consideration. Abraham Lincoln, a prominent Illinois lawyer and one-time Whig who had lost his seat in the House as a result of his opposition to the Mexican War, soon became a leading Republican force in his home state. His stand against the Kansas–Nebraska Act would propel him to the forefront of national politics.

At the same time, the Democratic Party gained strength in the South as pro-slavery southern Whigs defected to the Democrats, now seeing that party as the true champion of their interests.

Stephen Douglas had hoped that through the application of Popular Sovereignty, national attention would be diverted away from the divisive issue of slavery, thereby strengthening the Union and encouraging the nation's expansion westward. He had envisaged the Kansas–Nebraska Act as the first step in creating "a continuous line of settlements to the Pacific Ocean" and removing the political obstacles that stood in the way of the construction of a transcontinental railroad. Instead, his efforts led to open confrontation between pro- and anti-slave forces in Kansas as soon as the territory was opened for settlement in July of 1854. Rather than bring him national acclaim for his efforts to resolve the slavery issue, Stephen Douglas instead gained the enmity of both abolitionists and so-called "free-soilers" (those who opposed the spread of slavery only in the West).

The Kansas-Nebraska Act had alienated a significant number of free-soil Democrats in the South and in the border states. It had also caused the defection of northern free-soilers and abolitionists to the newly formed Republican party. In the presidential race of 1856, the Democrats declined to nominate Stephen Douglas as their candidate. To run the man most identified with the unpopular Kansas–Nebraska Act would no doubt cost them the election. Instead, they chose James Buchanan, who happened to be out of the country when the law was in the process of being passed.

In 1858, Douglas presented a bill before Congress that he hoped would lead to the realization of one of the primary goals of the Kansas–Nebraska Act: a railroad to the Pacific that followed the route from Chicago through South Pass to San Francisco. Yet by then sectional animosities had become so inflamed by the turmoil stirred up by the Kansas–Nebraska Act (and the subsequent Supreme Court decision in the Dred Scott case) that the South refused to approve any measure that would so greatly benefit the North.

Undaunted, Douglas responded with yet another sweeping compromise measure. He proposed that the government subsidize three railroads: one running along the northern route from Wisconsin to Puget Sound; another from Missouri or Iowa to San Francisco; and a southern route across Texas to Los Angeles or San Diego. Although the three-route plan presented a solution, Congress dragged its feet on the issue, refusing to pay so high a price for placating sectional interests.

Also in 1858, Douglas ran against Lincoln in his bid to secure his seat as senator from Illinois. In that contest, highlighted by the famous Lincoln–Douglas debates, Douglas' position on the extension of slavery and Popular Sovereignty now proved to be a liability; although he won reelection to the Senate, he lost national support among pro-slavery voters who now found his stand to be not extreme enough to their liking. The next year, he found himself caught in the middle of the congressional debate over a bill for a federal slave code, which if enacted could have imposed laws allowing slavery in a territory over the objections of a majority of its people. Douglas voted against the bill, maintaining that it violated his ideal of Popular Sovereignty. That further eroded his support among southerners.

In the presidential campaign of 1860, Douglas finally received his party's endorsement. But by this time the Democrats were so divided they nominated two candidates for president, Douglas and John G. Breckinridge, who backed the more extreme pro-slavery position that supported the federal government's right to legalize slavery in the territories. With the Democratic vote thus divided, Douglas lost the election to Abraham Lincoln.

BLEEDING KANSAS

In 1541–52, fifty years after Christopher Columbus first set foot in the Americas, Spanish explorer Francisco Vasquez de Coronado led a band of conquistadors eastward from New Mexico and across the Southern Plains into Kansas, hoping to find the fabled Seven Cities of Cibola. Led there by a Plains Indian with tales of gold, Coronado found the grass huts of Indian villages—probably Pawnee—near the site of present-day Lindborg, but no treasure.

Although nominally claimed by Spain, Kansas held neither precious minerals nor a large enough native population to exploit. Consequently, the Spanish tended to shun the area, viewing it as unsuitable for their usual pattern of colonization in the Americas. They made no efforts to establish settlements there, and in later years Spain's attention was diverted to her western dominions of New Mexico and California.

The French were next on the scene. When French explorer Robert La Salle traced the Mississippi to its outlet on the Gulf of Mexico in 1684, he claimed for France all the land adjoining every stream that drained into the mighty river. As a result, France soon came to view Kansas as part of the Louisiana Country, an idea that was not popular with the Spanish. But French traders made more inroads into the region. Although Spain protested, it did little to enforce its claim of sovereignty over any territory north of Texas.

The question was formally settled in 1763, when, in order to keep it out of the hands of the British, France ceded all of Louisiana to Spain. Spain held onto Kansas for the next 40 years then returned it to France—along with the rest of Louisiana—during the Napoleonic Wars. The region changed hands for the last time when it was acquired by the United States from France in the Louisiana Purchase of 1803.

The Missouri River region of Kansas was explored by Lewis and Clark in the course of their 1804–06 expedition. Zebulon Pike traversed Kansas in 1807, as did Stephen H. Long in 1819. In the early 1820s, traders from Missouri began crossing Kansas along the Santa Fe Trail. The first permanent white settlement was established at Fort Leavenworth in 1827. Later emigrants and gold-seekers of the 1840s passed through Kansas on the first leg of the Oregon Trail.

For the next 24 years, Kansas remained the heart of Indian Country. Seen as an empty expanse, unbroken by mountains and with little timber, most of Kansas offered neither the climate nor the type of soil to attract traditional frontier farmers of the 1820s and 1830s.

Yet eastern Kansas was not unlike the adjoining area of western Missouri whose pro-slavery farmers and plantation owners had, by the 1840s, begun to eye the region. Even though the Indian Intercourse Act of 1834 forbade white settlement, squatters persisted in carving out unlawful homesteads west of the Permanent Indian Frontier. The U.S. Army, charged with maintaining the region as a preserve for the Indians who lived there, evicted many of these pioneer trespassers, but many others merely left for a short time only to return and illegally settle on other lands on the eastern fringe of Indian Country. With the outbreak of the Mexican War in 1846, the army's attention shifted southward, leaving the way open for more illegal settlers to seep through the Permanent Indian Frontier and into eastern Kansas.

By the time the army returned to the region after 1848, the nation's military frontier had moved westward to the shores of the Pacific. As a result, Indian Country no longer served as a natural defensive barrier against foreign invasion, but now loomed as an impediment to white settlement. Just as King George's Proclamation Line of 1763, in the years prior to the onset of the American Revolution in 1775, had failed to keep American pioneers from moving into the Mississippi and Ohio valleys, the Permanent Indian Frontier had little hope of keeping the tide of settlement from pouring onto the Great Plains.

Throughout the 1840s, national perceptions about the so-called "Great American Desert" had begun to change. Western explorer John C. Fremont brought back reports that the region had the potential to support agriculture. Emigrants traveling westward with wagon trains could depend on the abundant grasslands to feed their livestock. Many pioneers in western Iowa and Illinois, equipped with new and improved farm implements and machinery, had already found that land able to support huge herds of wild buffalo could also be used to cultivate wheat. The root-matted subsoil of the prairies had long been an obstacle to cultivation, but in the 1840s a steel-bladed plow developed by John Deere of Illinois enabled

CYRUS McCORMICK AND HIS MECHANICAL REAPER

In 1831, the United States had just set aside most of the lands between the Missouri River and the Rocky Mountains as Indian Country. This vast area, which encompassed most of the Great Plains north of Texas, was viewed as unfit for agriculture and suitable only as hunting grounds for Indian peoples.

Yet in the summer of that year, in Rockbridge County, Virginia, a 22-year old farmer's son named Cyrus McCormick would demonstrate an invention that would bring drastic changes to what was long thought of as "The Great American Desert."

Cyrus McCormick grew up on his family's farm in Virginia's Shenandoah Valley. He worked closely with his father Robert, also a blacksmith and a part-time inventor who had spent years trying to perfect a machine that could reap grain. After 20 years without success, the elder McCormick gave up on the project and turned to running his iron foundry. Nonetheless, young Cyrus persisted in his efforts and, employing completely different principles, he succeeded in designing a working model of an automatic reaping machine.

In June of 1831, McCormick hitched his device to a team of horses and demonstrated his reaper to a crowd assembled in a field next to a local tavern. The reaper worked fine, but it made such a clatter that the horses pulling it had to be calmed by men walking alongside them.

McCormick did nothing with his invention for the next three years. It was only when he learned that Obed Hussey of Maine had developed a different type of reaper that McCormick applied for a patent on his machine, which he received in 1834.

Even then, McCormick did not try to market his invention, although he did produce a few reapers that he sold locally in Virginia beginning in 1841. By that time, he had improved his reaper so that it made less noise and could not only cut grain but bound it into sheaves. Soon afterward, he entered the farm machinery business in earnest. Sales grew to such an extent that by 1847 McCormick had opened a factory in Chicago and before long another one in Cincinnati. In 1851, he sold 1,000 reapers; six years later, the figure exceeded 20,000, and profits from his enterprise earned him more than a million dollars.

The McCormick Reaper consisted of a reel that gathered in the grain, a vibrating blade to cut it and

Cyrus McCormick (Photo courtesy of the Library of Congress)

a platform on which the cut grain was collected. The whole device was powered by a main drive wheel that turned as the horses pulled the device through the field.

McCormick's reaper could cut up to 12 acres of grain a day, as compared to only two acres that a man could do in a day by hand. The machine was to revolutionize farming by making it possible for small family farms to cultivate profitably much larger tracts of land. Moreover, larger farms no longer needed to rely on expensive seasonal labor to carry on harvesting, thereby increasing profits as well as output.

When McCormick's patent expired in 1848, he was faced with stiff competition from other farm equipment makers who were now free to manufacture his type of machine. To meet this challenge, he turned to innovative sales techniques. He advertised extensively, and he offered a warranty for his products. His greatest coup was offering to sell his reaper on credit. In this way, farmers with little cash could obtain his equipment, use it to harvest a profitable crop, then pay for the reaper in installments over the course of several seasons.

As a result of McCormick's invention, farm output skyrocketed. Even though tremendous farm surpluses forced prices down, farmers were producing so much that they still prospered. The farming revolution whetted farmers' appetites for larger and cheaper tracts of land. Their eyes turned to the West where government lands were still available at very low prices in Iowa and in the newly organized territories of Kansas and Nebraska.

In 1851, McCormick took his invention to England where he displayed it in the Great Exhibition in London. Even though the *Times* of London chided the design as resembling a "cross between a chariot, a wheelbarrow, and a flying machine," McCormick's invention won him the exhibition's first prize for farm machinery. Two years later, at an industrial exposition in New York City, McCormick was accorded similar high honors. The French Academy of Science later hailed McCormick as having "done more for agriculture than any man living."

What McCormick had done was also to have a great impact on the settlement of the nation's heartland. His reaper made prairie farming on a grand scale possible. It industrialized agriculture in the North and West in much the same way Eli Whitney's cotton gin created the southern Cotton Kingdom a half-century before. Yet unlike the cotton gin, McCormick's invention fostered the spread of free labor and not slavery. It encouraged both the large-scale farmer and the individual sodbuster of the prairies to cultivate huge tracts of land, undertakings that would have been unthinkable without the type of mechanization he introduced.

There were other sweeping effects. As farm production expanded by leaps and bounds, food costs plummeted. Workers could now afford to live on wages, causing many to abandon subsistence farming and flock to the industrialized cities of the North and East. The railroads of the Midwest and the Northeast, essential for transporting the farm products of the Midwest and the Old Northwest to markets in the East, likewise prospered. The slave-based agriculture of the South came to seem even more cumbersome and barbaric when compared to the mechanized agriculture that was booming on the prairies. One of McCormick's reapers, pulled by a team of horses, could turn an acre of wheat faster than 20 men equipped with hand-cutting tools.

Cyrus McCormick's business enterprise grew to become one of the largest manufacturers of farm equipment in the world. He later purchased the rights to other types of farm machinery, such as the automatic thresher and the twine binder. Upon his death in 1902, his son Cyrus, Jr., merged the company with two other firms to create International Harvester, which became an industrial giant in the 20th century.

After the Civil War and the demise of the slave-based agriculture of the South, McCormick's reapers helped spread industrialized agriculture to the Great Plains. The United States turned from importing grain to become the world's foremost grain-exporting nation.

The Mechanical Reaper (Photo courtesy of the Library of Congress)

western farmers to cut through it with ease. Factories in Chicago and Cincinnati were producing Cyrus McCormick's mechanical reaper and other farm machinery that enabled individual farmers to produce huge surpluses. Equally as dramatic as the increase in farm production was the rise in demand, as industrialization brought rapid economic and population growth to the cities of the Old Northwest and the East. As a result, wheat became an important cash crop, more than doubling in price between 1851 and 1855.

Along with the prospect of rising farm prices, the growth of railroads gave further incentive for the westward advance of agricultural settlement. In the 1840s, spurred on by financing from Boston, New York and Philadelphia, railroad construction had created a network of transportation links throughout the Ohio and Mississippi Valleys.

Built as extensions of such eastern lines as the Pennsylvania, Baltimore & Ohio, Erie and the New York Central, these western railroads provided a cheap way to ship goods and farm products between the eastern prairies and the river and Great Lakes ports of the Old Northwest and points eastward. Western lands once deemed too remote from the natural highways of the Missouri–Mississippi River system were now joined by a cobweb of rails that stretched throughout the Ohio and Mississippi Valleys, linking them with centers of trade at Chicago, St. Louis and Milwaukee.

In 1856, trains first rolled across the Mississippi River on the Chicago & Rock Island Railroad's newly opened bridge between Rock Island, Illinois, and Davenport, Iowa. Beyond Iowa lay Kansas, with its prairies newly deemed fertile and largely devoid of any significant white settlement. Coronado had been lured to Kansas by the fabled golden riches of Cibola. Now Kansas beckoned Americans with the promise of the wealth to be gleaned from golden fields of wheat.

The nation's appetite for more farmland had been whetted, and the Midwest seemed to present a ready and bountiful banquet of new opportunities for expansion. Within three years of the Fort Laramie Treaty of 1851 and subsequent treaties, the vast area between the Great Bend of the Missouri River and the Rocky Mountains had ceased to be considered as Indian Country. The Indian nations were cajoled and coerced into giving up their vast hunting grounds over which they had freely roamed for generations in exchange for presents, annuities and small reservations. The way was thus cleared for the organization of the Great Plains as territories.

Since the Northwest Ordinance of 1787, territories had been organized only after they had developed a population sufficient to warrant local government and representation in Congress. But both Kansas and Nebraska had been borne out of expediency; they were created mainly as a means to provide a band of bonafide real estate for the right of way of a proposed Pacific railroad.

As predicted, geography and not politics quickly settled the slavery issue in Nebraska. The area around the junction of the Platte and Missouri rivers, near present-day Omaha, drew the most settlers. Although their numbers were small, they were comprised mostly of free-soilers from Iowa and Illinois, and through the successful exercise of Popular Sovereignty, their territorial legislature easily enacted measures that discouraged slavery. Nonetheless, the territory's small population was in no hurry for admission as a free or any other kind of state, and so delayed achieving statehood until after the Civil War had resolved the slavery dispute.

Kansas would be a different story. Here was a new territory in which the slavery issue was to be determined by its people, but its people had not yet settled there. Kansas Territory, just one step away from statehood—with the principle of Popular Sovereignty to decide the issue—could possibly become a free state. That prospect alarmed pro-slavery and states' rights advocates in adjoining Missouri, who would be surrounded on three sides by free states and would have to contend with a new haven for runaway slaves to the west.

Moreover, the entire South had a vested interest in the outcome of the slavery issue in Kansas. Nearly all of Kansas lay north of the 36°30' line, beyond which the Missouri Compromise of 1820 had banned slavery. But in 1854 the Kansas–Nebraska Act had explicitly repealed that restriction on the spread of slavery; southerners, eager to assert their newly defined right to extend slavery into the new western territories, were not about to let Popular Sovereignty and the democratic process stand in their way.

Few southerners actually planned to use slaves in Kansas. Its prairies might yield wheat and corn, but the area was not especially inviting for the expansion of the Cotton Kingdom. Furthermore, most slave owners were reluctant to bring slaves into a region where they could risk losing their valuable human property should the vote go the wrong way. The real prize that Kansas presented for the South was increased power in the House of Representatives and two more southern votes in the Senate in support of states' rights.

In the North, opponents of slavery were equally alarmed at the possibility that Kansas could fall into pro-slavery hands. They condemned the existence of slavery anywhere in the nation as antithetical to the principles of liberty and freedom on which the country had been founded. If the slavery question were to be decided by Popular Sovereignty, the only way to assure a free Kansas would be to flood the territory with an overwhelmingly free-soil electorate.

In April of 1854, two months before the Kansas–Nebraska Act was signed into law, Eli Thayer—a prominent abolitionist and member of the Massachusetts legislature from Worcester—was already making preparations to manipulate Popular Sovereignty for the sake of the free-soil cause. In the 1840s, he was instrumental in establishing Oread College as the first four-year women's college in America. The school had been founded as a profit-making enterprise, thus joining the ideal of providing education for women with the practicality of a successful business venture. With his Massachusetts Emigrant Aid Company, Thayer hoped to accomplish a similar dual good: winning Kansas as a free state and making money for his investors.

The Massachusetts Emigrant Aid Company received its charter by an act of the state legislature on April 26, 1854. A week later, the company held its first meeting in Boston. Thayer planned to recruit a vanguard of several thousand New Englanders to settle in Kansas. Not only would the Emigrant Aid Company finance their journey, but it would also invest in real estate and develop townsites in Kansas. With the seeds of settlement thus sown, more free-soil emigrants would be encouraged to head for Kansas, their numbers drawn from the hundreds of thousands of Americans who migrated west each year as well as from the nearly half-million emigrants who arrived annually from foreign shores.

In this way, the company would not only attain the idealistic end of a free Kansas, but within a few short years, Thayer predicted, it would also earn a handsome profit from the sale of its Kansas holdings which by then would have markedly increased in value as a result of Kansas' growth as a free state.

Thayer proposed that the company aim to raise five million dollars to "plant a free state in Kansas." But Thayer's plan drew criticism from his wealthiest supporters, who were concerned that public opinion would charge them with being driven more by the profit motive than by the desire to keep slavery out of Kansas. As a result, the company was reorganized in early 1855 as the New England Emigrant Aid Society at the insistence of its chief benefactor, Massachusetts textile tycoon Amos Lawrence. Under the new charter, the group abandoned its plan to function as a business and instead became a charitable institution whose sole aim would be to insure that Kansas become a free state.

While the New England Emigrant Aid Society did manage to finance the emigration of a fair amount of anti-slavery settlers from New England to Kansas in the next few years, the number of settlers they actually sent did not exceed more than 1,500. Most northerners who did move West in the years 1854–58 headed for the more secure areas of the Ohio and Mississippi valleys, where plenty of good land was still available at low government prices.

Although Thayer's scheme never approached the grand scope he had envisaged, when news reached western Missouri of a $5 million Yankee plot to flood Kansas with free-staters, the reaction was one of alarm and anger. Even earlier, in 1853, pro-slavery Senator David Rice Atchison had urged supporters in Weston, Missouri to take up arms against this very possibility.

Originally from Frogtown, Kentucky, David R. Atchison became a lawyer on the Missouri frontier in the 1830s. He served in the state legislature before becoming a U.S. senator in 1843. Even though he strongly supported national expansion, Atchison was nonetheless a champion of Indian rights, and campaigned in the Senate to ensure the government upheld its obligations in carrying out the terms of Indian treaties.

Together with Senator Stephen A. Douglas, Atchison played a major role in bringing about the passage of the Kansas–Nebraska Act in 1854. He was especially instrumental in making sure that the new law explicitly repealed the Missouri Compromise's ban on the extension of slavery in the new territories west of the Missouri River. When he learned of the plan to import a free-soil population into Kansas, he responded by taking a leave from his seat in the U.S. Senate to lead Missouri efforts to make Kansas a slave state.

Atkinson declared that if need be, he would drive out slavery opponents by force, threatening to "Mormonize" the abolitionists by dealing out the same treatment that had forced the Mormons to flee Missouri in 1839. (Interestingly, Atchison had once been the attorney for the Mormons in Missouri.)

The Society of Missourians for Mutual Protection was established to counter New England-based efforts to meddle in the outcome of the slavery issue in Kansas. Its avowed purpose was to insure the right of southern emigrants to Kansas to keep their slave property. When the new territory was opened for settlement in July of 1854, such efforts were unnecessary since hundreds of pro-slavery Missouri squatters were already occupying claims in northeastern Kansas. This region west of Kansas City and Fort Leavenworth, lying between the Kansas and Missouri rivers, was the natural gateway for settlers. Easily accessible by steamboat from St. Louis and the river ports of the Mississippi, the area would be the scene of the conflict that became known as "Bleeding Kansas."

Starting in June of 1854, the first towns in the new territory were established by pro-slavery settlers at Leavenworth, Atchison and Lecompton. At about the same time, the New England Emigrant Aid Society founded its first town on the Kansas River, naming it Lawrence, in honor of Amos Lawrence. Soon afterward, they established Topeka to the west and Osawatomie to the south.

The first territorial governor of Kansas was Andrew H. Reeder of Pennsylvania. Appointed by President Franklin Pierce, he was sympathetic to southern rights but

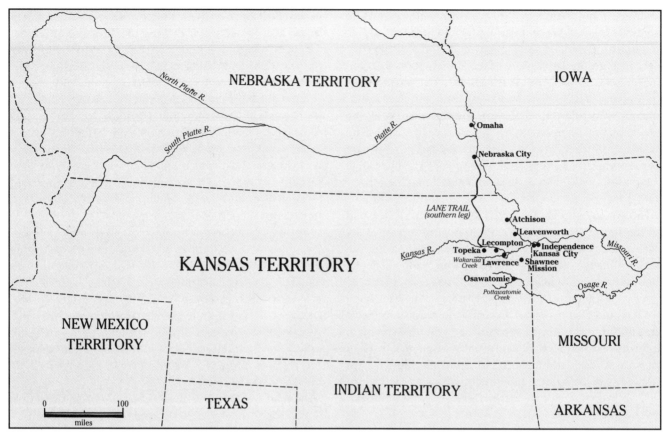

was also pledged to administer Kansas along the lines of Popular Sovereignty.

The first election in Kansas was held in November of 1854, the purpose of which was to elect a territorial delegate to Congress. At the time, pro-slavery and states' rights voters had a clear majority, their numbers swelled by the influx of settlers from nearby Missouri. Nonetheless, pro-slavery supporters were not taking any chances. To ensure the outcome in their favor, Atchison led a boisterous throng of pro-slavery Missouri frontiersman across the river and into Missouri to stuff the ballot boxes. Known as "Border Ruffians," they managed to cast more than 1,500 illegal ballots and win the election for the pro-slavery candidate. As it turned out, however, a subsequent census revealed that most of the legal votes had been cast by emigrants from Missouri and other slave states, and therefore, even without the aid of the bogus votes, the pro-slavery side would have easily won a victory without the help of the Border Ruffians.

The free-soilers and abolitionists protested, but were content to await the outcome of the election of the territorial legislature before taking any decisive action. That contest was held in March of 1855, and elicited a similar response from Senator Atchison and his pro-slavery Missouri followers. This time he brought an even larger

horde of Border Ruffians, numbering close to 5,000, who, plied with liberal amounts of free whiskey dispensed at booths near the polling places, overwhelmed the free-soil electorate and voted into office a pro-slavery majority to the legislature.

Free-soil settlers voiced their protests of fraud to Governor Reeder who ordered new elections. Yet the results of a second vote left the pro-slavery makeup of the Kansas territorial legislature unchanged. In response to the widespread election fraud, and to secure fair treatment for free-soilers, churches in New England and New York began sending rifles to aid the anti-slavery cause in Kansas. So many of the newly developed breech-loading Sharp's rifles were sent at the urging of Brooklyn, New York abolitionist preacher Henry Ward Beecher that the weapons soon became known as "Beecher's Bibles."

The pro-slavery legislature promptly passed laws that excluded anti-slavery adherents from holding public office, imposed fines for publicly advocating the abolition

Breech-loading Rifle (Molly Braun)

of slavery, and forbade the publication of any printed material that challenged the right to hold slaves in Kansas. Meanwhile, Governor Reeder protested the election fraud to President Pierce. The President, although a northerner from New Hampshire, held pro-southern sentiments, and he responded by removing Reeder from office and replacing him with another pro-slavery appointee, Wilson Shannon.

Kansas free-soilers refused to recognize what they considered a fraudulently elected pro-slavery legislature. Moreover, they held an election of their own to choose delegates to a constitutional convention that planned to petition the federal government for the immediate admission of Kansas as a free state. Needless to say, pro-slavery settlers boycotted the election.

The free-soil delegates met at Topeka in October of 1855 and established their own territorial legislature there. Soon Kansas had two elected governments, one at Shawnee Mission that was pro-slavery, and another at Topeka that was anti-slavery. Dr. Charles Robinson, a physician from Fitchburg, Massachusetts, and an organizer in Kansas for the New England Emigration Society, was named as the free-soil governor.

In November of 1855, tensions between the two sides erupted into violence after a free-soil farmer was killed by a pro-slavery settler in a dispute over a land claim. The pro-slavery man was not arrested, claiming self-defense. Demanding his prosecution, free-soilers reacted by burning the homes of pro-slavery settlers near Lawrence, by that time a stronghold of free-soil sentiment. Those responsible for this act were arrested by a pro-slavery sheriff, but free-soilers waylaid the sheriff and his posse and freed the prisoners.

Now it was the pro-slavery side's turn to vent their outrage. Again Missourians stormed into Kansas, and in the name of securing the rights of slaveholders, laid siege to the town of Lawrence. Prominent among them was David Atchison, in command of his so-called "Grand Army of Missouri," made up of some 1,500 Missouri frontiersmen. Governor Shannon, the pro-slavery appointee of President Pierce, managed to keep a lid on the situation and was able to get a pledge from the people of Lawrence that they would not resist the enforcement of territorial laws.

The calm that followed resulted more from the onset of severe winter weather than from the desire of either side to seek a peaceful resolution to the conflict. More isolated killings followed, committed by both free-soil and pro-slavery men. Reports sent back by journalists, mainly representing northern papers, tended to stress the atrocities committed by the pro-slavery side and to ignore the violence generated by free-soilers. As a result, public opinion went against the legally elected government of Kansas, and supported the struggle of the free-soilers whom the federal government deemed to be in rebellion.

Border Ruffians on the Way to Lawrence, Kansas (Photo courtesy of the Kansas State Historical Society)

The turmoil in Kansas reached a crescendo in May of 1856. A territorial judge pushed through an indictment of treason against the leaders of the illegal free-soil government. Many of these men lived in Lawrence, and that is where a horde of 800 Border Ruffians, now deputized as a posse, went to arrest them. After the town was surrounded, a peaceful settlement appeared at hand when the inhabitants of Lawrence decided to avert further violence and give in to the demands of the pro-slavery lawmen. Yet unexpectedly, a pro-slavery sheriff was shot and wounded in an isolated skirmish with free-soilers. Several days later, the army of pro-slavery Kansans and Border Ruffians descended on Lawrence and destroyed its principle building, the Free State Hotel, along with the offices of two free-soil newspapers. Shops were looted and the home of a the free-soil governor, Dr. Robinson, was burned to the ground.

Not far to the south, abolitionist John Brown heard of the attack on Lawrence while staying at his son's home at the settlement of Osawatomie. Originally from Connecticut, he had lived in New York and Ohio before becoming prominent as a leader of the anti-slavery cause in Pennsylvania. There he had been active with the Underground Railroad's efforts to aid fugitive slaves from the South on their flight to freedom in Canada. Brown arrived in Kansas in 1855 to join five of his sons who had settled there. To avenge what he took to be an insult to the honor of the abolitionist cause, on the night of May 23, 1855, he led a force of anti-slavery extremists to a settlement of pro-slavery sympathizers at Potawatomie Creek. Armed with cutlasses and guns, he seized five of the inhabitants; they were later found shot and hacked to death.

The "Potawatomie Massacre" instigated still more bloodshed. Free-soilers burned the homes of pro-slavery settlers, and pro-slavery advocates retaliated in kind against free-soilers. In reaction to the killings, armed pro-slavery forces barred free-soil emigrants and supplies bound for free-state settlements from reaching Kansas by way of the Missouri River and the overland routes from Missouri.

To circumvent the pro-slavery blockade, anti-slavery supporters in Chicago established a new overland trail from Iowa City, across Nebraska and southward to Topeka. Called the Lane Trail, after James Lane—a leader of militant anti-slavery forces in Kansas (known as "Jayhawkers," after a particularly ferocious bird of prey)—it was well-marked and dotted with aid stations for free-soil emigrants headed southward for Kansas. Soon the stream of free-state supporters and supplies resumed, with more direct aid funneled down the route from Chicago and northern Great Lakes cities.

Governor Wilson Shannon, exasperated by the futility of peacefully resolving a conflict between two sides who thought nothing of disregarding the law to achieve their respective ends, resigned in August 1856.

Shannon would be the second of the ten governors—six appointed by the President, and four sitting as acting governors—who would attempt to bring an end to the turmoil in Kansas between 1854 and 1861.

Meanwhile, the events in Kansas had stirred passions in Washington, D.C., on both sides of the issue. On May 19–20, 1856, as the pro-slavery forces were gathering for their assault on Lawrence, Senator Charles Sumner of Massachusetts delivered a stinging two-day diatribe against the Congressional supporters of the pro-slavery faction in Kansas. He verbally attacked "the Crime Against Kansas, the rape of a virgin territory, compelling it to the hateful embrace of slavery . . ."

In particular, his invective lashed out against Senate supporters of the Kansas–Nebraska Act, which he proclaimed had been enacted through "the mingled meanness and wickedness of the cheat." Sumner then singled out South Carolina Senator Andrew P. Butler, who he lambasted in lurid terms as: "A Don Quixote who had chosen a mistress to whom he has made his vows, and who . . . though polluted in the sight of the world, is chaste in his sight—I mean the harlot, Slavery."

These last remarks were too much for Butler's nephew, Preston Brooks, a congressman from South Carolina. A few days later, Brooks stormed into the Senate chamber and attacked Sumner with his gold-handled cane as the Massachusetts senator sat at his desk. Beaten severely about the head and shoulders, Sumner fell unconscious to the floor of the Senate. The attack left him disabled for the next three years. Southerners hailed Brooks as a defender of southern honor and states' rights. At the same time, the incident outraged northerners and incited many to rally around the anti-slavery cause in Kansas. For them, the specter of a "Bleeding Sumner" now joined "Bleeding Kansas" as embodying the tyranny that the South had foisted on the nation in its relentless campaign to spread slavery.

Back in Kansas, free-soilers had begun to arrive and stake out land claims in greater numbers than pro-slavery emigrants. For most settlers from free states, the desire for affordable land outweighed any concern to eliminate slavery. They tended to oppose slavery, but on economic rather than moral grounds. Enterprises based on free labor, they believed, would be at a disadvantage when pitted against an economy fueled by slavery.

Seeing that they soon might be outnumbered by a steady influx of free-soil settlers, pro-slavery forces in Kansas felt compelled to push through a pro-slavery constitution and seek admission as a slave state before it was too late. At a constitutional convention held at Lecompton in the fall of 1857, they proposed a pro-slavery constitution, although voters were presented with a choice of whether or not it would allow the further importation of slaves into Kansas.

Free-soilers, although permitted to participate in the constitutional convention, stayed away since to do otherwise would imply that they now recognized as legitimate a government that they believed had been established through fraud. In the territorial elections of December of 1857, free-soil men boycotted the polls. With mostly pro-slavery Kansas voting, the constitution naturally received approval with an overwhelming majority, even though nearly half of the 6,000 votes for it were later shown to have been fraudulently cast.

In the spring of 1858, having been ratified by at least one of Kansas' rival governments, the pro-slavery constitution was submitted to the president (by then James Buchanan, another pro-slavery northern Democrat), who endorsed it and passed it along to the Congress. By this time, however, the anti-slavery Republican Party had won enough seats in both the House and the Senate to halt Congressional approval of the Lecompton Constitution. Among those voting with the Republicans was Democratic Senator Stephen A. Douglas, who condemned the pro-slavery Lecompton Constitution as an affront to his principle of Popular Sovereignty. Although Democrats were able to maneuver passage of the pro-slavery Lecompton Constitution in the Senate, the House of Representatives succeeded in having it resubmitted to Kansas voters.

The free-soil legislature came to a dramatic end in July of 1856. It had planned to assemble at Topeka in direct defiance of an order from the President of the United States. On July 3, one day before the legislature was scheduled to meet, 200 federal mounted troops with light artillery, dispatched from Fort Leavenworth under the command of Colonel Edwin Sumner, arrived in Topeka. They lined up in front of the building where the legislature was meeting, their cannons poised and ready to fire. Colonel Sumner entered the assembly hall and ordered the legislators to disperse.

Many years earlier, a British officer had given this same order to a group of American rebels at Lexington, Massachusetts. His demand was then answered with "The shot heard round the world," which touched off the American Revolution. This time the rebels gave in. Thereafter, free-staters in Kansas worked to take control of the lawful legislature in order to win the state for their cause. Although they refused to take part in balloting that offered only a slave constitution, with their numbers swelled by the migration of predominantly free-soil pioneers, they soon won a majority in the Lecompton legislature.

Outbreaks of fighting still regularly plagued Kansas, with atrocities and attacks now carried out with equal vigor by both factions. Nonetheless, Popular Sovereignty was allowed to run its course. By August of 1858, enough free-soil votes could be mustered to defeat a referendum on the pro-slavery constitution by an overwhelming majority. Commenting on the outcome, J.H. Stringfellow, a leader of the pro-slavery side in Kansas, commented that the defeat of the Lecompton Constitution had shown that the issue of slavery "is settled against the South by immigration."

These election results notwithstanding, President Buchanan persisted in supporting the admission of Kansas under the pro-slavery Lecompton Constitution.

In the summer of 1859, free-soil Kansans drafted an anti-slavery constitution at Wyandotte. Although the admission of Kansas as a free state seemed assured, southern resistance in Congress and Buchanan's support for the Lecompton Constitution held the process up for the next two years.

By then Lincoln had replaced Buchanan, the anti-slavery Republican party had come to dominate both houses of Congress and all opposition from the southern states had become moot after many of them seceded from the Union. On January 29, 1861, Kansas, reduced to its present size, was admitted to the Union as a free state. By then its population had grown from a few hundred in 1854 to more than 100,000.

THE DRED SCOTT DECISION AND THE WEST

At a time when ballots, Border Ruffians and bullets were determining the future of slavery in Kansas, the U.S. Supreme Court stepped into the fray with its famous decision in the case of Dred Scott.

Dred Scott, a slave in Missouri, was owned by a U.S. Army surgeon. In the 1830s, his master had taken him to Fort Armstrong in Illinois, a free state under the Northwest Ordinance of 1787, and to Fort Snelling in Minnesota Territory, part of an area in which slavery had been prohibited by the Missouri Compromise of 1820. After residing for four years on free soil, Scott returned with his master to Missouri.

When Scott's owner died, the slave passed to his widow. She moved to Massachusetts to marry again, this time to a congressman with abolitionist sympathies. Scott remained behind in St. Louis, where he was hired out by an agent to do odd jobs. In 1846, encouraged by anti-slavery white friends (among them the son of one of his former owners), Scott was convinced to sue for his freedom on the ground that since he had resided in free territory he was no longer a slave. A lower court in Missouri agreed, but the Missouri Supreme Court reversed the decision. The case dragged on for nearly a decade until 1857, when the United States Supreme Court agreed to hear it.

The Supreme Court announced its decision in March of 1857, several days after James Buchanan took the oath of office as president of the United States, and while the conflict over slavery in Kansas was still raging. The court ruled that Scott's sojourns in Illinois and Minnesota Territory had no bearing on his status, and that upon his return to Missouri, he was still a slave.

That ruling alone would have settled the matter of Dred Scott, but Chief Justice Roger Brooke Taney, a southerner, was determined to use the case to pass judgment on the constitutionality of all federal bans against slavery. He declared that Scott had never resided in free territory since no territory could be made free by an act of Congress. To do so would be to prevent a slaveholder from bringing his property into a territory, and to ban property is to deprive its owner of the right to it. Therefore the Missouri Compromise, in banning slavery in the territory of the Louisiana Purchase north of the 36°30' line, was unconstitutional under the Fifth Amendment, which bars Congress from depriving a person of property without due process of law.

For northerners, even those who did not seek the abolition of slavery in the South, the Dred Scott decision meant that the spread of slavery into the western territories was now uncontainable. Any territory created by the federal government could be opened to slavery, despite any decision to the contrary based on Popular Sovereignty.

Pro-slavery and states' rights supporters in the South rejoiced at the news of the Dred Scott decision. Until that time, southerners were worried that with the addition of new free states in the West, they would soon be outnumbered in Congress. As a minority, they would then be subject to the will of the free states who some day could pass laws outlawing slavery throughout the nation. But with the Supreme Court's ruling in the Dred Scott case, westward expansion was no longer a threat to the South. The way was now open for the creation of new slave territories and states in the West that would help preserve slavery.

One immediate result was that President Buchanan, now empowered with the support of the federal judiciary, refused to recognize the free-state government in Kansas. The highest court of the land had deemed that slavery was a local and not a national issue; slavery could now be extended into the territories of Kansas and Nebraska and, theoretically, into every state of the Union.

The Dred Scott decision was denounced by abolitionists and northern moderates alike; they condemned it as part of a southern conspiracy to force slavery upon the nation. As a result, the South grew even more isolated as free-soil westerners became increasingly tied to the North, both economically and politically.

Within months of the ruling, abolitionist author and former slave Frederick Douglass prophetically stated that the Dred Scott decision, even though an "attempt to blot out forever the hopes of an enslaved people," would become a "necessary link in the chain of events leading to the downfall and complete overthrow of the whole slave system."

The case of Dred Scott had begun as a suit for the freedom of an obscure Missouri slave and had ended with a decision that added to the national furor over the extension of slavery in the West. Four years later, Frederick Douglass' prediction began to take shape when the southern states withdrew from the Union and an artillery attack on Fort Sumter in Charleston Harbor signaled the outbreak of the Civil War.

TIPPING THE BALANCE: THE WEST AND THE OUTBREAK OF THE CIVIL WAR

Since the nation's beginnings in 1776, foreign policy had shaped the geographic growth of the United States.

The Treaty of Paris in 1781 with Great Britain that ended the Revolutionary War also gave the nation its first western boundary at the Mississippi River. The Louisiana Purchase from France, in 1803, extended the nation farther west to the Continental Divide. The treaties with Spain and Great Britain that followed the end of the War of 1812 further defined the nation's western limits. The diplomatic settlement with the British over the Oregon Country in 1846, the military triumph over Mexico in 1848 and the Gadsden Purchase of 1853 finalized the nation's westward expansion.

But once achieved, these territorial gains were destined to strain to the breaking point the fragile ties that held the Union together. Of course, the issue of slavery was a major factor in the outbreak of the Civil War. Yet it was not the institution of slavery itself that actually ignited the conflict, but the question of whether slavery should be extended into the new western states and territories.

In late 1860, with the election of Abraham Lincoln, who opposed the creation of any new slave states, the southern states saw they would soon be outnumbered in Congress if more free states were to be created from the western territories. With that fate looming in front of them, they chose to secede from the Union rather than to submit to the will of the North.

There was a last-minute effort by Senator John Jordan Crittenden of Kentucky to avert the impending crisis.

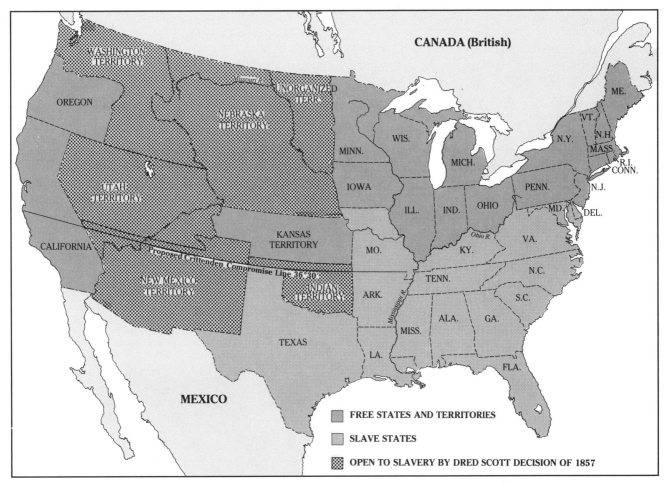

6.10 THE UNITED STATES IN 1860

Known as the Crittenden Compromise, it proposed a constitutional amendment that would have re-established the boundary between free and slave states set by the Missouri Compromise of 1820. Moreover, under the proposed amendment, the Missouri Compromise line of 36°30' would be extended to the Pacific Coast of California. Under this plan, the issue of slavery in the West would have been peacefully settled and the Union preserved.

Through the early months of 1861, even after the first southern states had withdrawn from the Union, the Senate and the House debated over ratification of Crittenden's proposed constitutional amendment.

But President-elect Lincoln had instructed his Republican supporters in Congress not to accept any proposal that would allow the creation of new slave states. For Lincoln, any compromise over the extension of slavery implied that slavery had equal rights with liberty. As a result, Senator Crittenden's measure failed to pass, and it was that failure that made the great schism inevitable—the Civil War.

Chapter 7
RESHAPING THE WEST (1861–1867)

THE EXODUS OF SOUTHERN STATES began in late December of 1860 when, in response to the election of Republican President Abraham Lincoln, South Carolina seceded from the Union. The next month saw the withdrawal of Mississippi, Florida, Alabama, Georgia and Louisiana. On February 4, 1861, the six secessionist states declared the formation of a new nation, the Confederate States of America. By May, they were joined by five more states: Texas, Virginia, Arkansas, Tennessee and North Carolina.

In the meantime, the departure of the southern states put an end to the controversy over slavery and westward expansion, leaving the way open for great changes in the organization of the Trans-Mississippi West.

On January 29, 1861, Kansas was admitted into the Union as a free state. One month later, out of the western part of what had been Kansas Territory plus a strip of eastern Utah Territory and the southeastern corner of Nebraska Territory, Congress created the new Colorado Territory. At the same time, Dakota Territory was carved from the northern and western expanse of Nebraska Territory, north of the 43rd Parallel and extending east to west between the Red River of the North and the Rocky Mountains. Farther west, the new Nevada Territory was formed from the western portion of Utah Territory.

The new state of Kansas, with its anti-slavery constitution—where open warfare over the spread of slavery had served as a prelude to the Civil War—was staunchly Republican and threw its full support behind the Union in the great conflict that erupted just three months after it had achieved statehood. With their new territorial governments, the miners of Colorado and Nevada now could more easily administer mining claims, and in gratitude for prompt recognition of their needs, were glad to

Abraham Lincoln (Photo courtesy of the Library of Congress)

rally to the Union cause. Nebraska Territory also benefited, for with its size reduced by the creation of Dakota and Colorado territories, it could be more effectively governed from its territorial capital at Omaha. This territory's loyalties had always been with the anti-slavery North, and it too put its full support behind the Union.

During the Civil War years, the West was further subdivided. In 1863, Arizona was formed from western New

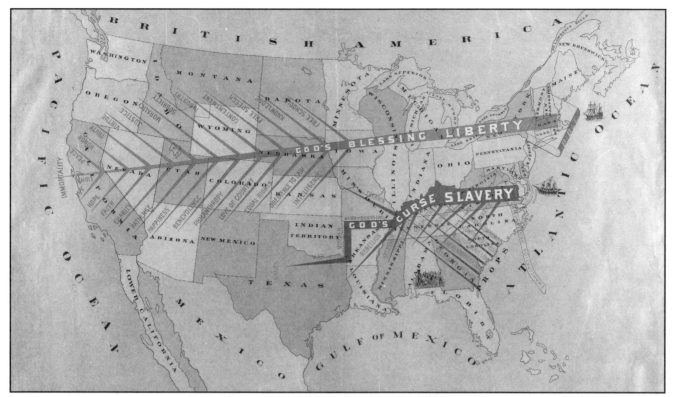

The Slavery Issue, from a Historical Map Published in 1888 (Photo courtesy of the Library of Congress)

Mexico Territory, and Idaho was formed from western Dakota Territory. Montana emerged as a territory in 1864, after a gold rush brought a surge of people into the western slopes of the Northern Rockies.

In the post-Civil War years, new western states loyal to the North, along with pro-northern western territories, would greet the southern states when they finally returned to the Union. As a result, the South would find itself outnumbered in Congress, with its political might as a region drastically diminished.

CONFEDERATE EXPANSION

East of the Mississippi River, where the major actions of the Civil War took place, the Confederacy waged a defensive war as it struggled for its very survival as a nation. An invasion by the Union army had to be repelled, and the strangling of southern trade by the Union naval blockade of southern ports had to be overcome.

In the West, however, the Confederacy stood to gain much by waging an aggressive campaign aimed at territorial expansion and the extension of slavery. In fact, the climate and soil of the West offered little prospect for the spread of slave-based agriculture. Even New Mexico Territory, which had a fair number of southern supporters, and which had enacted laws protecting the rights of slave owners, held less than 100 slaves in 1861.

The West nevertheless held other assets even more vital to the survival of the Confederacy. Gold and silver from the mining centers of California, Colorado, Nevada and southern New Mexico could provide the financial might the Confederacy needed to carry on the war. The capture of ports on California's Pacific Coast would enable the South to circumvent the Union blockade and would provide the Confederacy with both a trade outlet and a delivery route for armaments and supplies vital to the war effort.

In any case, if the Confederacy carried the conflict to the West, the Union would face a two-front war and, hopefully, would be compelled to divert some of its forces from the East. That would take some pressure off the Confederate defense of the strategically important regions of eastern Virginia and the lower Mississippi Valley.

In February of 1861, Texans voted 46,129 to 14,697 to secede from the Union. Sam Houston, who had led Texas through its war of independence in 1836 and nine years later helped engineer its annexation to the Union, was governor. Houston opposed secession; he hoped to remove Texas from the impending national conflict by declaring the state to be once again an independent republic. But he never got the chance. On March 16, the state legislature at Austin demanded that he swear allegiance to the Confederacy. When Houston refused to take the oath, the assembled delegates promptly removed him from office.

7.1 THE WEST AT THE OUTBREAK OF THE CIVIL WAR: 1861

General David E. Twiggs, commander of the U.S. Army's Department of Texas, was a Georgian with strong pro-southern sympathies. He was easily persuaded to turn over federal outposts and military supplies to the newly formed Confederate volunteer regiments. On February 16, Colonel Ben McCulloch of the Texas Rangers led a force of 1,000 armed men into San Antonio and formally accepted Twiggs' surrender. The incident occurred weeks before Lincoln took the oath of office and several months before the Confederate attack on Fort Sumter. The Confederate volunteer forces in Texas now held more than $1 million in federal arms and military supplies.

The Confederate army in Texas grew rapidly as newly enlisted volunteer units were combined with the state militia. Texas, now poised on the Confederacy's south-western frontier, was the natural launching point for an offensive into the Southwest and California. Twenty years earlier in 1841, the Republic of Texas had attempted to conquer New Mexico with the abortive Texas–Santa Fe Expedition. With the Union coming apart in 1861, the expansionist hopes of Texans were reawakened.

A grand scheme evolved to wrest New Mexico, Colorado and California from the Union. The Confederacy then would be in a strong position to purchase or conquer the northern Mexican states of Chihuahua, Sonora and Baja California. The way would be open for a railroad from the Texas Gulf Coast to the Mexican port of Guaymas on the Gulf of California. The line would span the continent and create an overland rail link between the Atlantic and the Pacific.

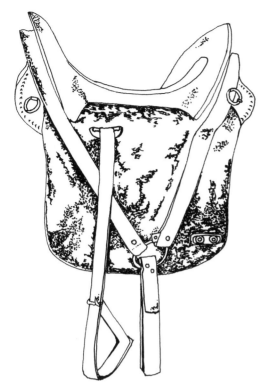

Civil War Saddle (Molly Braun)

In early summer of 1861, the Confederate advance began when a battalion of Texas Mounted Rifles, commanded by Colonel John R. Baylor, occupied Fort Bliss, opposite El Paso. Already abandoned by federal troops (along with all other Union outposts in Texas), Fort Bliss stood on the front line of a possible Union invasion of western Texas from New Mexico.

Such an attack was unlikely. The Union's frontier army, always thinly spread in the Far West, was now further reduced. More than 300 Union officers with ties to the South had left to join Confederate units in their home states. Union forces in the West, one soldier remarked, had become "an army without officers." Moreover, large numbers of Union troops had been pulled out of the West to reinforce the volunteer units now being mustered in the East.

Forty miles up the Rio Grande from Fort Bliss stood Fort Fillmore, the first line of defense for Union forces in New Mexico and the likely starting point for a Union move against western Texas. But many settlers in the nearby town of Mesilla were pro-Confederate, as were the miners around Tucson, 300 miles to the west. Colonel Baylor, who had been ordered to defend against a possible Union invasion from the upper Rio Grande, also

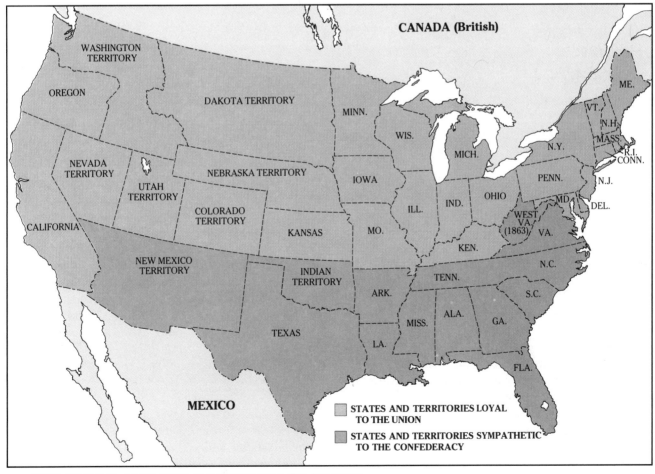

7.2 THE UNION AND THE CONFEDERACY IN 1861

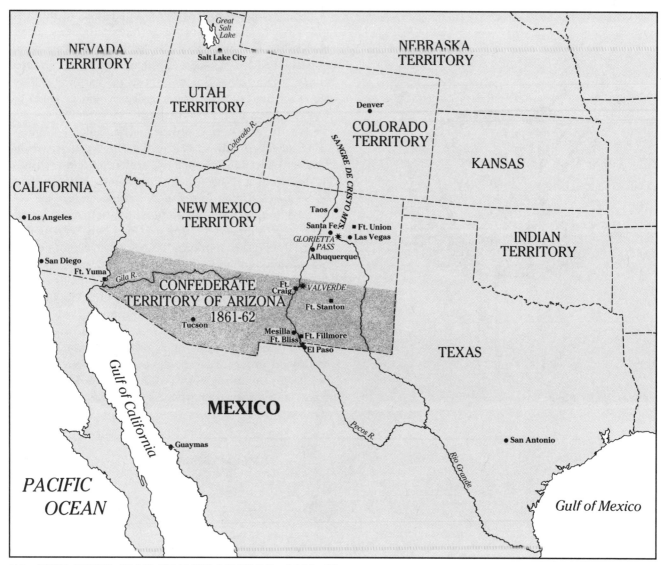

7.3 THE CIVIL WAR IN NEW MEXICO: 1861–62

had authority to launch an offensive northward into New Mexico. With the Confederate flag flying over Mesilla, and with Union defenses withdrawn to the East, Baylor felt confident that a push northward would succeed in seizing southern New Mexico for the Confederacy.

In late July of 1861, Baylor began his march northward. He soon entered Mesilla to the cheers of the prosouthern townspeople. Meanwhile, Major Isaac Lynde, commander of Union troops at Fort Fillmore, moved against Mesilla, hoping to dislodge Baylor and his Confederates. After a brief skirmish, however, Lynde withdrew to the fort. Unknown to Major Lynde, his 500 federal troops actually outnumbered the Confederates by two-to-one. Nevertheless, the Union commander decided to evacuate Fort Fillmore in the face of the Confederate advance, and he withdrew his men toward Fort Stanton, 140 miles to the east.

Major Lynde and his men never reached Fort Stanton. Before their departure, many of his troops had filled their canteens with whiskey pilfered from Fort Fillmore's medical stores. In the summer heat of the desert, their thirst intensified by drinking alcohol instead of water, many of them fell to the side of the trail. Meanwhile, Colonel Baylor and his Confederate forces were in pursuit and caught up with Lynde near San Augustin Springs, a few miles to the north of Mesilla. With his men in such poor shape, Major Lynde saw no alternative but to surrender his command to the Confederates. Without a shot being fired, Fort Fillmore had fallen to the Confederacy.

Only the isolated outpost of Fort Craig to the north now remained as the sole Union military presence in southern New Mexico. To the west, the way was open for a Confederate advance on California. But Baylor and his Mounted Texas Rifles were too small a force to carry out such an offensive. Instead, he remained in Mesilla to await reinforcements. On August 1, 1861, he announced that all of New Mexico Territory south of the 34th Parallel was now the Confederate Territory of Arizona. Several months later, a force of 100 Confederate soldiers headed westward to occupy Tucson. In January of 1862, the Confederate Congress officially declared Arizona to be part of the Confederacy.

Throughout the last months of 1861, Confederate General Henry Hopkins Sibley raised an army of more than 3,000 mounted troops to carry out the conquest of the rest of New Mexico. Equipped with rifles and artillery pieces seized from federal posts in Texas, Sibley and his command marched up the Rio Grande, and by January of 1862 they were 90 miles south of Fort Craig.

Meanwhile, Colonel Edward R.S. Canby, in command of Union forces in New Mexico, had massed 3,500 men at Fort Craig and awaited the Confederate onslaught. Ironically, Canby and Sibley had not only been classmates at West Point, but the two men were also brothers-in-law. In addition to regular army troops, Canby's command included units made up of New Mexico volunteers, including a regiment commanded by frontiersman Kit Carson.

Christopher "Kit" Carson (Photo courtesy of the Library of Congress)

Rather than risk a long siege against the well-entrenched Union forces at Fort Craig, Sibley decided to bypass the fort and head northward up the Rio Grande Valley toward Albuquerque and the territorial capital at Santa Fe. On February 21, 1862, Canby attempted to intercept Sibley at Valverde, a crossing point on the Rio Grande several miles upriver from Fort Craig. Despite a stand by Kit Carson and his New Mexican volunteers, the Confederates were able to drive Canby and his forces back across the Rio Grande to Fort Craig. The Battle of Valverde, the first major engagement of the Civil War in the Southwest, had ended with a Confederate victory.

Within a few weeks, Sibley marched into Albuquerque, and on March 10, 1862, occupied Santa Fe, the territorial capital. Days before, the territorial government had fled to the town of Las Vegas, 30 miles to the east on the Santa Fe Trail. The federal garrison at Santa Fe also headed eastward to take up positions at Fort Union, now the only remaining federal outpost in New Mexico standing between the advancing Confederate army and the goldfields of Colorado to the north.

The federal troops at Fort Union, numbering about 800 men, were no match for the Confederate troops poised to strike from Santa Fe. Reinforcements were desperately needed, but no troops could be spared from the East. A call went out in Denver for aid, and soon the First Colorado Volunteer Infantry Regiment was mustered into service. The Colorado regiment, comprised of about 900 miners and mountain men, as well as a fair number of frontiersmen drawn from Denver's saloons, soon set out for Fort Union. Although traveling mostly on foot and hampered by heavy snows in the Sangre de Cristo Mountains and through Raton Pass, the Coloradans covered the 400-mile distance to Fort Union in less than two weeks. In command was Colonel John P. Slough, a leading Denver lawyer turned soldier.

The "Pikes Peakers," as the Confederates called the Colorado volunteers, were eager to strike against Sibley's army, their fighting spirit aroused by news of the Union defeat at Valverde and the Confederate capture of Albuquerque and Santa Fe. Instead of following Canby's instructions to hold Fort Union against a possible Confederate attack, Slough took command of the garrison and marched his men down the Santa Fe Trail to confront the Confederate army at Glorietta Pass, some 20 miles east of Santa Fe.

At first, the Confederates appeared to win the day after they captured a stagecoach station known as Pigeon's Ranch. But soon afterward, on March 28, 1962, a detachment of the Colorado volunteers, led by Major John M. Chivington, undertook a daring maneuver that changed the course of the battle.

Chivington, a native of Ohio, had been a Methodist preacher and was an elder of Denver's First Methodist

Episcopal Church. Although he had been enlisted as the regimental chaplain, he opted to reject what he called a "praying" commission in favor of a "fighting" one.

Under cover of darkness, Chivington and 400 Pikes Peakers entered Apache Canyon at the western end of Glorietta Pass. They circled around the Confederate advance positions, and using ropes they descended to the foot of some cliffs where 73 Confederate supply wagons were gathered. They burned the entire wagon train, destroying ammunition, medical supplies, food and other materials that were vital for the proposed Confederate push into Colorado. Chivington's men then used their bayonets on about 500 mules and horses corralled nearby, destroying a large part of the Confederates' herd of draft animals.

Major Chivington's daring attack behind enemy lines put a sudden end to the Confederate northward advance into Colorado. Canby, now promoted to the rank of general, soon arrived with mounted Union troops from Fort Craig. Left without supplies, the Confederates were forced to fall back to Santa Fe, and from there they withdrew southward down the Rio Grande and back to Texas. The Confederate retreat was fraught with hardships. Food supplies were low and many of the men were wounded, and Sibley was forced to abandon many of his command along the way.

More bad news was waiting for Sibley at El Paso. There he learned that Colonel James H. Carleton was leading a federal force eastward from California to retake southern New Mexico. Known as the California Column, Carleton and his command had already recaptured Tucson and had sent advance units eastward toward the Rio Grande. On July 4, 1862, Carleton's men entered Mesilla and replaced the Confederate flag flying over the town with the Stars and Stripes of the Union. Meanwhile, General Sibley and his Confederate forces had hastened their retreat across western Texas. Some 3,000 Texans had set out to conquer New Mexico for the Confederacy. Of that number, less than half managed to straggle back into San Antonio in the summer of 1862.

The New Mexico campaign had been waged by Union and Confederate volunteer forces largely drawn from the West. The engagements in New Mexico would seem like mere skirmishes when compared to the titanic battles between the Blue and the Gray that were to be fought in the East. Yet the Union triumph demonstrated that its far western frontier could be defended without diverting the North's military might from the eastern theaters of conflict.

The defeat of the Texas Confederate forces at Glorietta Pass signaled the end of the Confederacy's plan to seize the Southwest and to expand to the Pacific. For this reason, the Union victory became known as the "Gettysburg of the West."

THE WAR ON THE CONFEDERATE FRONTIER

Since its creation in 1812, the state of Missouri had been the gateway to the American West. For years, St. Louis had been the headquarters of the upper Missouri River and Rocky Mountain fur trade. The western Missouri towns of Independence and Kansas City, at the eastern ends of the western trails, had served as the starting points for the great overland migrations to Oregon, California and the goldfields of the Pikes Peak Country.

As secession fever swept the South in the early months of 1861, Missouri found itself strategically perched astride yet another frontier—the central western frontier of the emerging Confederacy.

Missouri had always been a slave state with close economic and cultural ties to the South. Many of its inhabitants, especially in its southern and western parts, had roots in the South. The Missouri legislature was dominated by states' rights and pro-slavery Democrats.

In the election of 1860 (the same contest in which Lincoln won the presidency), Missourians elected Clairborne Fox Jackson as their governor. A native of Kentucky, Jackson had risen to prominence in Missouri as a lawyer and state legislator. A pro-slavery Democrat, he was instrumental in bringing about the defeat of Missouri's anti-slavery senator, Thomas Hart Benton. He later commanded bands of Border Ruffians in raids into Bleeding Kansas in the late 1850s.

In his inaugural address in January of 1860, Governor Jackson called on Missourians to follow the South's lead. "Common origin, pursuits, tastes, manners and customs . . . bind together in one brotherhood the States of the South," he declared, and urged his state to proclaim "her determination to stand by her sister slave-holding states."

Delegates elected to a state convention to decide the secession issue felt otherwise. They not only voted to remain in the Union, but soon afterward voted to unseat Governor Jackson, his lieutenant-governor, as well as the entire state legislature. Thereafter, and until the closing months of the Civil War, the pro-Union convention would rule Missouri in place of the deposed elected state government.

In the meantime, Jackson and his pro-secessionist followers had taken matters into their own hands, hoping that by swift action they could bring Missouri into the Confederacy. Jackson was still governor in April of 1861, when South Carolina artillery opened up on the federal garrison at Fort Sumter in Charleston Harbor. Immediately, President Lincoln called on all state governors to mobilize their state militias to defend the Union. By that time, however, Governor Jackson had organized several regiments of pro-Confederate Missouri militia. Instead of meeting Lincoln's request, Jackson called for an insurrection against federal authority in Missouri.

The federal arsenal in St. Louis held the largest concentration of arms in the slave states, and this became the target of Jackson's efforts. Although a smaller federal arsenal near Kansas City was seized by pro-Confederate militia, the huge supply of arms stockpiled at St. Louis was kept out of rebel hands through the able command of Captain Nathaniel Lyon of the U.S. Army. A West Point graduate and veteran of the Mexican War, Lyon had served with federal forces in Bleeding Kansas.

To meet the challenge of Governor Jackson and his pro-secessionist militia, Lyon raised four regiments of volunteers, drawn mostly from the predominantly pro-Union German emigrant population living in and around St. Louis. Meanwhile, Jackson had massed more than 700 armed men on the outskirts of St. Louis, at a site that quickly became known as "Camp Jackson." Several artillery pieces captured from the federal arsenal at Baton Rouge, Louisiana, were smuggled into Camp Jackson after Jackson had sent word to Confederate leaders asking for military aid.

On May 10, 1861, Captain Lyon surrounded the rebel encampment and forced the surrender of 700 Missouri militiamen without firing a shot. But Lyon made the mistake of parading his prisoners through the streets of St. Louis. Instead of arousing support for the Union cause, the event only aroused the ire of pro-Confederate sympathizers. Rioting erupted along the parade route and gunfire broke out. By the time it was over, 28 civilians and two of Lyon's troops lay dead in the street. Over the next several days, St. Louis saw more violence between civilians and soldiers.

Lyon sought to bring a prompt end to the fighting in St. Louis, and he agreed to meet with Governor Jackson and General Sterling Price, the newly appointed commander of the reorganized Missouri state militia. Price had led Missouri forces in the Mexican War in which he had put down a Pueblo Indian and Mexican uprising at Taos. A pro-slavery Democrat, he had served as a Missouri state legislator, Congressman and governor.

Governor Jackson and Price offered to keep Missouri neutral in the war if Lyon would agree to remove his troops from the state. But Lyon, by then a brigadier general, was a staunch Unionist from Connecticut and he took offense at a mere state governor and state militia commander offering terms to the U.S. Government. He refused to consider the proposal and stormed out of the meeting.

Before long, Lyon marched on the Missouri state capital at Jefferson City, where the pro-secessionist legislature was still in power. Outnumbered by federal troops,

Price's militia did not make a stand, and withdrew 50 miles up the Missouri River to Boonville.

By late June of 1861, General Price and his men had been driven southward across Missouri toward the Arkansas state line. Meanwhile, the pro-secessionist members of the Missouri state legislature had reconvened at Neosho in the southwestern corner of the state where, on November 3, they voted to secede from the Union. Three weeks later, the Confederate Congress in Richmond agreed to admit Missouri as the 12th Confederate state. But soon afterward, Missouri's Confederate state government was forced to flee the state in the face of advancing Union forces. For the rest of the war, it would remain as only a "shadow" government in exile.

Lyon's high-handed actions against the Missouri state militia had antagonized moderates as well as pro-slavery supporters. Bands of pro-Confederate guerrillas began to roam the countryside raiding farms and outlying areas. In response, groups of pro-Union partisans known as Jayhawkers began to pour in from Kansas to even the score. To supervise the volatile situation in Missouri, Lincoln appointed the erstwhile "Pathfinder" of western exploration, John C. Fremont, as major general in command at St. Louis.

Under Fremont's command, General Lyon was ordered to drive all Confederate-allied forces from Missouri. By August 10, 1861, he had chased Price and his Missouri state militia as far south as Springfield. By then, Price had joined up with Confederate units from Arkansas and Louisiana under the command of General Ben McCulloch.

Lyon thought he could overcome Confederate forces at Wilson's Creek, south of Springfield. Yet his forces numbered about 5,500, and his lines of supply to St. Louis were now thinly stretched across 200 miles of tenuously-held territory. In front of him was a combined force of about 13,000 Confederates. Although outnumbered by more than two-to-one, Lyon sent part of his army ahead to attack the Confederates from the rear.

The plan almost succeeded. The Confederates were driven forward by the rear attack. But the Union brigade that had outflanked the Confederates was stopped when it ran into a surprise attack by a Louisiana regiment. The maneuver ended in a rout when Confederate artillery opened up a devastating barrage on the besieged Union brigade.

Cut off from nearly one-third of his men and outnumbered by the enemy, General Lyon and the main part of his command now faced the combined troops of Price's militia and McCulloch's Confederates. In the battle that ensued, Lyon was killed when a bullet pierced his heart. Union forces, low on ammunition, were forced to retreat back to Springfield, and soon withdrew 100 miles further northward to Sedalia.

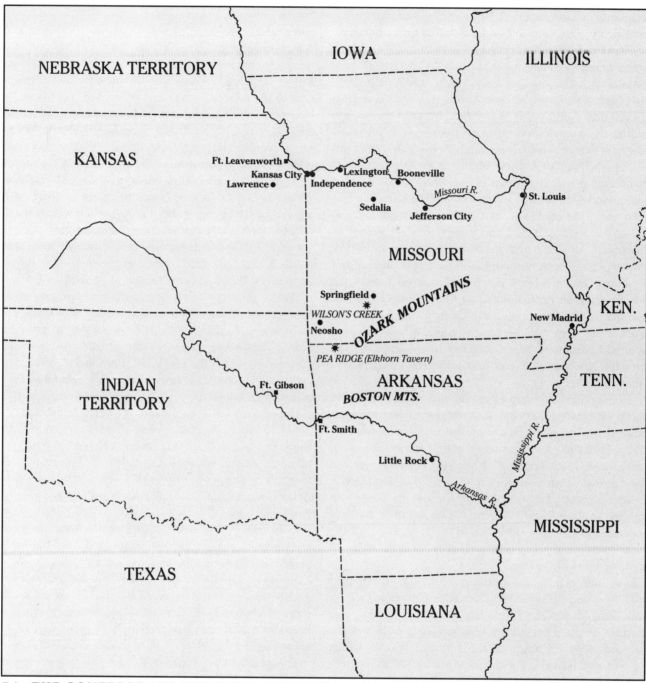

7.4 THE CONFEDERATE FRONTIER: MISSOURI, ARKANSAS AND THE INDIAN TERRITORY

Price took advantage of his victory in the Battle of Wilson's Creek and advanced northward to the Missouri River town of Lexington, which he captured.

As Price's militia units and pro-slavery guerrillas were spreading havoc throughout the state, Major General Fremont announced that he would shoot all Confederate partisans captured in Union-controlled regions, and that he would free the slaves of Confederate sympathizers. This last measure proved too much for Lincoln. Fearing that any hint of liberating slaves in Union-occupied terri-

tory would alienate the leaders of Delaware, Kentucky and Maryland (tree other slave states remaining in the Union), Lincoln removed Fremont from his command.

In early 1862, the Union army embarked on a three-pronged attack to secure the Mississippi River. The westernmost advance would be in southwestern Missouri, under the command of Brigadier General Samuel R. Curtis. Price was still active in that part of the state, but in the face of a larger Union army, he fell back into northern Arkansas to join up with Confederate forces under the command of General Earl Van Dorn and General McCulloch. Curtis then pursued McCulloch and Price into Arkansas until the Confederate generals agreed to make a stand.

The Confederate high command could see the value of a campaign into Missouri. Lying on the west bank of the Mississippi River, Missouri offered the Confederates an opportunity to outflank the Union offensive and save the vital Mississippi waterway from falling into Union hands. With the capture of St. Louis, the Confederacy would be able to mount a major counteroffensive down the Mississippi to dislodge Union forces in western Kentucky and Tennessee and halt the North's relentless drive into the South's heartland.

On March 7, 1862, General Curtis' men took up positions at Pea Ridge, a chain of low-lying hills in the Boston Mountains of northwestern Arkansas. Van Dorn surmised that his Confederate forces would not be able to dislodge the well-entrenched Union troops with a frontal attack. Instead, Van Dorn divided his army in an attempt to outflank Curtis. Confederate forces were augmented by about 1,500 pro-Confederate Cherokee warriors who had been recruited in the Indian Territory by the Confederacy's Commissioner of Indian Affairs, Albert Pike.

In the ensuing Battle of Pea Ridge, the Confederates made some initial advances, including a gallant charge by the Confederate Cherokees against the Union artillery. But the southern forces became too widely separated, and Curtis had received advanced word of the impending attack from one of his scouts, James Butler Hickok (who would later gain fame as the legendary frontiersman "Wild Bill" Hickok). Thus alerted, Curtis had time to turn his army around to meet Van Dorn's advance. Instead of attacking the Union rear, as planned, Van Dorn found himself facing the Union artillery and the full force of the Union troops.

Even though Van Dorn outnumbered Curtis in the Battle of Pea Ridge, the Confederate artillery was no match for the Union guns. In the end, the Union forces swept the Confederates from their positions at nearby Elkhorn Tavern and set the southerners on a retreat southward. General McCulloch lost his life in the battle. The Union forces advanced on the Mississippi River in Tennessee and at New Madrid, Missouri, effectively severing the Confederacy in half and depriving it of the vital river route to Texas and the Gulf Coast.

No other major engagements in the Missouri–Arkansas border region occurred after the Battle of Pea Ridge. The Union victory in that engagement was to keep Missouri firmly in Union hands throughout the War. In 1864, General Price led an abortive raid into Missouri but that ended when most of his troops deserted in the face of overwhelming resistance by Union cavalry along with Kansas and pro-Union Missouri militia units.

INDIAN RESISTANCE DURING THE CIVIL WAR

On the eastern end of the Great Plains, many of the Santee Sioux of Minnesota had grown disenchanted with reservation life. The lands assigned to them under the Fort Laramie Treaty of 1851 spanned the Minnesota River, about a hundred miles west of St. Paul. But whites, mostly Scandinavian and German emigrant farmers, had begun to edge onto Indian lands. Moreover, their annuities were late in coming, and traders defrauded them with overcharges and shoddy merchandise.

During the second summer of the Civil War, as thousands of loyal Minnesotans marched off to fight for the Union cause in campaigns in Virginia and other parts of the South, the Santee Sioux found themselves in dire straits. Those who had turned to farming suffered a poor harvest. But the Indian agent for the Santee Sioux refused to authorize the distribution of food supplies on credit, and demanded that the Indians wait until they received their annuity payment of $71,000. Yet while the Indians faced starvation, Congress delayed payment, debating over whether to pay the Indians in gold or in the newly issued paper money—greenbacks.

In August of 1862, when some of the Santee Sioux threatened to storm one of the reservation's government warehouses, Indian agent Thomas Galbraith relented and issued some provisions and trade goods. But traders at another government post refused to release their goods until the Indians' annuity money arrived. The Santee Sioux chief Little Crow seethed at the government agent's indifference to the Indians' plight, declaring that the Indians might have to take drastic steps to keep themselves from starving, warning that "When men are hungry they help themselves."

Soon afterward, a violent, seemingly isolated incident touched off the bloodiest single Indian uprising in U.S. history. A party of Santee Sioux hunters attacked and killed five whites at a farm near the settlement of Acton. When news of the killings reached Little Crow, he realized that the response of the whites would be swift and deadly. Since he saw no way of avoiding an all-out war against his people, he opted to throw in his lot with the younger Sioux braves who now saw this as an opportunity to drive the white interlopers from their lands once and for all.

Santee Sioux raiding parties swept through western Minnesota attacking settlers. A white trader named Andrew Myrick had refused the Indians' earlier desperate pleas to sell them food on credit, remarking "if they are hungry, let them eat grass or their own dung." He was among the first killed; his body was later found with his mouth stuffed full of grass.

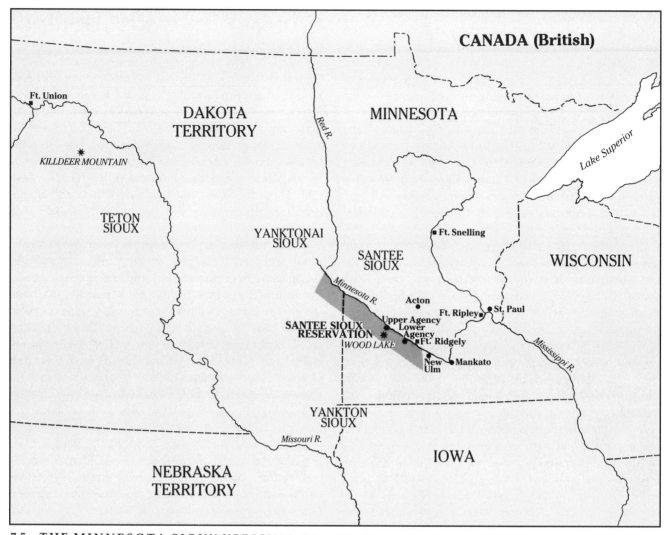

7.5 THE MINNESOTA SIOUX UPRISING OF 1862–63

After having failed in their assault on the town of New Ulm, the Indians attacked the garrison at nearby Fort Ridgely. With the help of several artillery pieces, the soldiers repelled the Sioux attack.

The Indians withdrew to continue their campaign throughout the countryside of 23 western Minnesota counties. They were soon joined by bands of Yankton Sioux from eastern Dakota Territory.

In response to the emergency, Minnesota governor Alexander Ramsey sent a relief column under General Henry Hastings Sibley (no relation to Confederate General Henry Hopkins Sibley of the New Mexico campaign) to suppress the Indian uprising in the Minnesota River Valley. Ironically, Ramsey and Sibley, who had each prospered in the fur trade, had been responsible for causing much of the Indians' discontent by skimming off a large chunk of the initial payments due the Sioux under the 1851 Fort Laramie Treaty, supposedly to cover alleged prior overpayments for furs and hides.

Sibley's forces, made up of newly mobilized federal volunteer troops as well as regiments of the Minnesota militia, managed to drive the Indians back to their reservation. The final blow to the Indian cause came in September of 1862 at Wood Lake. With the help of some influential Sioux who had opposed the uprising from the start, Sibley managed to secure the release of more than 250 captives and captured more than 2,000 of the rebels.

Sibley immediately set up a military court to try the Indians for atrocities against the white settlers. Three hundred and three of the Santee Sioux warriors were found guilty of murder or rape and sentenced to death. But before this summary justice could be meted out, President Abraham Lincoln interceded, at the urging of Indian reform leaders such as Minnesota's Episcopal bishop, Henry P. Whipple. Lincoln had a staff of lawyers carefully review the trial records of all the condemned warriors and, in the end, pardoned all but 38 of them. On December 26, 1862, these 38 were hanged from a giant scaffold at the settlement of Mankato. It was the largest mass execution in United States history. The rest of the Santee Sioux were exiled to smaller reservations on the Missouri River in present-day South Dakota.

Over the next year or so, the remnants of Little Crow's warrior bands fled westward into Dakota Territory. They were pursued by federal forces under General John Pope and General Alfred Sully, as well as by Minnesota militia under General Sibley. Among the ranks of the soldiers were several companies of "galvanized Yankees"—Confederate war prisoners who had agreed to fight Indians in the West in return for their freedom. By then, the Santees had been joined by other bands of Sioux, including Tetons, Yanktonais and Yanktons.

In July of 1864, the warring Sioux were defeated at the Battle of Killdeer Mountain in northern Dakota Territory. But aside from chastising the Santee Sioux for their uprising of 1862, the victory did little to bring peace to the Northern Plains. In the years that followed, the warfare continued and spread, involving nearly every Sioux band west of the Missouri River.

Plains Indian Headdress (Molly Braun)

Other tribes farther West had also grown weary of the federal government's broken promises and incursions onto protected lands. Beginning in 1859, hundreds of thousands of fortune-seekers, en route to the Pikes Peak Country of Colorado, and Idaho and Montana as well, trampled across the lands guaranteed to the Indians under treaties signed only a few years earlier. The Union's main concern in the West, aside from fending off the expansionist designs of the Confederacy, was to keep the overland trails open.

The federal government was hard-pressed to fight both the Confederacy and the Indian freedom fighters. Regular army garrisons were sent to the East, and local volunteer units took their place.

In the Great Basin, Shoshones, Bannocks and Paiutes in northern Utah and southern Idaho were raiding federally subsidized overland stage and freight routes, as well as attacking the increasing numbers of miners on traditional hunting grounds. In January of 1863, a regiment of volunteers from northern California, under the command of General Patrick Connor, fought a series of engagements against Bear Hunter's Shoshones at Bear River, north of Salt Lake City.

Two years later, in August of 1865, Connor's Powder River Expedition onto the Northern Plains attacked a peaceful Northern Arapaho band, led by Black Bear, at Tongue River in present-day Wyoming.

In the Southwest, the Apaches and Navajos, seeing that federal troops were being withdrawn to fight the Confederacy, seized the opportunity to drive white settlers from southern Arizona and New Mexico. General James Carleton's forces, known as the California Column, occupied southern New Mexico Territory and what was soon to become Arizona Territory. The first confrontation was at Apache Pass in July of 1862, when Chiricahua Apaches under Cochise and Mimbreno Apaches under Mangas Coloradas were repelled by Carleton's howitzers.

Union volunteer units from New Mexico and California, under the command of Colonel Kit Carson, pursued bands of Mescalero Apaches, subduing them by late 1862. General Carleton had them deported to Bosque Redondo, a reservation he established in eastern New Mexico.

Carson also won a decisive victory over the Navajos under Manuelito at Canyon de Chelly in northeastern Arizona Territory. In January of 1864, he trapped the Indians in their stronghold there, and after destroying hundreds of Indian horses and the peach orchards that the Indians relied on for food supplies, he forced more than 3,000 Navajos to surrender. Like their Apache neighbors, the Navajos were then compelled to accept confinement to reservation lands at Bosque Redondo.

By mid-1864, the western segment of the Santa Fe Trail was largely free of Indian raiding. Carson turned

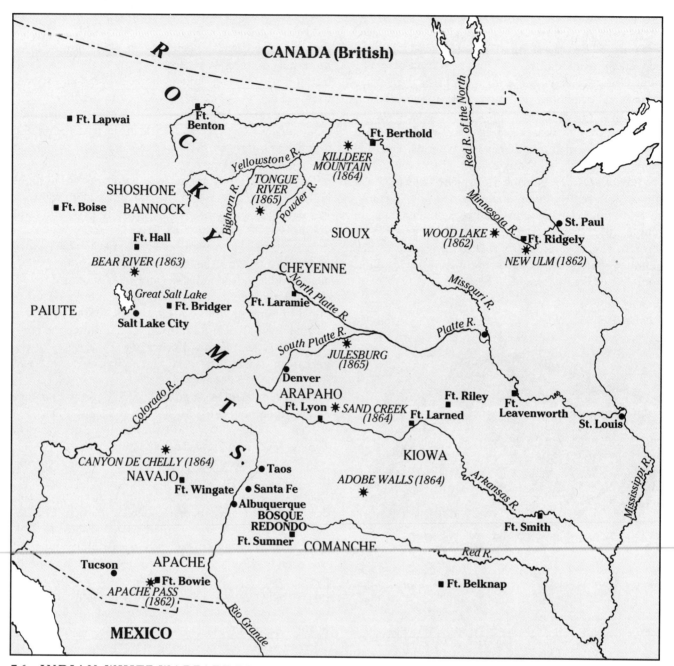

7.6 INDIAN-WHITE WARFARE DURING THE CIVIL WAR YEARS: 1861–65

his attention to the Comanche and Kiowa raiding parties to the east on the Southern Plains. In November of 1864, at Adobe Walls on the South Canadian River in the Staked Plain of Texas, Carson defeated Kiowas under Little Mountain and Satanta.

Meanwhile, the Cheyennes and Arapahos of the Southern Plains resisted the encroachments of miners and settlers of the Colorado Territory. In 1861, some of their chiefs had entered into a treaty under which they agreed to give up their reservation lands between the Arkansas and South Platte rivers for a smaller reservation at Sand Creek in southeastern Colorado. But many

of the Indians refused to acknowledge the treaty and conducted raids against stagecoach stations and outlying settlements all along the Platte River Valley.

As elsewhere in the West, federal troops were in short supply and for a while the Indian attacks went unchecked. In 1864, Colorado territorial governor John Evans pleaded with the War Department in Washington, D.C., to send military aid.

Even Colorado's own volunteer regiment could not be spared, since it was then involved in repelling a renewed Confederate assault on Missouri. Governor Evans took the defense of Colorado into his own hands and organized a new unit of volunteers, the Third Colorado Regiment, whose members had been drawn largely from Denver's saloons and from the mining camps nearby.

Black Kettle's Southern Cheyenne band had had enough of war as winter approached and were willing to settle down on their reservation at Sand Creek. Seeking peace, Black Kettle led his people along with a number of Southern Arapahos to Fort Lyon, near Sand Creek, where he offered to surrender to the officer in charge, Major Edward Wynkoop.

Unknown to Major Wynkoop, Governor Evans and the commanding Union officer of the Colorado region, General Samuel Curtis, had refused to accept any offers of peace from the Cheyennes, and instead they planned a punitive campaign against the warring tribes. Wynkoop—although without the authority to do so—provided Black Kettle and his people with provisions and directed them to encamp for the winter at Sand Creek.

Wynkoop's peaceful actions cost him his command. His replacement was soon joined by the newly organized Colorado Third Regiment, commanded by Colonel John Chivington, who had won fame for his part in the Battle of Glorietta Pass in the New Mexico campaign of 1862. At dawn on November 29, 1864, Chivington and his men attacked the sleeping Indian encampment at Sand Creek, reportedly killing hundreds. During the attack, chief Black Kettle hoisted an American flag and a white flag above his tepee. But the slaughter went on unabated, with many Indian women and children among the dead.

In the wake of the Sand Creek Massacre, as it became known, Cheyenne bands intensified their war on Colorado's white settlers. In January of 1865, they attacked and nearly destroyed the town of Julesburg, and for a time severed communication links between Denver and the outside world. News of the Sand Creek Massacre also prompted the Sioux to ally themselves with the Cheyennes and Arapahos and also raid stagecoaches, overland freight wagon trains and emigrants along the Oregon and Overland trails. In time, the warring Plains tribes withdrew, some northward to the Black Hills and others eastward to the Arkansas River.

Congressional investigations looking into the Sand Creek Massacre uncovered gross mismanagement in the handling of Indian affairs. Evans was forced to resign from his governorship in 1865, and the outrage fomented by the Sand Creek Massacre is thought to have helped delay Colorado's achieving statehood for a dozen years. Chivington avoided a court-martial when his term of enlistment expired in early 1865.

These revelations helped spawn a new federal post-Civil War "Peace Policy" under President Ulysses Grant to deal with the Indians of the West. The government now sought to enter into new treaties with the Plains tribes under which they would receive smaller reservations but would retain the right to hunt on unceded lands. But the Peace Policy would be short-lived.

THE HOMESTEAD ACT

Ever since his first years as a U.S. congressman from Pennsylvania in the early 1850s, Galusha Grow had campaigned for a radical change in the government's land policy. Until then, the surveyed lands of the public domain had been available to settlers for $1.25 an acre. But most small farmers lacked the cash to buy government land and could only do so by going into debt. Added to this was the cost of livestock, equipment and seed, as well as the expenses a farmer had to incur to support his family for two years until his farm became self-sufficient.

Born a Connecticut Yankee and raised on a farm in western Pennsylvania, Galusha Grow believed the lands of the public domain should be made available free of charge to any citizen. Naturally, frontier farmers in the West strongly favored a free land policy. Grow's views were also supported by such liberal-minded reformers in the North as *New York Tribune* editor Horace Greeley.

At first, the North also was the source of opposition to free land grants to pioneers. The growing industrial cities of the North demanded a huge work force and northern leaders feared that the promise of free land in the western states and territories would siphon off the labor supply. But that concern evaporated as the great tide of Irish immigration that began in the late 1840s promised to supply amply the North's need for industrial workers. And as industry expanded in the North, manufacturers began to look favorably on a free land policy since the rapid growth it would bring to the West would also create new markets for their products.

Galusha Grow first served as a member of the House of Representatives from 1851 to 1863. His interest in re-

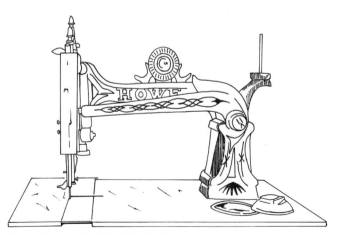

Howe Sewing Machine (Molly Braun)

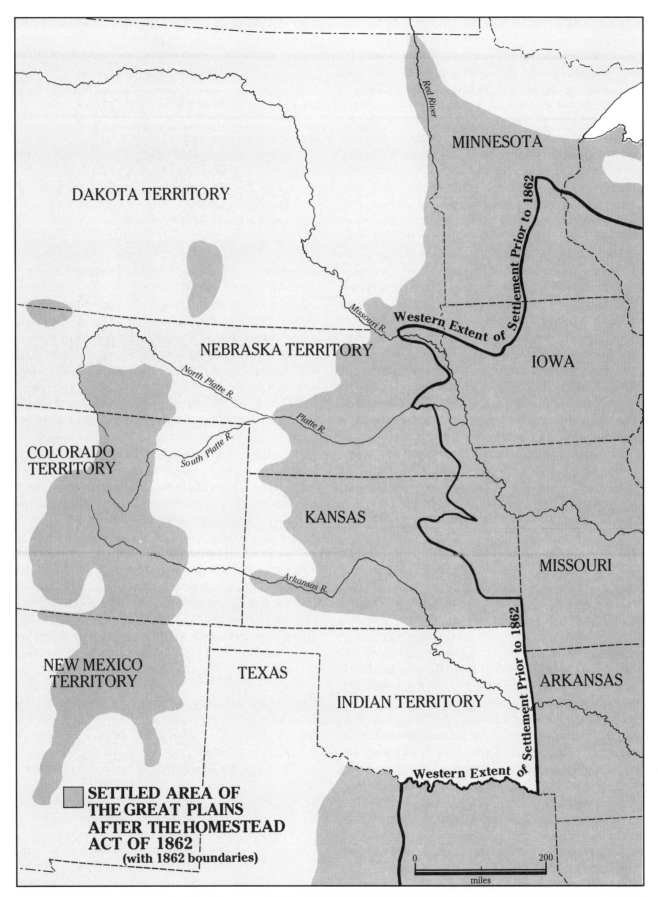

7.7 THE HOMESTEAD ACT OF 1862 AND SUBSEQUENT IMPACT ON SETTLEMENT OF THE GREAT PLAINS

forming the government's land policy prompted him to become chairman of the Committee on Territories. He campaigned tirelessly for the adoption of a free land policy, an idea that became embodied in the term "Homestead," referring to a family farm with all of its equipment and buildings.

Throughout the decade of the 1850s, Grow's efforts were blocked by the staunch opposition of southerners in both the House and the Senate. By then it was apparent that slavery had expanded about as much as geography would allow, and southerners feared that Grow's plan for free land grants would result in the western territories filling up with independent-minded free-soil farmers who were likely to establish states where slavery would be outlawed, undermining southern power in Congress.

Of more immediate concern for southerners was that a free land policy would put an end to land sales as a major source of government revenue. Higher tariffs on imports would be necessary to fill the gap, a step that would be harmful for the South where the prosperity of the cotton-based economy depended on free trade.

In 1852, a Homestead bill won approval in the House, but the southern-dominated Senate voted it down. Two more subsequent land-grant measures suffered similar defeats. In 1860, a Homestead bill did pass both the House and the Senate, only to be vetoed by outgoing President James Buchanan who, although a Pennsylvanian, sympathized with southern opposition to the proposed law.

In the meantime, anti-slavery adherents began to rally behind the call for Homestead legislation. The Republican Party, committed as it was to halting the spread of slavery in the western states and territories, seized upon the issue of Homestead to garner support in the Old Northwest, in the upper Mississippi Valley and in California, where voters were overwhelmingly in favor of a free land policy. In the presidential election of 1860, the Republican Party made support for some kind of Homestead legislation a major plank in their platform and as a result won many votes in regions where slavery was not a pressing issue.

Opposition to Grow's proposal for a free land policy quickly faded as the last of the southern states seceded from the Union in the spring of 1861. By then he was Speaker of the House of Representatives, and he saw his Homestead bill easily win passage in the Republican-dominated House and Senate. On May 20, 1862, the Homestead Act was signed into law by President Abraham Lincoln.

Under the terms of the Homestead Act, a grant of 160 acres of government land—a quarter of a square mile section—was available free of charge to "any person who is the head of a family, or who has arrived at the age of twenty-one years, and is a citizen of the United States,

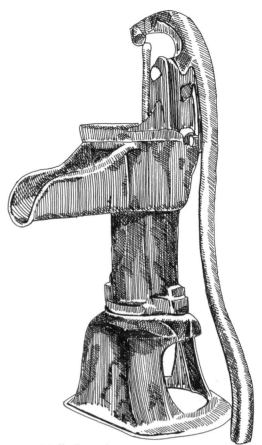

Water Pump (Molly Braun)

or who shall have filed his declaration of becoming such." All that was required was that the homesteader pay a $10 filing fee, construct a small dwelling on the property, make some minor improvements, cultivate the soil and reside on the land for five years. After that, the homesteader gained title to the property. He could also do so after only six months of occupancy by purchasing his claim from the government at the standard price of $1.25 an acre.

The first to claim a grant of free land under the Homestead Law was Daniel Freeman, a Nebraska farmer on leave from the Union army. The law was to go into effect on January 1, 1863, the day that Freeman was due to report back to his regiment. In order to take advantage of the new law, he persuaded the registrar of the land office at Beatrice in southeastern Nebraska to open the office at a few minutes past midnight to file his application, allowing him to return in time to his post in Kansas.

In the six months that followed, 224,500 acres in Nebraska were taken up under the Homestead Law. More settlers poured into the region in the next few years, drawn by the prospect of free land. The territory's population swelled from less than 30,000 in 1862, to more than 100,000 when it was admitted as a state in 1867.

In the years immediately following the Civil War, hundreds of thousands of returning Union war veterans took advantage of the new land policy. Provisions were added to the law that credited time served in the Union armed forces toward the residency period required to gain title to the land grants.

Over the next 30 years, more than half a million claims were filed, amounting to grants of 80 million acres of free lands. Yet there were problems with the size of the grant. A claim of one hundred and sixty acres was too small for subsistence farming on the semi-arid prairies, and not nearly large enough for large-scale agriculture and ranching. Unscrupulous speculators took advantage of loopholes in the law to acquire land titles. They would hire "pioneers" to file land claims and then transfer the claims to land companies after only six months of real or pretended residence. Sometimes a portable cabin on wheels was used to get around the requirement that a building be constructed on the land grant. Such a "building" could be moved from site to site to fulfill the law's demand that certain improvements be made on the homestead.

Congress attempted to remedy the situation by enacting supplemental laws aimed at enlarging the land grants, encouraging the growing of trees on the land and promoting irrigation. Abuses continued, however, and much of the public domain found its way into the hands of large land companies and railroads, which then realized a profit by selling the lands to individual "homesteaders."

Despite these abuses, the Homestead Act of 1862 began a process that led to the populating of the western half of the continent in less than one-tenth the time it had taken to settle the eastern half. In the period between 1870 and 1890, more lands were settled than had been in the previous 250 years. Furthermore, the passage of the Homestead Act in 1862 underscored the fact that the West had come into its own politically and would become a major sectional force in national politics.

Galusha Grow lost his congressional seat in 1862, the year in which he finally saw his Homestead Act passed into law. He remained out of office until 1894, when he was again elected to the House of Representatives. By that time, all of the public domain that had been available for settlement had been claimed under his and the subsequent federal laws aimed at the rapid disposition of unsettled lands.

In 1936, the site of Daniel Freeman's farm on Cub Creek, near Beatrice, Nebraska, the first settlement under the Homestead Act, was designated as the Homestead National Monument of America.

Double-barreled Shotgun (Molly Braun)

THE FIRST TRANSCONTINENTAL RAILROAD LINKS EAST AND WEST

The son of a minister, Theodore Dehone Judah was born in Connecticut and raised in Troy, New York, where he studied science at that town's Renssalaer Polytechnic Institute. He worked as a surveyor on several railroads in New York State and Massachusetts, and in 1854, at the age of 28, he headed west to California as surveying engineer for a short railroad line between Sacramento and the gold-mining area in the western foothills of the Sierra Nevada.

By that time, Judah had become a passionate transcontinental railroad enthusiast. From merchant Asa Whitney's vision in the 1840s, the idea that a railroad should span the continent had grown to become the focus of fierce congressional debates throughout the 1850s. The government had made surveys of several routes, but no progress could be made after the final decision became mired in the sectional differences between North and South.

In 1860, Judah undertook a survey of his own in search of a feasible way for a railroad to cross the crest of the Sierras. That summer, he determined that a railroad could be constructed near the emigrant route through Donner Lake, scene of the Donner Party tragedy of 1846. Armed with this information, Judah convinced four leading Sacramento businessmen, Collis P. Huntington, Mark Hopkins, Charles Crocker and Leland Stanford to back him in a plan to create what Judah termed as the initial segment of the "grand avenue of approach to the Pacific."

Huntington, Hopkins, Crocker and Stanford—later known as the "Big Four"—soon raised enough capital to charter the Central Pacific Railroad, with Judah as its chief engineer. Originally, the railroad was planned to link the booming silver-mining district of western Nevada's Comstock Lode region with Sacramento. But Judah, whose devotion to the transcontinental railroad project was so passionate that he was known locally as "Crazy Ted," envisioned the railroad as stretching far beyond the mountains of western Nevada.

Judah traveled to Washington, D.C., to lobby Congress for government aid in realizing his dream of a transcontinental railway. History was on his side. The South had just seceded and the attack on Fort Sumter had signaled the eruption of the Civil War. With the departure of the southern states also went any support for Jefferson Davis' proposed southern route. Moreover, Lincoln and the Republican Party had been elected on a platform pledged to build a transcontinental railroad.

On July 1, 1862, President Abraham Lincoln signed into law the Pacific Railroad Act. Under its terms, the Central Pacific was to build eastward along Judah's route across the Sierra Nevada to the California–Nevada line. The eastern half of the transcontinental railroad was to be built by the federally chartered Union Pacific. That line would begin at Omaha and proceed westward across the Great Plains and Rocky Mountains and eventually join up with the Central Pacific.

Financing for the first transcontinental railroad would come from generous land grants and government loans. For each mile of track they laid, the Central Pacific and the Union Pacific each received 10 square miles of public land along the right-of-way. Each railroad company would also get government subsidies in the form of loans, with the amounts varying according to the type of terrain through which they built. For each mile of track through flat land, they received $16,000; through the high desert and foothills of Nevada and Utah the lines would earn $32,000 per mile; and for every mile of track across the high peaks of the Rockies and the Sierra Nevada they would earn $48,000.

Although ground was broken in Sacramento for the Central Pacific in early 1863, the new line was short on cash and unable to begin the first 40 miles of track for the initial land grants and government loans requisite under the Pacific Railway Act. Undaunted, Collis P. Huntington managed to convince Lincoln that the western extent of the Sierra Nevada was actually just outside of Sacramento. As a result, the government designated 24 miles of flat land as mountains. This bit of "geological legerdemain" guaranteed that the Central Pacific would receive more than $750,000 in government loans for laying track in flat country, an amount far below the actual building costs. With this great infusion of government cash now imminent, Huntington and the Central Pacific soon attracted more investors from the banking establishment of the East and were able to commence laying their first tracks eastward.

Difficulties plagued the construction of the Central Pacific. Although there was an abundant supply of timber for railroad ties, most other items—including rails, nails, tools, locomotives and railroad cars—had to be transported by ship for the long voyage around Cape Horn to San Francisco Bay. Moreover, wartime demand and inflation had made goods scarce and prices high. By 1864, the Central Pacific had reached only 20 miles beyond Sacramento and it was again facing financial problems. Huntington again appealed to Washington and succeeded in persuading Congress and President Lincoln to enact the Pacific Railway Act of 1864, which doubled the land grants to 20 square miles for every mile of track laid and eased the credit terms on the government's loan bonds. The potential for larger land grants soon attracted more cash from investors.

Another problem that the Central Pacific had to overcome was a shortage of labor. Although there were plenty of able-bodied men in California, most would rather work for themselves in the gold and silver fields of Nevada and California than for wages on the Central Pacific. In 1865, Charles Crocker, who headed construction on the Central Pacific, decided to turn to California's population of Chinese. Many of these people had come from China in the 1850s to work leftover mining claims. Large Chinatowns had developed in San Francisco and Sacramento and it was from these communities that Crocker recruited his first Chinese laborers.

Many of the Irish laborers on the job objected to working alongside Orientals, and Crocker's chief construction foreman, James Strobridge, doubted that the frail-looking Chinese were up to the heavy work demanded by the railroad project. But Crocker responded by declaring that the ancestors of the Chinese had built the Great Wall of China and therefore they were worth trying out for work on his railroad.

As it turned out, the Chinese proved to be excellent railroad workers. They carved roads into the sides of mountains, and their knowledge of fireworks was easily adapted to proficiency with blasting powder and later with nitroglycerin. In all, the Chinese managed to do most of the heavy labor on the Central Pacific, digging as many as 15 tunnels through the Sierra Nevada.

The introduction of Chinese workers was so successful that Crocker soon exhausted California's available Chinese workforce and turned to recruiting thousands of laborers in the countryside around Canton, China. More than 13,000 Chinese came to America in this way, their passage provided by agents who would be repaid, with interest, from the Chinese workers' railroad wages.

By 1866, Crocker's army of Chinese workers was about to extend the railroad's tracks across the crest of the Sierra Nevada and into the easier flat land of the northern Nevada's Humboldt River Valley. The work was proceeding ahead of schedule, and the Central Pacific managed to persuade the government to permit the line to extend its tracks westward across Nevada and into Utah "until they shall meet and connect with the Union Pacific Railroad." With that, the Great Race to build the transcontinental railroad gained great momentum; the prize would be millions of dollars in government loans and thousands of square miles in land grants.

Meanwhile, the Union Pacific had gotten off to a late start in building the eastern half of the transcontinental railway. Eastern industrialists were making huge profits in the wartime munitions business and had little incentive to invest in the Union Pacific.

Thomas Durant, who was head of the Union Pacific, realized that the real money to be made from the railroad would come from profits on construction costs. Revenues from freight and passenger service would take a

HELL ON WHEELS

"Restaurant and saloon keepers, gamblers, desperadoes of every grade, the vilest of men and women made up this 'Hell on Wheels'." That was how Massachusetts newspaperman Samuel Bowles described the instant towns that sprung up along the Union Pacific's right of way as the railroad inched across Nebraska, Wyoming and northern Utah.

Kearny, Nebraska, was the first "Hell On Wheels" town. By August of 1866, the track had reached Fort Kearny, a frontier outpost 191 miles west of the railroad's starting point in Omaha. The thousands of "ex-Confederates and Federal soldiers, muleskinners, Mexicans, New York Irish, bushwhackers, ex-convicts" and ex-slaves from the South, who brought the roadbed and tracks through the Platte River Valley, were now far from civilization, in the midst of Indian Country, and sorely in need of place to spend their wages.

Help was not long in coming. Entrepreneurs, including cardsharks, whiskey sellers and "fallen women," were in pursuit. A tent city sprouted up opposite the fort, and as the Union Pacific continued building westward, the town of Kearny carried on a lucrative trade catering to the thirst and lust of the railroadmen.

In a few months, the railroad's base of operations—the end of the track—would move westward to a new location down the line, and the Hell On Wheels town would move right along with it. The name changed at every point, but the town remained essentially the same collection of dance halls, saloons, gambling casinos and bordellos. The scene was repeated over the next three years, with North Platte in Nebraska, and Rawlins, Cheyenne and Laramie in Wyoming springing up on the plains overnight.

Many Hell On Wheels towns lasted only several months, while some endured longer as the sites of the construction crews' winter quarters. A few managed to make the transition from "mobile Gomorrahs" to permanent townsites, especially Cheyenne, which stood at the junction of the branch line southward to Denver.

In June of 1867, when the railroad had been built as far as Julesburg, the Hell on Wheels town that mushroomed there was more upscale—at least in appearance. There was even a newspaper, the *Frontier Index*, which packed up its press and moved along with the town. Prefabricated wooden buildings had been added, known as "knockdowns," which were easily dismantled, loaded onto railroad cars and shipped down the track to become part of still another incarnation of a community whose primary industry was vice.

"There appears to be plenty of money here," newspaperman Henry M. Stanley wrote of Julesburg, "and plenty of fools to squander it."

But Julesburg was not all fun and games. There was a great turnover of population, and the town soon attracted outlaws, who preyed on each other and the railroad men alike. Far from having any organized communities with law enforcement officers, Julesburg was in the grip of anarchy, and Stanley told his readers that martial law would be the "only sure preventative of these murderous scenes."

Grenville Mellon Dodge, chief engineer of the Union Pacific, was also alarmed at the goings-on in Julesburg. While he had tolerated the outrageous conduct and rampant vice of the earlier Hell On Wheels towns, things were getting out of hand at Julesburg. Too many of the dead bodies that turned up daily were those of his workers, and venereal disease among the living was as high as 50 percent. As a former general, recently elected congressman from Nebraska and railroad company official, he felt duty bound to rectify the situation. With the nearest army troops preoccupied with keeping the Plains Indians from destroying the Iron Road, Dodge was forced to organize his own form of law and order. In early July of 1867, Dodge had his construction manager, Jack Casement, arm 200 of his toughest workers with rifles and head for Julesburg. Once there, he assembled the vice den proprietors and a number of women and announced that they had to either pay rent to the railroad company, buy their town lots or get out.

Julesburg's business community rejected the ultimatum with swear words and jokes about Casement's diminutive stature. The five-foot-four Casement ordered his men to open fire into the crowd. When the shooting stopped, more than 30 lay dead in the dusty street. A few dozen more were

Cheyenne, Wyoming, in 1876 (Photo courtesy of the National Archives)

strung up from telegraph poles. (Trees were few and far between on the Great Plains of western Nebraska.)

When Grenville Dodge paid a return visit, he noted that although it was still a den of debauchery, the town seemed under control. But Julesburg had not long to enjoy its status as a tamed Hell On Wheels town. Before the end of November, after less than five months of existence, the town was taken down in pieces, loaded onto flatcars and carried down the tracks to Cheyenne. A member of the train crew heralded the event by announcing to the relocated gamblers and railroad camp followers at the Cheyenne depot, "Gentlemen, here's Julesburg!"

The last Hell on Wheel towns were in Utah, not far from the site where the golden spike united the Union Pacific and Central Pacific. One, the first non-Mormon town in Utah, was called Corine, named by a Union Pacific real estate salesman in honor of his daughter—a designation that he soon regretted when the place quickly turned into a bawdy amusement park for off-duty track crews.

Most of the Hell On Wheels towns that moved west with the Union Pacific between 1866 and 1869 left behind little more than a few shacks or a water tower. Willow Station, Plum Creek, Sherman Summit, Fort Halleck, Medicine Bow, Carbon Station, Benton, Red Desert, Bitter Creek, Salt Wells and Bear River City were among the many "mushroom towns" that vanished without trace, not even leaving the abandoned buildings of a ghost town.

Despite the remote and desolate locale, the Hell On Wheels towns brought the first significant popu-

lation to the region. Although at the time it was the southwestern part of Dakota Territory, the Dakota territorial government wanted no part of the tumultuous Hell On Wheels settlements. Besides, there was no direct communication link since the area between the westernmost Dakota settlement and the nearest Hell on Wheels town was still controlled by the Indians.

Prompted by a petition unanimously endorsed by the Dakota territorial legislature, the federal government severed the western part of Dakota Territory, and by adding portions of eastern Idaho Territory and northern Utah Territory, created Wyoming Territory on July 25, 1868. Cheyenne was named the capital.

At the time, the railroad workers and the army of gamblers and women who followed them west numbered close to 20,000 people. But within two years, with railroad construction completed, the population rapidly dwindled to fewer than 10,000 white inhabitants.

The short but bawdy railroad-building period had brought an unusually large number of women to that part of the western frontier. But after the work was completed on that part of the line, Wyoming's population had diminished so much that every citizen in the new territory was valued as a potential voter, including women. That circumstance led Wyoming to pioneer in political equality. In December of 1869, as one of its first official acts, the Wyoming territorial government granted women the right to vote and to hold public office—the first territory or state in the United States to do so.

long time to recoup the initial investment, since there were few settlements along the railroad and freight business along the route was almost nonexistent. Instead, he planned to siphon off the money the railroad paid out for construction, and to this end Durant organized a company called Credit Mobilier (French for "moveable loan"), which charged the railroad exorbitant prices for material and labor. He and his partners ultimately realized more than $20 million from the scheme, and with Credit Mobilier stock they were able to buy the votes of congressmen who helped pass legislation favorable to the railroad and its investors.

Construction of the Union Pacific began after the Civil War's end in 1865. Supplies of material were now abundant, and capital diverted from the war effort now poured in to finance the Union Pacific. Manpower for the project came from thousands of Irish emigrants, from demobilized soldiers from both the Union and the former Confederacy, and it included a fair number of newly freed slaves from the South.

When the Union Pacific's chief engineer Peter Dey learned of the Credit Mobilier scheme, he quit in protest. He was replaced in 1866 by Grenville Mellon Dodge, who had just left the Union army after serving as a general in campaigns against the Indians on the Southern Plains and in Civil War campaigns in Georgia. He had been a surveyor and railroad builder; before the Civil War, he had explored the Platte River Valley and the South Pass for a railroad route. Under Dodge's direction, construction of the Union Pacific rapidly crossed Nebraska and by November of 1867, the railroad was approaching Wyoming's South Pass and the Continental Divide.

Construction of the Union Pacific across the flat terrain of the Great Plains proceeded with assembly-line precision. Three hundred miles ahead of the crews were the surveyors who plotted out the exact route. Then came the bridge builders and grading teams who built up the roadbeds. Next came the track-laying crews who managed to lay between three to five miles of track a day. Every 60 or 70 miles along the route, temporary settlements were established. For about two months, these towns of prefabricated buildings and tents served not only as supply depots but also catered to the recreational needs of the thousands of railroad workers. Each would contain several dozen saloons, gambling establishments and brothels. Known as "Hell On Wheels," these temporary towns would stand only as long as needed, usually no longer than a winter or several months. Then they would be taken down, loaded on flatcars and shipped down the track to be set up at the next site along the line. Some of them left a permanent settlements behind, which developed into western towns such as North Platte, Nebraska, and Laramie and Cheyenne in Wyoming.

By 1869, both the Central Pacific and the Union Pacific were building in opposite directions across northern Utah. Although they were slated to meet, the exact point where this would happen was still to be determined. For several months, the two lines were actually constructing parallel tracks, sometimes only a few hundred feet apart. Neither railroad wanted to stop laying track, since the more track each laid, the more they would earn in government land grants and loans. Finally, President Ulysses S. Grant stepped in to settle the issue. In a meeting with Grenville Dodge of the Union Pacific and Colis P. Huntington of the Central Pacific, it was agreed the two railroads would join at a site known as Promontory Point, north of the Great Salt Lake.

The great day came in May of 1869. As frontier journalist and poet Bret Harte described it, the Central Pacific locomotive *Jupiter* and the Union Pacific's *Number*

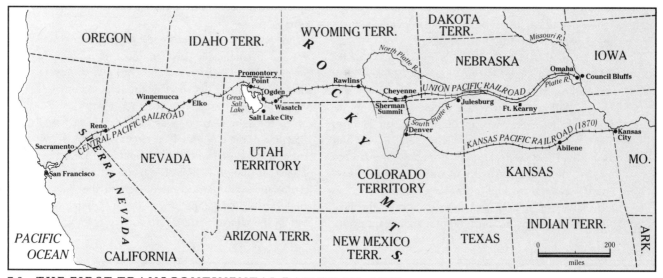

7.8 THE FIRST TRANSCONTINENTAL RAILROAD: 1869

119, faced each other "on the single track . . . . Half a world behind each back" as the final rails were set in place. A telegraph line was attached to a spike that would be hammered in and send an instantaneous signal to the world that the lines had been linked.

On May 10, 1869, Leland Stanford swung a silver hammer to drive in the final spike, which was made of gold. Although he missed it entirely, the message was sent out anyway. The news was received around the nation with great rejoicing. There were parades in Chicago and New York, and the Liberty Bell proclaimed the news to Philadelphia. In Buffalo, New York, crowds celebrated by pouring into the street singing "The Star Spangled Banner."

Grenville Dodge said to the workers assembled at the ceremony at Promontory Point: "Gentlemen, the great Benton [Senator Thomas Hart Benton] proposed that someday a giant statue of Columbus be erected on the highest peak of the Rocky Mountains, pointing westward, denoting that as the great route across the continent. You have made that prophecy today a fact. This is the way to India."

Theodore Judah did not live to see his dream of a transcontinental railroad become a reality. In 1863, on a trip across Panama en route to Washington, D.C., he contracted yellow fever and died soon after reaching New York. But the transcontinental railroad he had envisioned, and the ones that followed, entirely changed the pattern of western settlement.

THE ALASKA PURCHASE

Secretary of State William H. Seward was at his Washington, D.C., home playing cards on the evening of March 29, 1867, when he received a visit from Russian ambassador Baron Edward de Stoeckl. The Russian ambassador brought the news that Seward's proposal that the United States purchase Russian America—Alaska—had been approved by Czar Alexander II. Before dawn, the two men had ironed out a treaty that was submitted to the U.S. Senate that very morning, just hours before it was set to adjourn.

Vitus Bering, a Danish navigator in service to the Russian government, had discovered Alaska in 1741. Reports that the region was a rich source of sea otter skins soon brought on a great rush of fur hunters. By 1799, Russia had established a flourishing fishing and fur-trading colony in the Aleutian Islands and on the Alaskan mainland. The enterprise was run by the Russian American Company under a charter from the czar and dependent on the skill and labor of Aleut Indians.

Over the next decades, the Russian American Company extended its trade southward from Alaska along

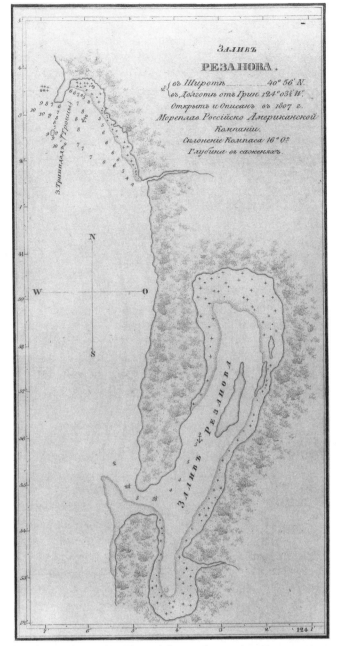

Russian Hydrographic Chart of the North American Coast, 1848–49 (Photo courtesy of the Library of Congress)

the Pacific coast of North America. Conflicts with the United States over fishing and shipping rights in those waters came to a head in the early 1820s, and in 1824 prompted President James Monroe to issue the Monroe Doctrine in which he warned foreign powers not to expand their colonial possessions in the Western Hemisphere.

In later years, Russia turned its attention away from North America to Central Asia, embarking on a program of "eastward expansion" into Siberia, with an eye on winning a foothold in India. In 1854, that policy helped bring about the Crimean War in which Russia was pitted against Great Britain.

Half a world away from European Russia, Alaska was too distant to protect from an armed takeover by the British fleet. To forestall that threat, the Russian government pretended to sell its North American colony to a San Francisco–based American company. But the plan was scrapped when the American government advised the Russians that the scheme would not fool the British.

As it turned out, the Russian American Company had subleased the southeastern Alaskan "panhandle" to the British-owned Hudson's Bay Company. Both big fur-trading concerns had good commercial reasons to keep the region in Russian hands, and they managed to persuade their respective governments to keep Alaska out of the sphere of the conflict.

Russia still had reasons to worry about protecting its Alaska holdings, as demonstrated by a new threat in 1857. There was a rumor that Brigham Young was planning a mass migration of Mormons to Alaska in the wake of the problems he was having with federal authorities in Utah. Although that report was never substantiated, it underscored Alaska's vulnerability.

The Russian government also feared that American expansionists, driven by the ideals of Manifest Destiny, might seize Alaska. Even by the late 1850s, the Russians were aware of some gold deposits in Alaska, and they were concerned that a significant strike could spark a sudden gold rush that would flood the region with Americans. And in the event of another European war, Alaska still remained easy prey for Russia's arch rival, Great Britain.

The Russian American Company was also becoming a problem. Despite prolonged Tlingit Indian resistance, the company had kept up its operations and had exploited the region's fur resources to the point where the sea otter was nearly extinct. Profits steadily declined after 1855, and by 1862, when its charter expired, the company was on the brink of bankruptcy.

Russia could either renew the ailing company's charter or take over direct administration of Alaska. Since either option would lose money, the Russian government chose to allow the company to carry on, but only on a year-to-year basis, with the hope that it might be revived. The idea of selling Alaska to the United States seemed more attractive than risking Alaska's seizure by a foreign power.

Russia had to somehow coax the United States to make the first move. If Russia were to offer openly to sell Alaska, the news could very well panic investors and creditors of the Russian American Company and wreak financial havoc on that already beleaguered enterprise. But in 1862, when Russia was ready to sell, the United States was in the grip of the Civil War and in no position to enter into negotiations for the acquisition of additional territory.

In 1861, newly elected President Abraham Lincoln appointed William H. Seward as his secretary of state. A former governor of New York and U.S. senator, Seward had been Lincoln's chief rival in the contest for the Republican presidential nomination in 1860. He was not only the Senate's most outspoken opponent of slavery, but he was also a passionate expansionist. "The popular passion for territorial aggrandizement," he once said, "is irresistible." For Seward, slavery was a moral wrong that stood in the way of the realization of the nation's Manifest Destiny.

Seward did not consider the Mexican Cession and the Gadsden Purchase as the end of national expansion; Manifest Destiny, he believed, meant the United States' taking all of North America. Although as secretary of state he was in a position to steer actively the nation toward the achievement of his goals, his ambitions for territorial growth were held up as long as the Civil War raged. In the midst of the conflict, he skillfully handled the Union's foreign affairs, dissuading the British from siding with the Confederacy and discouraging Louis Napoleon of France from carrying out his imperialist scheme in Mexico. On that April night in 1865 when Lincoln was assassinated by John Wilkes Booth, one of Booth's fellow conspirators broke into Seward's house and stabbed him. He survived the attack and continued on as secretary of state under the new president, Andrew Johnson.

With the war over and the Union victorious, the Russians renewed their efforts to sell Alaska. The Russians found their chance in 1867. The fishermen of Washington Territory had petitioned the United States government to help gain fishing rights for them in Alaskan waters. As secretary of state, Seward made the request on behalf of Washington Territory, but the Russian ambassador promptly told him that the Russian government would flatly refuse to grant any concessions to American fishermen. Just as the Russians had hoped, Seward then countered by offering to buy Alaska. The proposal was transmitted by the Atlantic cable to Czar Alexander in St. Petersburg, who quickly assented to the deal.

Ambassador Stoeckl had been authorized to accept nothing less than $5 million for Alaska, but when he saw how eager Seward was to complete the sale, he upped the price to $7 million. The Hudson's Bay Company still held leases to some Alaskan territory, but the United States, having had problems with that company since the War of 1812, did not want them as tenants. To buy them out, the Russians then received an additional $200,000, making the final purchase price for Alaska $7.2 million.

The treaty was finalized in the early morning hours of March 30, 1867. Seward presented the treaty to the Sen-

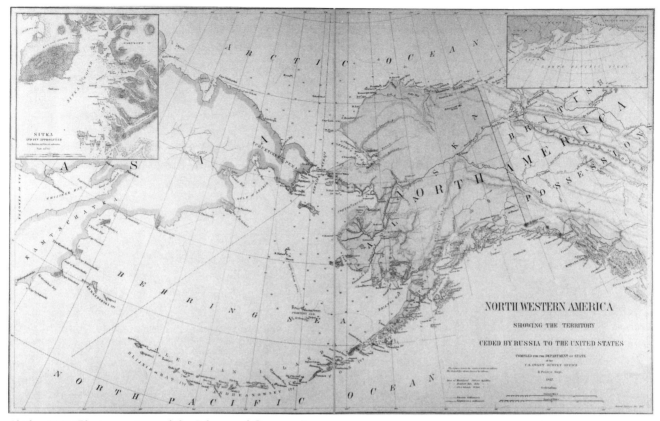

Alaska, 1867 (Photo courtesy of the Library of Congress)

ate that very day, and the Senate then convened in a special session to hear arguments for and against ratification. Most Americans knew little about Alaska. Except for the southeastern panhandle, most of the interior of the mainland was known by its Eskimo (Inuit) and Athapascan population, and not by whites. For many Americans, Alaska was a "frozen asset," a "barren, worthless, God-forsaken region" comprised of "walrus-covered icebergs." The press derided the proposed purchase as "Walrussia," "Johnson's Polar Bear Garden," "Seward's Icebox" and "Seward's Folly."

Seward had strong allies in the Senate. Among them was Senator Charles Sumner, chairman of the powerful Senate Committee on Foreign Relations. Although Sumner knew almost nothing about Alaska, he was aided by information gleaned from the Smithsonian Institution's natural history experts and thus able to deliver a three-hour speech to his Senate colleagues in which he extolled the region's natural resources and its strategic benefits to the United States. That greatly helped sway many senators, and the treaty was approved. Nevertheless, the measure won by a narrow margin, having passed by only one more vote than necessary.

The next hurdle was in the House of Representatives. Although the Senate had the authority to ratify the treaty, the House was responsible for giving its approval for the appropriation of the $7.2 million. President Johnson, who was in the midst of impeachment proceedings, had few friends in the House. Moreover, many members of the House were offended that the purchase price had been agreed upon without consulting them. They also resented the secrecy surrounding the treaty and characterized it as a "dark deal done in the night."

The fact remained that the treaty had already been ratified. If the government had to back out of the deal because the House failed to approve the money, the czar would be insulted. Four years earlier, in 1863, at the height of the Civil War, the czar had sent two small fleets of warships to the United States, one to New York and the other to San Francisco. Americans believed it was a gesture of Russian support for the Union and at the time Secretary of the Navy Gideon Welles remarked in gratitude, "God Bless the Russians." (Actually the Russian Navy had sent its ships to American waters in 1863 to keep them from being bottled up in the Baltic when a new war over Poland seemed about to break out between Russia and the major European powers.)

Some congressmen now viewed the proposed Alaska purchase as "an act of recompense to a tried friend" who had come to America's aid at the time of its greatest cri-

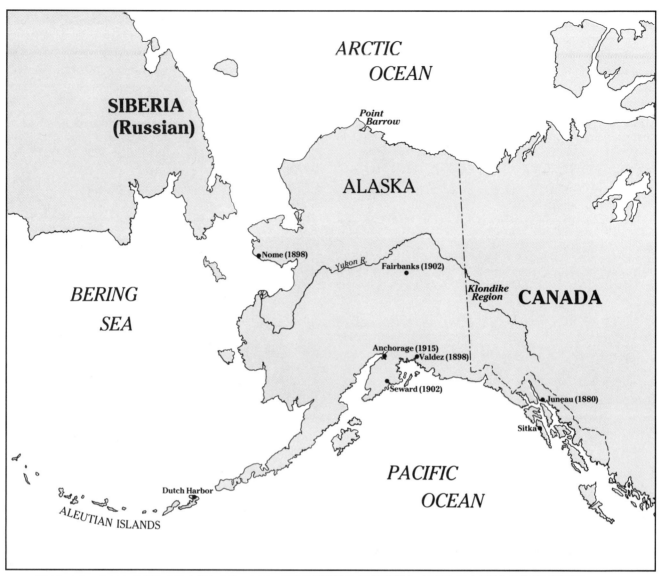

7.9 THE ALASKA PURCHASE OF 1867, SHOWING TOWNS AND DATES FOUNDED

sis. It would be a serious blow to friendly relations with Russia were the United States to throw the territory back in the "czar's face."

The debate over the Alaska purchase dragged on through Johnson's impeachment trial. But the president emerged triumphant from that ordeal, and by then public opinion had turned in favor of the Alaska purchase treaty. The *New York Herald* proclaimed that it was part of the nation's "inevitable destiny, which in time must give us the whole of the North American continent." In California, the *Sacramento Union* echoed that sentiment, declaring, "We approach the Pole . . . Our flag has advanced to the northern verge of the continent—the auroral land fringed by ice and the Arctic Sea."

The votes of a few congressmen were still needed. Russian ambassador Baron de Stoeckl, exasperated by the delays of the democratic process, then resorted to bribing some key representatives. His efforts apparently

paid off; the appropriation for the purchase of Alaska won final approval in the House on July 14, 1868.

Six months later, in his annual State of the Union address, President Andrew Johnson underscored Seward's ideals for national expansion when he declared that Alaska had been acquired "with the view of extending national jurisdiction and republican principles in the American hemisphere."

William Seward's deal with the Russians had increased the size of the United States by one-fifth. The territory was twice the size of the Mexican Cession without Texas, and had cost the United States less than two cents an acre for an area encompassing more than half a million square miles. Some congressmen saw the Alaska purchase as a first step in absorbing Canada, which would now "fall into our lap like a ripe apple."

Initially, Alaska was left to the management of the army and navy, and in 1879 it was put under the administration of the U.S. Customs Service. But in 1880, a prospector named Joe Juneau found gold in the Alaskan panhandle. The biggest gold mine in the world developed around the town that now bears his name. The initial gold discovery led to Alaska's organization as a territory in 1884, complete with a territorial governor and legislature.

More gold strikes followed, first in the adjacent Canadian Yukon and Klondike regions in 1896, which brought a stampede of hundreds of thousands of Americans through Alaska, and then in Alaska itself at Nome in 1898 and Fairbanks in 1902.

Fishing and mining caused the territory to grow throughout the 20th century. In the years after World War II, Alaska became strategically vital in the Cold War between the United States and Russia, and by 1959 had gained a sufficient population for admission as the 49th state.

"Seward's Folly" had proven to be a bargain after all. Within less than 30 years, Alaska had produced enough mineral wealth to repay the initial purchase price many times over.

Seward, Alaska, founded in 1902 as the ocean terminus of the Alaska Railroad, was named in honor of William H. Seward and his important role in making Alaska part of U.S. territory.

A NEW WEST

The United States emerged from the crisis of the Civil War as a nation transformed. The fierce debate over whether new western territories and states would be free or slave had been forever silenced by the roar of guns and cries of suffering of thousands on bloody battlefields.

In the early part of the war, the Union–Confederate borderlands of New Mexico and Missouri were scenes of decisive battles that left the West firmly tied to the Union. But at the same time, even greater bonds were being forged by the federal government in Washington. The withdrawal of the southern states had left Congress with a free hand to redraw the map of the West. In the absence of southern opposition, a new land policy was initiated that aimed to transform the Great Plains into the domain of free-soil farmers.

The turmoil of the Civil War years gave the western Indians an opportunity to rise up against the relentless tide of white encroachment. Warfare for them would continue until 1890.

The Civil War brought a sudden end to the sectional rivalry that had stymied efforts to construct a transcontinental railroad. Begun during the war and completed just four years after the war's end, the first transcontinental railroad linked the North and the West both physically and economically. The journey from the Atlantic to the Pacific that had once taken overland travelers several months could now be made in less than 10 days. But far more than a travel breakthrough, over the next 30 years, extensive railroad lines would change the course of western settlement. Millions of pioneers, drawn from the eastern United States as well as from Europe, would flock to the newly accessible lands and rapidly settle the western half of the nation, what was once considered the "Great American Desert."

As it turned out, the progress of westward expansion had not ended, but had only been interrupted by the struggle between the North and the South. In the years immediately following the Civil War, the revived spirit of Manifest Destiny led to the purchase of Alaska, bringing the nation's northwestern frontier to Asia's doorstep.

Chapter 8
FRONTIER'S END
(1868–1900s)

HE GILDED AGE WAS THE title of Mark Twain and Charles Dudley Warner's 1874 novel that satirized American life and culture in the post-Civil War years. It was a gilded age, and decidedly not a golden one. Beneath the glittering surface lay widespread political corruption at the highest levels of government, the ruthless business practices of so-called "robber barons" and unchecked exploitation of the nation's still-abundant but rapidly diminishing natural resources.

The "Gilded Age" came to identify the entire era from from the post-Civil War years to about 1912. It was a time when American business underwent phenomenal growth. Huge profits had been made during the war, and rich resources of timber, mineral wealth and fertile lands stood ready to exploit. The growing stream of immigrants from overseas provided an ever-expanding market for goods as well as a seemingly limitless supply of cheap labor.

The industrial centers of the East became booming markets for all the beef and bread that the West could produce. In the West, the Gilded Age reverberated with the rise of the great cattle empires and the rapid spread of farms and towns across the Great Plains.

The railroads were eager to reap the profits from the sale of the free western lands they had obtained from the government. For their lines to prosper, they needed to promote settlement along their western routes. Both these goals were achieved when they promoted one of the largest mass migrations in history. As a result of their efforts, the vast region of the nation's midsection—which only a few decades before had been regarded as a sparsely inhabited game preserve for native peoples and fur trappers—rapidly filled up with millions of newcom-

ers from the settled East as well as with hordes of immigrants from Europe.

This era also saw the final Indian military resistance against an expanding nation and land-hungry population. And it was toward the end of this era when the final act of the nation's century-long drama of territorial growth was played out: the opening of the remaining lands of the ever-dwindling Indian Territory to white settlement and the closing of the frontier.

THE FINAL INDIAN WARS IN THE WEST

In the years following the Civil War, the government sought a quick solution to Indian resistance to continuing white expansion. Officials shaped a new approach, a "Peace Policy" that would prevent massacres such as that at Sand Creek, while the army—now freed up from action in the East—showed its strength.

In October of 1867, representatives of the Southern Plains tribes signed a series of treaties at Medicine Lodge near Fort Larned in Kansas. They were granted reservations in the Indian Territory on holdings of the Cherokees, Chickasaws, Choctaws, Creeks and Seminoles, who were forced to forfeit portions of their reservations as punishment for some having sided with the Confederacy during the Civil War.

White development, however, such as along the Kansas Pacific Railroad, was closing in on the ever-shrinking Indian lands, and Indian raiding continued. Civil War heroes General William Tecumseh Sherman, head of the U.S. Army in the West, and General Philip Henry Sheridan, head of the Department of the Missouri, had a plan

Red Cloud (Photo courtesy of the National Archives of Canada)

to take away the Indians' ability to wage war—the same strategy they had used on the South.

In November of 1868, during a sustained winter campaign against militant factions, forces under Lieutenant Colonel George Armstrong Custer unexpectedly came upon Black Kettle's village on the Washita River in present-day western Oklahoma. More than 100 Indians were killed in the surprise attack, including Black Kettle, who had survived the Sand Creek Massacre four years before.

Meanwhile, on the Northern Plains, Sioux bands—under the Oglala Teton Sioux chief Red Cloud—had been waging a war against the federal government's efforts to develop a road northward from the Oregon Trail through the eastern foothills of the Bighorn Mountains. The new route followed the Bozeman Trail and promised to link the Montana and Idaho gold-mining country with the main east-west route. The proposed road cut right through the Powder River country, a favorite Sioux hunting ground. The army proceeded to construct forts along the route, including Fort Reno, Fort C.F. Smith and Fort Phil Kearny.

In December of 1866, a detachment of 80 men led by Captain William J. Fetterman were caught in a Sioux am-

bush near Fort Phil Kearny; Fetterman and his entire command were killed. In the months that followed, Red Cloud's warriors fought and won more battles along the Bozeman Trail, despite the army's new breech–loading repeating rifles.

The federal government, however, chose to make peace rather than continue the conflict that became known as the War for the Bozeman Trail or Red Cloud's War. In the spring of 1868, Red Cloud agreed to peace terms. The government gave up its plans for the Bozeman Trail route and abandoned the forts along the way. Under a new Fort Laramie Treaty, the Sioux received a large reservation in the Black Hills of present-day southwestern South Dakota. The Indians were also permitted to hunt in the Powder River country to the west—at least until the government decided to open the land for settlement.

Also during the years 1866–68, in southern Oregon and Idaho, the Snake War involved Northern Paiute bands under Paulina and Old Weawea against forces under Colonel George Crook. After relentless tracking and about 40 skirmishes, the army wore down the insurgents and forced a surrender.

A period of relative peace followed. But conditions were unchanged. Reservation conditions were generally miserable, and Indian lands were left unprotected. Governmental promises were inevitably broken.

In 1872–73, in a part of the Far West that had seen little Indian warfare since the Spanish occupation, Modocs under Kintpuash (Captain Jack) left their reservation in northern Oregon and made a stand against troops under General Edward Canby in northeast California. At the Lava Beds in January of 1873, a standoff occurred. On April 11 of that year, Canby was killed during a peace conference, making him the only general to die in the Indian wars. Captain Jack and three other warriors were hanged that October.

On the Southern Plains, in 1874–75, Comanches under Quanah Parker and Kiowas under Satanta, Lone Wolf and Mamanti resisted settlement on reservation lands in the Indian Territory in the Red River War, or Buffalo War. In June of 1874, a contingent of buffalo hunters with repeating rifles drove off allied Comanches, Kiowas, Cheyennes and Arapahos at Adobe Walls in Texas, where troops under Kit Carson had also won a victory 10 years before. Colonels Ranald S. Mackenzie and Nelson A. Miles moved on the insurgents. After the Indian defeat at Palo Duro Canyon in September of 1874, most militants surrendered.

On the Northern Plains in 1874, Lieutenant Colonel Custer led a scientific survey expedition through the Black Hills, and among his party were a few miners who found gold in the region. The news came on the heels of another national financial downturn, and the promise of ready wealth from placer mining in the Black Hills

8.1 INDIAN-WHITE WARFARE FOR THE WEST: 1866-90

soon brought tens of thousands of miners into the region.

The invasion threatened to bring about a new Sioux war, and to offset the impending conflict, the government offered to buy the Black Hills from the Sioux for $6 million. But the Indians refused to sell lands that they held as sacred. The Oglala-Brule Teton Sioux chief Crazy Horse spurned the offer, stating that "One does not sell the earth upon which people walk." And the Hunkpapa Teton Sioux leader Sitting Bull vowed to protect the Black Hills, declaring: "We want no white men here. The Black Hills belong to me. If the whites try to take them, I will fight."

The unchecked influx of gold-seekers into the Black Hills incensed the Sioux, and under Sitting Bull and Crazy Horse, thousands left their reservation to join bands of other Indian militants in the country around the Bighorn and Powder rivers. The government foresaw trouble. The large number of Indian freedom fighters in eastern Montana now threatened to interfere with the building of the Northern Pacific Railroad, then edging westward across the Northern Plains.

The government ordered all the Sioux back on their reservations by February 1, 1876. But Sitting Bull and Crazy Horse, now allied with bands of Northern Cheyennes, refused to obey and continued to mass warriors and supplies along the Little Bighorn River.

To meet the Indian challenge, a large-scale, three-pronged offensive was planned against the Sioux for the spring of 1876. From the North Platte, a column under General George Crook headed northward. From Fort Abraham Lincoln, near present-day Bismarck, North Dakota, a force under General Alfred H. Terry, including Custer and the 7th Cavalry, moved westward, and a third unit, under Colonel John Gibbon, proceeded eastward from western Montana. The three columns planned to converge on the Sioux and Cheyennes in the Bighorn River country.

On June 25, 1876, Custer and 265 men of the 7th Cavalry, having swung southward from the Yellowstone River, came upon a Sioux camp on the Little Bighorn River. Instead of rejoining Terry's command with the news, Custer impulsively decided to grab the glory of what seemed a ready military victory for himself, and launched an attack. But unknown to Custer, there were far more than the few hundred Indians he had seen in the camp. As he approached the Little Bighorn Indian encampment, he was surprised by several thousand Sioux and Cheyenne warriors. Within less than an hour, Custer and his entire command were wiped out. Only a lone Indian scout survived to relate what had happened.

News of Custer's defeat electrified the nation, which was only a week or so away from celebrating its 100th birthday. The Battle of the Little Bighorn became known as "Custer's Last Stand," but more significantly, it proved to be the last major victory of the Plains Indians.

The Sioux suffered defeats at War Bonnet Creek the following July, 1876, and at Slim Buttes in September, both in present-day South Dakota. Northern Cheyennes under Dull Knife were defeated in the Battle of Dull Knife on the Red Fork of the Powder River in Wyoming in November.

Most of the Sioux and their allies had surrendered by the spring of 1877. Crazy Horse, along with about 800 starving followers, turned himself in to federal authorities at Fort Robinson in northwestern Nebraska. Several months later, he was killed there in an altercation with soldiers. Meanwhile, Sitting Bull and a number of followers fled northward to seek refuge across the border in Canada. He remained there until 1881, when he returned to the United States and surrendered at Fort Buford in North Dakota. In 1885–86, Sitting Bull toured

Painting of Custer's Defeat at the Little Bighorn (Photo courtesy of the New York Public Library)

Chief Joseph (Photo courtesy of the National Archives of Canada)

with Buffalo Bill Cody's Wild West Show before settling down on the Sioux reservation.

In the aftermath of the Sioux War of 1876, the Sioux lost the Black Hills and were forced to accept a smaller reservation in the Dakota Territory.

In 1877, a new outbreak of Indian warfare occurred in the Pacific Northwest. The Nez Perces, under Chief Joseph and other leaders, refused to vacate ancestral homelands in eastern Oregon and Washington Territory. Gold miners, settlers and railroad developers coveted their lands, and the federal government ordered the tribe to a reservation in Idaho Territory. Fearing military retaliation after outbreaks of fighting between warrior bands and settlers, Chief Joseph chose instead to lead his people on a trek across the Bitterroot Mountains in an attempt to reach safety from persecution in Canada. In pursuit, federal troops under General Oliver Otis Howard chased the Nez Perces across 1,700 miles of wilderness. At one point, the Nez Perce retreat took the tribe through newly created Yellowstone National Park, where they briefly held several tourists as hostages before releasing them unharmed.

In September of 1877, at Bear Paw Mountain in northern Montana, just 40 miles from the Canadian border, General Nelson Miles caught the fleeing Indians in a trap, and Chief Joseph was forced to surrender. In giving up the fight, the Nez Perce leader declared: "Hear me, my chiefs. I am tired; my heart is sick and sad. From where the sun now stands I will fight no more, forever."

As punishment for their raids on white settlers, the Nez Perces were first exiled to a reservation in the Indian Territory of present-day Oklahoma. In that land, with a climate alien to the Nez Perces, many of the tribe became sick and died. But after Generals Howard and Miles protested this harsh measure, the government relented and allowed the Nez Perces to settle on more familiar country in Washington Territory.

There were other engagements in the struggle for the West between its native peoples and the bluecoats. White squatters on Indian homelands and hunting grounds, forced land cessions and broken treaties led to many outbreaks of violence. Small incidents led to larger ones and eventually to military campaigns.

In 1878, Bannocks, Paiutes and Umatillas under Buffalo Horn, Egan and Oytes resisted attacks from troops under General Oliver Howard out of Fort Boise in present-day Idaho. The insurgents grouped at Steens Mountain in southeastern Oregon, fighting battles at Silver Creek and Birch Creek in June and July. The final party of militants was captured that September. A band known as the Sheepeaters, probably Shoshones and Bannocks, living in the Salmon River Mountains of central Idaho, eluded cavalry patrols into the following year.

In 1879, the Ute War erupted in western Colorado, when Utes, dissatisfied with conditions at the White River Agency in western Colorado, rose up against the Indian agent Nathan Meeker. Warriors under Nicaagat (Jack), Colorow (Colorado), and Canalla (Johnson) fought Major Thomas Thornburgh's command at Milk Creek for a week in late September and early October. When troops finally reached the agency, they found Meeker and some of his white employees dead. Ouray negotiated on behalf of the militants, leading to a further reduction of Ute territory. One Ute, Quinkent (Douglas), who was thought to have raped Meeker's wife, was sentenced to imprisonment at Fort Leavenworth in Kansas and served a year.

During the late 1870s, the Apaches offered stubborn resistance to reservation life, escaping time and again and conducting raids in Arizona, New Mexico and northern Mexico. The Mimbreno Apache Victorio, leading members from a variety of bands living on the Warm Springs (Ojo Caliente) reservation in present-day southwestern New Mexico, conducted raids throughout much of the Southwest. Tracked by U.S. forces under Colonel Edward Hatch in New Mexico and Colonel Benjamin Grierson in Texas, Victorio was killed at the hands of

Mexican forces in October of 1880 at Three Peaks (Tres Castillos).

Similarly, in the 1880s, Geronimo resisted confinement on the San Carlos reservation in present-day eastern Arizona. He and a dedicated band of followers managed to elude capture until being tracked down by forces under now-general George Crook in 1886 at Canyon de los Embudos in Mexico on March 25, 1886. Geronimo agreed to the peace terms, but escaped while being led to Fort Bowie. Command was passed to now-General Nelson Miles, who forced Geronimo's final surrender on September 4, 1886, at Skeleton Canyon, about 65 miles south of the Apache Pass in present-day Arizona. Geronimo was imprisoned in Florida and Arizona, finally being allowed to return to the West in 1894. He never was permitted to return to Chiricahua country, however, but spent his remaining years in the Indian Territory.

The Indian Wars did not end with a battle, but a show of force and the suppression of a religious movement. By 1890, a revivalist fervor was spreading among the Indians of the West. The Ghost Dance religion had originated in the Great Basin among the Paiutes, founded by the prophet Wovoka (Jack Wilson). Its adherents believed that they could drive the whites from Indian lands

Reservation Indian Police Badge (Molly Braun)

if they followed traditional rituals and performed a certain ceremonial dance. They also believed "Ghost Shirts" would repel the army's bullets.

In December of 1890, Sitting Bull, whom government authorities had suspected of being a leader of the feared revolt, was killed in a struggle with reservation police at his home on the Standing Rock Reservation in North Dakota.

Federal authorities, fearing an organized rebellion, ordered troops to move on the Ghost Dancers. Troops surrounded a band of Sioux under the Miniconjou Teton Sioux chief Big Foot at Wounded Knee near the Pine Ridge reservation. Although the Indians had been disarmed, on the morning of December 29, 1890, shots rang out and the soldiers responded by opening up with rapid-firing cannons known as Hotchkiss guns. When the gunsmoke cleared, hundreds of Native Americans lay dead in the snow. Further demonstrations of force by the army ended gatherings of Ghost Dancers.

Sitting Bull (Photo courtesy of the National Archives of Canada)

Slaughtered Buffalo (Photo courtesy of the Library of Congress)

BUFFALO SOLDIERS

The Indians called them "Buffalo Soldiers," because the texture of their hair resembled the woolly coats of the Great Plains animal. These were the men of the African-American cavalry regiments that served in the campaigns against the western Indians in the years after the Civil War.

To meet the challenge of the Civil War, the ranks of the Union's armed forces had been swelled with hundreds of thousands of troops from volunteer and state militia units. But with most of these enlistments ending soon after the war's conclusion, the regular army was quickly reduced to peacetime strength. Yet there was still a great need for troops on the western frontier. To meet this demand, Congress passed legislation providing for the creation of several regiments of black cavalry troops in July of 1866.

Many blacks, recently freed from slavery but now facing poverty and unemployment, eagerly joined up, attracted by the prospect of room, board and clothing, as well as wages of $13 a month. There was no shortage of black recruits for the new cavalry regiments, but the plan still met strong opposition from military leaders. Despite the fact that more than 175,000 blacks had already served in the Union army in the Civil War, and that more than 30,000 of them had died for the Union cause, many high-ranking officers and War Department officials still doubted that blacks could be trained and they believed that black troops would panic in the face of combat.

Because of the need for frontier garrisons, these objections were dismissed. In August of 1866, the 10th U.S. Cavalry Regiment was mustered into service at Fort Leavenworth, Kansas. All of the officers were white, and all of the enlisted men were black. Their commander was Colonel Benjamin Grierson, a former music teacher from Illinois who had known Abraham Lincoln. In battles in Louisiana and Tennessee, Grierson had proven himself an able military leader, having risen through the ranks from private to brigadier general of volunteers.

The first challenges Colonel Grierson and his black regiment faced arose from the racial prejudice of Fort Leavenworth's commanding officer, who assigned the black troops to barracks in a damp and swampy part of the post. As a result, many of the black recruits were stricken with pneumonia and fever. The black soldiers were strictly segregated from white troops and they were not permitted to take part in official parades or other post functions. Racial prejudice was even reflected in the quality of the horses assigned the black cavalrymen, with many of their mounts made up of old or crippled leftovers from the Civil War.

Despite these difficulties, Colonel Grierson persevered in training his troops and managed to turn them into a highly effective unit of horse soldiers. They were soon detailed to Fort Riley in western Kansas, and in May of 1867 they saw their first action in the region between the Platte and Arkansas rivers in battles with Sioux and Cheyenne war parties.

Three months later, a detachment of the black cavalry regiment fought a six-hour battle with Cheyennes. Although the 34 troopers were outnumbered nearly two-to-one, they managed to repel their at-

---

The Wounded Knee incident, the last military campaign of its kind against the Indians, has come to be viewed as a symbol for a botched and cruel federal Indian policy and the destruction of the traditional Indian way of life.

A LOST WAY OF LIFE

The dispossession of Plains Indian culture did not come from military defeat alone. Disease played a large part, as did the extermination of the buffalo.

The Indians relied on the American bison for food, clothing and materials with which to make shelters. The herds were drastically reduced when white hunters shot hundreds of thousands of buffalo to provide meat for workers on the transcontinental railroad in the late 1860s. Among them was William "Buffalo Bill" Cody, who, by his own account, slaughtered 4,280 buffalo within an 18-month span. In the early 1870s, eastern tanneries developed a process that could turn buffalo hides into commercial leather. Thousands of white hunters flocked to the Great Plains to harvest the vast but rapidly dwindling herds of buffalo. In the years following the Civil War, as many as 15 million buffalo roamed the

tackers. Contrary to the views of skeptics in the War Department, they had stood their ground.

In September of 1867, while guarding railroad construction workers near Fort Hays, Kansas, a nine-man detail of the black regiment was pinned down in a ditch by a force of more than 70 Cheyenne warriors. Although facing overwhelming odds, the black soldiers managed to drive off their attackers.

In the late 1870s and early 1880s, the army's regiments of black horse soldiers took part in the struggle against the Apaches in southern New Mexico, where they became adept at the Indians' guerrilla warfare techniques. In 1880, they played a significant role in driving the Apache warrior chief Victorio into Mexico, where he was ultimately defeated and killed by the Mexican army.

Taking part in that campaign was Lieutenant Henry Ossian Flipper, the first black officer in the regular army, and the first black man to graduate from West Point. In the subsequent war against Geronimo and his Apache followers, Sergeant William McBrayar, a black cavalryman from North Carolina, performed with distinction and won the Congressional Medal of Honor for himself and for his entire regiment.

White officers who served with the black cavalry regiments also won fame. Among them was General John J. Pershing, commander of the American Expeditionary Force in World War I, who earned the unflattering nickname "Black Jack" because of his strict command of the Buffalo Soldiers on the southwestern frontier.

The morale and esprit de corps of the Buffalo Soldiers remained unmatched. The desertion rate of soldiers in the black regiments was the lowest in U.S. military history. Proud of their reputation as In-

Buffalo Soldiers (Photo courtesy of the New York Public Library)

dian fighters, the black soldiers of the frontier army incorporated the buffalo in their regimental coat of arms.

Long after the Indian wars on the western frontier had ended, the spirit of the Buffalo Soldiers lived on. In honor of the gallant tradition of their predecessors, the black divisions who served in the segregated army of World War I and World War II continued to display the buffalo as the centerpiece of their official emblem.

Great Plains. But by the early 1870s, more than half had been slaughtered.

By the mid–1880s, the great herds of buffalo had vanished from the Plains. By 1903, fewer than 40 wild buffalo were left in North America. The end of the buffalo brought the end of Indian independence. From then on, Plains Indians were doomed to either subsist on government handouts or adopt the Euroamerican way of life.

For years, the Plains Indians and the tribes of the mountains and Southwest had posed a formidable barrier for the expansion of American settlement in the West. But through disease, warfare, forced relocation to reservations and the destruction of the buffalo herds, the

power of the western Indians had been broken and their way of life altered forever. While their numbers and landholdings dwindled, railroad men, cattlemen, inventors and homesteaders were establishing new western traditions.

RAILROADS CRISSCROSS THE WEST

Other transcontinental railroad projects were not long behind the joining of the Union Pacific and Central Pacific in 1869. The Kansas Pacific Railroad, originally de-

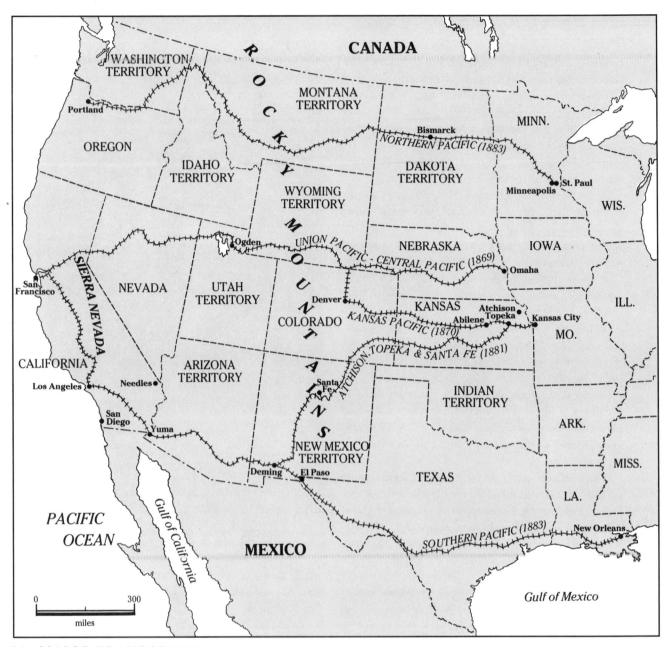

8.2 MAJOR TRANSCONTINENTAL RAILROADS IN 1883

signed as a southern spur line to connect the Union Pacific with Kansas City, was built westward south of the main line to Denver where a branch line joined that city with the Union Pacific at Cheyenne. Another branch line linked Salt Lake City with the Union Pacific at Ogden, Utah, near Promontory Point.

While the Central Pacific was pushing its way across the Sierra Nevada and the deserts of northern Nevada, its owners were developing the Southern Pacific, which eventually linked San Francisco and New Orleans. Over the next decade, the Southern Pacific built eastward to join with another transcontinental line, the Atchison, Topeka & Santa Fe Railroad that spanned the Southern Plains and southern Rockies from Topeka, through southern Colorado and Santa Fe, New Mexico. Across the Northern Plains and Northern Rockies, the Northern Pacific Railroad had linked St. Paul, Minnesota with Portland, Oregon, by 1883.

The construction of the western railroads did more to populate the West than any land cession won through diplomacy or victory in war. Railroad companies advertised throughout the eastern United States and the Mississippi Valley announcing lands for sale along the newly established lines. Their agents went to Europe with the news, and hundreds of thousands of emigrants arrived from overseas to buy and settle upon the lands the railroads had won from the government. Between the Union Pacific and the Central Pacific alone, enough

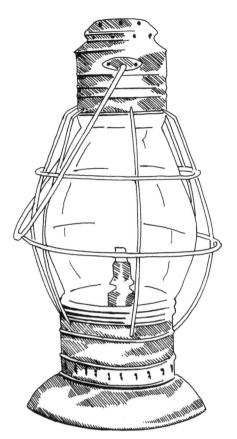

Railroad Lantern (Molly Braun)

land had passed from the public domain into private hands to encompass the states of New York, Massachusetts, Rhode Island and Vermont.

In the past, the frontier had crept slowly westward or had sprung up in isolated mining boom areas. With the advent of the western railroads, towns and farming communities rapidly grew up along railroad lines. The railroads not only linked the East and West, but also increased white settlement in the vast stretches—the domain of the Native American—in between.

COWBOYS, CATTLE TRAILS AND THE CATTLE KINGDOM

At the close of the Civil War, the Great Plains still loomed large and were sparsely populated. Long shunned by westering pioneers as too arid for farming, the region had been left as a hunting reserve for the nomadic, buffalo-hunting Plains Indians. Written off as the "Great American Desert," in less than two decades the Great Plains would be hailed as the "Garden of the West." The cattle industry on the Southern Plains helped spur post–Civil War development and settlement. Multitudes of cows—Texas longhorns—would be driven to railheads in Kansas, Nebraska and Wyoming by "cow-

boys," who became the most prevalent symbol of all the pioneer figures spawned by the western frontier.

Although Texas had largely been spared the physical ravages of warfare, the Civil War had left the Texas economy a shambles. The Union blockade had bottled up its Gulf Coast ports. Midway through the war, the Mississippi River had fallen under Union control, severing trade ties between Texas and her sister Confederate states. Among the industries hardest hit by these disruptions was the Texas cattle business.

Cattle-raising had been introduced into the grasslands of southeastern Texas by Spanish colonists in the early 18th century. Anglo-Americans who had followed Stephen Austin into the region between the Rio Grande and Nueces River brought cattle of their own, and these had interbred with the Spanish Andalusian cattle to produce the hardy Texas longhorn. Sturdier and larger than its Spanish ancestors, with a set of horns that could measure up to seven feet across, the Texas longhorn was raised by Americans mainly for tallow and hides.

The Mexican *vaquero* (cowherder) developed the riding and roping skills needed to care for cattle from horseback, and these were handed down to American settlers, who became known as "buckaroos" and more commonly as "cowboys."

Cattle were usually shipped by steamboat to New Orleans or driven overland to nearby Mississippi River ports. In the decade before the Civil War, the railroads had reached the Mississippi Valley, and some cattlemen began driving their herds northward along the Shawnee Trail for shipment by rail to meatpackers in St. Louis and Chicago. In the spring of 1853, two Illinois men drove about 150 cows overland from Texas some 1,500 miles northward to Indiana, where they were shipped by train another 600 miles eastward to New York City. Although the enterprise earned a handsome profit, the trouble and danger involved discouraged most cattlemen from making it a regular practice.

After the Civil War, Confederate veterans returning to southeastern Texas found their ranches in disrepair and their cattle herds scattered across the open grasslands, living in a semi-wild state. The war had completely dis-

Ivory-handled Colt .45 Peacemaker (Molly Braun)

Cattle Round-up (Photo courtesy of the National Archives)

rupted the cattle trade. The cattle left untended for more than four years—that would have been rounded up yearly and shipped to markets outside Texas—had grown fat and numerous. Up to five million head of cattle roamed the open ranges of southeastern Texas in 1866. Some bore identifying brands, but many were "mavericks"—unbranded cattle born in the wild—with unknown ownership.

Due to the huge cattle surplus, cattle prices in Texas had plummeted to less than five dollars a head. But there was a great demand for beef in growing northern cities. The war effort had drained the North of available cattle, and in the first year after the war there was an acute shortage of beef. The federal government would also buy beef on the hoof; frontier military posts and newly-established reservations for the Plains Indians had to be supplied with fresh meat.

By 1866, railheads had reached St. Joseph and Sedalia in western Missouri. Cattle dealers there were paying as much as $50 a head for Texas longhorns to transport by rail to meatpackers in St. Louis and Chicago.

The potential for huge profits was not hard to imagine. In dire need of a way to replace now worthless Confederate dollars with Yankee greenbacks, and with little other opportunities to make any money, many Texans were willing to risk the hazards of the long cattle drive northward.

In the spring of 1866, the ranchers organized the first big post-war cattle roundup. Cows with brands were "cut out" from the huge wild herds and given over to their proper owners. Unbranded "maverick" calves could sometimes be identified if they followed their branded mothers. But unmarked cattle that had grown up in the wild were often simply divided up among the ranchers. Mavericks were so numerous that more than a few cowboys managed to muster their own herds together just by rounding up the unbranded animals.

More than 250,000 cattle had been rounded up for the 1866 drive along the Shawnee Trail to Sedalia and St. Joseph. Individual herds numbered about 2,500. Each "outfit" had about 10 cowboys and was equipped with a "chuck wagon" manned by a cook. A trail boss or professional "drover" commanded each herd. The work was hard and dangerous. Cowboys spent their entire working day in the saddle. The more experienced ones rode "point," leading the herd. Alongside the length of the herd were the "swing" riders whose job was to keep the herd from straying along too wide a path. At the rear, novice cowboys—greenhorns—rode "drag," their duty being to make sure the slower and lazy cows did not lag too far behind the rest of the herd.

Even after the herd had been bedded down at a watering spot for the night, the cowboy's work was not done. Each took turns for two hours a night riding around the cattle to calm them and avert a stampede. To avoid startling the resting beasts, cowboys would sing songs as they circled the herd on horseback. Whether moving on the trail or bedded down, Texas longhorn cattle were extremely nervous creatures. A clap of thunder, the snap of a piece of brush or the striking of a match could panic them and touch off a mad rush that could leave them scattered across the Plains.

Gaining control of stampedes was one of the cowboys most dangerous tasks. The technique involved a rider outrunning the lead cows and attempting to turn them around so that they milled with the onrushing cattle and slowed the stampede. There was always the danger that a cowboy and his horse would be knocked down in the midst of the panicked and charging herd and be trampled to death.

Stampedes could be costly in dollars as well as lives. Some of the scattered cattle were never recovered. Cattle that had lost their footing were crushed where they fell. Cattle injured in the stampede could no longer be driven and had to be shot. Furthermore, after a run at high speed over a few miles, a cow could lose up to 50 pounds of its weight, diminishing its sale price at the end of the trail.

Rivers were another routine hazard. Between Texas and Missouri, there was the Brazos, the Colorado, the Red and the Arkansas; each had to be crossed and there were no bridges along the route. Usually the water was shallow enough for the cattle to wade across, but spring floods sometimes raised water levels so that the cows had to swim. Generally a tame cow or oxen would lead the herd across. To get cattle across a deep river, the herd had to keep moving forward. If part of the herd turned and began to mill, the animals could become confused and drown.

Other natural dangers came from prairie fires and tornadoes—the latter known as "Idaho Brain Storms" in cowboy jargon. Lightning was always a problem when the skies were overcast; a mounted cowboy was often the most prominent target for a lightning bolt on the treeless landscape of the Great Plains.

Once across the Red River, the cattle drive was in Indian Territory, the land of the Cherokees, Chickasaws,

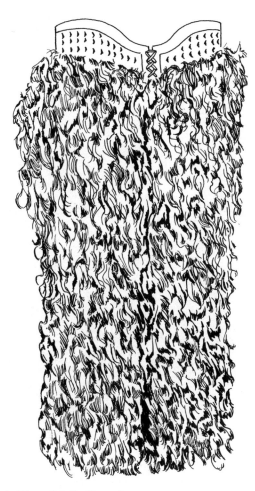

Goathair Chaps (Molly Braun)

Choctaws, Creeks and Seminoles, who been removed from their lands in the Southeast earlier in the century. Often they asked for some tribute from the cattlemen, usually a steer or two, and sometimes charged a toll of about 10 cents a head for allowing the herd to cross their lands and eat their grass. If the cowboys refused to comply, the Indians might intentionally stampede the cattle, then make off with a number of the scattered animals.

The cattlemen's challenges were not over even after they had crossed into southeastern Kansas at Baxter Springs. Kansas farmers were alarmed that the Texas cattle would infect their farm animals with Texas fever, a fatal cattle disease borne by ticks that Texas longhorns carried northward up the trail. Although the Texas cattle were immune from the disease, the fever ticks could rapidly spread to livestock and domestic cattle along the Shawnee Trail in Missouri. Bands of farmers armed with guns turned out in force to block the cattle drive. Many of the herds were turned back while a few managed to get through only by means of a long and costly detour through the difficult forested hill country of northeastern Arkansas.

In southern Missouri the cowboys of the first big cattle drive had to contend with Jayhawkers, the remnants of the paramilitary guerrilla bands that had terrorized the Kansas–Missouri border country during the Civil War. Like the Indians of the Indian Territory, they threatened to stampede the cattle if they were not paid off. On more than one occasion, cowboys were killed in attacks by armed Jayhawkers who sometimes made off with an entire herd.

The cattle drive of 1866 did not bode well for the future of the Texas cattle business. Of the quarter of a million cattle that had started out, only about 35,000 managed to reach the railheads in Missouri. Many of the cattle that did arrive were in such poor shape that the prices they commanded were lower.

Not all the cattle driven north from Texas that year wound up in Missouri. Among the drovers was Nelson Story. Originally from Ohio, he had been an overland freight wagon driver on the Oregon and Bozeman trails before coming to Texas. In western Montana Territory, he had managed to scrape $30,000 in gold from an abandoned mining claim at Alder Gulch. Story then went south to Texas to cash in on the possibilities of driving cheap cattle northward to Kansas City.

In Texas, Story purchased 3,000 head of longhorns and drove them north to the Missouri border. Rather than pay the Jayhawkers, he decided to drive his herd northward across the Plains all the way to the gold-mining towns in western Montana Territory. Gold strikes had drawn hordes of gold–seekers to the new boom towns of Bozeman City, Bannack and Virginia City. The region was bustling with thousands of miners and merchants, and Story knew the demand for fresh beef was

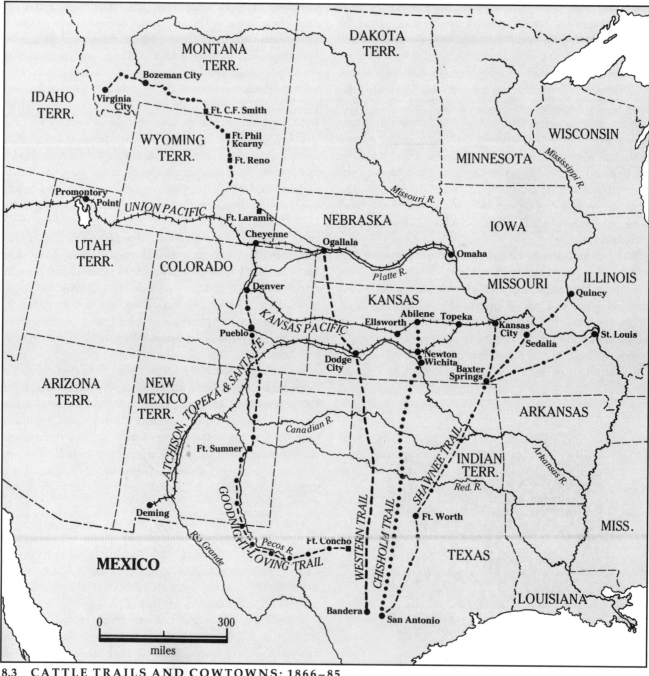

8.3 CATTLE TRAILS AND COWTOWNS: 1866–85

so high there that even a cow in the poorest shape would bring a hundred dollars in gold.

Story's outfit of 28 cowboys drove the herd northward across the entire width of Kansas to Fort Leavenworth. From there, the group followed the Oregon Trail westward along the Platte River to Fort Laramie, then headed northward through the Powder River country and up the Bozeman Trail toward Bannack and Virginia City.

This was in the summer of 1866, when the Sioux chief Red Cloud was resisting the army's efforts to develop the Bozeman Trail as a road to the Montana mining country. Although outnumbered 10-to-one, Story and his men were able to fend off raiding parties with newly developed Remington repeating rifles and six-shooters.

Story wintered his cattle on the Montana plains, then drove the 3,000 head into Virginia City and Bozeman. He sold most of his herd in the mining towns for about $100,000 in gold and cash. With the remaining cattle, he established a ranching operation on the open range around present-day Livingston, Montana. His cattle enterprise prospered by supplying beef to the local Crow Indian reservation and to nearby army posts. He later went into real estate in Los Angeles, his best-known project the Story Building, the first skyscraper to rise above the city.

Another cattleman who pioneered a route for the long drive north was Charles Goodnight. Born in Illinois, he was raised in Texas and became a Texas Ranger. During the Civil War, he had fought Comanches on the Texas frontier. After the war, he returned to his ranch on the Brazos river and managed to gather up a herd of about 2,000 head of cattle. More than a few of them were unbranded mavericks that he had not owned before the war.

While most Texas cattlemen were risking the troublesome route to Missouri, Goodnight decided to take his cattle through New Mexico to the Colorado mining towns. He soon joined up with another Texas cattlemen, Oliver Loving, who in 1858 had driven the first herd of Texas cattle overland to Chicago. Two years later, Loving had pioneered a cattle route north from Texas to Denver by way of the Indian Territory and the Arkansas River. But in the spring of 1866, the Kiowas and Comanches were attacking travelers along that trail. To avoid trouble, Goodnight and Loving first took their herd from Fort Belknap into northwestern Texas along the former route of the Butterfield Overland Mail.

With an outfit of 18 cowboys, they drove their cattle across nearly 100 miles of waterless country. By the time they approached the Pecos, the cattle were maddened by thirst and the herd bolted in a stampede toward the river. About 100 cows were lost in the rush to the water; some were trampled in the stampede, while others were drowned in the Pecos when they poured headlong over a six-foot embankment into the stream. This loss was in addition to the 300 head that had died of thirst in the trek across the arid wastes of western Texas.

Goodnight and Loving then drove the cattle northward up the Pecos River Valley, the herd now depleted by about one-fifth. They soon came upon Fort Sumner and Bosque Redondo, the Navajo and Apache Indian reservation in eastern New Mexico. The Indians were in desperate need of food, and the Indian agent bought most of the Goodnight and Loving's herd, for a substantial profit to the cowboys. While Goodnight returned to Texas with some of the cowboys and $12,000 in gold, Loving took the rest of the cattle northward to Denver where he sold them to cattleman John Wesley Iliff. Over the next few years, Iliff became a major supplier of beef for Union Pacific Railroad construction crews in Wyoming. His cattle operation along Colorado's South Platte River Valley grew to become one of the largest on the Great Plains.

The route that the two partners had blazed became known as the Goodnight–Loving Trail. On the next year's trail drive, Loving died as a result wounds suffered in an attack by a Comanche war party. Goodnight continued in the cattle business, utilizing the Goodnight–Loving Trail to bring tens of thousands of cattle northward into New Mexico and Colorado. He later developed a huge ranching operation on the Arkansas River, near Pueblo, Colorado.

Meanwhile, back in Texas, the cattlemen who had attempted the 1866 drive into Missouri were still smarting from their losses. But in 1867, Joseph G. McCoy, an Illinois cattle dealer, came up with an ingenious plan that would alleviate the problems the first long drive had faced and revolutionize the cattle business.

With the Kansas Pacific railroad then extending its tracks across Kansas, McCoy hit upon the idea of establishing a new railhead for cattle at a point several hundred miles west of the troublesome areas of southern Missouri. In the spring of 1867, McCoy bought up 250 acres near the Kansas Pacific tracks in Abilene. He had shipping pens and corrals built that could hold up to 1,000 cattle at a time. Then he sent agents south to Texas to spread the word to ranchers setting out for Missouri and to those already on the trail that more welcome facilities awaited them northwest of the Shawnee Trail.

Cattlemen driving herds northward accepted the invitation and swung west near Forth Worth, then headed northward through the middle of Indian country, along a route known as the Chisholm Trail. Years before, a Cherokee-Scottish trader named Jesse Chisholm had brought wagons along the route to and from his trading post in southern Kansas, and it was along the wheel-rutted tracks of this road that the first cattle from Texas reached Abilene.

Thirty-five thousand head of cattle were brought to Abilene that first year. They were sold there for half a million Yankee dollars. The profits flowed back to Texas, and encouraged more cattlemen to bring their herds to Abilene.

Soon there were more cattle than dealers to buy them, and so McCoy set about promoting his new cattle dealing center by sending a freight car east with wild buffalo and horses. In Chicago and St. Louis, cowboys he had hired staged roping and riding exhibitions. The publicity helped bring in more cattle dealers from the East, and by 1870 as many as 300,000 cattle were being driven north from Texas to Abilene annually.

Abilene was the first cowtown on the Great Plains. In addition to cattle pens and corrals, McCoy had built a three-story hotel to house the visiting cowboys, called the Drover's Cottage. Saloons, gambling casinos, dance halls and brothels began to sprout up along a stretch of town that became known as Texas Street. Cowboys, seeking to blow off steam and spend their wages in a wild spree, poured in at the end of the long drives. Three hundred cowboys a day arrived during the height of the season, eager to squander their hard-earned wages for the chance to have "a year's fun in a week."

The cowtowns spawned the image of the Wild West. Exuberant Texas cowboys, far from home and with money to spend, often rode into town with guns blazing. Alcohol flowed freely, and drunken disputes were often settled with gunfire. Unlike the railroad and mining towns, the cowtowns also maintained a year-round population of respectable citizens who resented the lawlessness that the cattle drives brought to their communities.

Things got so out of hand that a correspondent for the Topeka *Commonwealth* declared: "At this writing, hell is now in session in Abilene." But townspeople also knew that the cattle drives were the foundation of their prosperity. In order not to interrupt the steady flow of cattle and cash that poured up the trail from Texas, and at the same time contain the lawlessness that came along with it, laws were passed to restrict certain unseemly activities to a confined area of the town.

Conditions were still difficult to handle at times. In 1870, Abilene's leaders hired a marshal to deal with the situation. Two St. Louis lawmen first applied for the job, but they departed the first day on witnessing cowboy rowdiness. The man selected as Abilene's first marshal was Thomas J. Smith, a former New York City police officer. Smith knew that "whiskey and pistols were a combination beyond control," and the town soon complied with his request to pass a law against carrying guns. Smith himself maintained the peace with his soft-spoken but firm manner, backed up by his fists rather than firearms. The plan worked for about six months until he was killed in a scuffle with a local Abilene farmer who he was trying to arrest for murder.

Abilene's next marshal was James Butler "Wild Bill" Hickok, a former army scout in the Civil War and in the 1868 campaign against the Cheyennes. Unlike his predecessor, Hickok had no qualms about firearms. He was lax about enforcing Abilene's ban on carrying guns. He usually carried two pistols at his sides, and was not shy about using them. Gunfights were common during his tenure, which lasted only about five months. Although fast on the draw and a crack shot, Hickok was also trigger-happy, and in a gunfight with an unruly cowboy, he accidentally killed one of his own deputies. After that, the town fired him.

The summer of 1871 turned out to be Abilene's last year as a cowtown. At that time, the town had 10 saloons and more than a few houses of prostitution. Gunfights were common and the wild antics of off-duty cowboys had become too much for the community's law-abiding citizens to tolerate.

Seeking to shed the town's reputation as the vice capital of the Southern Plains, Abilene's leaders decided that the cattle drives would have to find a different destination. They formed the Farmers' Protective Association, which in early 1872 circulated a notice in Texas newspapers requesting "all who have contemplated driving Texas Cattle to Abilene the coming season to seek some other point for shipment, as the inhabitants . . . will no longer submit to the evils of the trade."

The people of Abilene got their wish, but it was not entirely as a result of their published petition. By then, the Atchison, Topeka & Santa Fe Railroad had built tracks westward to Newton, a point on the Chisholm Trail south of Abilene and more convenient for trail drives.

In 1871, 40,000 head of cattle were shipped from Newton by rail to meatpackers in Kansas City. Soon afterward, the Kansas Pacific Railroad established a new railhead for Texas cattle 70 miles west of Abilene at Ellsworth. Since it was west of the settled farming areas around Abilene, cattlemen did not have to contend with county quarantine laws against bringing fever tick-bearing Texas cattle into that part of the state.

While Abilene settled into its more sedate existence as the center for the region's wheat farmers, those who had prospered from the cattle drives moved on to the new cowtowns. A portion of the Drover's Cottage was dismantled and moved to Ellsworth to cater to the hordes of cowboys that poured into that town starting in 1872. In its first year as a cowtown, Ellsworth attracted as many as 100,000 head of cattle to its corrals and loading chutes.

Wichita was the next cattle center to emerge on the Kansas prairies. Its location farther south on the Chisholm Trail made the cattle drive there shorter. The branch line that the Atchison, Topeka & Santa Fe Railroad built in 1872 soon deflected most of the cattle drives to it. Merchants and saloonkeepers flocked to Wichita to cater to the hundreds of cowboys who arrived daily with the cattle drives. In its first year as a cowtown, close to half a million Texas longhorns passed through Wichita on their way to slaughterhouses in Chicago and Kansas City. Wichita also became a center for buyers of cattle that were then driven overland to Indian reservations to the north.

Throughout the 1870s, the pattern was repeated. As wheat farming spread in Kansas, the cattle trails and cattle drives were pushed farther westward. Cowtowns at railheads at the end of the trail moved with them until 1875, when Dodge City, the terminus of the Western Trail, rose to prominence as the "Cowboy Capital."

The same raucous scenes were repeated, and saloons and "houses of ill-repute" proliferated amid a climate of general lawlessness. Over the next decade, as many as 250,000 cattle arrived at Dodge City's stockyards each year, filling up more than 3,500 freight cars with cows headed for Kansas City, Chicago and the dinner tables of the East. Dodge City's infamous "Boot Hill" cemetery also filled up with unlucky cowboys whose violent sprees ended suddenly when they "died with their boots on."

But the days of the long drive were soon to end. Cattlemen had long known that the grass of the Great Plains could support their herds even through the winter months. Cattle could paw through the snow-covered grasslands and thrive with little outside attention. Cattle ranching on the Great Plains was not possible, however, until the buffalo herds had been diminished and the Plains Indians had been confined to reservations. These conditions came to pass by 1876, after which cattle herds that had formerly been driven north from Texas were kept on the open range around the cowtowns.

As homesteaders moved in, the cattlemen shifted their operations northward and westward into Nebraska, Wyoming and the high plains of Montana. Ogallala, Nebraska and Cheyenne, Wyoming, along the route of the Union Pacific, now garnered the cattle trade that had begun 10 years before in Texas and Kansas.

In the first years of the western cattle boom, cattlemen used the lands of the public domain for pasturage. But as more and more of the Great Plains was settled by homesteaders, the open range began to diminish. Barbed wire fences were first introduced by farmers seeking to protect their government-granted homesteads from the huge herds of freely roaming cattle.

At first, cattlemen responded by cutting down the fences, sometimes leading to open warfare between cowmen and farmers. Soon, however, the cattlemen themselves began fencing in large tracts of land. Filing homestead claims in the names of their employees, cattlemen were able to carve out huge ranches of tens of thousands of acres from the public domain. Herds reached tremendous size, and the type of cattle changed as well. The Texas longhorn, while hardy enough to be raised on the open range, produced beef that was not tender enough for eastern tastes. Hereford and Angus cattle were introduced and interbred with the longhorn to produce the type of western beef cattle whose meat was more marketable.

Cattle-raising became big business. Capital from Wall Street financiers and syndicates in Great Britain and Europe organized huge operations on the Great Plains. The Prairie Cattle Company and the Swan Land and Capital Company, both owned by investors in Scotland, each controlled ranches encompassing as much as a 100 square miles of Wyoming and Montana real estate. The XIT ranch in Montana controlled as much as 15,000 square miles of range land. These large-scale operations held up to 100,000 cattle at a time. With the end of the cattle drives, the free and easy life of the cowboy turned into the more mundane routine of the ranchhand. His duties now included tending fences as well as cattle.

Millions of cattle now grazed on the grasslands of the Great Plains where the great herds of buffalo had once roamed. Grass, once in limitless supply, diminished as the cattle business expanded. Cattlemen had to resort to growing grass, and mowing hay in the off-season became yet another new and mundane task for the cowboy, who now found himself working more on foot than on horseback.

Grass suitable for raising beef cattle could also be used to support sheep. In the early 1880s, from the valleys of New Mexico and California sheepherders brought their wooly stock onto the Great Plains, attracted by newly opened cheap and abundant grazing grounds.

Some cattlemen, realizing that sheepraising had a lower overhead and could earn a higher profit margin than cattle, turned to sheep as an alternative. Most, however, scorned the invasion of sheep as unwanted competition. They believed the sheep wore down the grazing lands by eating the grass down to a point close to the ground, leaving nothing but bare stubble for cattle.

Open warfare between cattlemen and sheepmen sometimes erupted. More than half a million sheep were destroyed by irate ranchers, whose cowboys would often drive a sheep herd over the edge of a cliff or shoot and

Barbed-wire Fence (Molly Braun)

BILLY THE KID

Along with the cowboy and the sodbuster, the West of the post–Civil War years spawned yet another type of frontiersman—the gunfighter.

The railroad towns, cowtowns and mining boom towns that sprang up far from the centers of established law and order quickly became meccas for gamblers and fugitives from justice. Ranchers, plagued by unchecked cattle rustling on the open range, often resorted to their own brand of justice, which was frequently dispensed from the barrel of a six-shooter or the end of a rope.

Individuals on both sides of the law took advantage of the wide-open nature of frontier society to use their skill with the six-shooter as a way of earning a living. Both lawmen and outlaws left behind a legacy of violence. One of the most notorious of those figures—whose gun-toting exploits helped characterize the frontier's closing years as the "Wild West"—was a young desperado named Billy the Kid.

His real name was William Bonney. A native of New York City's Lower East Side, he was left fatherless when young. His mother took him west, eventually settling in Silver City, New Mexico Territory. His mother's death in 1874 left him an orphan at the age of 14. Three years later, while working for the army as a wagon driver in southeastern Arizona Territory, he quarreled with a blacksmith who had called him a pimp. The dispute ended with Billy pulling his gun and shooting the man to death. That marked the first of a long line of killings that would ensue in the course of his short but violent career as a western gunfighter.

Although jailed by the army, Billy escaped within a few days and fled to the Pecos River valley of New Mexico. There he found work as a cowhand for a wealthy British rancher named John Tunstall. When Tunstall was killed by rival cattlemen in the "Lincoln County War," Billy took it upon himself to revenge the death of the man he had come to see as his benefactor. He joined the posse that tracked down Tunstall's killers. When the two men responsible surrendered after a five-hour gunfight, Billy was among the party that escorted the culprits back to Lincoln, the county seat, to stand trial. But Billy, who had his own ideas about justice, killed the two men in cold blood, along with a member of the

Billy the Kid (Photo courtesy of the Library of Congress)

posse who made the mistake of trying to save the prisoners.

From then on, Billy the Kid, as he soon became known, embarked on a career of murder and cattle rustling. After he had killed the sheriff and the deputy who tried to arrest him for the murder of the two prisoners, he became the leader of a band of outlaws who preyed on cattle herds of local ranchers and those of a nearby Apache Indian reservation. In late 1878, New Mexico Territory's newly appointed governor, Lew Wallace (later to earn fame as the author of the classic novel *Ben Hur*), offered Billy amnesty for his crimes if he would testify against those involved in the Lincoln County War.

Billy took up the offer and surrendered. Although he complied by providing damning evidence against one of his late employer's enemies, the local district attorney refused to honor Governor Wallace's amnesty pledge. But before he could be brought to trial for killing the sheriff and the deputy, the Kid escaped from jail. He then fled to the region around Fort Sumner in eastern New Mexico Territory. There he made the fatal mistake of befriending Pat Garrett,

a bartender at a local saloon. Soon afterward, in the fall of 1880, Garrett was elected sheriff of Lincoln County, and one of his initial duties was to bring the fugitive Billy the Kid to justice.

Billy and his gang of rustlers were tracked down and captured at an abandoned ranch house. He was brought to the town of Mesilla where he stood trial and was found guilty of murder. After he was sentenced to hang, he made a daring escape in which he wriggled out of his shackles and killed two guards with guns stolen from Sheriff Garrett's office.

Pat Garrett, however, was soon on his trail again. He found Billy hiding out in the cabin of one of the Kid's friends near Fort Sumner, and there, on July 15, 1881, surprised the Kid in a darkened bedroom and shot him dead. In the days before his death, Billy the Kid had boasted that he had killed 21 men—"one for every year of my life."

club the animals to death in an effort to preserve the Great Plains as the domain of the cattleman.

More than the encroachment of homesteaders and sheepmen, the real threat to the Great Plains cattle empires came from overstocking the range. Overproduction of cattle caused prices to fall both at the cattle-shipping centers and at meatpacking centers in Chicago. In 1885, President Grover Cleveland issued an executive order commanding ranchers who had illegally leased lands in the Indian Territory to remove their herds. As a result, hundreds of thousands of head of cattle were driven to the already overburdened ranges of Colorado, Kansas, Nebraska and the Dakota and Wyoming territories.

The terrible winter blizzards of 1886–87 were the death knell for open range cattle raising. Grass had withered in the droughts of the previous two years and streams for watering cattle had dried up. When the first fierce snows of January blanketed the plains that winter, close to two million head of cattle were caught in the open. In past years, cattle could move with the drifting snow, eventually find shelter and paw through the snow cover and find adequate grass underneath. But the grass was sparse, and fences now blocked the moving herds. The cows piled up in heaps against the barbed wire fences to freeze and starve to death. Tens of thousands more were buried in ravines and dry streambeds.

The cattle losses became known as the "Big Die-Up." Cattlemen lost 60 percent of their stock. In the spring of 1887, the Great Plains were littered with the carcasses of millions of cattle. Theodore Roosevelt, who ran a ranching operation in Dakota Territory while taking a break

from his political career in the mid–1880s, described the devastation as a "perfect smashup all through the cattle country . . . The losses are crippling."

Many ranchers, both large and small, were left bankrupt. Those whose businesses survived had to make ex-

Enamel Coffee Pot (Molly Braun)

tensive changes. Herds were cut down to more manageable sizes. The practice of wintering herds on the open range was replaced by raising stock in smaller fenced-in areas known as feedlots.

The end of the cattle boom also marked the passing of the cowboy era in the West. But the colorful garb of wide-brimmed Stetson 10–gallon hat, chaps for protection from longhorns and brush and the high-heeled boots with spurs for controlling a mustang cowpony would shape western fashions for decades afterward. Cowboy culture would persist well into the 20th century and become the stuff of thousands of movies and television shows long after the last cattle drive had ended and the last cowtown had closed down its corrals and loading chutes. And in music, the image of the singing cowboy—originating from the mournful tunes sung to calm the herds—evolved into the style known as country and western.

From the era of the cattle boom emerged the legend of the West. Part truth, and beefed up with a good measure of exaggeration, the legend endured in literature, art and music. In John Ford's 1962 Hollywood western, *The Man Who Shot Liberty Valance*, a cowboy tells a newspaperman, "This is the West. When the legend becomes fact, print the legend."

NEW TECHNOLOGIES FOR THE WEST

Until the end of the Civil War, the semi-arid Great Plains had posed a barrier to the advance of the farming frontier. West of the 98th Meridian, rainfall was usually less than 20 inches a year, not enough to support the kind of agriculture practiced in the more humid regions east of the Missouri River.

The turf of the Great Plains, thickly matted with the deep roots of prairie grass, did not yield to the type of plows and other farming implements settlers customarily used. Trees grew only in widely scattered river bottoms, making timber scarce for building houses, barns and fences. Unlike the Old Northwest and the Mississippi Valley, the region lacked a system of navigable rivers that could provide the cheap transportation that had spurred settlement east of the Missouri River.

Yet in the three decades that followed the Civil War, the Great Plains would see the greatest expansion of settlement in the history of the United States. More territory would be claimed and cultivated from 1870 to 1900 than had been occupied since the establishment of Virginia's original Jamestown colony in 1607. What made

8.4   THE UNITED STATES IN 1876

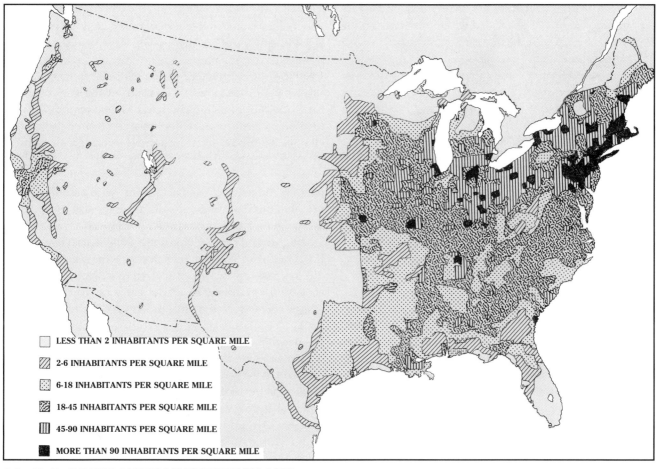

LESS THAN 2 INHABITANTS PER SQUARE MILE

2-6 INHABITANTS PER SQUARE MILE

6-18 INHABITANTS PER SQUARE MILE

18-45 INHABITANTS PER SQUARE MILE

45-90 INHABITANTS PER SQUARE MILE

MORE THAN 90 INHABITANTS PER SQUARE MILE

8.5   U.S. POPULATION DENSITY IN 1870

this rapid growth possible was the introduction of new methods of farming and new developments in farm technology. Most of all, it was the efforts of a new kind of pioneer—the sodbuster—that was to transform the "Great American Desert" into the nation's breadbasket.

In 1874, Moses Armstrong, Dakota Territory's delegate to Congress, declared, "Nearly one-half the area of our American domain is yet but sparsely settled," and he urged the federal government to enact "generous laws" to encourage white settlement of the West.

The Homestead Act of 1862 made it possible for individual citizens and qualified emigrants to claim 160 acres of the public domain free of cost. Under the Pre-emption Law of 1841, a homesteader could enlarge his holdings by another 160 acres by purchasing up to 160 acres of public land at $1.25 an acre. The Timber Culture Act of 1873 granted settlers an additional 160 acres if one-fourth of it was planted with trees within a four-year period. Yet it would take more than the attraction of free or low-cost land to populate the Great Plains. The challenge of farming in a region that lacked sufficient water and timber as well as adequate transportation would have to be met before Moses Armstrong's vision could become a reality.

Industry in the Northeast had boomed during the Civil War when necessity had carried the Industrial Revolution into high gear. Production of machinery to replace manual farm labor was in great demand, prompted by the shortage of manpower during the war years. Innovations continued into the post-war years, resulting in the development of new farm machinery that enabled more food to be produced with less labor.

These developments were particularly important for pioneers on the semi-arid Great Plains, where large tracts of land had to be cultivated just to provide a subsistence income for farm families. But the newcomers who dared the challenges of Great Plains agriculture in the late 1860s and early 1870s were interested in more than subsistence. Rapid industrialization had swelled the populations of eastern cities, sparking demand for food in areas where little food was produced. Wheat was bringing more than a dollar a bushel, making it an extremely attractive cash crop. Exports of American farm products were also increasing yearly, guaranteeing farmers a ready and expanding market in Europe.

One basic improvement that helped open the Great Plains to agriculture was the invention of a chilled-iron plow. With its smooth-surfaced mold-board, farmers

Farming the Plains in the 1870s (Photo courtesy of the New York Public Library)

could easily cut through the dense cover of roots that carpeted the topsoil of the Great Plains. Several years after this innovation, developed by James Oliver of Indiana in 1868, an improved version was introduced with a steel-sheathed plowshare.

The demand for better farm implements encouraged the development of a wide variety of low-cost "sulky plows." This enabled the farmer to ride upon the machine, greatly reducing the amount of labor that had to be expended and increasing the acreage that could be cultivated. A major adaptation of the sulky plow was the addition of multiple plowshares, enabling one farmer to plow up to three furrows at a time.

Planting on the Great Plains was made easier with improved machinery equipped with spring-toothed harrows specially adapted to the prairie soil. By 1874, new types of automatic seeders had been introduced that opened seed furrows and deposited seed grain into the ground. High demand had spurred the development of better mowing and reaping machinery. By the late 1870s, a practical cord binder was available that not only cut wheat but also bound it into sheaves. This enabled two men and a team of horses to harvest an acre in one day, a task that previously had taken more than a score of workers.

Although improved machinery was essential for extensive agriculture on the Great Plains, no farmer could hope to succeed on the open grasslands without suitable fencing. When a homesteader staked out his claim, he marked it out by running a furrow around his land. But as farmers ventured farther westward onto the Plains, they came increasingly in contact with the vast cattle kingdom. The cattle drovers and ranchers who used the open range of the public domain as a free pasturage were not about to respect such flimsy property lines. Timber for fencing, so abundant in the forested East,

was virtually nonexistent on the Great Plains. Simple wire fences would not do; wandering cattle herds could work a hole through them with their heads and then trample a farmer's crops.

In 1874, Joseph D. Glidden, a De Kalb, Illinois farmer, solved the problem when he devised the first practical barbed wire for fencing. By braiding two strands of wire together and placing pointed metal barbs in between the strands, he produced an affordable fencing material that was an effective deterrent to the onslaught of cattle. Mass production of barbed wire came soon afterward, when a Worcester, Massachusetts, wire-manufacturing firm went into partnership with Glidden and began making the wire with steam-driven machinery.

The problem of water for Great Plains farmers was one that could not entirely be solved by the innovations of the machine age. Early settlers on the Great Plains could seek out lands along or near streams or rivers. But such choice spots were limited, and they were often bought up by speculators or were part of the lands granted to railroads.

Homesteaders fortunate enough to stake their claim within five miles of a spring or river could haul water by wagon or by foot. Most, however, were not as lucky, and had to rely on tapping the water table beneath the prairies. An underground supply of water might be found within 10 or 20 feet of the surface in areas near rivers. But the majority of farmers, with lands far from streams and riverbeds, had to dig several hundred feet down before they could hope to reach the ground water beneath the prairie. By the late 1870s, well-drilling machinery that had been developed for the burgeoning oil industry in the East was adapted to the quest for water on the Great Plains.

Although this method was effective in hammering pipes deep enough to reach the water table, there still remained the problem of bringing the water to the surface. With wells sometimes 300 feet below the ground, the traditional "old oaken bucket" hoisted by a rope simply was not practical.

The winds of the Great Plains that constantly swept across the unbroken landscape were a natural power source that could be harnessed to solve this problem. An improved type of windmill had been developed by a Connecticut mechanic named Daniel Halliday in 1854. Using the principals of centrifugal force, he made his device self-governing, allowing it to turn at a constant speed as the velocity of the wind changed. By employing the power generated by the windmill to power a pumping device, the relentless winds of the Great Plains could be used to bring water from deep below the surface with no manual effort. By the 1880s, these types of windmills were in wide use throughout the Great Plains region.

Windmill-driven pumps, however, were not a solution to the lack of rainfall. Water pumped from underground could provide a farmer's family and his livestock with an adequate water supply, but it would never be enough to irrigate his lands. The answer lay in adapting farming methods to the region's climate.

To meet the challenge of cultivating the semi-arid lands of the Great Plains, agricultural scientists developed the technique of "dry farming." Farmers would loosen the soil by plowing furrows deeper than was customary, and in this way allow capillary action to bring ground water closer to the surface. Immediately after every infrequent rainfall, a farmer would rush to harrow his fields in order to spread a protective cover of fine soil that would slow the evaporation of whatever water had accumulated.

The main factor that opened the Great Plains to agriculture was the building of the western railroads. The federal government had granted the railroads close to 200 million acres of land along their right of ways. By 1871, the railroads had become the largest landowners in the nation. The railroad companies needed to sell this land to recoup the millions of dollars that had been expended in constructing the iron roads now spanning the West. Moreover, towns needed to be developed along the railroad routes in order to provide the volume of through-traffic needed to make the lines profitable. Even the sale of remaining government lands to homesteaders would benefit the railroads because of more potential business along a route.

Eager to sell their lands, the railroads launched a massive advertising campaign to lure settlers to the West. They peppered the East with pamphlets that publicized the Great Plains as a virtual farmer's paradise, depicting it as a land where "mocking birds and gorgeous parakeets and cockatoos warble musical challenges to each other amid the rich foliage of the sweet-bay and mango trees." Railroad immigration bureaus sent agents to Europe to spread the word, filling the minds of hopeful peasants with visions of owning their own lands. Low-cost or free transportation was offered to prospective land buyers. Steamship companies were also active, offering free passage to returning emigrants if they agreed to encourage their countrymen to seek new lives as farmers on the Great Plains.

HOMESTEADERS ON THE PLAINS

The "America Fever" took hold in Europe, especially in Scandinavia, Germany and Ireland. Peasant farmers with no hope of possessing lands in their native countries were lured to Minnesota, Nebraska, Kansas and Dakota Territory.

The immigrant tide was so great that, in the 1880s, travelers in eastern Dakota and other parts of the Great Plains reported that Scandinavian languages were more commonly heard than English.

As alluring as the promise of prosperity on the Great Plains may have been, the first settlers were presented with problems and hardships that no previous generation of pioneers had to face. Although the treeless prairies required none of the back-breaking labor of clearing forests, there was little or no timber to build log cabins.

Pioneer Family in Nebraska (Photo courtesy of the National Archives)

WOMEN OF THE WEST

In the 18th and 19th centuries, men were the politicians and soldiers and, with a few exceptions, the explorers, miners, railroad workers, cattle drivers and gunfighters as well. Although male names pervade the history of westward expansion, men were only part of the story. At the heart of shaping the nation also were women.

Some women's names and stories have survived for us:

- **Marie Dorion** of the Iowa tribe, who—like the Shoshone woman Sacajawea with the Lewis and Clark Expedition—proved essential to the Astorians as a guide, interpreter and peacemaker in their trek from St. Louis to Oregon in 1811–12.

- **Cynthia Anne Parker,** a white captive of the Comanches as a nine-year-old in 1836, who went on to become a devoted wife of tribal leader Peta Nocono and mother of Quanah Parker, the war chief, principal chief, religious leader and tribal statesman.

- **Narcissa Whitman and Eliza Spalding,** mission-

A Teacher and Her Pupils in Front of a Sod Schoolhouse During the 1890s (Photo courtesy of the National Archives)

Shipping in lumber from the forests of the Old Northwest by rail was beyond the means of most pioneers on the Great Plains.

For housing, Great Plains pioneers resorted to using the thick sod of the prairie. A settler's first shelter was usually a dugout, a dwelling carved into the side of a low hill with an opening covered with boards from packing crates. He would soon after construct a sodhouse with strips of the tough prairie turf cut with a special plow. The sod strips, which came to be known as "Nebraska marble," were firmly held together by the enmeshed roots of prairie grass. They would then be laid in brick-like tiers to form the walls of the sodbuster's new home. For a roof, some cottonwood poles were hauled from a local streambed that would be used as a frame which was then covered with layers of sod. The sodhouse's earthen walls were a perfect insulator, making the sodhouse cool in summer and warm in winter,

aries who became the first known non-Indian women to cross the Rocky Mountains in 1836.

- **Biddy Mason,** a black woman who came to California from Mississippi as a slave in 1851, but managed to win freedom for her family in 1856, arguing successfully in court that since her master had resided in California, a free state, he should not be permitted to take her and her family to Texas, a slave state.
- **Esther Morris,** Wyoming's "Mother of Suffrage," whose efforts led to the passage Council Bill Number 70, granting women the right to vote in Wyoming Territory in 1869. She went on to serve as Justice of the Peace of South Pass City, the first woman in all of the United States to hold such a position.
- **Mary Anna Hallock,** a New Yorker who moved west with her husband in 1876, living in New Almaden, California, and later Leadville, Colorado. She later wrote novels about western life under the pseudonym Mary Foote, including *The Led-Horse Claim* (1883) and *The Chosen Valley* (1892).
- **Mary Achey,** an army wife, who, from the 1860s until her death in 1885, painted scenes of the West.
- **Evelyn Jephson Cameron,** an Englishwoman who came to Montana with her husband in 1889 and photographed its people and places. She was also reputed to be the first woman in all of Montana to ride astride a horse, not sidesaddle.
- **Sarah Winnemucca,** a Paiute Indian lecturer, writer and educator, who lobbied for the rights of her people from the 1860s through the 1880s.
- **Belle Starr** who led a gang of cattle thieves in the Oklahoma Territory in the 1880s.
- **Annie Oakley,** a sharpshooter and member of Buffalo Bill Cody's Wild West show in the late 1800s.

Nampeyo, a Pueblo Indian Potter (Photo courtesy of the National Archives of Canada)

In addition to those individuals whose names and contributions we know, there were many others whose work affected the course of western history: Indian wives, pioneer wives, army wives, missionary wives and mail-order brides; unmarried or widowed homesteaders, farmers and ranchers; storekeepers, launderers, cooks and domestics; prostitutes and outlaws; singers, dancers and actresses; lawyers, doctors and nurses; cowgirls; and school teachers. Frontier women all.

and despite being dark and dingy, these dwellings proved an effective home for a pioneer family's first years on the Great Plains.

Fuel was another basic necessity that had to be improvised from the Great Plains environment. With no wood to burn, early pioneers turned to using buffalo chips—dried pieces of manure left by the huge but diminishing herds of buffalo that still roamed the Plains in the early 1870s.

After the extinction of the buffalo herds, farmers resorted to using dried cow manure left behind by the herds of cattle that were driven through from Texas. But the advancing farming frontier pushed cattle drives farther westward, and farmers had to find other means to cook their food and heat their homes. Some used the dried stalks of sunflowers, while others burned hay in specially designed stoves. Neither of these methods were altogether satisfactory, since they filled a sod house

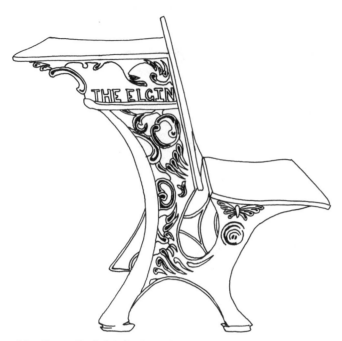

Schoolhouse Desk (Molly Braun)

with smoke and harmful gases. Coal shipped in by railroads in the 1880s finally solved the problem of fuel for farmers on the Great Plains.

The climate of the Great Plains offered another challenge. Few pioneers were prepared for the severe winter blizzards in which temperatures could plunge to 40° below zero. Fierce winds would drive snow and sleet as high as the tops of the sod homes, coating farm animals with sheets of ice. For weeks at a time, farm families were reduced to huddling in their homes along with their smaller livestock.

The "school-children's storm" of 1888 was one of the worst. It struck on a day in early January that had begun deceptively cloudless and mild. Children walking home from school were caught in it when it hit in later afternoon. The sky was quickly enveloped with dark clouds and the wind suddenly picked up. Hundreds of small children, dressed for warmer weather, found themselves lost in the blowing snow. Many were unable to find shelter, and several hundred in Dakota and Nebraska were found frozen to death in snowdrifts, huddled together in a futile attempt to keep warm.

The extreme heat of summer was bad enough, but it was made worse when a searing wind swept across the land, withering whatever crops were in its path. Prairie fires were common in dry spring and fall seasons, touched off by lightning or a chance spark from a campfire. Flames would spread rapidly across the plains, consuming everything for miles around. A farmer could usually protect his home by burning off the grass around his house to create a firebreak, but there was little he could do to save his crops from being destroyed.

Another devastating hazard of farming on the Great Plains was the plague of grasshoppers that descended on the land during the extremely dry fall seasons of the years 1874 to 1877. Millions of the insects, borne by the wind, came in great clouds from the eastern Rocky Mountains and carpeted the ground for miles. The grasshoppers swarmed into the settlers sod huts, devouring clothes and harnesses. They even ate the handles of farm implements, attracted by the residue of human sweat in the wood.

Many prairie farmers, ruined by the grasshopper plagues, faced starvation and had to rely on handouts from state and territorial governments. For thousands of others, the grasshoppers were the last straw, and unwilling to face the terrible trials of life on the Great Plains, they packed up their wagons and headed eastward, some displaying signs declaring, "From Kansas, where it rains grasshoppers, fire and destruction."

Despite the hardships of nature, many remained to develop their farms. Those that prospered were able to afford lumber for frame houses. Settlers followed the railroads as they built out across the flatlands of Kansas and Nebraska. In Dakota Territory, railroads from Chicago spread the movement westward toward the Missouri River. The first "Dakota Boom" gained momentum after 1868, when the Sioux Indians were confined to their reservations in the Black Hills. Settlement of the Northern Plains was slowed by the Panic of 1873, precipitated by the bankruptcy of the Northern Pacific Railroad. A few years later, in an effort to recover their losses, the owners of that line initiated the practice of "Bonanza Farming" in the Red River Valley of western Minnesota and eastern Dakota. They granted expert wheat farmer Oliver Dalrymple 18 square miles of fertile lands, and he brought in gangs of workers equipped with carloads of farm machinery. The large-scale operation was an unqualified success, yielding a phenomenal 25 bushels of wheat per acre on 4,500 acres, bringing in a profit of more than 125 percent on the initial start-up costs.

The promise demonstrated by "Bonanza Farming" soon attracted eastern capital. Large tracts were quickly bought up along the 300-mile long Red River Valley, pouring much-needed new financing into the coffers of the Northern Pacific. As a result, the line was able to resume its construction, and within a few years reached across the Great Plains and Rocky Mountains to Portland, Oregon. An additional spur to the rapid settlement of Dakota was the Black Hills Gold Rush. After 1876, Dakota settlers could depend on the tens of thousands of miners who had flocked to the region as a ready market for their farm products.

Another railroad, the Great Northern, was instrumental in bringing about the rapid settlement of the lands

8.6 THE WEST IN 1889

north of the Union Pacific. Headed by James J. Hill, the line inched its way across northern Dakota to Fargo and Grand Forks. By 1890, the line was completed with its western terminus at Seattle, in Washington Territory. Hill's achievement is noteworthy because unlike previous transcontinental lines, his railroad received no land grants from the government. Instead, he had to rely on immigration to build up settlements along the route in order to develop way traffic. His advertising campaign brought in thousands of settlers from Europe, induced by free transportation, loans to farmers just starting out and agricultural innovations such as model farms and specially bred livestock.

Along the western fringe of the Great Plains in eastern Montana and Wyoming, farming settlement also bloomed, made easier with irrigation provided by the rivers that ran down the eastern slopes of the Rocky Mountains. The booming mining towns of Billings, Glendive and Miles City provided an instant market for farmers of the western Great Plains.

The rising population on the Great Plains soon prompted the region's territorial governments to seek admission as states. Political obstacles first had to be overcome. Dominated through the late 1870s and early 1880s by the Democrats, Congress was reluctant to admit the predominantly Republican Northern Plains territor-

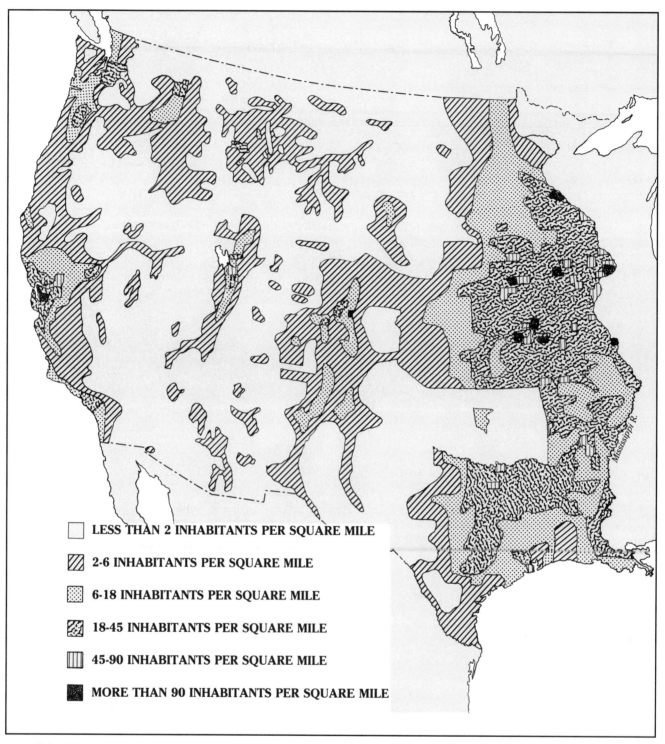

LESS THAN 2 INHABITANTS PER SQUARE MILE

2-6 INHABITANTS PER SQUARE MILE

6-18 INHABITANTS PER SQUARE MILE

18-45 INHABITANTS PER SQUARE MILE

45-90 INHABITANTS PER SQUARE MILE

MORE THAN 90 INHABITANTS PER SQUARE MILE

8.7 POPULATION DENSITY OF THE WEST IN 1890

ies. But after the election of 1888, in which Republican candidate Benjamin Harrison was elected president, the Republicans found themselves with a slight majority in both the House and the Senate.

With enough new Republican congressmen to support the measure, the Dakota Territory was divided in two, giving the Republican party an extra two votes in the Senate. In 1889, the "Omnibus Bill" was enacted, which

not only admitted North Dakota and South Dakota, but also authorized the admission of Washington and Montana as states. A year later, in 1890, Wyoming and Idaho followed their sister western states into the Union.

The march of the frontier was nearly complete. The pioneer trailblazers that spearheaded settlement into the Ohio and Mississippi valleys had been followed by the mountain men and fur traders who were the first to occupy the Far West. The territories and states carved from the Great Plains had risen from the efforts of the cowboys and cattlemen. They had finally given way to the relentless advance of pioneer farmers.

BOOMERS AND SOONERS INVADE OKLAHOMA

In 1854, the Kansas–Nebraska Act had reduced the Indian Territory to a 40,000 square-mile area, which now comprises the present-day state of Oklahoma. It was bounded on the north by Kansas, on the south and west by Texas and northeastern New Mexico and on the east by Arkansas and southeastern Missouri.

On the map, the remaining land assigned to the Indians appeared as a peninsula jutting out from the West into the settled areas of the Mississippi Valley. Since 1834, white settlement in the Indian Territory had been banned by federal law. The government had promised the Indians that the land would be theirs for "as long as the sun rise and go down . . . as long as grass grew . . . as long as the water runs."

But in the Civil War, factions of Creeks, Seminoles, Cherokees, Chickasaws and Choctaws had sided with the Confederacy. After the war's end, the federal government had punished these tribes for their disloyalty by forcing them to cede a portion of their western reservation lands in the Indian Territory. This area was intended for the resettlement of other western Indians and for freed blacks who had been slaves in the Indian Territory. The government had also demanded that the Indians grant rights-of-way for railroad construction through their lands.

After the Cheyennes and Arapahos had been given reservations on the ceded Cherokee and Seminole lands, there still remained close to two million acres of Indian Territory that had not been assigned to any tribe. These Unassigned Lands—the Oklahoma District—stood as a tempting morsel of territory for many homesteaders who had been overwhelmed by the hardships of settling the drought-stricken and grasshopper-plagued Great Plains to the north, south and west of the Indian Territory.

The area's abundant rivers were the main attraction. The fertile and well-wooded valleys of the Arkansas, Cimarron, Canadian and Red rivers were a virtual Garden of Eden when compared to the semi-arid and treeless wastelands of western Kansas and Nebraska.

In the 1870s, Texas cattlemen had begun leasing Cherokee lands in the northern part of the Indian Territory. By the 1880s, white ranchers were stringing barbed wire on the open range of the Indian Territory in an effort to separate their herds from rival cattlemen. These developments prompted Kansas farmers to protest that wealthy cattlemen profited from Indian Territory, while homesteaders seeking homes and farms were excluded.

A call to open some of the lands of the Indian Territory first came from the railroads that planned to construct routes through the region. Backers of the Atchison, Topeka & Santa Fe, the Missouri, Kansas & Texas, and the Atlantic & Pacific railroads knew that their business would flourish if farms, towns and cities developed along their lines.

Ironically, the demand for opening the Indian Territory to white settlement found one of its most outspoken voices in an Indian. The son of a leading Cherokee family, Elias C. Boudinot had served as a colonel with Indian forces allied with the Confederacy in the Civil War, and had been the Cherokees' representative to the Confederate government in Richmond. In the 1870s, he worked as an attorney in Washington, D.C., and served as a clerk with the House Committee on Private Land Claims.

Boudinot's earlier pro-southern stance had caused him to lose favor among Cherokee leaders. In Washington, he joined with railroad and government officials to promote the opening of the Indian Territory to white settlement. He may have hoped that by helping to bring about the new era of prosperity that the railroads would usher in, he might regain a leadership position with his people.

In early 1879, Boudinot published an article in the Chicago *Times* in which he claimed that millions of acres in the Indian Territory that had been ceded by the Creeks, Seminoles and other tribes were now part of the public domain and legally open to settlement under the Homestead and Pre-emption laws. In addition, he offered prospective settlers free maps of the area and detailed information about the opportunities for homesteading on the Unassigned Lands of the Oklahoma District.

Newspapers in Kansas, Missouri, Arkansas and Nebraska reprinted Boudinot's article, spreading the word to land-hungry homesteaders. The news soon sparked a popular movement to open the Indian Territory to white settlement. Adherents to the cause became known as "boomers." By the spring of 1879, a group known as the Oklahoma Colony had been organized under the leadership of David L. Payne.

Originally from Indiana, Payne was a distant cousin of frontiersman Davy Crockett, who had died at the Alamo in 1836, the year in which Payne was born. In 1857, young Payne had set out for the West, settling on public land near Fort Leavenworth, Kansas. He was not much of a farmer; instead he found employment as a scout for private and government expeditions on the Southern Plains. At the outbreak of the Civil War in 1861, Payne enlisted in a Kansas volunteer regiment with which he served in military operations in Arkansas and Missouri. Later in the war, he saw action in Virginia, and was with

General Grant's forces when Lee surrendered at Appomattox in 1865.

In the years immediately after the war, Payne was elected to the Kansas legislature. In 1868, he re-entered the army to serve as a captain in a military expedition against the Cheyennes in western Kansas and the Indian Territory. It was in the course of this campaign that Colonel George Armstrong Custer destroyed Black Kettle's Cheyenne encampment in the Battle of the Washita. About a year later, Payne served as a scout in the Wichita Mountains of Indian Territory, and it was then that he first learned of the rich bottom lands of the Oklahoma District.

Throughout the early 1870s, Payne made numerous attempts at homesteading in western Kansas, but repeatedly mortgaged his claims and lost them to foreclosures. In 1877, he won an appointment as assistant doorkeeper to the House of Representatives in Washington, D.C. He lost that position in 1879 when the head doorkeeper was dismissed for official misconduct, forcing the dismissal of his entire staff.

It was during his tenure in Washington that Payne became acquainted with Elias C. Boudinot, and it was with Boudinot's encouragement that Payne returned to Kansas to take up the leadership of the movement to open the Indian Territory to white settlement. In the summer of 1879, Payne arrived in Wichita, Kansas, where he soon organized several thousand boomers into a group known as the "Oklahoma Colony."

By the spring of 1880, Payne was ready to launch his first invasion of Indian Territory. Leading a party of 21 followers, he evaded army troops guarding the border, and managed to cross the Cherokee Outlet into Oklahoma District. On a site near present-day Oklahoma City, the group constructed a stockade and sent out surveying crews to locate claims for the colonists.

Within days, however, a detachment of army troops arrived on the scene and ordered Payne and his party out of the region, escorting them back to the Kansas border.

Undaunted, Payne launched another attempt a few months later. He and his group were arrested and brought before federal judge Isaac Parker at Fort Smith, Arkansas. This was exactly what Payne wanted—a chance to bring the issue in a test case before a federal court.

Judge Parker ruled that the Unassigned Lands of the Oklahoma District were still part of the Indian Territory, and that Payne and his followers were guilty of violating federal law against settling there. Payne was fined $1,000, but this punishment was meaningless to the Oklahoma Colony leader since he had no property and the fine could therefore not be collected. The law provided no other penalty, leaving Payne free to resume his campaign to settle the Oklahoma District.

Over the next four years, Payne continued to play cat and mouse with the army. On many occasions, he led other groups of colonists into the Oklahoma District. Each time federal troops would find him, arrest him for trespassing and bring him out again. In the meantime, he gained thousands of additional supporters and his Oklahoma Colony amassed a war chest of over $100,000 from its members.

In November of 1884, shortly after a boomer rally in Wellington, Kansas, Payne died of a heart attack. Leadership of the Oklahoma Colony then passed to Payne's chief lieutenant, William L. Couch. Just over a week after Payne's death, Couch led several hundred boomers, including women and children, into the northeastern region of the Unassigned Lands near present-day Stillwater, Oklahoma. When ordered to leave by federal troops, Crouch refused. Instead of forcibly evicting the trespassers, the commanding army officer simply surrounded them, cutting off their supply lines. After a few weeks of this siege, with food supplies running low, Couch and his boomers were forced to return to Kansas.

Meanwhile, a new wrinkle had developed in the issue of the Unassigned Lands. In early 1885, Secretary of the Interior Henry M. Teller, who supervised Indian affairs, recommended to President Chester A. Arthur that the Indian lands be opened to settlement. In March 1885, Congress passed legislation that authorized the president to negotiate with the Seminoles, Creeks and Cherokees for the cession of their surplus lands in western Indian Territory.

No action was taken until January of 1889, when Creek leader Pleasant Porter formally declared his tribe's desire to sell their western land. Similar offers were made by leaders of the Seminoles. The subsequent treaties provided the Indians with payments of more than $4 million for the unassigned lands of the Indian Territory.

On March 23, 1889, President Benjamin Harrison, who had just been inaugurated, issued a proclamation declaring that at noon on April 22, 1889, the Unassigned Lands of the Oklahoma District would be open to settlement under the Homestead and Pre-emption laws. Over the next few weeks, more than 100,000 hopeful home-seekers crowded the borders of southern Kansas and northern Texas in anticipation of the opening of the new territory.

Several days before the official opening, the prospective settlers were permitted to cross the Indian Territory to the borders of the Oklahoma District. Fifteen special trains, deployed at Arkansas City on the Kansas border, were packed with homesteaders, many hanging onto the sides and piled atop the roofs of the cars. Thousands of others massed along the boundary line, awaiting the signal that would launch "Harrison's Hoss Race."

At noon on April 22, 1889, the report of pistols fired by soldiers announced the opening of the Oklahoma

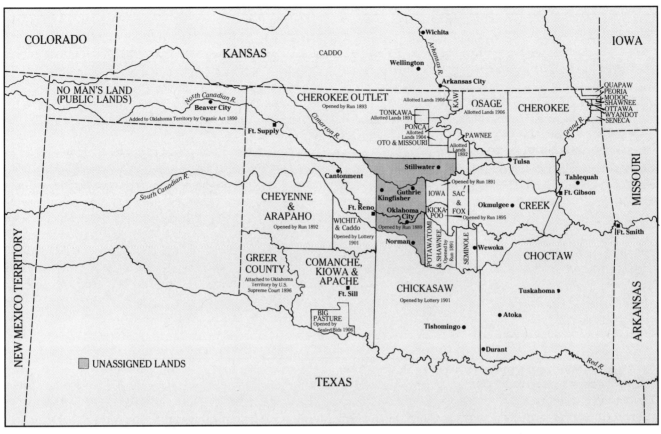

8.8 INDIAN TERRITORY AND OKLAHOMA LAND OPENINGS: 1889–1906

District. The trains slowly inched across the border, maintaining a pace equal to a walking horse so as not to give an unfair advantage to the boomers aboard. As they passed into the Oklahoma District, the homesteaders leaped from cars in a mad scramble to claim free lands. At the same time, thousands of others swarmed across the border, in wagons, on horseback and some even on bicycles. Among the horde of settlers was a group of four circus midgets riding on a single horse. Within hours, the cities of Guthrie, Oklahoma City, Kingfisher and Norman had sprung into existence on lands that a day before had been barren prairie.

Some of the participants in the Oklahoma Land Rush, as it came to be known, had literally "jumped the gun." These settlers had managed to evade army patrols, and sneaked in to stake claims before the designated time. Some of these "Sooners" were apprehended and their claims declared invalid, but most managed to elude the authorities. In later years, Oklahoma was nicknamed the "Sooner State."

By nightfall on April 22, 1889, all of the 1,920,000 acres of the Oklahoma District had been claimed by settlers. Oklahoma City and Guthrie each boasted initial populations of well over 10,000 people. William L. Couch became Oklahoma City's first mayor.

Formal government for the new settlements came in May of 1890, when Congress passed legislation creating the Territory of Oklahoma. Over the next few years, more Indian lands were opened to settlement and these areas were joined to the Oklahoma Territory. Another land rush took place in September of 1893, when the Cherokee Outlet was opened, bringing another 6 million acres of land into the Territory.

The Dawes Severalty Act of 1887 provided for the allotment of individual homesteads to members of tribes that still held Indian lands. These allotments of 160 acres left millions of acres of surplus land open for settlement. By 1905, only the Cherokee, Choctaw and Creek lands

Oklahoma Land Run in the Cherokee Outlet, 1893 (Photo courtesy of the New York Public Library)

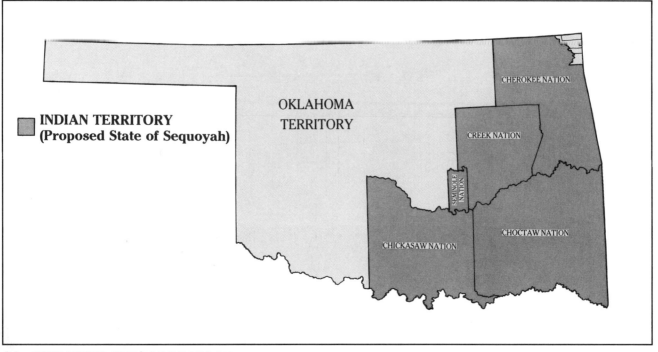

INDIAN TERRITORY
(Proposed State of Sequoyah)

OKLAHOMA
TERRITORY

CHEROKEE NATION

CREEK NATION

SEMINOLE NATION

CHOCTAW NATION

CHICKASAW NATION

8.9   THE TWIN TERRITORIES IN 1905

in what is now eastern Oklahoma remained as Indian Territory.

By then, Oklahoma Territory and the Indian Territory, which together had become known as the Twin Territories, were likely candidates for statehood. Leaders of the Indian tribes attempted to have the Indian Territory admitted as a separate state and held a convention for this purpose at Muskogee in August of 1905. The proposal to create the Indian state of "Sequoyah" was tabled by the House of Representatives. President Theodore Roosevelt also rejected the idea declaring, "There is no obligation upon us to treat territorial subdivisions, which are matters of convenience only, as binding us on the question of admission to statehood."

In the meantime, the Senate passed legislation to merge the Twin Territories into one and admit it as a single state. On November 16, 1907, Oklahoma entered the Union as the 46th state.

THE GROWTH OF STATEHOOD

In 1890, Utah, New Mexico and Arizona territories—more than half the area acquired in the Mexican Cession of 1848—still remained outside the Union.

The Mormons who first settled Utah Territory applied for admission as the State of Deseret as early as 1849. But their bid for statehood was repeatedly rejected because the federal government did not approve of the Mormon practice of polygamy. The Mormon church finally advised its members to refrain from plural marriages in 1890, after the government stepped up its efforts to enforce federal antipolygamy laws.

By then, the growth of railroads and mining in Utah Territory had brought a sizable non-Mormon population into the region. In the early 1890s, the new influx had caused the Mormon People's Party to lose its hold on the territorial government. In 1895, the territory submitted a new proposed state constitution to Congress that explicitly outlawed polygamy and forbade church control of the government. Congress approved the constitution, and on January 4, 1896, President Grover Cleveland endorsed the bill that made Utah the 45th state.

New Mexico and Arizona originally had been organized as a single territory in 1850. In 1863, the federal government set aside the western portion of the region as Arizona Territory soon after Union troops were able to reoccupy the region and end its brief career as a Confederate territory.

Both New Mexico and Arizona territories grew in population with the development of railroads and mining, prompting a call for statehood by the late 1880s. In 1905, a plan was proposed in Congress for making a single state of New Mexico and Arizona. But the inhabitants of Arizona Territory wanted only separate statehood. Its mostly Anglo-American inhabitants did not want to fall under the political domination of New Mexico's larger Mexican–American and Indian population.

Congress, however, had political reasons of its own for opposing separate statehood. Both New Mexico and

8.10 THE GROWTH OF THE UNITED STATES BY STATEHOOD

Arizona were then overwhelmingly Democratic. At that time, the Republicans held sway over both houses of Congress. Two new Democratic states could threaten the Republican majority by sending as many as four new Democrats to the Senate. As a result, statehood for both territories was held up for the next several years.

The political wrangling came to an end in 1912 after the Democrats had gained a stronger position in Congress. The necessary legislation was passed, and on January 6, 1912, New Mexico entered the Union as the 47th state. (In 1907, Oklahoma had become the 46th state.)

President William Howard Taft welcomed the citizens of the new state of New Mexico, declaring, "I am glad to give you life. I hope you will be happy." One month later, on February 4, Arizona was admitted as the 48th state.

In January of 1959, Alaska, the 49th state, was added to the 48 continental states. The roll of the states was completed in August of 1959, when the Hawaiian Islands—which the United States had annexed in 1898—entered the Union as the 50th state.

Epilogue

THE REAL SIGNIFICANCE OF THE FRONTIER

FOR MORE THAN half a century, the American frontier was truly a frontier in the Old World sense: the area of the country that faced or bordered upon another country. First it had been the line between the British colonies of the eastern seaboard and the French territory west of the Appalachians. Then it had shifted westward to define the line between the United States and the Spanish possessions west of the Mississippi River. The last frontiers with British Oregon, the Republic of Texas and the northern Mexican provinces of California and New Mexico evaporated in a flurry of diplomatic and military endeavors that marked the course of Manifest Destiny in the late 1840s.

Since colonial times, the West had been a child of the South. The first westward push into the Ohio and Mississippi valleys had been spearheaded by Daniel Boone and other pioneers from the Carolinas and Virginia. The first great acquisition of western lands, the Louisiana Purchase, had been prompted by the South's desire to open New Orleans as the principal gateway for the West's agricultural output.

U.S. involvement in what turned into the War of 1812 had many opponents in the North; the issue had brought the New England states to the brink of seceding from the Union. But the South saw that conflict as an opportunity to drive the Spanish out of West Florida and strengthen its hold on the agricultural trade of the entire Mississippi Valley.

The United States underwent its greatest periods of territorial expansion during the first half of the 19th century. By 1853, the nation had expanded to its present boundaries. Significantly, at every critical point in that process a southerner occupied the White House.

Thomas Jefferson, a Virginian, was responsible for the Louisiana Purchase in 1803. In 1819, James Monroe, another Virginian, was in charge when Florida was acquired from Spain and Great Britain ceded the Red River Basin. The Oregon Country became part of the U.S. during the presidency of Virginian John Tyler, and the greatest western prize of all—California and the Southwest—was wrested from Mexico under the presidency of James K. Polk, a North Carolina native raised in Tennessee. Even Millard Fillmore, although a native of New York, nevertheless had southern interests in mind when Jefferson Davis of Mississippi encouraged him to endorse the Gadsden Purchase of 1853.

In the first decades of the 19th century, the rise of the Cotton Kingdom generated a booming agricultural economy in the South. In a sense, the South became a self-contained colonial empire, with its immense pool of slave labor serving the same purpose as the Asian and African colonies of France and Great Britain.

When the controversy over the slavery issue threatened to undermine the very foundations of that empire, the South looked to the acquisition of additional territory in the West. With more territories and states open to

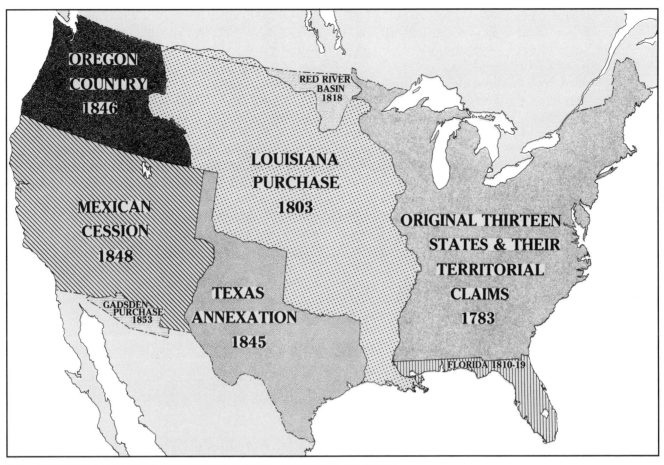

E.1 WESTWARD EXPANSION OF THE UNITED STATES

slavery, the South could bolster its power in the national government, and thereby forestall northern efforts to enact federal laws banning slavery.

The war with Mexico that erupted in 1846 was a campaign mostly fought by southerners. It resulted in the addition of a large area of territory that the South eyed as a region in which slavery could be extended. Even in areas of the Mexican cession in which the environment made slavery impractical, new states and territories could nevertheless be carved that would support southern interests.

While the South may have gained political strength with the acquisition of new territory, each phase of westward expansion further aggravated the slavery issue. The Louisiana Purchase of 1803 ultimately led to the first big showdown between North and South that ended peaceably with the Missouri Compromise of 1820. The vast territory brought into the Union by the Mexican Cession in 1848 renewed the controversy that was again calmed, albeit temporarily, with the Compromise of 1850. From that agreement emerged the concept of "Popular Sovereignty," an ideal that was acceptable to the North and South only if the populations involved adhered to each section's respective views on slavery.

Abraham Lincoln, commenting on the Dred Scott decision in 1858, declared: "A house divided against itself cannot stand. I believe this government cannot endure permanently half slave and half free . . . Either the opponents of slavery will arrest the further spread of it . . . or its advocates will push it forward till it shall become alike lawful in all the States, old as well as new, North as well as South." His words proved prophetic; the issue of the spread of slavery into the western territories—an area that the South had been so instrumental in acquiring—soon pushed the nation into its bloodiest conflict.

In the Civil War, the abortive Texas campaign to capture New Mexico, Colorado and California may have been an attempt by southerners to seize what they viewed as rightfully theirs. But the Union forces of the North managed to hold onto the West through sheer military might. After the defeat of the South, the bonds between the North and the West were strengthened with a liberal policy of free land and federal support for the building of the transcontinental railroad. When mining or agricultural opportunities opened up in the West, the first pioneers to arrive on the scene often relied on the northern-dominated federal government to send in troops to overcome Indian resistance.

After the Civil War, the West itself emerged as a distinctive section, replacing in importance the former agricultural might of the South. This new agricultural empire was first based on cattle, then on wheat and corn. But the West held other riches—mineral wealth of gold, silver and copper—that helped finance the growth of the industrial cities of the North.

In time, however, westerners of the farming and mining frontiers came to feel that they were being exploited by the more industrialized regions of the East. Dissatisfaction with national monetary policies and the growth of industrial trusts that dictated just how much western farmers could earn led to a widespread popular revolt among westerners. The West struck back with the rise of the Populist movement in the 1890s, and the creation of a new political party—the People's or Populist Party.

Although the westerners who supported the Populist Party failed to put a candidate in the White House, many of their demands were realized a few decades later. Ultimately, the western-born movement helped bring about new federal regulations regarding interstate commerce, a reform of national monetary policy and the direct election by voters of U.S. senators.

For the American colonists, the Revolutionary War was a struggle for independence. But when that conflict spilled over across the Appalachians, for the Indians of the Ohio and Mississippi valleys it became a war against white encroachment that dragged on until the conclusion of the War of 1812. The nearly 50 years of relative peace that ensued ended with the outbreak of the Civil War. It was then that the Plains Indians began to fight against the spread of white settlement across the Great Plains. By the time the Indians suffered their ultimate military defeat at Wounded Knee, South Dakota in 1890, the frontier had vanished and the Native American population had been decimated.

The exploits of fur trappers, miners, cowboys and hardy homesteaders gave rise to the popular mythology

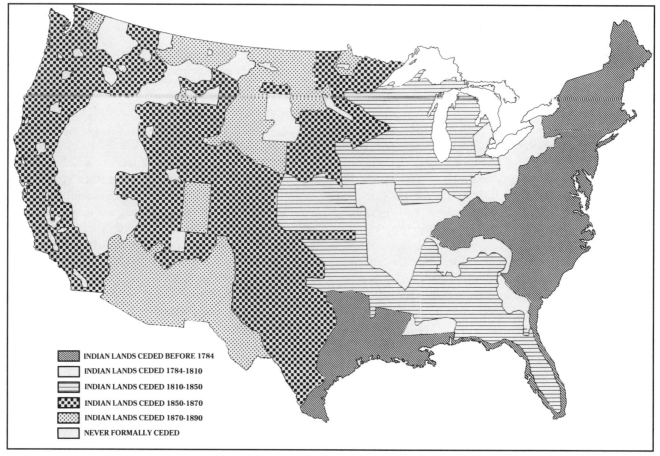

INDIAN LANDS CEDED BEFORE 1784
INDIAN LANDS CEDED 1784-1810
INDIAN LANDS CEDED 1810-1850
INDIAN LANDS CEDED 1850-1870
INDIAN LANDS CEDED 1870-1890
NEVER FORMALLY CEDED

E.2 THE APPROPRIATION OF INDIAN LANDS

that it was the efforts of these intrepid pioneers who "tamed the West." In fact, the West was settled largely through the efforts of American big business.

The mineral riches of western mines could only be adequately exploited with huge infusions of capital. After the Civil War, cattle-raising rapidly grew into a large-scale commercial enterprise. As for the pioneer farmer on the Great Plains, his presence there was largely the result of another huge industrial endeavor—the construction of the western railroads.

The mass migration induced by the railroads' advertising and publicity campaigns brought in hundreds of thousands of settlers. They cultivated the virgin grasslands of the Great Plains with dry farming methods that were at best moderately successful in times of greater-than-usual rainfall, and failed altogether during periods of prolonged drought.

Modern environmental historians claim that the Great Plains should never have been cultivated. They blame the pioneer sodbusters' dry farming practices for destroying the grasslands' protective cover that left the land vulnerable to the disastrous Dust Bowl conditions that devastated the Great Plains in the early 1930s.

When economic depressions stemmed the flow of private capital into the West, the federal government took up the slack by expending billions of dollars for land reclamation and irrigation projects and for the construction of dams to harness the waters of western rivers. Even earlier, the federal government had indirectly subsidized the great cattle boom of the 1870s and 1880s by allowing the herds to graze free of charge on the federal lands of the public domain.

One hundred years after the closing of the frontier, 500 million acres of the West—nearly one-fifth the area of the entire United States—remain under the control of the federal government's Bureau of Land Management and the Forest Service. Throughout the 20th century, these lands have been available at no cost (or at very low rates) to corporations involved in large-scale cattle-raising, mining and logging operations.

Facts indicate that the settlement of the West came about largely through the involvement of big government and big business. Nonetheless, the bold dreams and romantic hopes of those individuals who first ventured into the West undeniably played a large role in shaping the way in which Americans view themselves.

Appendix A
Profile of U.S. Territorial Expansion (1783–1898)

DATE	TERRITORY ACQUIRED	STATES & PARTS OF STATES FORMED
1783	The territory of the 13 original states and adjoining western territory, as recognized by Great Britain under the Treaty of Paris	Virginia, New York, Massachusetts, New Hampshire, Maryland, Connecticut, Rhode Island, Delaware, North Carolina, New Jersey, South Carolina, Pennsylvania, Georgia, Vermont, Kentucky, Tennessee, Ohio, Indiana, Mississippi, Illinois, Alabama, Maine, Michigan, Wisconsin, West Virginia
1803	The Louisiana Purchase (from France)	Louisiana, Missouri, Arkansas, Iowa, Minnesota (southeastern), Kansas, Nebraska, Colorado (eastern), North Dakota, South Dakota, Montana (eastern), Wyoming (eastern), Oklahoma (eastern)
1810–13	Annexation of West Florida (taken from Spain by American settlers)	Southern portions of Alabama, Mississippi and Louisiana
1819	East Florida (ceded by Spain under Adams–Onis Treaty)	Florida
1845	Annexation of Texas (Republic of Texas & adjoining territory)	Texas, Colorado (central), Kansas (southeastern), Wyoming (south central), Oklahoma (panhandle), New Mexico (eastern)
1846	Annexation of the Oregon Country (end of joint occupation with Great Britain)	Oregon, Montana (western), Washington, Idaho, Wyoming (western)
1848	Mexican Cession	California, Nevada, Colorado (western), Wyoming (southeastern), Utah, New Mexico, Arizona
1853	Gadsden Purchase (from Mexico)	Southwestern New Mexico and southern Arizona
1867	Alaska Purchase (from Russia)	Alaska
1898	Annexation of the Hawaiian Islands	Hawaii

Appendix B
Chronology of U.S. Territorial Expansion (1750–1917)

1750
Frontiersman Christopher Gist explores lands granted to the Virginia-based Ohio Company in the Ohio River Valley; the company establishes a post, Fort Cumberland, in the Allegheny mountains of western Maryland.

1752
In the Treaty of Logstown, the Delawares and Iroquois acknowledge the Virginia colony's claim to territory south of the Ohio River.

The French react to the increased British presence in the Ohio Valley with an attack on the British trading post at Pickawillany.

1753
The French construct forts between the south shore of Lake Erie and the Allegheny and Ohio rivers.

George Washington travels to the Ohio Country to warn the French out of the region.

1754
The French occupy the strategic Forks of the Ohio (at present-day Pittsburgh) and construct Fort Duquesne; British settlers are driven out of the Ohio Valley.

Initial conflict of the French and Indian War occurs near the Forks of the Ohio when George Washington and a force of Virginia militia defeat a small French reconnaissance unit; he later surrenders to a larger French force and withdraws to Virginia.

1755
British General Edward Braddock leads a large military expedition westward from Fort Cumberland to the vicinity of Fort Duquesne; his army is defeated and he is killed in the ensuing battle with the French.

1756
The French and their Indian allies mount successful offensives along the northern Appalachian frontier, forcing British colonists to flee the Mohawk Valley.

1758
British forces under General John Forbes mount an offensive against the French in the Ohio Valley; the French are compelled to abandon and destroy Fort Duquesne; the Forks of the Ohio fall to the British, opening the Trans-Appalachian region to settlement from Virginia.

1759–60
The British achieve major victories over the French at Quebec, Montreal and Detroit.

1762
In the secret Treaty of Fountainbleau, France transfers to Spain all its territory west of the Mississippi River.

1763
The Treaty of Paris brings the French and Indian War to an end; France cedes its North American territory to Great Britain; Virginia lays claim to western lands as far as the Mississippi.

Pontiac's Rebellion erupts on the Great Lakes frontier, from Detroit to Fort Niagara.

The Proclamation of 1763, issued by King George III, limits English settlement to the lands east of the Appalachian Mountains; the lands west of the mountains are reserved for the Indians.

1764
French fur traders establish St. Louis on the Mississippi, near the mouth of the Missouri River.

1766
Pontiac surrenders to British forces at Oswego.

1768
Westward frontier advance: In the North, the Iroquois sell their lands in southwestern New York, western Pennsylvania and parts of present-day West Virginia, Kentucky and Tennessee; in the South, the Creeks and Cherokees agree to give up territory in western South Carolina and western Georgia.

1769
Daniel Boone begins explorations of eastern Kentucky.

1770
Westward frontier advance: Virginia colony acquires western lands from the Cherokees.

1771
Daniel Boone returns to North Carolina.

1773
Daniel Boone, leading settlers into Kentucky, is forced to turn back after an Indian attack at Cumberland Gap.

1774
Lord Dunmore's War: The Shawnees are defeated at the Battle of Point Pleasant; in the ensuing treaty, the Indians agree to open more of their lands south of the Ohio River to white settlement.

1775
In the Treaty of Sycamore Shoals, Judge Richard Henderson buys a large portion of present-day Kentucky from the Cherokees.

Daniel Boone blazes a trail through the Cumberland Gap to the Kentucky River; establishes Boonesborough.

The Revolutionary War erupts as fighting breaks out in New England between colonial militia and British troops.

1776
British-allied Indians attack settlements all along the Appalachian frontier.

Virginia annexes Kentucky.

1778
George Rogers Clark leads an American military expedition down the Ohio and captures British strongholds at Kaskaskia and Vincennes in the Illinois Country.

1780
Nashborough (later Nashville) is established on the Cumberland River.

1783
The Treaty of Paris formally ends the Revolutionary War.

Westward frontier advance: Great Britain recognizes U.S. territory as extending westward to the Mississippi River.

1784
Settlers in eastern Tennessee separate from North Carolina and organize themselves as the State of Franklin.

1785
Under the Land Ordinance of 1785, the Old Northwest—the area north of the Ohio River between the Appalachians and the Mississippi—is to be organized into townships and sections in preparation for the sale of public lands to settlers.

Fort Harmar established on the Ohio River at the mouth of the Muskingum River.

1787
Congress enacts the Northwest Ordinance of 1787, which provides for the organization of the Old Northwest into as many as five territories and outlines how these territories can eventually be admitted to the Union as states; the extension of slavery into territories and states formed from the Old Northwest is banned.

Marietta, Ohio is founded by Rufus Putnam and the Ohio Company, the first permanent U.S. settlement in the region organized under the Northwest Ordinance.

1788
Present-day Cincinnati is established at the junction of the Miami and Ohio rivers.

1789
The State of Franklin is dissolved and the area is rejoined to North Carolina.

1791
The Indians of the Old Northwest rise up under Little Turtle in what becomes known as Little Turtle's War.

1792
General "Mad" Anthony Wayne takes over command of U.S. troops in the ongoing Indian war in the Old Northwest.

1794
General Wayne defeats Little Turtle and his followers at the Battle of Fallen Timbers.

Under the terms of the Jay Treaty of 1794, Great Britain agrees to vacate its garrisons and Indian trading posts in the Old Northwest.

1795
Westward frontier advance: In the Treaty of Fort Greenville, the Indians of the Old Northwest cede their territory in present-day southwestern Ohio and southeastern Indiana.

Westward frontier advance: In the Treaty of San Lorenzo (the Pinckney Treaty), Spain assures U.S. navigation rights on the Mississippi and recognizes what is now Mississippi and Alabama as U.S. territory.

1800
In the Treaty of San Ildefonso, Spain agrees to return the Louisiana Country to France.

1802
Indiana territorial governor William Henry Harrison obtains cessions of Indian lands in present-day southern Indiana and Illinois.

1803
Ohio becomes the first state formed from the Old Northwest.

Westward frontier advance: France sells the Louisiana Country to the United States, extending the nation's western boundary to the Rocky Mountains and giving the U.S. control of the entire Mississippi River.

1804
Lewis and Clark and the Corps of Discovery set out from St. Louis to explore the Missouri River into the Far West.

The area acquired in the Louisiana Purchase is organized into the Territory of Orleans and the District of Louisiana.

1805
Lewis and Clark travel from the upper Missouri across the Continental Divide to the mouth of the Columbia River on the Oregon coast.

Zebulon Pike leads a U.S. Army expedition up the Mississippi into present-day north-central Minnesota.

1806
Lewis and Clark return to St. Louis from their explorations of the Northern Plains, the Northern Rockies and the Pacific Northwest.

1806–07
Zebulon Pike explores western Missouri, present-day Kansas and southern Nebraska and crosses into Spanish territory when he enters the upper Rio Grande Valley of New Mexico.

1807
Manuel Lisa launches his first fur-trading venture up the Missouri and into the Northern Rockies; one of his trappers, John Colter, explores the Teton Mountains and the area around present-day Yellowstone Park.

1810
Andrew Henry, Manuel Lisa's partner, establishes a trading post near the Three Forks of the Missouri in present-day southwestern Montana.

Baton Rouge and the surrounding area of Spanish-held West Florida are seized by American settlers and, soon after, annexed to the United States.

1811
John Jacob Astor's fur company establishes Fort Astoria at the mouth of the Columbia River on the Oregon coast.

Governor William Henry Harrison of Indiana Territory leads a military expedition up the Wabash River to attack the Shawnees at Prophetstown; the engagement becomes known as the Battle of Tippecanoe.

The Shawnee leader Tecumseh leads his people in an uprising against American frontier settlements in the Old Northwest.

The first steamboat to navigate on the western rivers, the *New Orleans*, travels down the Ohio from Pittsburgh to the mouth of the Mississippi at New Orleans.

1812
Louisiana is admitted to the Union; Missouri Territory is organized.

Outbreak of the War of 1812: Mounting international tensions stemming from British infringement of U.S. rights on the high seas, as well as suspected British involvement in the Indian uprising on the frontier, leads the United States to declare war on Great Britain.

The U.S. suffers defeats at Detroit and Fort Dearborn (present-day Chicago).

1813
Commodore Oliver Hazard Perry defeats British naval forces in the Battle of Lake Erie.

Harrison leads U.S. forces to victory in the Battle of the Thames in which Tecumseh is killed.

Creeks massacre American settlers in an attack on Fort Mims, in present-day Alabama.

General Andrew Jackson leads Tennessee militia against the Creeks.

1814
General Andrew Jackson, in command of frontier militia force, defeats Creeks in the Battle of Horseshoe Bend; the Indians are forced to cede a large portion of their homelands in the Treaty of Fort Jackson.

British invasion force is stopped in northern New York in the Battle of Lake Champlain.

The United States and Great Britain agree to the Treaty of Ghent, bringing an end to the War of 1812; under its terms, the United States neither gains nor loses territory.

1815
The United States wins a victory over the British in the Battle of New Orleans; news that a peace agreement had already been reached does not reach America until weeks after the battle.

1817
The Rush-Bagot Agreement between the United States and Great Britain limits naval forces on the Great Lakes and sets the precedent for the unguarded boundary between the United States and Canada.

Construction of the Erie Canal begins at Rome, New York.

1818
Under the terms of the Convention of 1818, the United States and Great Britain reach agreement on the northern boundary of the Louisiana Purchase and consent to joint occupation of the Oregon Country for the next 10 years.

The National (or Cumberland) Road reaches from Baltimore and Cumberland, Maryland to Wheeling on the Ohio River.

1819
The United States and Spain enter into the Adams–Onis Treaty (ratified by Congress in 1821), which provides for the cession of East Florida to the United States, and establishes the southwestern boundary of the Louisiana Purchase and the northern boundary of Spanish California.

The Panic of 1819 causes hardship among western farmers; many face eviction when they are unable to meet payments on government land purchases.

1820
The Missouri Compromise allows the admission of Mis-

souri as a slave state and Maine as a free state; under its terms, slavery will be prohibited in the remaining territories and states formed from the Louisiana Purchase north of the southern Missouri state line.

Major Stephen Long leads a U.S. Army exploration into the eastern Colorado Rockies; in his official report, he characterizes the Great Plains as the "Great American Desert."

1821

Mexico wins independence from Spain.

William Becknell pioneers the Santa Fe Trail as a trade route between the Missouri Frontier and Santa Fe, New Mexico.

Russia announces that its Alaskan territory extends into the northern portion of the Oregon Country to the 51st parallel.

Stephen Austin establishes an American colony in Texas.

1822

In a second trade expedition to Santa Fe, Becknell introduces the use of wagons to carry goods westward across the Southern Plains.

William Henry Ashley launches his first fur-trading expedition to the Missouri River region and Northern Rockies.

1823

Arikara Indians attack Ashley and his men on the Missouri River in present-day South Dakota.

Colonel Henry Leavenworth commands punitive military expedition against the Arikaras, the first U.S.–Indian conflict west of the Mississippi River.

Jedediah Smith and a party of mountain men head overland across the Plains to the Rocky Mountains in present-day Wyoming.

President James Monroe warns the European powers that the Western Hemisphere is now off-limits to colonization; his declaration becomes known as the Monroe Doctrine.

1824

Jedediah Smith and his companions cross the Continental Divide by way of South Pass and explore the Green River in present-day southwestern Wyoming and northeastern Utah.

In a treaty with the U.S., Russia withdraws its earlier claim on the northern region of the Ore-

gon Country, and agrees that the southern boundary of Russian Alaska is at 54° 40'.

Mountain man James Bridger comes upon the Great Salt Lake.

1825

The first annual fur trappers' rendezvous is held at Henrys Fork of the Green River.

The Erie Canal opens, linking Lake Erie at Buffalo with the Atlantic Ocean at New York City.

Jedediah Smith leads a party of trappers across the Great Basin to California; he explores the San Joaquin Valley and returns eastward across the Sierra Nevada to Bear Lake in northern Utah.

1826–37

Smith, on his second trip to California, travels into Oregon and returns to the Green River by way of the Columbia and Snake rivers.

1830

President Jackson signs the Indian Removal Act, providing for the relocation of the remaining eastern tribes to lands west of the Mississippi River.

1831

Cyrus McCormick invents a device for harvesting crops; his mechanical reaper will revolutionize agriculture on the Great Plains.

1832

Nathaniel Wyeth and Captain Benjamin Bonneville mount separate fur-trading efforts to the Far West.

The Black Hawk War: Chief Black Hawk of the Sauk tribe resists government efforts to remove his people to lands west of the Mississippi in Iowa; he is defeated in a battle at the mouth of the Bad Axe River in present-day Wisconsin.

1834

Nathaniel Wyeth establishes Fort Hall, the first permanent American settlement west of the Continental Divide.

1835

Discontent in the American colonies in Texas gives rise to a movement for independence from Mexico.

Texas revolutionaries seize San Antonio.

1836

Texans suffer losses at the Alamo and Goliad; having de-

clared their independence from Mexico, they defeat Mexican forces at the Battle of San Jacinto; Mexico withdraws from Texas, but does not recognize the independence of the Republic of Texas.

1837

President Andrew Jackson extends recognition to the Republic of Texas.

1839

Most of the remaining Five Civilized Tribes (Cherokee, Chickasaw, Choctaw, Creek and Seminole) are relocated to lands in present-day eastern Oklahoma and Arkansas.

1841

The first large wagon train travels westward from Independence, Missouri across the Plains by way of the Oregon Trail, bringing a large influx of American settlers into Oregon's Willamette Valley.

1843

James Bridger opens Fort Bridger in present-day southwestern Wyoming.

1845

Westward frontier advance: The United States annexes Texas.

Manifest Destiny becomes the ideological basis for aggressive government policy of territorial expansion.

1846

A border dispute along the Rio Grande erupts into the Mexican War.

U.S. wins victory over Mexican troops in the Battle of Palo Alto.

U.S. forces under Colonel Stephen Watts Kearny occupy New Mexico and march on southern California.

Combined U.S. land and sea forces capture California from Mexico.

Westward frontier advance: The Oregon boundary is settled with Great Britain; joint occupation ends, with the U.S.–Canada boundary now set at the 49th parallel.

1847

U.S. troops occupy Mexico City.

The Mormons, under the leadership of Brigham Young, establish a settlement near the Great Salt Lake in Utah and organize what becomes the State of Deseret.

1848

Westward frontier advance: The Mexican War ends with the Treaty of Guadalupe Hidalgo; the province of New Mexico (comprising present-day Arizona, western Colorado, Utah and part of Wyoming) is ceded to the United States along with California; the Rio Grande is recognized as the Texas border with Mexico.

Oregon is organized as a U.S. territory.

News of the discovery of gold at Sutter's Mill in California brings on the Gold Rush of 1849 and leads to an immediate influx of thousands of Americans into California.

1850

In the Compromise of 1850, California is admitted as a free state, territorial governments are established in New Mexico and Utah and Texas is reduced to its present state boundaries.

1851

In a treaty with the Sioux, the U.S. acquires Indian lands in Iowa and Minnesota.

1853

Washington Territory is separated from the northern section of Oregon Territory.

The U.S. government commissions officials to survey land for a transcontinental railroad.

In the Gadsden Purchase, the United States buys from Mexico a strip of territory extending southward from the Gila River; the area is seen as vital for a proposed transcontinental railroad route.

1854

Congress enacts the Kansas–Nebraska Act, establishing Kansas and Nebraska as territories with the right to self-determination in regard to the question of slavery.

1855

A railroad across the Isthmus of Panama is completed, providing easier transportation links between the eastern and western United States.

Fighting erupts between pro- and anti-slavery forces in Kansas; guerrilla warfare breaks out throughout the territory.

1857

In the Dred Scott decision, the United States Supreme Court declares that the Missouri Compromise of 1820 is unconstitutional and federally imposed laws banning slavery in the territories are likewise invalid.

Federal troops arrive in Utah to put down a rebellion against U.S. territorial authority.

1858
The Butterfield Overland Mail Company begins regular stage coach service between St. Louis and San Francisco.

Western frontier advance: Yankton Sioux cede their lands in southeastern Dakota to the United States.

1859
Oregon is admitted to the Union as the 33rd State.

Discovery of rich deposits of gold and silver—the Comstock Lode—leads to a rush of settlers into western Nevada.

1860
The Pony Express begins regular runs between St. Joseph, Missouri and Sacramento, California; letters between these two points can now be delivered in 10 days.

1861
Outbreak of the Civil War: 11 Southern states, including Texas, secede from the Union.

The Arapahos and Cheyennes agree to give up their lands in Colorado and relocate to a reservation between Sand Creek and the Arkansas River.

The Territory of Nevada is organized by act of Congress.

The Indian Territory (present-day Oklahoma) is left to the Confederacy; the Five Civilized Tribes sign alliances with the Confederate government.

Civil War in the West: Confederate troops from Texas occupy New Mexico.

The first transcontinental telegraph line is completed, linking San Francisco with Washington, D.C.

1862
Confederate troops capture Albuquerque and Santa Fe.

In the Battle of Glorietta Pass, Confederate troops are routed; they retreat down the Rio Grande and return to Texas; Union control is restored over the Southwest.

Congress passes the Pacific Railway Act, authorizing the Union Pacific Company and the Central Pacific Company to undertake the construction of the

nation's first transcontinental railroad between Omaha, Nebraska and Sacramento, California.

The Santee Sioux of western Minnesota stage a six-week uprising against white settlers in the area; the rebellion is put down by U.S. troops and Indian leaders are taken into custody; 38 Santee Sioux are later hanged for crimes committed during the uprising.

The Homestead Act is signed into law by President Abraham Lincoln; under its terms, by paying a small registration fee a settler can obtain ownership of up to 160 acres of public land if he farms it for five continuous years.

1863
Idaho Territory established.

1865
The Confederacy surrenders to the Union at Appomattox, Virginia, ending the Civil War.

Construction begins at Omaha and Sacramento of the first transcontinental railroad.

1866
Indian warfare erupts on the Northern Plains in the Powder River region between U.S. troops and the Sioux under Red Cloud.

1867
Nebraska is admitted to the Union as the 37th state.

The United States purchases Alaska from Russia.

The War for the Bozeman Trail pits U.S. frontier garrisons against Sioux and Cheyenne warriors in what is now south-central Montana.

1868
The Fort Laramie Treaty ends the War for the Bozeman Trail; for the time being, the region is left to the Indians.

Wyoming Territory is created by act of Congress.

Lt. Colonel George Armstrong Custer conducts a campaign against the Cheyennes in present-day western Oklahoma.

1869
The nation's first transcontinental railroad is completed when its eastern and western segments are joined at Promontory Point, Utah.

John Wesley Powell explores the Grand Canyon.

Wyoming Territory grants women the right to vote.

1871
An Apache uprising begins in New Mexico and Arizona and will persist until 1886.

1872
Yellowstone National Park, the nation's first national park, is created by act of Congress.

The Modoc War in northern California breaks out when U.S. troops attempt to force the Modocs to leave northern California and return to their reservation near Klamath Lake, Oregon.

1873
Jesse and Frank James undertake their first train robbery in western Iowa.

1874
Indian warfare on the Southern Plains ends as Kiowas and Comanches surrender to U.S. troops at Fort Sill (Oklahoma), thus bringing an end to the Red River Wars.

1875
Lt. Colonel George A. Custer reports finding gold deposits in the Black Hills, leading to an influx of whites into the region, and incurring the animosity of the Sioux, for whom these lands are sacred.

1876
The Sioux of the Dakotas and Wyoming, under Sitting Bull and Crazy Horse, defy government orders to relocate to reservations.

An offensive against the Sioux in eastern Montana results in disaster for U.S. forces under Custer; at the Little Bighorn River, his command of over 220 men is wiped out by an overwhelming force of Sioux, Cheyenne and Blackfoot warriors.

Colorado enters the Union as the 38th state.

1877
After a 1,300-mile flight from federal troops, Chief Joseph and his Nez Perce tribe surrender in northern Montana.

1881
The nation's second transcontinental railroad is completed when the Southern Pacific, extending eastward from southern California, links up with the Atchison, Topeka & Santa Fe Railroad at Deming, New Mexico.

At Tombstone, Arizona, Wyatt Earp and his brothers, along with their friend Doc Holliday, shoot down three ranchers; the conflict, known as the Gunfight at the OK Corral, arose out of a dispute involving Holliday's complicity in a stagecoach robbery.

1883
The Northern Pacific Railroad spans the continent from St. Paul, Minnesota to the Oregon coast.

1886
Apache leader Geronimo surrenders to General Nelson A. Miles at Skeleton Canyon, Arizona, ending 15 years of Indian warfare along the Arizona–Mexico border.

1887
The Dawes Act becomes law; Indian tribal lands are to be divided and distributed to individual Indians.

1889
Oklahoma Territory, which has been set aside from the Indian Territory, is opened to settlement in a mad scramble that becomes known as the Oklahoma Land Rush.

Washington, Montana, North Dakota and South Dakota are admitted to the Union.

1890
Much of the Great Sioux Reservation between the Missouri River and the Black Hills is open to white settlement.

Oklahoma Territory established.

Idaho enters the Union as the 43rd state.

Wyoming granted statehood by presidential order.

At Wounded Knee, South Dakota, an outbreak of violence between Sioux and U.S. troops leaves over 175 of the 350 Indians dead; this marks the last major conflict between U.S. troops and the American Indians.

1891
Results of the Census of 1890 reveal that what had been defined as the frontier—the habitable regions of the United States with less than two inhabitants per square mile—is no more.

1892
In Wyoming, tensions between cattlemen and settlers flares into the Johnson County War; an army of hired gunmen hunt down and kill suspected cattle

rustlers; the conflict is eventually put down by federal troops.

Three million acres of Crow Indian lands in Montana are opened to white settlement.

1898
The United States declares war on Spain; the conflict had developed over the issue of Cuban independence.

Hawaii is annexed to the United States by a joint Congressional resolution.

After three months, the Spanish–American War ends with Spain's cession to the United States of the Philippines and Guam in the Pacific, and the acquisition of Puerto Rico in the Caribbean.

1899
The Alaska Gold Rush begins with the discovery of gold deposits near Nome.

1903
Construction of the Panama Canal begins.

1906
Oklahoma and the Indian Territory are combined into one single territory.

1907
Oklahoma is admitted to the Union as the 46th state.

1912
New Mexico is admitted as the 47th state and Arizona is admitted as the 48th state; the contiguous area of the United States is now fully organized into states.

Alaska is organized as a U.S. territory.

1914
The Panama Canal is completed; the United States maintains sovereignty over the man-made waterway with leased rights on the Canal Zone.

1917
The United States purchases the Virgin Islands from Denmark for $25 million; the islands are of strategic value because of their position on the approach to the Panama Canal.

Bibliography

Adams, Alexander B. *The Disputed Lands: A History of the American West.* New York: G.P. Putnam's Sons, 1981.
———. *Sunlight and Storm: The Great American Plains.* New York: G.P. Putnam's Sons, 1977.
Adams, James Truslow. *Atlas of American History.* New York: Charles Scribner's Sons, 1943.
Athearn, Robert G. *Forts of The Upper Missouri.* Englewood Cliffs, N.J.: Prentice-Hall, 1967.
Babcock, Willoughby M. "The Fur Trade as an Aid to Settlement." *North Dakota Historical Quarterly* 7 (1993). 82–93.
Bailey, Thomas A. *A Diplomatic History of the American People.* Englewood Cliffs, N.J.: Prentice-Hall, 1980; first published, 1940.
Bakeless, John. *The Eyes of Discovery: The Pageant of North America As Seen by the First Explorers.* New York: Dover Publications, 1961; first published, 1950.
Barnard, Edward S., ed. *Story of the Great American West.* Pleasantville, N.Y.: Reader's Digest Association, 1977.
Bell, William Gardner. "Attack Outside Fort's Walls." *Wild West,* February, 1993.
Bernstein, Richard. "Unsettling the Old West: Now Historians are Bad-Mouthing the American Frontier." *New York Times Magazine,* March 18, 1990.
Billington, Ray Allen. *The Far Western Frontier: 1830–1860.* New York: Harper, 1956.
———. *Westward Expansion: A History of the American Frontier.* New York: Macmillan Co., 1949.
———. *The Westward Movement in the United States.* New York: Van Nostrand, 1959.
Bowen, Ezra, ed. *This Fabulous Century: Prelude: 1870–1900.* New York: Time-Life Books, 1970.
Bowman, John S., ed. *The World Almanac of the American West.* New York: World Almanac, 1986.
Brinkley, Alan. "The Western Historians: Don't Fence Them In." *New York Times Book Review,* September 20, 1992.
Britt, Albert. *Toward the Western Ocean: The Story of the Men Who Bridged the Continent, 1803–1869.* Barre, Mass.: Barre Publ., 1963.
Brown, Dee. *Bury My Heart at Wounded Knee.* New York: Holt, Rinehart & Winston, 1971.
———. *Hear that Lonesome Whistle Blow.* New York: Holt, Rinehart & Winston, 1977.

Burke, John. *Buffalo Bill: The Noblest Whiteskin.* New York: G.P. Putnam's Sons, 1973.
Burt, Olive W. *Mountain Men of the Early West.* New York: Hawthorn Books, 1967.
Butterfield, Roger. *The American Past: A History of the United States from Concord to the Nuclear Age.* New York: Simon and Schuster, 1957.
Carley, Kenneth. *The Sioux Uprising of 1862.* St. Paul: Minnesota Historical Society, 1976.
Carpenter, Allan. *The Encyclopedia of the Central West.* New York: Facts On File, 1990.
———. *The Encyclopedia of the Midwest.* New York: Facts On File, 1989.
Caruso, John Anthony. *The Great Lakes Frontier.* Indianapolis: Bobbs-Merrill, 1961.
———. *The Southern Frontier.* Indianapolis: Bobbs-Merrill, 1963.
Chittenden, Hiram M. *The American Fur Trade of the Far West,* 3 vols. New York: Harper, 1902, rev. 1935.
Clark, Dan Elbert. *The West in American History.* New York: Thomas Y. Crowell, 1937.
Cleland, Robert Glass. *This Reckless Breed of Men: The Trappers and Fur Traders of the Southwest.* New York: Alfred A. Knopf, 1963.
Clokey, Richard M. *William H. Ashley: Enterprise and Politics in the Trans-Mississippi West.* Norman: University of Oklahoma Press, 1980.
Coit, Margaret L. *The Sweep Westward.* New York: Time-Life Books, 1963.
Cooke, Donald E. *Atlas of the Presidents.* Maplewood, N.J.: Hammond, 1964.
Custer, Elizabeth Bacon. *Boots and Saddles; or Life in Dakota with General Custer.* New York: Harper and Brothers, 1885; rep. 1961.
———. *Following the Guidon.* Norman: University of Oklahoma Press, 1966; first published, 1890.
———. *Tenting on the Plains; or, General Custer in Kansas and Texas.* Norman: University of Oklahoma Press, 1971; first published, 1887.
Custer, George Armstrong. *My Life on the Plains, or Personal Experiences with Indians.* Norman: University of Oklahoma Press, 1962; first published, 1874.

Dale, Harrison Clifford. *The Ashley–Smith Expeditions and the Discovery of a Central Route to the Pacific: 1822–29.* Cleveland: A.H. Clark Co., 1918.

Daniel, Clifton, ed. *Chronicle of America.* Mount Kisco, N.Y.: Chronicle Publications, 1989.

Davis, Kenneth S. *Kansas: A Bicentennial History.* New York: W.W. Norton, 1976.

De Voto, Bernard. *Across the Wide Missouri.* Boston: Houghton Mifflin, 1947.

———. *The Year of Decision: 1846.* Boston: Little Brown, 1950.

———. *The Course of Empire.* Boston: Houghton Mifflin, 1952.

Dippie, Brian W. *Nomad: George Armstrong Custer in Turf, Field & Farm.* Austin: University of Texas Press, 1980.

Dunlop, Richard. *Great Trails of the West.* New York: Abingdon Press, 1971.

Egan, Timothy. "Sweeping Reversal of U.S. Land Policy Sought by Clinton: Big Change for the West." *New York Times,* February 24, 1992.

Farrar, V. J. *The Annexation of Russian America to the United States.* New York: Russell & Russell, 1966; first published, 1937.

Fehrenbach, T. R. *Lone Star: A History of Texas and the Texans.* New York: American Legacy Press, 1968.

Fehrenbacher, Don E. *The Era of Expansion, 1800–1848.* New York: John Wiley & Sons, 1969.

Ferrell, Robert H., and Richard Natkiel. *Atlas of American History.* New York: Facts On File, 1988.

Forbis, William H. *The Cowboys.* New York: Time-Life Books, 1973.

Frantz, Joe B. *Texas: A Bicentennial History.* New York: W.W. Norton, 1976.

Frazier, Ian. *Great Plains.* New York: Farrar, Straus, Giroux, 1989.

Garraty, John A. *The American Nation: A History of the United States Since 1865.* New York: Harper & Row, 1983.

Goetzmann, William H. *New Lands, New Men.* New York: Viking, 1986.

Goodwin, Cardinal Leonidas. *The Trans-Mississippi West: 1803–1853.* New York: Russell & Russell, 1922.

Hafen, LeRoy R., and Carl Coke Rister. *Western America.* Englewood Cliffs, N.J.: Prentice-Hall, 1941.

Hagan, Kenneth J. *This People's Navy: The Making of American Sea Power.* New York: The Free Press/Macmillan, 1991.

Hale, Edward Everett. *Kansas and Nebraska.* Freeport, N.Y.: Books for Libraries Press, 1972; first published, 1854.

Hassrick, Royal B. *The Colorful Story of the American West.* London: Octopus Books, 1975.

Hedges, James B. *Henry Villard and the Railways of the Northwest.* New Haven: Russell & Russell, 1930.

Heffner, Richard D. *A Documentary History of the United States.* New York: New American Library, 1965; first published, 1952.

Hillman, Martin. *Bridging a Continent (Encyclopedia of Discovery and Exploration, Vol. 8).* London: Aldus Books, 1971.

Hoig, Stan. *The Sand Creek Massacre.* Norman: University of Oklahoma Press, 1961.

Holbrook, Stewart H. *The Story of American Railroads.* New York: Crown, 1947.

Horn, Huston. *The Pioneers.* Alexandria, Va.: Time-Life Books, 1974.

Howard, Robert West. *The Iron Trail: The Story of the First Transcontinental Railroad.* New York: G.P. Putnam's Sons, 1962.

Howarth, Stephen. *To Shining Sea: A History of the United States Navy, 1775–1991.* New York: Random House, 1991.

Jackson, W. Turrentine. *Wagon Roads West: A Study of Federal Road Surveys and Construction in the Trans-Mississippi West, 1846–1869.* New Haven: Yale University Press, 1965; first published, 1952.

Josephy, Alvin M. Jr. *The Civil War in the American West.* New York: Alfred A. Knopf, 1991.

———. *War on the Frontier: The Trans–Mississippi West.* Alexandria, Va.: Time-Life Books, 1986.

Ketchum, Robert M., ed. *The Pioneer Spirit.* New York: American Heritage Publishing Co., 1959.

Keyes, Nelson Beecher. *The American Frontier: Our Unique Heritage.* Garden City, N.Y.: Hanover House, 1954.

Klose, Nelson. *A Concise Study Guide to the American Frontier.* Lincoln, Neb.: University of Nebraska Press, 1964.

Lamar, Howard. R., ed. *The Reader's Encyclopedia of the American West.* New York: Harper & Row, 1977.

Latham, Frank. *The Transcontinental Railroad 1862–69; A Great Engineering Feat Links America Coast to Coast.* New York: F. Watts, 1973.

Lavender, David. *The Great West.* New York: American Heritage Publishing Co., 1965.

———. *The Overland Migrations: Settlers to Oregon, California, and Utah.* Washington, D.C.: National Park Service, 1980.

Lesley, Lewis Burt. *Uncle Sam's Camels.* Glorietta, N.M.: Rio Grande Press, 1970; first published, 1929.

Linton, Calvin D. *American Headlines: Year by Year.* New York: Thomas Nelson, 1985.

McCormick, Charles H.; Robert G. Ferris, ed. *Founders and Frontiersmen: Historic Places Commemorating Early Nationhood and the Westward Movement, 1783–1828.* Washington, D.C.: National Park Service, 1967.

McPherson, James M. *Battle Cry of Freedom: The Civil War Era.* New York: Oxford University Press, 1988.

McReynolds, Edwin C. *Oklahoma: A History of the Sooner State.* Norman: University of Oklahoma Press, 1954.

Menig, D.W. *The Shaping of America: A Geographical Perspective of History.* New Haven: Yale University Press, 1986.

Mirsky, Jeannette. *The Westward Crossings: Balboa, Mackenzie, Lewis and Clark.* London: A. Wingate, 1951.

Momaday, N. Scott. "New Mexico: Passage into Legend." *New York Times Magazine: The Sophisticated Traveler,* October 18, 1992.

Monaghan, Jay. *The Overland Trail.* Indianapolis: Bobbs–Merrill, 1947.

Moody, Ralph. *The Old Trails West.* New York: Thomas Y. Crowell Co., 1963.

Morgan, H. Wayne, and Anne Hodges Morgan. *Oklahoma: A History.* New York: W.W. Norton, 1977.

Morgan, Dale L. *Jedediah Smith and the Opening of the West.* Lincoln: University of Nebraska Press, 1964.

———. *The State of Deseret.* Logan: Utah State Univ., 1987.

Morison, Samuel Eliot. *The Oxford History of the American People: Volume Two, 1789–1877.* New York: Oxford University Press, 1965.

———. *The Oxford History of the American People: Volume Three, 1869–1963.* New York: Oxford University Press, 1965.

Morris, John Wesley. *Historical Atlas of Oklahoma*. Norman: University of Oklahoma Press, 1986.

Moskowitz, Milton, Michael Katz, and Robert Levering, eds. *Everybody's Business: The Irreverent Guide to Corporate America*. New York: Harper & Row, 1980.

Nadeau, Remi A. *Fort Laramie and the Sioux Indians*. Englewood Cliffs, N.J.: Prentice-Hall, 1967.

National Geographic Society. *Into the Wilderness*. Washington, D.C.: National Geographic Society, 1978.

Nevin, David. *The Mexican War*. Alexandria, Va.: Time-Life Books, 1978.

Nichols, Alice. *Bleeding Kansas*. New York: Oxford University Press, 1954.

O'Meara, Walter. *Guns at the Forks*. Englewood Cliffs, N.J.: Prentice-Hall, 1965.

O'Neil, Paul. *The End and the Myth*. Alexandria, Va.: Time-Life Books, 1979.

Osgood, Ernest Staples. *The Day of the Cattleman*. Chicago: University of Chicago Press, 1929.

Parkman, Francis. *The Oregon Trail*. New York: New American Library, 1978; first published, 1847.

Paul, Rodman. *The Far West and the Great Plains in Transition: 1859–1900*. New York: Harper & Row, 1988.

———. *Mining Frontiers of the Far West*. New York: Holt, Rinehart and Winston, 1963.

Pletcher, David M. *The Diplomacy of Annexation: Texas, Oregon and the Mexican War*. Columbia: University of Missouri Press, 1973.

Richmond, Robert W., and Robert W. Mardock, eds. *A Nation Moving West: Readings in the History of the American Frontier*. Lincoln: University of Nebraska Press, 1966.

Riegel, Robert E. *America Moves West*. New York: Henry Holt & Co., 1955.

———. *The Story of the Western Railroads: From 1852 Through the Reign of the Giants*. Lincoln: University of Nebraska Press, 1964.

Rister, Carl Coke. *Land Hunger: David Payne and the Oklahoma Boomers*. Norman: University of Oklahoma Press, 1942.

Roosevelt, Theodore. *The Winning of the West*. New York: Hastings House, 1963; first published, 1889.

Ross, Alexander; Kenneth A. Spaulding, ed. *The Fur Hunters of the Far West*. Norman: University of Oklahoma Press, 1956.

Sandoz, Mari. *The Beaver Men: Spearheads of Empire*. New York, Hastings House, 1964.

Scherer, John. "The Eighth Wonder." *NAHO*, Fall 1975 (New York State Museum and Science Service).

Schlesinger, Arthur M., Jr., ed. *The Almanac of American History*. New York: G.P. Putnam's Sons, 1983.

Schlissel, Lillian. *Women's Diaries of the Westward Journey*. New York: Schocken, 1982.

Seidman, Lawrence I. *Once in the Saddle: The Cowboy's Frontier 1866–96*. New York: Facts On File, 1991.

Selby, John. *The Conquest of the American West*. Totowa, N.J.: Rowman and Littlefield, 1976.

Shirley, Glenn. "Cattle Drive Through Hell." *Old West*, Spring 1993.

Shoemaker, Earl Arthur. *The Permanent Indian Frontier: the reason for the construction and abandonment of Fort Scott, Kansas, during the dragoon era: a special history study*. Washington, D.C.: National Park Service, 1986.

Singletary, Otis A. *The Mexican War*. Chicago: University of Chicago Press, 1960.

Sosin, Jack M. *The Revolutionary Frontier, 1763–1783*. New York: Holt Rinehart and Winston, 1967.

Sparks, Edwin Erle. *The Expansion of the American People*. New York: Scott, Foresman & Co., 1900.

Steiner, Stan N. *The Waning of the West*. New York: St. Martin's Press, 1989.

Stewart, George Rippey. *Ordeal by Hunger: The Story of the Donner Party*. Lincoln: University of Nebraska Press, 1986; first published, 1960.

Tanner, Ogden. *The Ranchers*. Alexandria, Va.: Time-Life Books, 1977.

Thompson, John. *Closing the Frontier: Radical Response in Oklahoma, 1889–1923*. Norman: University of Oklahoma Press, 1986.

Trachtman, Paul. *The Gunfighters*. Alexandria, Va.: Time-Life Books, 1974.

Turner, Frederick Jackson. *Frontier and Section*. Englewood Cliffs, N.J.: Prentice-Hall, 1961.

———. *Significance of Sections in American History*. New York: Henry Holt and Co., 1950.

Van Every, Dale. *The Final Challenge: The American Frontier: 1804–45*. New York: William Morrow, 1964.

Voices of Freedom: Sources in American History. Englewood Cliffs, N.J.: Prentice Hall/Allyn & Bacon, 1987.

Waldman, Carl. *Atlas of the North American Indian*. New York: Facts On File, 1985.

———. *Encyclopedia of Native American Tribes*. New York: Facts On File, 1988.

———. *Who Was Who in Native American History*. New York: Facts On File, 1990.

Walton, George, H. *Sentinel of the Plains: Fort Leavenworth and the American West*. Englewood Cliffs, N.J.: Prentice-Hall, 1973.

Webb, Walter Pescott. *The Great Plains*. Waltham, Mass.: Blaisdell, 1931.

Wexler, Alan, and Carl Waldman. *Who Was Who in World Exploration*. New York: Facts On File, 1992.

Wexler, Sanford. *Westward Expansion: An Eyewitness History*. New York: Facts On File, 1991.

Wheeler, Keith. *The Railroaders*. New York: Time-Life Books, 1973.

———. *The Townsmen*. New York: Time-Life Books, 1975.

Winther, Oscar Osburn. *Via Western Express and Stagecoach*. Lincoln: University of Nebraska Press, 1968; first published, 1945.

Wishart, David J. *The Fur Trade of the American West, 1807–1840*. Lincoln: University of Nebraska Press, 1979.

Worcestor, Don. *The Chisholm Trail: High Road of the Cattle Kingdom*. Lincoln: University of Nebraska Press, 1980.

Wukovits, John F. "Dire Warning Ignored." *Wild West*, April 1992.

INDEX

This note is arranged alphabetically letter by letter. Illustrations and captions are indicated by *italic* page numbers. Maps are indicated by *"m"* following the page number.

Grow, Galusha 169, 171–172
Grundy, Felix 45
Guadalupe Hidalgo, Treaty of (1848)
110, 222
Guam 224
gunfighters 198–199
Gunnison, John Williams 139
Gunnison Massacre (1853) 139
Gwin, William 137

H

Haiti 26
Half King (Tanacharison) (Seneca
leader) 5
Halliday, Daniel 202
Hallock, Mary Anna (Mary Foote)
205
Hamilton, Alexander 35
Hamilton, Henry 11, 14, 16
Hard Labor, Treaty of (1768) 8
"hard money" 53
Harmar, Josiah 20, 22
Harmar's Defeat (1790) 21m
Harrison, Benjamin 208, 210
Harrison, William Henry 42–44, 46,
52, 89, 221
"Harrison's Hoss Race" 210
Harrodsburg (Kentucky) 11, 13, 14
harrows, spring-toothed 202
Harte, Bret 176
Hastings, Lansford W. 112, 113
"Hastings Cutoff" 112
Hatch, Edward 186
Havasupai Indians 103m
Hawaii 213, 224
hayforks 3
Hays, John Coffee 87
headdresses 167
Hearst, George 127
Hecete, Bruno 98
"Hell On Wheels" 174–175, 176
Henderson, Richard 11, 24, 220
Henry, Andrew 36, 68–71, 221
Henry, Patrick 14
Henry's Fort 35m, 36
Hereford cattle 197
Hickok, James Butler ("Wild Bill")
165, 196
Hidatsa Indians 68m, 122m, 123
hides 110
Hill, James J. 207
Holladay, Ben 136
Holliday, Doc 223
Homestead Act (1862) 170m, 171,
201, 223
homesteaders 203, 203–212, 204

Hoopa Indians 103m
Hopi Indians 103m
Hopkins, Mark 172
horses 121, 123, 135–136
Horseshoe Bend, Battle of (1814) 47,
221
Hotchkiss guns 187
Houston, Sam 83–85, 157
Howard, Benjamin 46
Howard, Oliver Otis 186
Hualapai Indians 103m
Huc, Abbé 141
Hudson's Bay Company 65, 69, 72,
77, 99, 100, 178 see also Fort
Vancouver
Hull, William 42, 45–46
Hunt, Wilson Price 37, 71
Huntington, Collis P. 116, 172, 173,
176
Huron (Wyandot) Indians 3, 14, 19,
20m
Hussey, Obed 146

I

Idaho 157, 208
Idaho Territory 101, 223
Ide, William B. 114
Iliff, John Wesley 195
Illinois 19, 44, 50–51, 51m, 64, 75m
Illinois and Michigan Canal 64, 64m
Illinois Confederacy 42
Illinois Indians 14, 20m
Illinois Territory 42
impressment 48, 49
Independence (Missouri) 81
Indiana 19, 50, 51m, 64
Indiana Company 8
Indian Affairs, Bureau of 125
Indiana Territory 42, 44
Indian Country 84, 89m, 93, 95,
123–124, 145
Indian Intercourse Act of 1834 145
Indian Police, U.S. 187
Indian Removal Act of 1830 92, 93,
222
Indians, American see Native
Americans; specific tribe (e.g.,
Cherokee)
Indian Territory 182, 193, 209, 211m,
212, 212m, 223
Interior, U.S. Department of the 125
Iowa 28
Iowa Indians 122m, 126
Irish immigrants 62, 84, 169, 173, 176,
203
iron 53

Iroquois Confederacy 10, 20m
Iroquois Indians 3, 8, 10, 12–13, 19,
220

J

Jackson, Andrew
California purchase bid made 111
Indian removal policy 90–93, 222
in Indian wars 221
Oregon Country monitored 100
Texas purchase bid made 83
Texas Republic recognized 84, 222
in War of 1812 47–48, 48
Jackson, Clairborne Fox 162, 163
Jackson, David 73, 74, 75, 77
Jackson, George A. 132
James, Edwin 66, 67
James, Jesse and Frank 223
Jay, John 18, 22
"Jayhawkers" 152, 163, 193
Jay Treaty (1794) 22, 221
Jefferson, Thomas
exploration favored 16, 28
Indian relocation favored 88
Lewis and Clark expedition backed
29
Louisiana cession to France alarms
25
Louisiana Purchase arranged
26–28, 214
on Missouri Compromise 58
Jicarilla Apache Indians 122m
Johnson, Andrew 178–180
Johnson County War (1892) 223
"Johnson's Polar Bear Garden" 179
Joliet, Louis 1
Jones, Thomas Ap Catesby 111
Joseph, Chief (Nez Perce leader) 186,
186, 223
Judah, Theodore Dehone 172, 173,
177
Julesburg (Nebraska) 168m, 174–175
Juneau, Joe 181
Jupiter (locomotive) 176

K

Kalispel Indians 103m
Kansas 28, 142–144, 145, 148–153,
150m, 156
Kansas-Nebraska Act of 1854
142–144, 143m, 149, 152, 222
Kansas Pacific Railroad 176m,
189–190, 190m, 195, 196
Kansas Territory 130–131
Kaskaskia (Illinois country) 14, 43m
Kaskaskia Indians 42, 126

Mexican-Americans 212
Mexican Cession (1848) 110m, 118
Mexican War (1846-48) 85, 106–110,
  107m, 109, 114–115, 222
Mexico 59, 73, 82–85, 111, 222 see also
  Mexican Cession; Mexican War
Miami and Erie Canal 64, 64m
Miami Indians 1, 14, 19, 20m, 22, 126
Michaux, Andre 29
Michigan 19
Michigan Territory 46, 50
Milan, Benjamin 83
Miles, Nelson A. 183, 186, 187, 223
Milk Creek, Battle of (1879) 184m, 186
Mimbreno Apache Indians 167
Mingo Indians see Seneca Indians
mining 126–133, 127m see also gold
  rushes
Minnesota 28
missionaries 99–100
Mississippi 50, 156
Mississippi Company 8
Mississippi River 23m, 28, 32–33, 45,
  54, 55, 92m, 221
Mississippi Territory 47
Missouri 28, 56, 70, 75m, 162–165, 222
Missourians for Mutual Protection,
  Society of 149
Missouri Compromise (1820) 56,
  57m, 58, 143, 149, 155, 221
Missouri Fur Company 36
Missouri Gazette (St. Louis
  newspaper) 68
Missouri Indians 122m
Missouri Intelligencer (newspaper) 79
Missouri River 31, 68–71, 72m, 75,
  123, 221
Missouri Territory 28, 51, 221
Mitchell, David 125
Miwok Indians 103m
Mobile (Alabama) 49
Modoc Indians 103m, 183, 223
Modoc War (1872) 223
Mohawk Valley 220
Mojave Indians 73, 103m
molasses 54
Monroe, James 27, 59, 67, 88, 177,
  214, 222
Monroe Doctrine 59, 60m, 62, 177, 222
Montana 28, 157, 208, 223
Montcalm, Louis 6
Monterey (California) 111, 114
Mormon Battalion 104
Mormon Corridor 105, 105m
Mormons 101–106, 104m, 115, 178,
  212, 222

Mormon Trail 104m, 105
Mormon War (1856-57) 105–106
Morris, Esther 205
Morse, Jedediah 88
"Mother Lode" 116
Mountain Branch (of Santa Fe Trail)
  80
Mountain Meadows Massacre (1857)
  106
"mountain men" 68, 110, 123
Mount Davidson (Nevada) 127, 128
mules 78
Myrick, Andrew 165

N

Nampeyo (Pueblo Indian potter) 205
Napoleon Bonaparte 26, 28
Nashville (Tennessee) 220
National Road (Cumberland Road)
  52, 53m, 62, 221
Native Americans see also specific
  tribes (e.g., Cherokee Indians)
  effect of westward expansion on
    xii, xv
  in fur trade 69
  homelands of Far West tribes 103m
  homelands of Old Northwest tribes
    20m
  homelands of Plains Indians 122m
  homelands of Upper Mississippi
    92m
  lands ceded in Old Northwest 43m
  population density in 1500 xivm
  removal policy 85–96
  resistance by 182–188, 184m
    in Civil War period 165–169,
      168m
  Western homelands assigned to
    Eastern Indians 95m
Nauvoo (Illinois) 103, 104m
Nauvoo Legion 103
Navajo Indians 103m, 167
Nebraska 28, 223
"Nebraska marble" 204
Nebraska Territory 142–144, 156, 171
Nevada 129
Nevada Territory 106, 129, 156, 223
New England Emigrant Aid Society
  149
New Mexico 78–79, 85, 108–110, 118,
  160–162, 160m, 212–213, 224
New Orleans (Louisiana) 25–28
New Orleans (steamboat) 54, 221
New Orleans, Battle of (1815) 221
New Spain 34m
New Ulm, Battle of (1862) 168m

New York City 63
New York Herald (newspaper) 180
New York Herald Tribune (newspaper)
  132
New York State 18, 62 see also Erie
  Canal
Nez Perce Indians 32, 68m, 103m,
  186, 223
Nicaagat (Ute leader) 186
Non-Intercourse Act (1809) 45
Nootka Indians 37, 103m
North America
  Compromise of 1850 119m
  early maps of 13m, xiim
  European claims in 1754 2m
  European claims in 1763 7m, 9m
  European incursions onto Indian
    lands xiiim
  Native American population
    density in 1500 xivm
  non-Indian claims in 1783 17m
  non-Indian claims in 1800 26m
North Carolina 18, 18m, 24, 156
North Dakota 28, 208, 223
Northern Pacific Railroad 190, 190m,
  206, 223
North West Company 38m, 65, 97
Northwest Ordinance of 1787 19, 118,
  221
Northwest Territory (Old Northwest)
  20, 21m, 22
Number 119 (locomotive) 176–177
Nye, James W. 129

O

Oakley, Annie 205
Ohio 19, 64, 221
Ohio, Forks of the 1, 4, 5, 220
Ohio and Erie Canal 64, 64m
Ohio Company 1, 3–4, 19, 220, 221
Ohio River 54, 55
Ohio Valley 1, 3–6, 8, 220
Ojibway Indians see Chippewa
  Indians
OK Corral, Gunfight at the (1881) 223
Oklahoma 28, 209–212, 211m, 224
Oklahoma Colony 209, 210
Oklahoma Land Rush (1889)
  210–211, 223
Oklahoma Territory 211, 212m, 223
Old Spanish Trail 76m
Old Weawea (Paiute leader) 183
Oliver, James 202
Omaha Indians 122m, 126
Omnibus Bill (1889) 208
"one big reservation" 123, 124, 126

principal population centers in
1810 38*m*

statehood dates 213*m*

territorial annexations 1845-53
120*m*

territories and states in 1800 26*m*

territories and states in 1814 49*m*

territories and states in 1821 57*m*

westward expansion 215*m*

*United States Magazine and Democratic
Review* 96

United States Steamship Company
133

"upland cotton" 40, 41

Utah 106, 118, 175, 212

Utah Territory 105, 129

Ute Indians 101, 133, 139, 186

Ute War (1879) 186

Utica (New York) 62

V

Valverde, Battle of (1862) 161

Vancouver, George 98

Van Dorn, Earl 165

Vasquez, Louis 77

Velez de Escalante, Silvestre 101

Victorio (Apache leader) 186, 189

Villard, Henry 132

Vincennes (Illinois country) 14, 43*m*

Virginia 18*m*, 64, 156

Virginia City (Nevada) 127, 128*m*, 129

Virginia Colony 3–6, 11–12, 220

Virgin Islands 224

Vizcaino, Sebastian de 97, 110

W

Wabash and Erie Canal 64, 64*m*

Wabash River, Battle of (1791) 22

wagon trains *100*, 124, 125, 126, 222

Walker, Joseph Reddeford 76, 76*m*,
110

Walker, Samuel H. 86

Walker, Thomas 10

"Walker Colt" (revolver) 87

Walker Pass 76

Walk-In-The Water (steamboat) 55

Wallace, Lew 199

Walla Walla Indians 103*m*

"Walrussia" 179

War Bonnet Creek, Battle of (1876)
184*m*, 185

warclubs *16*

War Department, U.S. 125, 137, 140

"War Hawks" 45, 49

Warner, Charles Dudley 182

War of 1812 38, 44–49, 47*m*, 48*m*, 62,
221

Warrior (steamboat) *55*

Washington (state) 208, 223

Washington, D.C. 48

Washington, George
in American Revolution 13, 16
in British diplomatic mission 4–5,
4*m*
canal proposed by 64
in French and Indian War *5*, 220
in Indian punitive expeditions 20,
22
Mississippi Company headed by 8
Ohio Company stockholdings 1

Washington Territory 101, 222

Washita, Battle of (1868) 184*m*

Washoe Mountains 127

water pumps *171*, 202

Wayne, Henry C. 140

Wayne, "Mad" Anthony 22, 221

Weatherford, William *see* Red Eagle

Webster, Daniel 111, 118

Weiser, Conrad 3

Weller, John B. 133

Welles, Gideon 179

Wells Fargo & Company 136

Western Engineer (steamboat) 65

Western Trail 194*m*

whaling 59, 98, 110

wheat 45, 53, 64, 196

Whigs 109, 117, 118, 144

Whipple, Amiel W. 139

Whipple, Henry P. 166

White House 48

White Stick Creeks 47, 48

Whitman, Marcus 99–100, 101

Whitman, Narcissa 99–100, 101,
204–205

Whitney, Asa 137, 172

Whitney, Eli *40*, 40–41, 87

Whitney Company 87

Wichita (Kansas) 196

Wichita Indians 122*m*

Wilderness, Battle of the (1755) 5

Wilderness Road 11, *11*

Wild West Show 186, 205

Wilkinson, James 33, 35, 47, 49, 81

Willamette Cattle Company 100

Willamette Valley 100

Wilmot, David 117–118

Wilmot Proviso 118

Wilson, Jack *see* Wovoka

Wilson's Creek, Battle of (1861) 163,
164*m*

Winchester, James 46

windmills 202

Winnebago Indians 88, 89, 90

Winnebago Uprising (1827) 89, 91*m*

Winnemucca, Sarah 205

Wisconsin 19

Wolfe, James 6

women 175, *204*, 204–205, 223

Wood Lake, Battle of (1862) 168*m*

Woods, Abraham 1

Worcester v. State of Georgia (1832) 93

Wounded Knee, Battle of (1890)
184*m*, 187, 223

Wovoka (Jack Wilson) 187

Wurteh (mother of Sequoyah) 94

Wyandot Indians *see* Huron
(Wyandot) Indians

Wyeth, Nathaniel J. 76*m*, 77, 99, 100,
222

Wynkoop, Edward 169

Wyoming 28, 208

Wyoming Territory 175, 223

X

XIT Ranch 197

Y

Yakima Indians 103*m*

Yanktonai Sioux Indians 122*m*, 167

Yankton Sioux Indians 122*m*, 166, 223

Yavapai Indians 103*m*

Yellowstone (steamboat) 75

Yellowstone Expedition 65, 66

Yellowstone National Park 186, 223

Yellowstone Packet (keelboat) 69

Yellowstone River 69

Yokuts Indians 103*m*

"yonder siders" 126

Young, Brigham 102, 103–106, *104*,
178, 222

Young, Ewing 99, 100, 110

Yuchi Indians 10

Yuma Indians 103*m*

Z

Zuni Indians 103*m*